W9-BLR-370

PRAISE FOR *UNCARING*

"No one is better qualified to write about what ails healthcare than Robert Pearl. *Uncaring* ought to trigger a rethinking of the professional culture of American medicine."

—Malcolm Gladwell, author of five *New York Times* bestsellers

"In *Uncaring*, Dr. Robert Pearl provides an X-ray examination of the medical profession and how it has both promoted and adversely affected American healthcare. It's deep, insightful, and can be considered the modern version of what Francis Peabody wrote almost a century ago: 'The secret of the care of the patient is in caring for the patient.' We need to get that back."

—Eric Topol, MD, professor at Scripps Research and author of *Deep Medicine*

"In this hard-hitting, immensely valuable book, Robert Pearl pulls back the veil from the face of the culture of medicine. He reveals the truths, both good and bad, about what drives physicians and the system of care. As an accomplished surgeon, admired executive, sophisticated policy analyst, and master storyteller, he does that with both expertise and compassion, as few others could. His recommendations—tough, clear, and right—for what needs to change provide a roadmap for all who seek better health and care."

—Donald M. Berwick, MD, president emeritus and senior fellow at the Institute for Healthcare Improvement

"How do so many young doctors who enter medicine filled with idealism and the desire to do good end up decades later as cynical professionals, caring about money, prestige, success—everything but the patient? Dr. Robert Pearl, in this riveting examination of the physician culture, diagnoses the pathologies in the system that too often strips the 'caring' out of healthcare."

—Elisabeth Rosenthal, editor in chief of *Kaiser Health News*, and author of *An American Sickness*

"Dr. Robert Pearl has peeled back the curtain and revealed major challenges facing the culture of medicine. His insights are a must-read for anyone who wants to improve our healthcare system, and in so doing, provide better care and save lives."

—Leana Wen, MD, public health professor at George Washington University, and author of *When Doctors Don't Listen*

"*Uncaring* is a brilliant and incisive dive into physician culture, both its seamy underbelly and the moments that inspire. Pearl's vast experience as a physician steeped in the culture, and as leader of one of the largest healthcare systems in America, allows him to write with authority, yet in a personal and engaging way, and at the end to offer solutions. The result is a wonderful and compelling read."

—Abraham Verghese, MD, professor of medicine, Stanford University, and author of *Cutting for Stone*

"Culture squashes innovation. And this may just be a defining truth for the practice of medicine today. Pearl takes a probing look at America's medical practice and reveals the sacrosanct clinical hierarchy, entrenched clinical biases, financial drivers, and physician burnout. He's pressing on the tender and sensitive spots. And while conventional medicine might suggest that this won't hurt a bit, it will. As Pearl suggests, denial isn't the path to recovery. *Uncaring* provides an honest history and physical of medicine today, with a bold vision to define and protect the very best of care."

—John Nosta, technology innovationist, Google Health Advisory Board, and World Health Organization technology expert

"Dr. Robert Pearl's *Uncaring* is a deeply readable, empathic, and insightful exploration of the status of twenty-first-century American physicians—their heroism, their altruism, their limitations, and the shared culture that too often makes them less than they could and must be to heal our healthcare system. Healthcare leaders, policymakers, and physicians can all benefit from understanding the lessons *Uncaring* teaches."

—David Blumenthal, MD, MPP, president of the Commonwealth Fund

"The history and culture of medicine has set the stage for the way our current system of care is organized and delivered. In these unprecedented times, this book offers insights into the way our system of care is both working and failing the people that it serves. Pearl spells out the case that to really understand how the healthcare system works you must really understand how physicians work. Through storytelling and personal reflections of a career in medical leadership with distinction, Pearl shares how physicians view their patients and themselves. This rare 'under the covers' view of medicine offers insights into tough issues that plague our system but also offers a path forward for improving healthcare. This personal and fascinating read shows doctors as humans and offers hope for those wanting to see empathy and compassion remain an essential part of the way we deliver care in the future. I highly recommend this book to all who seek a better understanding of healthcare and want to make a difference in improving the way it works."

—The Honorable David J. Shulkin, MD, ninth secretary,
US Department of Veterans Affairs

"Dr. Robert Pearl's *Uncaring* explains the unique challenges of the healthcare system in providing quality care in an equitable manner. He distills the issues down to the salient points, providing a roadmap to make the necessary changes. Now is our time to act! Dr. Pearl provides the way."

—John Whyte, MD, MPH, chief medical officer, WebMD

"*Uncaring* lifts the veil on the deeply conditioned culture that drives American physicians and our multi-trillion-dollar healthcare system. To solve our biggest challenges, we can't ignore this elephant in the room, and Dr. Robert Pearl never flinches once. Sunlight is the best disinfectant, and *Uncaring* illuminates the shadows that many doctors themselves are reluctant to see."

—Zubin Damania, MD, host of *The ZDoggMD Show*, the
internet's most popular live medical show and podcast

"Dr. Robert Pearl is uniquely qualified to take us inside physician culture and provide key insights on the medical mind. Physicians are the key resource in our healthcare system. *Uncaring* is a sweeping must-read exploration of physician culture, bringing together poignant stories, deep research, and vast professional experience to help us all understand how physician culture shapes healthcare. Patients, physicians, and policymakers will all benefit from this invaluable and highly engaging book that teaches us what works and what needs to change in the future."

—Ian Morrison, PhD, author and healthcare futurist

"Dr. Pearl writes with authority, having served as CEO of two successful Kaiser Permanente medical groups, one on each coast, leading 12,000 physicians. He traces the evolution of physician culture, which has come into conflict with modern demands for accountability in cost and quality. This has led to frustration and physician burnout. He explains how, 'A healthcare organization that is integrated, prepaid, and tech savvy can bring out the best in physicians—enabling better collaboration, cooperation, prevention . . . creating a set of behaviors that lead to superior clinical outcomes.' Dr. Pearl's prescription for the United States could make us one of the world's healthcare leaders. It would be a powerful and effective treatment for a very ill healthcare system."

—Alain C. Enthoven, PhD, Marriner S. Eccles Professor of Public and Private Management (Emeritus), Graduate School of Business, Stanford University, and member of the National Academy of Medicine

"The relationship between doctors and technology is complicated. On one hand, technological advances have made it possible for physicians to prevent cancer, greatly reduce deaths from heart attacks, and streamline overall patient care. On the other hand, doctors bemoan computers and medical technologies because they stand in the way of the most important relationship—the one between the physician and the patient. Thanks to the rapid digitization of healthcare, many of the doctor's time-honored skills and virtues have become irrelevant or obsolete seemingly overnight. In a profession now fueled by clinical algorithms, electronic health records, and sophisticated machinery, physicians are being told their clinical intuition and decades of expertise no longer matter—and could even prove harmful to patients. In *Uncaring*, Dr. Pearl traces the historical rise of technology in medicine and explains how physicians arrived at this critical juncture. In the end, he details how doctors can find an increased sense of purpose in a profession that seems to be leaving them behind, revealing that the solutions of the past can't adequately address the challenges of today."

—Kevin Pho, founder of KevinMD, social media's leading physician voice

"In *Uncaring*, Robert Pearl takes on all of healthcare's inconvenient truths through the lens of an increasingly beleaguered component of the US healthcare system: American physicians. Physicians have never been more central to solving America's healthcare problems. But, in some ways, they have never been more sidelined. Pearl offers a thoughtful diagnosis and treatment plan that aims to restore what we all want to be front and center: the physician-patient relationship."

—Sachin H. Jain, president and CEO of SCAN Group and Health Plan, and former CEO of CareMore Health

"We often hear that what ails US medical care is the structure of our healthcare system itself. In *Uncaring*, Dr. Robert Pearl reveals a problem that runs much deeper: how physician culture fails both doctors and the patients they so eagerly aim to help. What if healthcare providers aren't just operating within a flawed system, but are also operating out of a flawed philosophy? Dr. Pearl provides an expert examination of the history of medical culture, how it has shaped our current healthcare system, and most importantly, how we must rectify it."

—Avik Roy, president, The Foundation for Research on Equal Opportunity

"In a well-documented, panoramic narrative, an insider demystifies what makes many doctors tick."

—*Kirkus*

UNCARING

UNCARING

How the Culture
of Medicine Kills
Doctors & Patients

Robert Pearl, MD

PUBLICAFFAIRS

New York

PublicAffairs
Hachette Book Group
1290 Avenue of the Americas, New York, NY 10104
www.publicaffairsbooks.com
@Public_Affairs

Printed in the United States of America

First Edition: May 2021

Published by PublicAffairs, an imprint of Perseus Books, LLC, a subsidiary of Hachette Book Group, Inc. The PublicAffairs name and logo is a trademark of the Hachette Book Group.

The Hachette Speakers Bureau provides a wide range of authors for speaking events. To find out more, go to www.hachettespeakersbureau.com or call (866) 376-6591.

The publisher is not responsible for websites (or their content) that are not owned by the publisher.

Print book interior design by Amy Quinn.

Library of Congress Cataloging-in-Publication Data

Names: Pearl, Robert, author.
Title: Uncaring : how the culture of medicine kills doctors and patients / Robert Pearl.
Description: First edition. | New York : PublicAffairs, 2021. | Includes bibliographical
    references and index.
Identifiers: LCCN 2020046925 | ISBN 9781541758278 (hardcover) | ISBN 9781541758254
    (ebook)
Subjects: MESH: Delivery of Health Care | Physician's Role | Quality of Health
    Care | United States Classification: LCC R697.P45 | NLM W 84 AA1 | DDC
    610.73/72069—dc23
LC record available at https://lccn.loc.gov/2020046925

ISBNs: 978-1-5417-5827-8 (hardcover), 978-1-5417-5825-4 (ebook)

LSC-C

Printing 1, 2021

In loving memory of my mother, Lilian Pearl

CONTENTS

Introduction   1

PART ONE: DIAGNOSING PHYSICIAN CULTURE

Chapter One   Bloodletting, Handwashing,
and Gorilla Watching   13

Chapter Two   A First Look at Physician Culture   24

Chapter Three   Heroes and Fools   30

Chapter Four   A Two-Part History of Today's Physician Culture   35

Chapter Five   *The People v. Physician Culture*   50

PART TWO: THE PHYSICIAN'S PAIN

Chapter One   Did We Kill One of Our Own?   69

Chapter Two   The Rise of Burnout, the Rebirth of Moral Injury   81

Chapter Three   The Problem with Prestige   90

Chapter Four   How the Mighty Fell   99

Chapter Five   Doctors and Self-Determination Theory   104

Chapter Six   Bored Stiff   114

PART THREE: HELPING OR HARMING PATIENTS?

Chapter One   Quality Isn't a Given   123

Chapter Two   A Tale of Two Emergencies   127

Chapter Three   Human Shields   133

Chapter Four   The Real Price of Rx   141

Chapter Five   A Great Inconvenience   149

Chapter Six   The Language Barrier   155

Chapter Seven   Impersonalized Medicine   161

Chapter Eight   The Truth Is Complicated   169

Chapter Nine   The Doctor's Double Standard   177

PART FOUR: THE SOCIAL LADDER

Chapter One   A Culture Without Answers   187
Chapter Two   On Death and Dying   191
Chapter Three   The Young and the Breathless   206
Chapter Four   Colorblind   219
Chapter Five   Does Sex Matter?   230
Chapter Six   Discomfort with Difference   237
Chapter Seven   The Last Straw   252

PART FIVE: THE EVOLUTION OF PHYSICIAN CULTURE

Chapter One   Economic Desperation   263
Chapter Two   Between Scylla and Charybdis   271
Chapter Three   Two Paths, Both Fraught with Peril   277
Chapter Four   Denial, Anger, Bargaining, and Depression   289
Chapter Five   Acceptance and the Five *C*s of Cultural Change   295
Chapter Six   The Virtues of Being Difficult   312
Chapter Seven   Medicine: A Love Story   322

                 Acknowledgments   *335*
                 Bibliography   *339*
                 Index   *367*

INTRODUCTION

U NDER A MICROSCOPE, STRUCTURES AND organisms too small for the naked eye become magnified, visible, spectacular. Through the ocular lens, you can see the beautiful and complex machinery at work inside a droplet of water, a blade of grass, or a strand of hair. There is something at once intoxicating and inspiring about these views. By amplifying what's otherwise hidden, we discover deeper, more interesting truths about the world around us.

So it was throughout the year 2020, when a submicroscopic agent reminded us of the immense power contained within the things we cannot see. Sizewise, the novel coronavirus, known to scientists as SARS-CoV-2, is teenier than tiny. Measuring a tad over a hundred-billionth of a meter in diameter, the virus is four thousand times smaller than a poppyseed, even smaller than a wavelength of light.

The infectious agent is biologically unimpressive as well. Its fragile genetic makeup consists of a few shards of RNA, surrounded by a thin lipid shell with skinny florets of protein extending outward. Left on a park bench or a door handle, the coronavirus dies in hours. It's no match for a bar of soap, household disinfectants, or most forms of alcohol.

Not until you see it under the lens of an electron microscope does the coronavirus begin to look the villainous part. Once illuminated through beams of accelerated electrons, the virus becomes a menacing vision, a brooding orb, a flailing mace capable of penetrating human cells and replicating itself into a pathogen with unspeakable might.

ON JANUARY 7, 2020, THE *New York Times* was the first US newspaper to report that a mysterious SARS-like infection had sickened fifty-nine people in China. On January 21, the Centers for Disease Control and Prevention reported the first confirmed case of COVID-19 in the United States, detected in a thirty-five-year-old man from Washington.

Within a matter of weeks, the itsy-bitsy virus had begun taking lives and devastating complex adaptive systems—political, educational, economic, and social—throughout the United States. The disease shook financial markets, dominated news coverage, and disrupted human existence in ways most Americans had never experienced.

Perhaps no system was hit harder than healthcare. Hospitals overflowed, equipment grew scarce, and the very foundation of American medicine crumbled beneath our feet. As we look back at this acutely difficult moment in medicine, it is easy to forget that trouble had been brewing for some time. Independent research had, by the early 2000s, rated the US healthcare system the most expensive and least effective in the developed world, a label that stands to this day.

Well before the coronavirus outbreak, American healthcare had staggered, and doctors had been stumbling for decades. The signs of failure were clear and present. Medical costs had already bankrupted millions of patients and sent millions of others deep into debt. This was already a system that allowed doctors to send surprise (out-of-network) medical bills to the people they treated and then sue the patients who couldn't afford to pay. This was already a system in which a third of medical procedures performed were scientifically proven to add no clinical value. This was a system in which "pill mill" physicians spawned a deadly prescription drug epidemic, which took more than sixty thousand lives a year and contributed to a three-year decline in US life expectancy. This was an industry of professionals, trained in science, who had failed to follow evidence- and science-based approaches, leading to half a million avoidable deaths each year.

And yet, despite the medical system's well-documented disappointments, healthcare professionals remain among our society's most beloved and lionized figures. We labeled them heroes of the coronavirus pandemic. Patients won't soon forget the sacrifices of doctors, nurses, and clinical staff who charged in to battle against the invisible enemy, month after month, despite spike after spike of new cases.

During the first few weeks of the outbreak, the internet erupted with images of doctors and nurses donning garbage bags for smocks and salad lids for facial shields. These "frontline soldiers" looked more like a ragtag militia than a properly equipped army. Through it all, news outlets documented their struggles and triumphs. Americans watched from home as physicians with darkened and drooping eyelids fought off exhaustion and continued fighting COVID-19. They worked from morning to night in substandard and often dangerous conditions, brimming all the while with looks of determination. They ended their shifts with deep red lashes on their faces, markings left by the snug-fitting N95 masks they were forced to reuse, day after day.

Communities across the country expressed their appreciation in every way imaginable. Signage outside hospital entryways informed new arrivals that "Heroes Work Here." Local restaurateurs, themselves struggling to stay afloat during lockdown orders, sent sandwiches and pizzas to healthcare workers toiling in ICUs and ERs. Sewing clubs fashioned hand-stitched masks for nurses who couldn't get their hands on the personal protective equipment they needed. Blue lights beamed onto historic landmarks, from the Space Needle in Seattle to the Empire State Building in New York City, in solidarity and support of essential frontline workers. Yard signs adorned suburban lawns, while heart-shaped cutouts graced city windows, all in shows of gratitude for the paramedics, doctors, and other first responders who risked their lives to save others.

In New Jersey, a team of doctors, nurses, and staff were brought to tears when they looked outside the hospital window and saw a man holding a hand-drawn sign that read, "Thank you for saving my wife's life. I love you all."

These are the images of the American doctor we cherish. Like their predecessors who battled the Spanish flu and smallpox, the coronavirus fighters stared death in the face and charged forward, not just during the initial wave of hospitalizations but through multiple resurgences of the disease. Their acts of heroism will remain forever imprinted on our national consciousness.

For hundreds of thousands of doctors, it was all part of the job, as it has been for centuries. Dating back to the medieval plagues, physicians battled diseases with few medical weapons and sparse scientific knowledge. And even when the weapons improved, and their scientific understanding caught up with the deadliest of illnesses, doctors continued to hold dear the qualities of courage, dedication, and selflessness. In the medical profession, these characteristics are foundational, indispensable, and deeply embedded in the culture.

———————

AS AMERICANS LONG FOR A return to normalcy, they find themselves standing amid the ruins of financial devastation, tasked with the duty to rebuild their systems: political, educational, economic, social, and, perhaps most challenging, healthcare.

But where to begin? American doctors, policy experts, and academic scholars may offer differing visions, but they are united on at least one point: we need to fix healthcare's *systemic issues*.

By this they mean freeing doctors from the red tape and bureaucratic burdens that bog them down. A now common refrain in medical circles is "let doctors be doctors." Proponents of this mantra insist that American healthcare would improve by leaps and bounds if we simply eliminated annoying administrative matters, pesky prior authorization requirements, and cumbersome computers that (literally) sit between physicians and their patients. Doctors point out that these barriers to better care were put in place by a self-serving array of healthcare-system players: health insurers, governmental regulators, computer manufacturers, and hospital executives. Indeed, these groups, along with pharmaceutical companies and medical technology firms, are guilty of holding healthcare back while inflicting harm on patients and doctors alike. Correcting their deficiencies will be central to healthcare reform. But if those are the only changes our nation accomplishes, then everyone—including doctors and patients—will be sorely disappointed with the results. Contrary to what most people believe, fixing the US healthcare system won't be enough.

We must also address the invisible and highly influential *physician culture*. Founded on the ideals of compassion and commitment, the culture of physicians has been passed down through generations of professionals who possess a deep desire to help people in need. This culture proves capable of inspiring superhuman achievements and has spurred some of the greatest advancements in human civilization, from organ transplantation to cancer immunotherapy to the marvels of modern surgery. But this same culture carries a dark underbelly, which is responsible in many ways for the rising costs and decaying standards of medical care that permeate our nation's inpatient and outpatient facilities. Physician culture contains a duality of human motives and actions, leading to outcomes that range from life-saving to life ending.

The coronavirus crisis offers a clear example of this dualism. In the context of providing care to extremely ill patients, a defining principle of physician culture is to "save a life at any cost," words that still echo in my ears from more than a decade of medical training. On one hand, this is what doctors did magnificently in response to the surging disease. They resuscitated and revived patients (repeatedly, when necessary), no matter how great the costs or how nominal the patient's chances of survival. That virtuous life-saving creed buoyed doctors during the worst phases of the pandemic, giving them a clear sense of mission as they drove to work each day, knowing full well the personal health risks they faced. It enabled the kind of selfless and heroic actions that would seem reckless or extreme in nearly any other line of work.

With hospitals overwhelmed and ICU beds running low, doctors did everything they could to treat the sick. And they were forced to get creative quickly. Seemingly overnight, physicians figured out how to place two patients with rapidly evolving pneumonia (a consequence of the virus) on a single ventilator, saving both. Patients and the media joined the medical community in rejoicing in the ingenuity. Absent from the kudos, however, was a difficult truth: The doctors who believe in saving a life at any cost had not, in fact, done everything possible to save lives. The very culture that drove them to rescue the sickest of the sick during the pandemic also allowed them to ignore their clinical shortcomings and dismiss the power of preventive medicine.

To explain, let's revisit New York City in April 2020. The Big Apple was, at the time, the epicenter of the outbreak in the United States. There epidemiologists discovered that 94 percent of hospitalized coronavirus patients had at least one major chronic health condition like diabetes, chronic lung disease, obesity, heart failure, or hypertension. A whopping 88 percent of them had two or more.

Had physicians invested more time and effort over the years in preventing and better managing these types of chronic diseases, many of the patients who died would never have become critically ill in the first place. Most would not have even required hospital admission. And they would be alive now. Through a combination of medications, preventive care, patient willingness, and behavioral change, conditions like heart disease and adult-onset diabetes are often avoidable or entirely manageable. Time and again, studies show that when healthcare organizations place a high value on primary care (including family and internal medicine), evidence-based care, and various preventive approaches, they reduce the prevalence of chronic disease among patients by up to half compared to national averages.

However, physicians and healthcare organizations across the United States do not invest nearly enough time and energy in successfully preventing chronic illness or helping patients avoid its complications. Some of the problem and cause for failure is systemic. For instance, doctors on the whole get reimbursed too little for the time it takes to prevent disease, and they often lack the information technology systems needed to provide well-coordinated care.

But a large (and largely unseen) part of the problem is rooted in the values and priorities of physicians. Today, primary care is undervalued, even looked down on, by much of the medical community and by specialists in particular. Research has shown that hospital executives and academic leaders place a higher premium on training interventional specialists than on training primary care doctors who help patients avoid major health problems. As a result of its lower average salary and overall lack of esteem, primary care sits near the bottom on the list of desired residencies for medical students. Because physician culture elevates intervention over prevention too, many human lives have been lost to COVID-19. And because of the dysfunctions of both the US healthcare system and physician culture, American patients became unwilling yet ideal hosts for the deadly coronavirus.

This pandemic has brought out the best in physicians and, simultaneously, highlighted their weaknesses. Despite the clear link between avoidable chronic disease and excessive COVID-19 deaths, not a single doctor or physician association has stepped forward to claim responsibility for the problem or vow to do better in the future.

In our time of great need, Americans saw and celebrated an army of physician heroes. And in doing so, they overlooked an uncomfortable reality. Doctors are neither heroes nor villains. They are humans who share a culture that produces both remarkable successes and abysmal failures.

Until now, this culture has remained largely invisible. But like a virus, it affects people even if they can't see it. Physician culture wields tremendous influence over the lives of patients, doctors, and the nation as a whole, regardless of whether people acknowledge (or are even aware of) its existence.

Uncaring tells the story of a profession that is both triumphant and dangerously flawed, filled with people who aspire to help others, yet who sometimes act coldly, callously, and indifferently toward the pain of others. This book takes you inside the doctor's world, revealing unique insights about their training, their daily practices, and the culture they share. It is a book about people striving for perfection and about the impossibility of achieving it. It sheds light on the norms, rules, and expectations of doctors, and shows how culture shapes their thoughts and beliefs. It deciphers their evolving language, symbols, and codes. It highlights what brings doctors together and what isolates them from their colleagues and patients. Finally, this book examines the elements of physician culture that need to be corrected, the ones that should be preserved, and how to accomplish both.

The exploration begins by diving into the meaning and relevance of "culture," an abstract concept with myriad definitions and applications. Part One, "Diagnosing Physician Culture," takes you behind medicine's protective curtain. There you'll be introduced to the rituals, icons, and beliefs physicians share.

Part Two, "The Physician's Pain," explores the complex interplay between the healthcare system and physician culture, showing how both have contributed to a burnout crisis that is now wreaking havoc on US doctors.

Part Three, "Helping or Harming Patients?," focuses on the impact physician culture has on patients and the ways it contributes to the deterioration of our nation's overall health.

Having detailed the reasons doctors feel overwhelmed, fatigued, and in perpetual conflict with the world around them, Part Four, "The Social Ladder," looks at how changes in society are ratcheting up the discomfort physicians experience. Like the proverbial straw that breaks the camel's back, each new societal influence seems, on the surface, relatively insignificant and completely manageable. But together, these changing norms are proving too much for physicians to handle.

Part Five, "The Evolution of Physician Culture," offers patients, doctors, business leaders, and elected officials a difficult but necessary choice—one they will need to make in a world now socially, economically, and politically ravaged by the coronavirus. As the nation's "new normal" takes shape, all the options involving the future of American medicine will be painful and risky. This section outlines those choices and the path toward making US healthcare, once again, the best in the world. Through the process, physician culture has an opportunity to change for the better.

By the end of this book, having observed physician culture under the proverbial microscope, you will be able to see in fine detail what has long remained invisible. You'll better understand the doctors who provide your medical care and how you can protect yourself from their cultural shortcomings. Some of the stories in this book will inspire you and generate a deeper appreciation for the role doctors play in your life. Others will sadden you, opening your eyes to the many ways that physician culture compromises your health, harms our economy, and holds our country back.

The pages that follow tell the stories of dedicated people who aim to heal and who have, for centuries, earned the respect of their patients. You will come to understand the effects of a system and a culture held over from the last century. These relics served their purpose in simpler times.

But their time has passed. With facts, research, and personal stories, this book spotlights the valiance of American doctors and exposes their vices. It was written with the hope that our nation will protect the best parts of physician culture and seize on necessary improvements in medicine while also abandoning those cultural elements that cause harm to patients and doctors alike.

PART ONE

DIAGNOSING PHYSICIAN CULTURE

BLOODLETTING, HANDWASHING, AND GORILLA WATCHING

Invisible things are the only realities; invisible things alone are the things that shall remain.

—*William Godwin*

Humans are both fascinated by and fearful of what they cannot see. For centuries, unseen forces have fueled the world's most important academic endeavors. They led Sir Isaac Newton to theorize of an invisible force pulling matter toward the earth. They inspired Adam Smith's mystic principle of an "invisible hand" moving the world economy.

In our modern lives, the possibility of a hidden world governed by invisible entities has given way to some of our wildest conspiracy theories and greatest anxieties. We are fascinated by books and movies about secret societies, hidden agendas, and coded messages.

The root of my interest in the ever elusive physician culture was embedded in my professional experience of leading ten thousand doctors for eighteen years as CEO of the nation's largest medical group. During that time, I came to realize that physician behaviors are driven by something more than meets the eye. Without an invisible force guiding their thoughts and decisions, their day-to-day actions would seem nothing short of illogical. But with an understanding of this unseen influence, the contradictions of medical practice begin to make sense.

To help pull back the curtain on the invisible yet highly influential physician culture, here are two historical-medical examples, along with one plucked from modern psychological literature.

=====

GEORGE WASHINGTON DIED ON DECEMBER 14, 1799, two years after completing his second term in office. He lived to be sixty-eight, a remarkable life span considering the average person born in the Americas at that time died at age thirty-five. His impressive longevity notwithstanding, Washington might have lived several more years were it not for the medical care he received immediately prior to his death.

Washington, a former general, spent most of December 12, 1799, riding his horse in the snow and sleet around his Mount Vernon estate in Virginia. The next day, he came down with a sore throat. His doctors would eventually diagnose it as quinsy, a term that once meant throat inflammation. Medical historians would later call it croup, or acute epiglottitis (although it might have been a peritonsillar abscess instead). Regardless of what we call it, his throat infection was not the only thing that killed him.

In the early morning hours of December 14, the general suddenly awoke in great pain and informed his wife that he felt unwell. He could hardly speak and breathed with great difficulty. By sunrise, when the maid arrived to light the fireplace, she found Washington in severe respiratory distress.

Mrs. Washington sent the maid to fetch Colonel Tobias Lear, Washington's personal secretary. Observing his boss struggling with each passing breath, Lear sent for Albin Rawlins, the estate overseer, who prepared a medicinal mixture of molasses, vinegar, and butter. When Washington tried to swallow the concoction, he experienced what was described as an episode of "convulsive suffocation," yet another term that has not survived the centuries but is thought to mean a fit of coughing.

Hours later, and still not feeling better, Washington ordered Rawlins to perform a procedure commonly used at the time to restore health: venesection, better known as bloodletting.

As his condition continued to deteriorate, a third and final message was sent from the estate. This one went to Washington's personal physician, Dr. James Craik, who upon arrival later that day found the president's health status alarming. After assessing his patient, the doctor concluded that Washington's blood must still be tainted. In response, he performed two more venesections, draining about 1.2 liters each time. Still unsatisfied with Washington's clinical progress, Dr. Craik repeated the procedure several times throughout the evening, removing 3.75 liters of blood in all (from a body that would have contained no more than 5.5 liters total).

As Washington's life began slipping away, he wheezed and coughed out his dying requests. He asked that his aides finalize any unfinished letters and settle his books. He also insisted on being observed for three days prior to his burial just to be sure he was dead. Then, as night approached, Washington uttered his final words: "'Tis well."

The former president's official cause of death, to this day, is throat infection. In a time before antibiotics and ENT (ear-nose-throat) specialists, bacterial epiglottitis was indeed a common cause of death. However, with the aid of modern medical science, we can form a broader, more educated theory about what actually killed him. When medical historians and scientists examine the available evidence, most believe Washington's demise came not so much from a fatal infection as from a series of misguided medical interventions. To our nation's first commander-in-chief, and to his doctors, the removal of large volumes of blood was the surest path to healing. Today, we recognize bloodletting as a shortcut to death.

Venesection as a "healing" measure predates the rise of the Roman Empire by at least five centuries and is believed to have taken the life of King Charles II of England in 1685. The ancient practice of puncturing and draining blood from the human body originated at a time when medical knowledge left much to be desired. Blood was thought by some to be one of four bodily humors that had to remain in proper balance to preserve good health. Each humor was thought to be centered in a particular organ—brain, lung, spleen, and gallbladder—and all related to a specific personality type. Doctors believed that bloodletting rebalanced these humors, which is why it remained the most common medical practice performed for at least three thousand years.

During the Middle Ages, requests for bloodletting grew so great that doctors alone could not satisfy the demand. Barbers who were already skilled at using sharp, straight blades on their customers began performing bloodletting procedures in their chairs. At the end of each treatment, they'd hang their bloodied towels on sticks outside, a practice that lent itself to a now-familiar symbol: the traditional red-and-white-striped barber pole.

From the 1500s to the 1700s, hardly any doctors raised doubts about the advantages of bloodletting. Their concerns were intuitive, anecdotal, and largely ignored. But in the 1800s, the evidence against the practice turned scientific. Pierre Charles Alexandre Louis, a French physician with four first names, had been studying the use of venesection on patients with pneumonia. He found that 44 percent of those who were bled within the first four days of diagnosis went on to die. Only 25 percent of those patients who were bled *later* in their illness succumbed. He deduced that patients relieved of their blood later on had survived because they'd already passed through the worst phases of the disease. They could, therefore, better withstand the blood loss.

Louis was right, of course. Bloodletting was not then or now a useful treatment for pneumonia or for anything else (with the rarest exception to treat a condition called *hemochromatosis*, which involves excess iron storage in the body). Despite the accuracy of his conclusion, bloodletting's popularity persisted well into the twentieth century. In fact, Sir William Osler, considered by many to be the father of modern medical practice, was a conspicuous proponent. His textbook, *The Principles and Practice of Medicine*, had long been regarded as the definitive word on medical diagnosis and treatment. Strange as it might seem, bloodletting was included in this text as an acceptable medical practice up until the 1923 edition, nearly one hundred years after Louis scientifically demonstrated its harmful effects.

Given the carnage this practice inflicted throughout history, one might expect that doctors of the past century would lament their folly and have begged the belated forgiveness of the thousands, perhaps millions, of patients who died unnecessarily. On the contrary, you'll find little evidence of embarrassment or contrition in the medical literature. One recent account in the *British Journal of Haematology* celebrates the profession's wisdom, proclaiming that "the story of bloodletting illustrates how, over two thousand years, dogma was supplanted by scientific medicine." As recipients of medical care, we can be thankful that science did, eventually, win out. But would anyone consider a ninety-five-year delay in the acknowledgment of proven science to be a historical triumph?

The failure to advance medical practice in the face of controlled scientific evidence is, unfortunately, a trend that continues in modern times. In 2013, an article published in *Mayo Clinic Proceedings* reported that over one-third of well-established medical practices are ineffective, potentially dangerous, or both. But that's not all. Researchers from the National Institutes of Health looked at ten years of clinical papers from the *New England Journal of Medicine* and found that subsequent scientific evidence contradicted established practice in 146 of the 363 studies published. This means that 40 percent of the time, prevailing medical wisdom was (and still is) wrong.

We might assume that physicians would have learned from history's mistakes. We might hope that doctors, as a matter of cultural correction, would now cloak themselves in humility. We would be disappointed.

———

DOCTORS OF THE TWENTY-FIRST CENTURY point with pride to the incredible innovations and discoveries that have advanced modern medical practice. Magnetic resonance imaging (MRI) machines give physicians an unobstructed view inside the human body, allowing them to diagnose a multitude of conditions, from torn ligaments to malignant tumors. Heart-lung and ECMO (extracorporeal membrane oxygenation) machines enable doctors to stop and restart the human heart, bypassing the patient's own cardiopulmonary system completely. Scientists can now sequence the human genome, down to its last nucleic acid, paving the way for ever-more effective cancer treatments.

Despite all this scientific progress, physicians today often fail to fulfill basic clinical expectations. The story of an obstetrician named Dr. Ignaz

Semmelweis gives twenty-first-century observers a clear insight into the origins of this strange inertia. Let's join the German-Hungarian physician at his workplace in nineteenth-century Austria.

Fresh out of medical school in 1844, Dr. Semmelweis found himself perturbed by the maternal death rate in the obstetrical ward of the Viennese hospital where he worked. He calculated that as many as one in four mothers did not make it out of childbirth alive. He also observed a strange inconsistency: although his unit, run by doctors, had a high but typical mortality rate for the time, the adjacent labor and delivery unit, run by midwives, had a death rate two-thirds lower. Given that his fellow physicians had far more training and much higher occupational prestige than the midwives, Semmelweis was both perplexed and embarrassed by these mortality statistics.

Semmelweis knew these mothers were dying from a devastating uterine infection called puerperal fever, but he could not be sure what was causing it. (Mind you, it would be another fifty years before Louis Pasteur discovered the existence of bacteria and germs.) The accepted theory among Semmelweis's contemporaries had to do with the existence of miasmas. According to Europe's leading scientists at the time, miasmas were nasty little particles in the air that were associated with bad smells. These particles supposedly wafted from the streets and sewers of well-trafficked cities up into hospital rooms, where they were inhaled by mothers, who consequently suffered infection.

Short of burning down hospitals filled with these invisible particles, doctors of the 1800s believed there was nothing physicians could do to avoid or eliminate the problem. But if miasmas were the cause of this fatal fever killing mothers, then why was the mortality rate so much lower in the adjacent obstetrical unit run by midwives?

One day, a doctor who worked alongside Semmelweis accidentally nicked his finger while performing an autopsy on a woman who had just died from puerperal fever following childbirth. The doctor, in turn, developed a nasty hand infection and succumbed from an illness that seemed identical to the puerperal fever that had taken the life of his patient. Semmelweis recognized the significance of this occurrence. He postulated that the cause of postpartum uterine infection had nothing to do with tiny stink particles floating through the air. Rather, it had everything to do with the doctors who were performing the deliveries.

He hypothesized that the physicians who marched around the hospital with blood-stained hands and pus-splattered aprons were responsible for transmitting diseases to laboring moms. Based on this theory, Semmelweis ordered physicians in his unit to change their aprons and disinfect their hands by dipping them in a chlorine antiseptic solution before examining new patients. The results were astounding. The maternal death rate in the hospital plummeted from 18.27 percent to 1.27 percent.

In 1861, Semmelweis published his principal work, *The Etiology, Concept, and Prophylaxis of Childbed Fever*, outlining his research and the steps required to prevent the spread of disease. Knowing the results were indisputable and his findings capable of saving countless lives, he sent the paper to Europe's most prominent obstetricians and medical societies. He then personally addressed open letters to professors of medicine in other countries around the world, heralding the discovery.

Then he waited. And he waited some more. And nothing happened. Most doctors ignored Semmelweis's recommendations. Those who offered comment were openly critical of his theory. For years, his findings were either unheeded or outright rejected by the global community of doctors. Thanks in part to the widespread dismissal of his work, Semmelweis had trouble finding a job, and in 1865 he died alone in a mental institution.

Nearly 160 have passed since Semmelweis's breakthrough discovery. Medical knowledge, hospital cleanliness, and clinical practice today bear little resemblance to the filthy conditions and unenlightened routines of nineteenth-century Vienna. Doctors now understand the existence of bacteria and the spread of viruses. More than that, they have determined the exact genetic makeup of these submicroscopic organisms and identified their chemical composition down to the cellular membrane. As part of obtaining hospital admitting privileges, physicians must pass tests on hospital-acquired infections, including their origin and prevention. On written exams concerning the importance of handwashing and the dangers of spreading germs, doctors score perfectly.

However, contrary to what most patients assume, there exists a huge gap between what physicians know and what they do. Despite the pinpoint accuracy of the answers they provide on the tests, doctors across the country regularly fail to wash their hands (or use gel-based disinfectants) when going from one patient's room to the next. How regularly? According to the published findings of numerous research studies, doctors in US hospitals fail to wash their hands *one out of every three times* they enter a patient's room.

As in Semmelweis's time, the consequences remain dire. Healthcare-acquired (or associated) infections are the fourth-leading cause of death in the United States, affecting 1.7 million Americans each year and killing almost 100,000 of them. The spread of these harmful infections, particularly those caused by the deadly organism *Clostridium difficile* or *C. diff*, often results from doctors carrying the bacterium on their unwashed hands when going from one patient's room to the next.

Though these habits are extremely concerning, perhaps equally concerning is the blasé reaction doctors have to these mortality statistics. I have sat through dozens of hospital staff meetings where the issue of hand hygiene has been raised by infectious disease experts. The typical response from doctors is indifference. On occasion, when physicians speak up, it is to defend themselves. "I always wash my hands, except when I don't plan to touch the patient," one doctor will say to the agreeable head nodding of others. Or "I make sure to always wear gloves when I enter a patient's room," ignoring the fact that bacterium can spread when the gloves are put on and taken off. When the infectious disease experts at these educational sessions explain that handwashing remains vital, the physicians generally say nothing, preferring to disregard them, just like Semmelweis's colleagues.

How do we reconcile this continuation of poor hand hygiene, now more than a century after miasma theory was discarded and replaced by the germ theory of disease? The answer lies in physician culture—in the shared perceptions that doctors have about themselves and their colleagues. As healers, doctors desire respect and feel they must convey to patients, both verbally and symbolically, that they are consummate professionals and experts who know exactly what they are doing at all times.

In Semmelweis's time, doctors had a disgusting way of preserving the positive perceptions of patients and showcasing their expertise. Then it was assumed that the more dried blood and pus caked upon the doctor's leather apron, the more experience he had and the more respect he deserved. Surely any physician covered in guts must be well trained and extremely knowledgeable. Therefore the merest suggestion that the doctor's apron or the physician himself could be spreading disease was medical heresy. Doctors don't cause illness or harm patients. They heal them. Period.

Looking back, we can conclude that it was naïve and foolish of Semmelweis to assume doctors would simply discard their aprons and forfeit assumptions about their own professional excellence. They saw themselves as highly dedicated doctors, not as potentially contaminated sources of infection. It is no wonder they found Semmelweis's conclusions absurd and dismissed his recommendations.

Today the filthy leather apron has been replaced with the long white coat, a modern symbol of physician exceptionalism. Those who don it are presumed to be esteemed healers, not purveyors of harm. Implicit in the coat's color is the enduring cultural belief that physicians are pure, uncontaminated, and incapable of transmitting infectious disease. When a patient dies from a hospital-acquired infection, each treating physician assumes it was someone else's fault, probably the housekeeping staff or one of the nurses. These denials aren't scientific or logical. They are cultural.

Make no mistake, there is nothing that keeps doctors from observing proper hand hygiene. Soap, water, and paper towel dispensers are available in every patient's room. For physicians worried about damaging their skin, there are soothing alcohol-based antibacterial liquids adjacent to the sinks. The time required to practice good hygiene, especially with fast-acting disinfectant gels, is less than two seconds. And yet, nearly two hundred years since Semmelweis demonstrated the value of handwashing, US doctors omit this life-saving step one-third of the time. And just as they did then, physicians look the other way when their colleagues do the same.

━━━━━━

People who are immersed in a culture, any culture, including physician culture, seem sublimely unaware of its existence and its powerful influence. As they go about their lives, making decisions that they assume are independent of external forces, they view themselves as autonomous, rational thinkers. In doing so, they fail to notice or consider an important fact. They've been culturally conditioned to behave just like those around them.

To outsiders looking in, this failure to notice something so evident may seem impossible. Can people really overlook such a dominant force? Research from Harvard University answers this question in the affirmative. Let's go there now.

It's 1999, and in a large classroom located on the Harvard campus in Cambridge, Massachusetts, researchers are showing students a grainy VHS video. In it, six students are split into opposing teams of three: one team is dressed in white, the other in black. Both squads have a basketball and are standing in a vacant elevator bank.

Those watching this video are instructed to count the passes of the team in white as all six participants weave about in a formation that loosely resembles the warm-up routine for the Harlem Globetrotters. After about a minute, the tape ends, the lights in the classroom come back on, and the students are asked to report the number of passes. Most get the answer correct: thirty-four, or maybe thirty-five—it doesn't really matter for reasons that will soon become clear.

The students are then asked the following question: "Did you happen to notice anything unusual while you were doing the counting task?" As researchers Daniel Simons of the University of Illinois and Christopher Chabris of Harvard explain it, "We weren't really interested in pass-counting ability. We were actually testing something else."

That something else appears at about thirty seconds into the video while test takers are diligently following the bouncing balls. From the right side of the screen, someone enters the picture wearing a cheap-looking gorilla costume. This person—a female Harvard student, according to the study's authors—walks directly into the middle of the passing frenzy, thumps her chest, and then exits to the left of the screen after about nine seconds.

Here's the incredible and informative part: according to Simons and Chabris, half the students participating in the study failed to see it happen. As they explain in their best-selling book, *The Invisible Gorilla*, the researchers have repeated this study hundreds of times for different audiences all over the world. Every time, the results are about the same. Half the people never see the gorilla.

"We think we experience and understand the world as it is, but our thoughts are beset by everyday illusions," the duo explains. Often, what we see and what we don't is labeled "selective attention." When our job is to count passes, we don't notice anything else, even a gorilla. Under the right circumstances, most people won't see what's happening right under their noses, even when it's completely obvious to others. The same is true of culture. Culture is all around us, and yet we are unable to recognize its impact on our lives.

In American medicine, when doctors "follow the bouncing balls," they focus on what they can count: the growing number of patients they must see each day, the dwindling minutes they get to spend providing care, the declining rate of reimbursements per procedure, and the outrageous number of computer clicks required to document an office visit. In other words, they see the failures of the *healthcare system* while failing to notice an equally sizable problem staring them in the face. Physician culture is medicine's gorilla. It accompanies doctors everywhere, altering their perceptions and shaping their decisions. And yet they are unaware of its presence.

But it needn't remain this way. Even though physician culture is invisible, doctors don't have to stay oblivious to its existence. After all, once the participants in the Harvard experiment were told about the primate on the screen, they never again failed to notice their fellow student in that absurd gorilla costume. Once doctors begin to recognize the powerful role physician culture plays in their own practices, they'll never again overlook it.

PART ONE | CHAPTER TWO

A FIRST LOOK AT PHYSICIAN CULTURE

I N 1952, AMERICAN ANTHROPOLOGISTS ALFRED Kroeber and Clyde Kluckhohn published the outcomes of a painstaking research effort: documenting all known classifications and codifications of the word "culture" in English literature between 1871 and 1951. Hoping to better comprehend its usage and meaning, they compiled a list of 164 different definitions—a list that has grown, not shrunk, in the decades that have followed.

Culture remains an abstract and often confusing term. Entire library stacks are dedicated to its many manifestations in and effects on human civilization. Though there is doubtless intellectual and sociological merit in sorting through the various definitions and subtypes, this book takes a less punctilious approach when explaining culture's role in medicine.

This chapter outlines five of the most important facets of physician culture. Together they provide a foundation for understanding the ways doctors learn, practice, and pass on their shared knowledge, values, beliefs, and behavioral expectations.

1. PHYSICIAN CULTURE IS UNCONSCIOUSLY ABSORBED

From a young age, I've been disgusted by cigarette smoke. I can't stand within ten feet of a lit cigarette without coughing uncontrollably. When it was legal to smoke in bars and airport lounges, I remember watching the patrons gathered together inside, wholly unbothered by, and seemingly unaware of, the dense fog of smoke surrounding them.

Physician culture works much the same way. When you're in it, among it, and breathing it in, day after day, you don't notice the things that seem odd or offensive to outsiders. If you are encountering physician culture for the first time, you may find the customs, rituals, and norms described in these pages as inexplicable and disturbing as I find a room filled with smoke.

In the process of learning medicine and becoming part of the culture, doctors stop noticing the peculiarities of the profession. And it happens without notice. During initial clinical rotations, medical students are horrified by the off-color jokes told in the operating room and the deprecating comments made about doctors in other specialties. Yet, by the time these young professionals finish their residencies, it's all second nature: they observe the same customs themselves.

Physician culture is acquired through a decade or more of intense training. The lessons, stories, and beliefs that doctors hold dear are handed down from one generation of physicians to the next. Thus, how people think and behave, whether in the operating room or near an ashtray, is the result of cultural conditioning as much as it is their intrinsic values, intellect, or rational decision making.

2. PHYSICIAN CULTURE GIVES DOCTORS MENTAL SHORTCUTS

In the book *Thinking, Fast and Slow*, Nobel Prize–winning psychologist Daniel Kahneman explains two different systems of thought. One consists of the "slow" (or controlled) operations of the brain, which are deductive and in depth, requiring conscious and methodical analysis. Doctors rely on this pathway to solve the most complex medical and ethical problems they face.

The other is the "fast" (or automatic) system of thought, which is hardwired into the brain's circuitry. It allows people to know, without much thought, what actions to take. Culture is intimately connected with this "fast" thinking approach. It enables physicians to make snap judgments about what's wrong with a patient and helps them reach a quick and confident conclusion about the best treatment. Without these automatic associations, physicians could never get through a typical day. They would ruminate at length about every little decision, overwhelming themselves with the intricacy and gravity of each potential choice.

New doctors spend a lot of time figuring out what is expected of them, which rules to follow, and how to earn the respect of their leaders. Once they internalize the ins and outs of the physician culture, doctors don't have to think so hard about what to do. They just act.

On the plus side, this quick-sorting process reduces anxiety, helping doctors prioritize tasks and solve problems swiftly. On the negative side, these shortcuts leave physicians vulnerable to overlooking unusual medical problems, stereotyping patients, and falling into routines that can be harmful to themselves and those they treat.

3. PHYSICIAN CULTURE EVOLVES SLOWLY, IF AT ALL

When workplace cultures adapt, it's often in response to extreme external pressures. As a result, the process of managing change is rarely comfortable, quick, or successful. But it can happen. A rare and applicable success story happened in the 1990s at IBM.

For most of the organization's history, the corporate culture was notoriously insular and stiff. The salesforce dressed the conservative part, with the men clean-shaven and clothed in the classic uniform of a dark suit, white shirt, and "sincere" tie. Think: the opposite of Silicon Valley, where today's standard work attire includes T-shirts and jeans. IBM at the time sold reliable (even if creatively uninspired) computer hardware, earning itself the industry catchphrase: "Nobody was ever fired for buying IBM."

But when smaller personal computers began to threaten IBM's market position and revenue share, the board fired the CEO in 1993 and hired Lou Gerstner. As an outsider, Gerstner knew large mainframe computers would soon be antiquated. So he shifted IBM's business strategy from hardware to consulting. He also laid off 100,000 employees and ultimately sold the entire PC division. Over the decade that he served as CEO, the company became faster, nimbler, and more diversified. The culture shifted in lockstep, not because its employees wanted to but because they had to. The future of their business depended on it.

Today's IBM is a powerful player in the field of artificial intelligence. It's a fast-moving, progressive organization with a lax work-from-home policy, a wide open-door policy, and a dress code that has IBMers looking more like Silicon Valley entrepreneurs than their pressed-suit predecessors.

Cultural change is rarely a matter of choice. It's usually a matter of survival, brought on by outside pressures that make it impossible to maintain the status quo. Healthcare, however, has remained an outlier. In fact, of the one hundred or so companies and industries I have examined in my role on the faculty of the Stanford Graduate School of Business, healthcare's lack of change stands apart, particularly given how inefficient, inconvenient, and technologically outdated the industry is. The reason for its unchanging consistency is simple. Doctors benefit too much, financially, from the way things are and stand to lose too much, culturally (their prestige and privilege), by changing.

4. PHYSICIAN CULTURE IS FACTIONAL AND HIERARCHICAL

Cultural allegiances can be dangerous. For proof, look no further than "the beautiful game." Even before the coronavirus outbreak, some soccer matches around the world had to be played without spectators—not for fear of spreading disease but for fear that fans would kill one another, literally. The word "fan," short for fanatic, is a fitting designation for loyalists of English football clubs.

In one British study, researchers recruited subjects who "strongly identified" as fans of Manchester United (soccer's version of the New York Yankees, a franchise that's historically successful, well financed, and hated by many). After a brief intake, fans were sent one at a time to a building all the way on the other side of a university campus. Along the way, the research subjects all witnessed the same thing: a choreographed accident during which an actor toppled over in pain. In two different versions of the experiment, the victim who fell down was wearing either a Manchester jersey or the jersey of its much-hated rival, the Liverpool Football Club. The results speak powerfully to views we harbor about people from other "tribes." When the victim was thought to be a Manchester fan, the participants lent assistance on twelve of thirteen occasions. In contrast, when the victim wore the Liverpool jersey, he received assistance only three of ten times.

Similar factions and allegiances exist within physician culture. For example, surgeons deride primary care doctors as those who "contemplate their navels" as they search for "zebras" (very unusual diseases). In turn, primary care physicians accuse surgeons of following the sequence "ready, fire, aim," implying they rush patients to the operating room before they've adequately analyzed and diagnosed the problem. Orthopedists have been called "strong as an ox, and twice as smart," but certainly not by fellow orthopedists. Meanwhile, the everlasting battle between community doctors and those at academic medical centers has all the usual rancor of a "town and gown" rivalry.

The evaluation of other cultures according to the standards of one's own is called ethnocentrism. Since these judgments of others are invariably negative, one of the more dangerous consequences of tribalism is the tendency to perceive one's own norms, values, and customs as superior. This sense of hierarchy permeates medicine, creating an "us versus them" attitude among medical specialties. In fact, these negative perceptions extend to anyone physicians see as an "outsider," including insurers, hospital administrators, nurses, and even patients.

5. PHYSICIAN CULTURE IS COMMUNICATED THROUGH LANGUAGE AND SYMBOLS

Like barbers today who brand their businesses with red and white poles, doctors adorn themselves with specialty-specific symbols.

Pediatricians attach stuffed animals to their jackets. Internal medicine doctors drape stethoscopes around their necks. Otolaryngologists (doctors who focus on the ears, nose, and throat) wear headlights, reminiscent of white-coated miners. These symbols serve practical purposes. The toys help pediatricians win the trust of children. Stethoscopes are needed to evaluate the heart and lungs. Headlights help ENT doctors gaze inside the dark caverns of the human nose, mouth, and throat.

Of equal significance, these emblems are worn as badges of pride, no different from the color combinations that represent every college football team in the country. That's why neurologists, members of a highly contemplative specialty, frequently wear bow ties, while surgeons prefer OR greens, even when they're rounding in places outside the operating area.

Cultural symbols communicate powerful messages to future doctors, beginning on day one of medical school with the "white coat ceremony." Before the first day of classes, families gather to watch their offspring slip into one of the most recognizable symbols in all of medicine. Members of the academic physician faculty place white coats on the newly matriculated students.

The only exception to this ritual occurs when the future doctor's parents are, themselves, physicians. Those parents are allowed to help their sons and daughters into their new coats. This prohibition might seem strange: Why not allow all parents to participate in the ceremony and demonstrate their pride? And why is this specific exception made? The answer to both questions is cultural. Contrary to what an observer might presume, the ceremony isn't about the pride of the parents. Rather, it marks the transition of the inductees from their birth family to their new one. As parents sit on the sidelines, they symbolically agree to relinquish control of their offspring. No longer will they instruct their sons and daughters on how to dress, eat, or behave in public. The role of authority figure has been taken on by the medical school faculty. The message on that day is clear: only those who are steeped in the physician culture can be trusted to pass on the right values, beliefs, and norms to the next generation.

HEROES AND FOOLS

MONDAY MORNINGS ARE CHAOTIC FOR junior surgical residents. First, they have to get up to speed on all the patients admitted over the weekend. Next, they must prep for a full day in the operating room. Their mantra: stay alert, and be ready for anything.

I'd arrived at Stanford University Hospital promptly at five thirty one summery Monday morning to prepare for rounds at six. I grabbed a cup of coffee before heading to the ICU to scan patient charts. I hadn't even thumbed through the first file when a "code red" cracked over the paging system, summoning me to the emergency room.

A man's life was ending, and my job was to save him. Bounding down the stairs and racing around the corner, I could see three emergency medical technicians (EMTs) hovering outside the patient's room.

"Eighteen-year-old-pedestrian-struck-by-a-fast-moving-car-with-multiple-rib-fractures-abdominal-bruising-and-hypotension," said one paramedic in trademark staccato, covering all the essentials in a single, incomplete sentence.

I raced into the room and glanced at the monitor. The man's blood pressure was crashing at 60 over 20, his pulse racing at 140. As two ER physicians plunged IVs into each arm with pas de deux synchronization, a technician raced to the blood bank to retrieve four units of "packed cells" (red blood cells that have been separated from the liquid plasma for rapid transfusion). I called for a central-line kit and inserted a large-bore IV catheter into the internal jugular, a vein with a direct portal to the heart.

I hoped the massive infusion of fluid would keep the patient alive until the blood arrived. As his color faded, I asked, "Where's the technician with that blood?"

He entered the room seconds later, holding both bags in one outstretched hand like an Olympic relay racer passing off a baton. The nurse took the exchange, verified that the blood type matched the patient's, and hung two units immediately. A radiology tech wheeled in a portable X-ray unit, and five minutes later we had the film in front of us.

The diagnosis was as clear as the sunny California day outside: pneumothorax. There was air surrounding and compressing the right lung. Unless we provided an egress, the mounting pressure inside his chest cavity would prevent the heart from pumping well-oxygenated blood to the body. I asked for a chest tube set, painted the man's thorax with an antiseptic betadine, and inserted the plastic cylinder just above the bruised rib. His blood-oxygen level sprang back to normal. It was good to see, a step forward, but not enough. With a quick glance at the blood pressure monitor, I learned the man was still hypotensive. As fast as we could pour blood in through the neck vein, he was losing it from somewhere in his abdominal cavity. Our window to save this patient's life was slamming shut.

As I turned toward the nurse who was monitoring the patient's vital signs, I caught a glimpse of the clock on the wall. Twenty-five minutes had passed since the code red jolted me into action. Silicon Valley was still asleep. Most working folks in the Bay Area hadn't yet picked the morning paper off the lawn. As I said, Mondays are chaotic for junior surgical residents.

I instructed one of the nurses to page Dr. Paul Patterson, the attending surgeon on call, and to alert the operating room: "Tell them we're on our way and this patient will die without immediate surgery."

That was true. The human body is evolved to keep blood flowing to the vital organs even after a massive hemorrhage, but there's only so much human physiology could do for this eighteen-year-old body in front of me. We had to stop the bleeding. No time to waste.

The on-call senior and junior resident from the night before were still in the hospital, occupying the adjacent operating room, treating an equally unstable drive-by shooting victim. Dr. Patterson arrived just as our patient was being intubated. As we scrubbed our hands for surgery, he turned to me and asked, "What incision do you want to make?"

This was unusual. Junior residents usually aren't handed the knife for such a complex and risky procedure, but I leapt at the opportunity. "I'll make a long, vertical, midline incision," I said.

The poor kid. One-hundred-sixty-odd pounds of flesh and bone versus a two-ton automobile. I asked the nurse for a number 10 blade. With its curved cutting edge, I slit the abdominal tissue, observing extensive bruising along the entire upper half of the abdomen along with profuse internal bleeding in the abdominal cavity itself. Over the next two hours, we removed the ruptured spleen, cauterized the bleeding liver, and put hemostatic sponges over the oozing areas.

Operations like these distort your mental acuity. It's like trying to complete a jigsaw puzzle inside a sensory-deprivation tank. The next time I looked at the clock, it was eight thirty a.m. Two and a half hours had seemingly evaporated.

With the bleeding stopped, I closed the abdominal incision and bandaged the wound. After writing postoperative orders, I helped wheel our patient to the ICU with strict instructions to notify me should his blood pressure fall.

With that, I scrubbed into my scheduled surgeries. It wasn't yet halfway to lunchtime—not that I'd have time to eat. Throughout the day, I checked in on the car-accident victim between cases. With all the blood he'd lost, and all the fluid he had been given, it would've been easy for his sodium and potassium levels to become alarmingly abnormal. So I kept close tabs on his vital signs, electrolytes, and hematocrit (the volume percentage of red blood cells).

As a junior resident, I was on call every third night in the hospital, meaning one night in three I worked thirty-six hours straight. On good nights, I'd get a couple hours of interrupted sleep. On bad ones, none. I finished my elective surgeries around six that evening, saw a couple of minor consults in the ER, and got paged to the ICU just after midnight. It was the teenager from earlier that day. His blood pressure was crashing again. I palpated his abdomen, which felt like an overfilled water balloon.

This was going to be a long night. Alongside the attending surgeon on call, a different one than the day before, we reopened the abdomen and suctioned two liters of blood. I was worried a suture had come undone in the area of the splenectomy. It would have been a major technical error on my part. Thankfully, the splenic bed (located where the organ had previously been in the left upper abdomen) was dry. The problem was his pesky liver, which had suffered extensive bruising and tearing. Unlike the spleen, you need a liver, so you can't just take it out to stop the bleeding. Once again we sutured, cauterized, and placed hemostatic sponges on the surface of this essential organ. I stayed by the young man's bedside until morning.

Twenty-four hours after driving to the hospital and without a wink of sleep, I made rounds and headed to the OR. I had a full slate of surgeries ahead of me but felt fine. At six that night, just before heading home, my pager beeped. It was the ICU. The dike had broken again, and the young man's blood pressure was plunging for the third time in forty-eight hours. I should have started driving home at that point. Someone should have made me go.

The attending handed me the knife. I could have passed on the re-sponsibility to my co-resident, who had been assigned to work that night, but I told him I'd staff the surgery. I felt personally responsible. He understood. He'd insist on the same if our roles were reversed. It's just the culture.

By Wednesday morning, the teenager had turned a corner. His bleeding had stopped. I downed a cup of coffee, took three bites of a donut, and began morning rounds. Day three. By six that night, I only had one more task to complete. I needed to make sure all the patients who would be operated on Thursday had signed their consent forms.

The last patient I saw that evening was a sixty-year-old gentleman scheduled to have his colon resected first thing in the morning. He had a large so-called apple-core cancer, named after its appearance on a barium X-ray. I sat in the chair by his bed. As he turned his neck to face me, I felt my eyes closing. I jerked to attention. Had he noticed? Had my eyes actually shut, or had I only imagined it?

"Sir, did you complete your intestinal clean out already?" I asked him, the words spilling out of my mouth like warm soup. The next thing I remember, the patient was squeezing and shaking me, trying his best to wake me up. I opened my eyes to see his legs draped over the edge of the bed, and his bony fingers resting on my shoulder. "Go home, doc," he said. "You're in worse shape than I am."

He was right to be concerned. Sixty-some hours had passed after that first code red. In that time, I'd played the role of hero. I saved one life and improved a dozen more. I didn't lose a single patient during that sleepless marathon, nor had I harmed anyone to the best of my knowledge. But two and a half days without sleep had also turned me into a fool. I believed I was invincible and irreplaceable. I'd convinced myself I was capable of providing the best medical care despite my lack of sleep. In my self-deception, I had potentially and inappropriately put a man's life at risk. I own that responsibility. And I know that I was abetted by a physician culture that encouraged both sets of behaviors: the heroic ones and the foolish too.

Doctors are expected to be white knights, battling death for as long and as hard as it takes to save the day. Culture drives doctors to go above and beyond, to help and to heal, to perform what patients believe to be miracles. It forms the glue that bonds patients to their doctors and instills in both parties a mutual faith that everything will turn out all right.

Yet these same cultural expectations also drive doctors to their breaking points and beyond. Not every physician who stays up days at a time does so without incident. Sleep deprivation can lead to mistakes—even catastrophes.

Today's "duty-hour" limitations cap the resident's workweek at eighty hours (averaged over four weeks, with residents required to leave the hospital after thirty straight hours). Yet the unspoken expectations and unyielding demands placed on doctors still leave them feeling triumphant one moment and pathetic the next. Even now, physician culture turns heroes into fools.

A TWO-PART HISTORY OF TODAY'S PHYSICIAN CULTURE

MEDICAL PRACTICE DATES BACK MORE than five thousand years, to the agrarian civilizations of India and to the Middle Eastern villages of antiquity. In the Western world, the culture of medicine began taking shape approximately twenty-five hundred years ago with the oath of Hippocrates, a text that made sacred the physician's vow to honor patient privacy and treat the sick to the best of one's ability.

For most of medicine's history, diseases tormented doctors. Plagues killed millions, including the physicians who left the safety of their homes to comfort the sick and attempt to heal the dying. Before the introduction of modern diagnostic and therapeutic technologies, the doctor's experience, wisdom, and intuition were the best and only defenses against injury and illness. Lacking the scientific tools and understanding they have today, physicians rarely won their battles against disease. Entire civilizations died gruesome deaths with doctors at their bedsides. And yet the willingness of physicians to care for the sick despite constant threats earned them generations of admiration, gratitude, and esteem.

Across centuries, doctors have been respected and revered as healers, heroes, and valued members of their communities. Patients, even in the process of dying, have long expressed appreciation for the kindness, empathy, and compassion physicians provide. In return, doctors have remained willing to risk their lives to care for the sick, and they do so today with a powerful and righteous sense of mission. The result of this long-lasting, mutual bond is a relationship that has sustained the practice of medicine to this day.

Though it might be hard to imagine now, it was just two generations ago that doctors possessed only three diagnostic tools: a stethoscope, a reflex hammer, and a combination otoscope/ophthalmoscope (the hand-held instrument doctors stick in your ears and shine in your eyes). Though this armamentarium may sound archaic—even pathetic by today's standards—patients of a bygone era nevertheless had high regard for the physicians who used them. Rather than looking down on the profession, patients were appreciative of and deeply loyal to their doctors.

Fast-forward to the present day. Physicians now rely on sophisticated diagnostic machinery rather than human touch or the outdated triad of medical instruments. They use handheld ultrasounds to diagnose heart problems with far greater precision and accuracy than the stethoscope. Doctors now peer inside, and understand the inner workings of, the human body with the use of powerful CT, MRI, and PET scanners. These multimillion-dollar pieces of equipment allow doctors to quickly identify abnormalities that once required surgical exploration. Medications, treatments, and operations have advanced so rapidly that life expectancy has increased by more than twenty years in the past century.

Behind this stunning clinical success is an important cultural paradox: despite having more tools and knowledge to effectively treat their patients, American doctors are less respected than even a generation ago. While physicians maintain their respected status in American society, many doctors feel that their values (and their relative value) are under attack.

The courage of the coronavirus fighters no doubt placed a temporary halo over the heads of medical practitioners, but gratitude today is fleeting. Younger patients, especially, have begun gravitating away from the traditional doctor's office and toward any place that offers faster access, greater convenience, and lower out-of-pocket prices. Healthcare, like many "services" these days, is becoming less personal and more transactional. To understand the doctor's decline in esteem, it's best to begin with a look back at medicine's golden era.

THE ERA OF THE PIONEERS: TWO STEPS FORWARD

The discovery of penicillin, an antibiotic originally derived from a common mold, created modern medicine. This fortuitous finding by Alexander Fleming in 1928 kicked off decades of scientific fervor, helping to push antibiotics into ubiquity shortly after World War II. Around that time, doctors found themselves armed with a host of new and powerful drugs. The profession, once hampered by a lack of scientific research and clinical know-how, was by the 1960s racing toward ever-greater medical discoveries, giving doctors both the confidence and the ability to push the boundaries of medical practice.

Cancer was one of the first and biggest targets of this brave new era. The leaders in this fight, the earliest oncologists and radiation therapists, believed the disease needed to be battled with vengeance. They declared war, embarking on a period of relentless medical innovation, glorious achievements, and regrettable sacrifices.

The experimental weapons in the battle against cancer were primitive and inexact. Agents like nitrogen mustard, a product of chemical warfare, showed promise in killing cancer cells. These chemotherapeutic derivatives were generously infused into the bodies of patients, where they destroyed much more than cancer.

Deep down, America's oncology pioneers knew these drugs, yet to be refined, would bring their patients closer to death than to a cure. Administering them to children and young adults was a terrible burden for doctors to bear. It was also a necessary evil if there was to be any hope of curing leukemia.

Siddhartha Mukherjee's Pulitzer–winning book *The Emperor of All Maladies* brings readers face-to-face with the outsized personalities of these cancer-fighting pioneers. Stationed at the Dana Farber Institute in Boston, they were scorned by their more conservative colleagues for crossing the line that separates compassionate care from patient torture. Mukherjee, a masterful storyteller and researcher, links some of the success these pioneers experienced to their zeal and rebelliousness. In the book, they come across as rash and impetuous, bold and groundbreaking, like the Sex Pistols of oncology.

As a resident at Stanford, I worked alongside many of the West Coast cancer pioneers. A decade before my residency, they, too, had begun the same pursuit as their colleagues out East. Except the physicians at Stanford did not strike me as callous or irresponsible. They were not "ruled by none," as the Sex Pistols once described themselves. Like their colleagues in Boston, Stanford's oncologists were ambitious, caring, and driven.

What struck me as different about them was their ability to overlook the consequences of what they did (and had to do) each day in the name of progress. These pioneers coped with the anguish of harming their pediatric subjects by employing a powerful set of psychological defense mechanisms.

Based on my observations, *repression* and *denial*, not rebelliousness, kept these doctors going during the days of human experimentation in the war against cancer. In psychoanalytic theory, repression is the exclusion of distressing memories, thoughts, or feelings from the conscious mind. Denial, a close cousin, allows individuals to refrain from confronting uncomfortable truths, freeing them to take actions they otherwise couldn't.

Denial and repression have been part of the physician culture for centuries. In the Middle Ages, the logical fear of dying from the plague could have kept physicians locked in their houses. Instead, these subconscious coping mechanisms enabled doctors to go out into plague-infested streets to offer succor. These same psychological defenses allowed physicians in the era before anesthesia to amputate gangrenous limbs and go to sleep each night without the screams of patients echoing in their ears.

I will note that my observation of these pioneers was extended beyond the professional to something much more personal. While at Stanford, I also watched these medical giants care for my cousin Alan.

Growing up, Alan and I lived a few blocks from each other in Great Neck, a Long Island suburb about twenty miles east of Manhattan. If you were to enter Alan's boyhood bedroom, a ten-by-twelve-foot rectangular box at the end of a first-floor hallway, you'd be greeted by a long window on the far end, revealing the property's verdant backyard. Look at the other three walls, and you'd get a picture-perfect view into Alan's youth.

To the right is a wall lined with bookshelves, cramped with hardcover classics, dozens of biographies of world leaders, and various prayer books in Hebrew. Look left: games, playing cards, and an impressive stamp collection. Conspicuously absent are any posters of rock bands or scantily clad actresses. You'd find no decorative nunchucks, autographed baseballs, or trophies honoring athletic achievements. Instead, on the wall nearest the door, atop a dresser, sits Alan's most prized possession: his violin. Next to it, on the table, are hundreds of scores from classical compositions.

In school, Alan dragged his feet to gym class but ran through the halls to his German lessons. He joined the yearbook club and earned first-chair violin in the school orchestra. On weekends, while neighborhood kids played Little League, Alan and his mother listened to orchestral masterpieces on the family record player. My cousin would swirl his index finger in the air as if conducting the performances himself. In high school, when his classmates quoted the leading liberal politicians, Alan shot back with the words of conservative commentators like William F. Buckley.

Not wanting to be shoehorned into an easily categorized persona, Alan surprised everyone after graduation by enrolling at Oberlin, an institution that the *American Conservative* once called "An Insane Asylum" of radical liberals. Once on campus, he chose Asian Studies for his major and minored in Chinese. From the first day of college, he set his sights on a law degree from Harvard.

By this point, we had lost touch, as young men often do, which is why I was not aware that during his junior year, Alan made a discovery that would change his life forever. One November evening, while showering before bed, Alan felt a painless lump in his groin. Believing it to be a hernia, he flew back to New York over winter break to have it repaired by his father, a general surgeon.

My uncle Herb had three loves in his life: his wife, his children, and medicine. He was a skilled clinician who, after examining his son, suspected there was something not right about the mass. It didn't feel like the typical inguinal hernia. So rather than scheduling Alan for surgical repair, Herb biopsied the mass under local anesthesia and sent the tissue to the pathology department in the basement of the North Shore hospital where he worked. Two days later, the pathologist called with concern in his voice. My uncle raced out of a patient's room, took the elevator down, and examined the slides under a microscope himself.

Staring back at him through the ocular lens were the dreaded "owl-eyed" Reed-Sternberg cells, indicative of Hodgkin's lymphoma, a malignancy of the body's lymph tissue. Herb ordered a chest X-ray, which showed a mediastinal mass enlargement of the lymph nodes directly under the sternum. With lymph node involvement both above and below the diaphragm, Alan was designated "stage three."

In 1968, stage three Hodgkin's lymphoma was a death sentence, carrying a life expectancy of two years at most. My uncle, desperate to save his firstborn son, went to the medical library and scoured the literature for rays of hope. After weeks of investigation, he learned of two physicians at Stanford, one an oncologist and the other a radiation therapist, who were trying out a radical and aggressive experimental treatment for this particular cancer. Their approach threw the kitchen sink at the malignancy, hitting it with a potent cocktail of chemicals while bombarding it with radioactive emissions. The combination was likelier to devastate the body than rid the patient of the disease, but it was Alan's only hope.

Without hesitation, my cousin and his father flew across the country where Alan became one of the first patients in the United States to undergo aggressive cancer therapy for Hodgkin's lymphoma.

Every two weeks, doctors on the West Coast administered a series of powerful and extremely poisonous intravenous chemotherapy agents, producing in my cousin intense and prolonged abdominal spasms, along with vomiting that lasted all weekend. This was the reality for all patients enrolled in the protocol. Following chemotherapy, he underwent radiation treatments, which produced total-body weakness with diffuse lung damage.

All the while, despite the suffering they inflicted, Alan's doctors never blinked. They didn't hide from patients or families in their research labs or leave the day-to-day care to others. They were on the cancer ward, zipping from room to room, day and night, providing Alan and the other patients with compassion, encouragement, and hope. Throughout their workdays, these doctors managed to repress the apparent pain they caused, denied near certain failure, and celebrated their rare successes.

Neither Alan nor his parents ever thought about giving up. The physicians made sure of it. They knew the treatment was a long shot, but low odds were better than no odds. Over the next year, Alan flew cross-country, month after month, more than five thousand miles round-trip, for ongoing treatment and follow-up monitoring, consenting to whatever approach the doctors recommended to keep death at bay.

About a year after his chemotherapy ended, Alan received miraculous news: all his tests for cancer were negative.

My cousin felt as though he had a new lease on life and vowed to make the most of it. He received a master's degree from Harvard in Asian studies. He traveled to China for a year and became fluent in Mandarin, later returning to Harvard to complete law school, just as he had dreamed. By the time he graduated, Alan had become a true Renaissance man: a law expert, a global adventurer, an accomplished musician, and a polyglot.

With diplomas in hand, he moved to San Francisco to join the legal staff of a multinational telecommunications and transport company, rising quickly through the ranks. Before long, Alan and two of his friends split from the organization to build what would become a multibillion-dollar container shipping business.

Around the same time that Alan moved to the West Coast, I began my residency at Stanford, a short car ride from San Francisco. With distance no longer a barrier, it took us no time to rekindle our relationship. I loved driving to his condo near the Embarcadero, where we could see the lights of the Bay Bridge from his living room. True to the man Alan had become, his apartment was impeccably decorated with modern furniture, accented with Asian art. We dined in the city whenever we could. Alan enjoyed taking me to Chinatown, and I relished the looks on the waiters' faces when my cousin placed our orders in perfect Mandarin. Periodically, he'd take me to the symphony, or the opera, with comped tickets from his firm. He was always eager to offer a detailed analysis of the program as well as a biography of the featured violinist.

While in medical school, I'd become knowledgeable about Alan's disease and its treatment. As a resident, I followed his clinical progress closely, and for the next few years we would meet for lunch in the hospital cafeteria during his follow-up visits.

One day, during my sixth and final year of residency, Alan confided in me that he felt weak. He had just returned from a business trip to Asia and thought he might be coming down with the flu. I was careful not to alarm him, but I took it upon myself to check his laboratory test results that night (something no longer acceptable under current patient privacy laws).

The blood test showed an elevated white-cell count. Alan was told to return the next day for evaluation. The oncologist performed a bone marrow biopsy. Forty-eight hours later, Alan consented to restarting chemotherapy for acute myeloblastic leukemia, this round even more aggressive than the ones before.

In an era before the advent of bone marrow transfer, Alan's chances of being cured weren't just low. They were zero. Both his oncologist and hematologist knew the treatment would be futile. In fact, everyone at the hospital knew it—everyone except Alan and his family. No one had the heart to tell them.

I, too, said nothing. Though it was ultimately Alan's choice to take the chemotherapy, someone should have stepped in. Like my colleagues, I had been taught and trained to never let the patient lose hope, even when the prognosis was hopeless. I had not yet learned that the majority of patients and their families prefer truth over fantasy.

The drugs quickly destroyed Alan's remaining bone marrow, wiping out his white cells and leaving him vulnerable to infection. Two days after restarting treatment, he developed pneumonia that progressed to respiratory failure. Alan spent the next two weeks intubated in the ICU. They would be the last two weeks of his life. He died one month short of his thirty-first birthday.

When I think about the origins of present-day physician culture, both its triumphs and its failures, I'm reminded of my cousin. Alan was the first close relative of mine to die. My aunt and uncle stayed with me for the next several weeks. During that time, their faces grew gaunt and their shoulders slumped. They both aged a decade in the months that followed.

My uncle had lost two of his greatest loves. When Alan died, so did Herb's passion for medicine. He was never the same person or doctor after that.

Today's patients owe a debt of gratitude to the oncology pioneers of yesterday and to the psychological defenses that allowed them to push the medical frontiers. Repression and denial, the subconscious by-products of physician culture, gave Alan's doctors the confidence and courage they needed to cure his lymphoma. Their collective hubris and selflessness helped extend his life by a full decade, opening the door to future cancer-fighting innovations. However, these same cultural attributes made it impossible for them to admit defeat at the end of Alan's life, even when they knew the treatments they provided couldn't succeed.

This is the yin and yang of physician culture. "Save a life at any cost" inspires doctors to chase the elusive cure and refuse to quit. It also keeps them from facing the reality that, sometimes, there is no cure to be found. Over time, hiding from the truth became a cultural norm, as much for the benefit of the physician as the patient.

Today, the same defense mechanisms that propelled medical science forward in the era of the pioneers is now holding medical progress back and killing patients. Here's how it happened.

THE COMPUTER ERA: ONE GIANT LEAP BACK

The leading physician researchers and surgical superstars of the 1960s and '70s helped to accelerate medical science, making new discoveries and attacking diseases once considered invincible. They were true pioneers of the profession.

So profound was their impact on the medical sciences that American healthcare, by the 1980s, had reached world-leading status. US medicine was progressing at a pace never before seen. Research laboratories were quickly unraveling the mysteries of DNA, discovering the genetic basis for disease, identifying new types of viruses, and homing in on potential treatments for HIV/AIDS, even before the epidemic erupted.

American clinicians were riding intellectual highs and earning international awards—taking home three times more Nobel Prizes in physiology and medicine than scientists and researchers from any other country.

In parallel to these laboratory breakthroughs, researchers were beginning to uncover the origins of cardiovascular, pulmonary, and oncologic diseases that had befuddled doctors for decades. Year after year, physicians gained deeper insight into the perils of smoking, high blood pressure, and elevated blood lipids. Their findings educated the public and redefined the role of physicians. Novel drugs provided them with the tools to effectively lower blood pressure and prevent strokes. Doctors could not only treat heart attacks but prevent them by prescribing cholesterol-lowering statins. And, for the first time, doctors had cancer screening tools capable of identifying malignancies at their earliest stages, allowing them to intervene sooner, diminishing the likelihood of mortality from this most dreaded infirmity.

As medical knowledge soared, evidence-based practices and treatment protocols emerged. Ongoing research validated the notion that the most effective and life-saving care indeed came from science-based recommendations and well-defined algorithms. It did not, as doctors had previously assumed, come from their "clinical intuition," flawed recall of anecdotal experiences, or reliance on personal preference when treating patients. In this era of scientific innovation, the cherry on the top of American clinical triumph was the introduction of the personal computer. The information technology era had arrived, and the potential seemed limitless.

In the early 2000s, electronic health records (EHRs) slowly began to replace old-fashioned paper records as the preferred documentation method. The digital version churned out large quantities of useful clinical data that, in turn, brought about opportunities to systematize, streamline, and transform the delivery of medical care.

Through the computerization of scientific and medical data, healthcare systems could embed in their EHRs a series of step-by-step checklists for doctors to follow. These new protocols made it possible for all physicians, not just the smartest, to provide excellent, error-free medical care almost every time. Computers were now capable of instructing doctors on how best to prevent disease and treat problems. Physicians could easily and quickly access these clinical "how to" guidelines while the patient sat in the exam room or lay on a gurney in the ER. Although some patient issues proved too complex or rare for computerized approaches, the overwhelming majority of diseases had a clear, well-defined path for diagnosis and treatment.

As data became more readily available, hospitals, insurance companies, and government health agencies joined forces in the spirit of continuous improvement to equip doctors with detailed evaluations of their performance. For the first time in history, physicians could be ranked from best to worst in dozens of clinical areas based on quantifiable, objective outcome measures.

Like pro athletes, physicians now had "stats," which were placed in front of them each month in the form of a performance report. In these reports, doctors could compare their complication rates following surgery to those of their colleagues. They could see their success or failure in preventive medicine, patient satisfaction, and myriad other measures. Consumer groups quickly jumped on board, pushing for more metrics, more consistency, and ever-greater improvements.

Never before had physicians had so many tools and so much information at their disposal. With all of it, they could prevent diseases, avoid complications, and save lives like never before. And so you might think these newfound opportunities to extend life would be cause for celebration among American physicians. You would be wrong.

Had our nation's doctors chosen to follow the science, adhere to the checklists, and embrace the newest information technologies, Americans today would be among the healthiest patients in the world, beneficiaries of a brave new world of clinical science and high tech. When presented with these twenty-first-century solutions, physicians did not respond with gratitude or grace. Instead, they went on the attack, rejecting the notion that medical practice could or should be standardized. Rather than promoting the scientific merits of consistent care delivery, physicians saw comparative performance reports and algorithmic approaches as threats to their intelligence, intuition, and hard-earned independence.

If you find it hard to excuse the doctor's resistance to technology and science in the era of computers, imagine yourself an up-and-coming physician whose training predated widespread IT systems. While your friends were traveling the world and having kids after college, you were cramming your head with thousands of anatomical terms, biochemical pathways, and pharmaceutical dosage recommendations. During residency, you worked eighty to one hundred hours a week. All in all, you devoted more than a decade of your prime years to mastering the ins and outs of the profession, believing that your ingenuity, experiences, and problem-solving abilities were perfectly suited for what your mentors hailed as the "art of medicine." Finally, it's your turn to reap the reward of your efforts. You feel you deserve the praise of your patients, the respect of your colleagues, and the opportunity to exercise your clinical judgment without anyone looking over your shoulder. As a well-trained clinician, you are confident that your intelligence places you in the upper echelon of all doctors. Now is your time!

Then, suddenly and without warning, the computer era forces you to check your ego at the exam room door. You are confronted with clinical outcome data that flip your perceptions upside down, undermining your confidence and shattering the illusion that you are "special" or even in the top half of your specialty. According to these new performance reports, the difficult truth is that you, like most of your colleagues, are average, not exceptional.

Practically overnight, algorithms and evidence-based expectations have rendered your intuition and independent judgment relatively insignificant and, potentially, deadly. Though these performance reports are disseminated with the intent to help you improve patient care, they feel like a slap in the face.

This conflict between science and medical culture existed in the nineteenth century, too, when Semmelweis's contemporaries rejected the idea of handwashing. And it continues today. If you ask doctors whether medicine is an art or an applied science, they will insist it is more the former than the latter. Type "the art of medicine" into Google and the search engine will present a litany of articles by physicians who bemoan the loss of artistic expression in clinical care, by which they usually mean that they miss the freedom to practice as they prefer.

If you eavesdrop on discussions in hospital conference rooms, you'll hear physicians from every specialty castigate the influx of computerized checklists and algorithmic solutions. "Cookbook medicine," they call it with contempt. Medical care isn't, in their minds, some recipe to be followed but rather a craft, a creative skill, a showcase of personal experience and individual judgment.

With a sneer, they complain the profession is being overrun by "metrics," implying that clinical outcome measures are irrelevant statistics, time wasters, and meaningless expectations that only make the physician's job harder. Doctors use these derisive terms to defend the status quo and the freedoms they value. Their response might seem strangely antiscientific to outsiders. Medicine is, after all, a profession anchored in biology, chemistry, anatomy, and physics. But here's the thing: physicians do not reject science. They merely resent how it is being used to control and judge them. They reject any expectation that they need to improve. All doctors believe they are outstanding and exceptional. How dare the comparative performance reports challenge and undermine that assumption?

In the parlance of physician culture, the word "science" carries a positive connotation. Science is all about facts, rigor, and pragmatism, which are essential for the practice of medicine. But implicit in the word "art" are the highest ideals of the profession. These values include vocational freedom, personal preference, and individual creativity.

Physicians view medicine as a uniquely creative venture. To them, the doctor's role is to solve complex puzzles, engage with colleagues in serious clinical discussions, and produce one-of-a-kind medical masterpieces for the benefit of patients. That is what they were promised in medical school and why they trained so intensely for so long.

Doctors fancy themselves great artists: masters in the same vein as Rembrandt, Monet, or Picasso—all different but uniquely expert in their craft. As absurd as it would seem to replace history's greatest painters with a lesser-trained apprentice, so, too, it would be outrageous to substitute a doctor's skill with a computerized algorithm or a nurse practitioner who did not undergo the same rigorous training.

Yet when it comes to objective measurements of medical outcomes, doctors who rely on their individual experience, intuition, and "creativity" lag their colleagues who adhere to standardized, evidence-based approaches. Regardless of the doctor's preferences, or the culture's lingering values, the most effective care is the kind that adheres to proven clinical protocols. Despite the great value doctors place on their "artistic" abilities, the best medical outcomes come from medicine's version of a paint-by-numbers kit. Physicians today are caught between how they want to practice and how they're expected to practice, forcing them to grapple with a disconcerting possibility no previous generation of doctors had to consider: Are we replaceable?

As medicine becomes increasingly standardized, evidence-based, and algorithmic, physicians can feel their position at the top of the socio-professional hierarchy slipping. This is a tough realization for the men and women of a proud professional culture. But regardless of how doctors feel, the science is clear: There are better and worse approaches for treating patients. Whether it's controlling high blood pressure, managing diabetes, or performing surgery, there is almost always a best way to do things.

Faced with facts that contradict their cultural norms and values, doctors are increasingly unhappy and unfulfilled. They are responding negatively, often with outward expressions of anger. They hurl their collective hurt onto the proponents of scientific progress and technological change. Psychologists call this *projection*, and like repression and denial, doctors use this defense mechanism as a way of dealing with unwanted emotions.

Instead of admitting that variation in clinical care leads to poorer patient outcomes, doctors accuse performance-report proponents of wrongdoing. I once heard a community physician say that algorithmic approaches were designed to "turn great doctors into average ones." In practice, such approaches elevate the outcomes of all clinicians. Psychologically, physicians feel caught between the creative profession they chose and the more mundane job that medicine has become.

Doctors today project their feelings unconsciously, as a safeguard against the overwhelming sensation that the profession they love is leaving them behind.

When the fight against cancer (and the more recent one against the coronavirus) called for heroes, doctors utilized their intelligence, fortitude, and defense mechanisms to meet the challenge head-on. Through repression and denial, they held their fears and emotions in check for the betterment of all humankind.

Yet when scientific discoveries and information technologies call for greater consistency in medical practice, doctors choose to rebel. They lash out at the data, the checklists, and the constraints placed on their practice. Frustrated and unfulfilled, doctors blame others for their unhappiness and decry the broken system in which they work. As a result, patients are suffering and dying. So, too, are physicians.

THE PEOPLE V. PHYSICIAN CULTURE

Two symbols represent the medical profession. One, the Caduceus, features two snakes coiled around a winged staff. This ancient emblem dates back to 1400 BCE and today adorns the white coats of doctors, along with prescription pads and the covers of countless medical textbooks. The other symbol is the Rod of Asclepius, a single snake wrapped around a wingless staff. It serves as the official emblem of the World Health Organization and more than one hundred other healthcare bodies around the globe.

To those unfamiliar with the origins of these symbols, a logical set of questions may emerge. Why does medicine have two similar-looking logos? And why do they both feature snakes and staffs?

As for the question of snakes, one theory connects the fact that these reptiles shed their skin with the metaphor of regeneration and restoration, two outcomes doctors have sought for patients throughout history. The staff is most likely a reference to an ancient treatment for patients infected by the guinea worm (*Dracunculus medinensis*), a parasite that enters the human body through the consumption of contaminated water before traveling through the blood stream to the arms or legs. Once trapped in an extremity, the worm burrows its way toward the skin where it produces intense itching, pain, and burning. In time, a blister surfaces and soon ruptures. That is when the snakelike head of the guinea worm protrudes. Healers of the past would wind the creature's head around a stick (the noble staff) and slowly pull the parasite out, thus curing the patient and leaving medicine with its famed emblem of healing.

Although the two symbols are nearly identical, they have different origins and meanings. In mythology, the Caduceus, a symbol of the Greek deity Hermes, is associated with commerce and identified with thieves, merchants, and messengers. In contrast, Asclepius is the ancient Greek god of medicine and health.

The image of the Caduceus first became popularly (mis)associated with doctors when the US Army Medical Corps adopted it as their symbol in 1902 and placed the image on the uniforms of medical officers. Though the mix-up was unintentional, the emblems inadvertently symbolize the two divergent roles of the physician culture.

Because medicine is simultaneously a healing profession and a lucrative trade, one can link the Caduceus to the economic well-being of doctors and the Rod of Asclepius to the profession's higher sense of purpose. Doctors today find themselves drawn to both of these competing interests. At times, they feel pushed to act on their own self-serving financial interests, and at other times, as during the coronavirus pandemic, they're pushed in the direction of their millennia-old mission to heal.

On occasion, the forces of mission and money align, such as when plastic surgeons use revenues from cosmetic cases to fund global surgical trips. Once landed, they provide free reconstructive surgery to children with cleft lips and palates. Most often, however, the two motivations compete.

When we look at the declining state of American healthcare today, it seems difficult to defend the consequences of physician culture. It has led doctors to turn their backs on evidence-based guidelines and IT solutions. It has enabled factually inaccurate and tone-deaf declarations that American healthcare is the best in the world. It leaves doctors in a defensive posture when confronted with data on the hundreds of thousands of deaths caused each year by medical error in the United States.

Yet, despite its flaws, it would be wrong to ignore the undeniable dedication, commitment, and zeal for excellence the culture engenders in physicians. It deserves to be judged fairly.

Asked to defend physician culture in a court of opinion, I believe I'd have a winnable case. On the first day of trial, I'd arrive in a long-sleeved white coat, knowing its ivory crispness would catch the eyes of all twelve jurors, communicating cleanliness, honesty, and purity—qualities deeply embedded in the culture of medicine. With its tailored three-button front, the coat would create a sleek silhouette. Its fancy embroidery, reading Robert Pearl, MD, would command respect while evoking a deeper sense of trust than if I had arrived wearing a dark suit, white shirt, and conservative tie.

During opening arguments, the prosecution would doubtless lambast doctors for their failures in prevention, avoidable medical errors, and excessive costs. Opposing counsel would label physicians arrogant, stubborn, and self-important. With those objectionable character attacks still hanging in the air, I'd begin my defense.

Rising from the defendant's table, I'd stride to the front of the jury box and acknowledge right away that physician culture, like any culture, has its flaws. Doctors could do better, far better than they do today. But as I shift gears, I'd ask the members of the jury to think about *their* doctors and all the times physicians have helped them and their family through difficult times. I would trumpet the heroic sacrifices of those who risked their lives during the coronavirus pandemic. I'd go on and on about the physician volunteers who leave the comforts of their offices to help the less fortunate, and volunteer their precious nights and weekends to treat uninsured patients in community clinics. After pausing to let the jurors bathe in the warm, emotional affinity they have for their own physicians, I'd begin to describe the doctor's pain.

Ladies and gentlemen of the jury, please recognize that physicians would never intentionally harm a patient. To do so would be antithetical to the culture they hold dear. Instead, the harm they inflict is more like collateral damage, an unintended result of a chaotic set of circumstances. To explain, I'd ask you to put yourself in your doctor's shoes. From this vantage point, you can see the past few decades have been most unkind. Doctors today suffer great dissatisfaction, unhappiness, and disillusionment. The scientific evolution of medicine and the insurgence of information technology have wreaked havoc on their psyches, not unlike the toll that automation and globalization have taken on the American factory worker. These are not excuses for the mistakes of doctors but explanations for their failings. They are mitigating factors worthy of your consideration and compassion.

The doctor's dual loss of status and control over the past two decades has been psychologically devastating. Despite dedicating their adult years to learning and practicing the art and science of medicine, physicians feel less valued and less important than ever before. They feel cheated out of the profession they were promised. What it once meant to be a doctor is not at all what it means to be a doctor today.

To illustrate the tragic loss of esteem, I would then recount an experience from the fall of 2017, which puts the doctor's pain in context. For me, it encapsulates the resilience, grace, and beauty of physician culture in the face of so much degradation and disrespect.

I TOOK AN EARLY MORNING flight from Washington, DC, to a prestigious academic medical center in the Northeast. I've chosen to omit the institution's name in deference to the physicians and residents who work there and who deserved better treatment than they received that cold autumn day.

After completing a lecture on the future of American healthcare in the main auditorium, I joined some of the hospital's residents for lunch in the cafeteria.

While I was waiting in line, the hospital's CEO, whom I'd met earlier that morning, cut ahead of our group with three young men in tow. They were all wearing business suits. One of the residents from our group, clad in his OR greens, asked what they were doing. The CEO replied, "I'm getting lunch for my busy administrative fellows."

In that moment, the four residents standing patiently in line learned a valuable lesson about where they rank in the healthcare hierarchy. In the culture of hospital administration, the people accorded highest status include financial analysts, chief financial officers, and department managers. Save for a few doctors who bring in a disproportionate sum of the hospital's revenue, most physicians don't make the cut. Strange as it may seem, administrators value MBAs more than MDs. Through the lens of the hospital CEO, those who manage the facility's finances are more important than those who provide the medical care. Thus they are entitled to eat first in the cafeteria, marking a 180-degree reversal from just a generation or two ago when the opinions and concerns of doctors carried the most weight.

As the residents and I placed our trays at our table and pulled out our seats, I expected to hear a barrage of snide comments about the rudeness that just took place. There was none of that. Instead of bemoaning the slight, the residents began talking about potential solutions for the problems confronting the American healthcare system. I was impressed by their insights, ideas, and civility.

I asked the two men and two women in our group about their interest in healthcare policy. The pair of residents sitting across from me had both worked in safety-net programs for disadvantaged segments of their communities and planned to return to them after residency. The tall gentleman to my left came from a small rural town in Montana and hoped to work alongside the only other doctor in the area following his training in family medicine. The fourth resident, a woman with a master's degree in public health, told us she would be returning to Washington, DC, after surgical training so she could split her time between her practice and a healthcare policy group focused on expanding Medicaid.

I was inspired by their dedication to medicine and their personal commitment to their respective communities. It's possible that I simply got paired with an exceptional group. Perhaps their co-residents were pursuing medicine mainly as a means to a privileged lifestyle. But based on the conversations I've had with numerous medical students and dozens of residents from across the country, I am confident that most view medicine as a calling, not a cash cow.

So I ask you, men and women of the jury, how would you feel if you were a young doctor about to embark on a thirty-year career in medicine? Wouldn't you feel frustrated, insignificant, and small if the hospital CEO so callously devalued you? Now multiply that emotion across an entire profession. Every day, doctors feel stripped of their dignity and decision-making abilities. They are forced to jump through bureaucratic and regulatory hoops. They're expected to follow the checklists embedded in their computers, not to think creatively.

Making eye contact with the juror who seemed most sympathetic to the distress of doctors, I'd add:

Yes, physicians need to follow the science more regularly. But despite what the other side has told you about the superiority of evidence-based approaches and computer-derived protocols, remember that there are times when science and technology are wrong. If there is even a slight chance that your medical situation might be unique, falling outside the averages and algorithms, wouldn't you want your doctor, a trusted human, to step in and override the guidelines? Don't get me wrong: technology and science serve a vital function in medical care, but the physician culture has, time and again, proven its distinctive value. To demonstrate that value, let me call my first witness.

―――――――――

GLORIA (NOT HER REAL NAME) sought me out a few years after my residency, still early in my career as a plastic and reconstructive surgeon. Looking at her chart, I could see she had recently moved to California and joined Kaiser Permanente as a member, the organization's preferred term for "patient."

She had been referred to me by a primary care physician to evaluate and treat the hemangioma on her face. And because Gloria was a new member, I wasn't sure what to expect when I knocked on the exam room door. Hemangiomas are benign tumors, dense overgrowths of blood vessels in one area of the body. Sometimes they're little more than a red dot, an ink spot on the skin with the diameter of spaghetti. Other times, these vascular malformations grow much, much bigger.

I opened the door to greet Gloria and could see right away her problem was extensive. The tumor was beet red and larger than two fists. It swelled the entire left side of her face. She told me that young children passing her in the street would often point at her or cling to their parents in fear. Gloria's rendition of her daily struggles touched me.

She had already undergone more than a dozen procedures by plastic surgeons on the East Coast. Sitting opposite her, I asked why she was interested in going through yet another surgery.

She had just moved here to begin an import-export business with co-headquarters in Asia, she said. It was a once-in-a-lifetime opportunity, and she wanted to pursue it with utmost confidence. I doubt that many people with her degree of deformity would be willing to venture every day into a world that can be intensely cruel, no matter how enticing the business prospects.

"I'd be grateful for any improvement you could make to my overall appearance," she said. I hesitated, trying to figure out how to be empathetic while voicing my sincere doubt that surgery would result in any noticeable improvement. Uncomfortable and unsure how best to articulate my concerns, I probably came across as insensitive in my reply. "Any additional treatment would have limited cosmetic benefit. I'd recommend you not take the risk."

After six years of surgical training, I knew it would be dangerous to operate on someone with a hemangioma as extensive as Gloria's. Because her vascular abnormality was thick and infiltrating her facial muscle, attempting a complete excision of the tumor would paralyze her face, creating a problem far worse than the one she had to endure now. A scaled-back procedure, debulking the tumor, would require incising the vascular lesion itself, potentially causing major hemorrhage or death. And even if the operation went without complication, there were a litany of postoperative risks, including infection and poor healing.

Despite all those concerns, I knew the greatest risk wasn't technical. Instead, for patients like Gloria, it's that they usually come to surgeons with unrealistic expectations, hoping for a miracle.

The warnings of my plastic surgery instructors rang in my ears. *When a patient has undergone multiple surgical procedures without successful resolution, and has no fear of undergoing another, consider it a red flag and a huge medical-legal risk.* I could see the graph I'd committed to memory early in my residency. Along the horizontal axis was "likely improvement" and on the vertical axis was "patient expectation." A 45-degree line divided the rectangular space in two. People whose expectations exceed the most likely reality will always be disappointed. And it's invariably the last surgeon to operate whose reputation is marred.

Had Gloria's request been transmogrified into a question on a plastic surgery board exam, the correct answer would be to deny her another operation. And had I relied on a computerized treatment algorithm for guidance, it, too, would recommend no further intervention.

Science-based guidelines exist to temper the doctor's "gut feelings," reducing the likelihood of error while increasing the probability of a safe outcome. By calculating the averages, these computerized care models prove extremely successful in saving the most lives and preventing the gravest harms. However, they do so without regard for the uniqueness of individuals. They are not designed to recognize exceptions to the rules.

The *science* of medicine calculates risk and identifies the safest path forward for both doctor and patient. The *art* of medicine, by contrast, elevates individuality, finding beauty in life's most precious exceptions.

If Gloria had been any other patient, I would have sided with conventional wisdom and held my ground. But I did not turn Gloria away that day. After talking at length, I sensed there was something different about her situation.

My conclusion wasn't statistical but intuitive. Contrary to what I'd been taught about patients like her, I was convinced Gloria was not in denial. Based on our discussion, my *intuition* told me that her courage to pursue her dreams despite the obvious deformity on her face meant that she harbored no delusions about what surgery could achieve. I was confident she was an exception to the rules.

Gloria accepted that nature had dealt her a cruel card. Despite the nasty stares, the rude questions, and the looks of revulsion on the faces of children, she was eager to travel across the Pacific in pursuit of new life experiences, new opportunities, and new social interactions. She relished life and all its opportunities. For her, surgery wasn't a panacea. It was a reason to lift her chin ever-so-slightly higher when walking into a room. That was, at best, all I could give her. And in my heart, I believed it would be good enough for Gloria.

Over the next ten years, I operated on her more than a half dozen times. Most of the procedures were very minor, frequently under local anesthesia as an outpatient. After each surgery, Gloria sent me a handwritten thank-you card. I couldn't be sure if she was more grateful for the small aesthetic improvement or for the fact that I believed in her.

There is great danger in doctors who default to anecdotal experience and intuition over science. As Gloria's story demonstrates, there is also danger in stripping doctors entirely of their ability to exercise independent judgment. Anecdotes and one-off experiences are no substitutes for rigorous analysis and statistical significance, but our lives and our world would lose much of its humanity and meaning without these people-centered cornerstones of physician culture.

As you can see, ladies and gentlemen of the jury, Gloria is an example of how physician culture complements science and elevates the profession for the benefit of patients. My second and final witness will speak to the priceless moments when physician culture not only lifts up doctors and patients but rescues them as well.

———

THE KITCHEN PHONE RANG ON a bright spring morning. It was slightly after eight o'clock on a Saturday. On the line was a pediatric oncologist I knew from Kaiser Santa Clara asking me to consult on a hospitalized pediatric patient with leukemia. The girl was now in her third course of chemotherapy. It sounded urgent.

Within the hour, I was standing at the bedside of a ten-year-old girl named Kathy. Her lightly freckled skin glistened with sweat. She was running a fever of 102 degrees. Thin rays of California sunshine pierced the window shades of her room, a small and sterile space tucked in the corner of the pediatric intensive-care ward on the hospital's seventh floor.

Kathy's mother and father, both gowned and masked, took turns mopping their daughter's forehead and neck. I closed the medical chart and leaned over so that the patient and I could speak face-to-face.

"Hi Kathy, my name is Dr. Pearl. I am a plastic and reconstructive surgeon. How are you feeling?" Her pale blue eyes shied away from me, toward her mom, as if seeking permission. Kathy's mother scrunched her nose and eyebrows, nodding as if to say, "It's okay, sweetheart, you can answer the doctor." Kathy whispered, "Not very good," still keeping her eyes on her mother.

Of course, I knew Kathy wasn't well. From my conversation with the oncologist, I was aware that she had a severe infection, although the physicians caring for her couldn't be certain of its exact nature or location. I also understood the girl's reticence. New doctors bring out shyness in pediatric patients.

It's common for children to feel helpless in hospitals. All day, they sit in bed and on the fringes of important medical discussions, trapped in a strange, self-detached reality. Their bodies and diseases become the center of conversations to which they are not invited. Expressionless physicians scurry in and out of the room firing questions and observations at the parents as if the child were invisible: *How is she feeling today? We need to run some more diagnostic tests on her.* White-coated strangers rudely pull parents aside and fill the room with indecipherable terms. They speak in hushed tones as if telling diabolical secrets. Orderlies appear abruptly and whisk the children away—off to the next series of scary tests or painful procedures. In hospitals, urgency takes precedence over the kind of patience and tenderness that builds trust.

In my tenure as a surgeon, I worked hard to master the art of conversing with younger patients. One key to success was giving kids an expanded (if somewhat artificial) sense of control. I did that by speaking with them directly, hoping to make all the chaos and confusion feel a tad more tolerable.

I leaned in closer to Kathy, looked at her, and asked, "Does it hurt anywhere?"

Perhaps sensing my sincerity, Kathy craned her neck in my direction, tilting her chin toward her right upper arm. There the area was inflamed with a fiery red discoloration. Her eyes showed me the exact location of the pain and the depth of her discomfort.

Four hours earlier, the nurse had used a black felt pen on Kathy's arm, marking the boundary between her normal freckled skin and the bright-red erythematous area. Examining the girl's arm, I could see angry red streaks extending well beyond the black ink, some reaching as high as her armpit, an area doctors call the *axilla.* Throughout the morning, physicians administered a variety of powerful antibiotics to douse Kathy's infection. All produced negligible improvement, like dropping a slurry of water on a raging forest fire amid the blustery Santa Ana winds.

As I studied her arm, the room fell eerily silent. The *drip, drip, drip* of Kathy's IV fluid echoed in the plastic tubing. The hospital room itself was a foreboding space devoid of flowers, balloons, or well-wishing friends. The sparseness was a necessity in Kathy's case. Any exposure to germs, no matter how innocuous, presented a great risk because of the high-dose chemotherapy, which had thrashed the infection-fighting white blood cells in her body.

My mind sifted quickly back through Kathy's medical record, review-ing its contents for relevant facts. I started with the pediatric resident's progress note, written just minutes before I arrived: *The patient, a 10 Y.O. girl with leukemia, admitted to the pediatric ICU Friday morning following third round of chemo. On admission, temperature was 102 with a rapid pulse. Blood pressure normal. White blood-cell count precipitously low.*

That's the problem with chemotherapy, I thought. Too much of it and the patient can die from the medication. Too little and she dies from the cancer itself.

My mind continued flipping through the patient's medical informa-tion: *By yesterday afternoon, Kathy's white cell count was less than 10% of nor-mal, significantly compromising her body's ability to ward off infection. Slight redness was spotted at the site of her IV last evening, which has spread over-night above the elbow. The plastic surgeon* (that's me) *was consulted at 8 a.m.*

In that moment, at her bedside, my job was to figure out the depth of Kathy's infection. And like a detective fresh on the case, I had but a few clues to go on, along with a litany of complicating factors. It's difficult to accurately diagnose infections in patients receiving high-dose chemo. The usual signs of infection, like a sudden rise in the white-cell count, tend not to present. Even the magnitude of fever can be distorted by the med-ications or underlying disease.

There were three conditions that could explain Kathy's symptoms. One possibility was cellulitis, which meant the bacteria would be con-fined to the skin and superficial dermal tissues, thus attacking her body a mere fraction of an inch below the surface of her arm. If that was the diagnosis, high-dose antibiotics were the best solution. Option number two would have been a welcomed diagnosis, though I knew it was a long shot. If Kathy's infection was an abscess (a collection of pus residing deeper in the tissues), I could incise and drain the site, thus giving the infection a channel for egress. Unfortunately, further probing ruled this option out.

A third and final possibility remained. It was the most terrifying. What if the bacterial infection had not only penetrated deep into Kathy's extremity but was now spreading along the fascia, the poorly vascularized gristle surrounding the underlying muscles, nerves, and blood vessels of the arm?

Doctors call this kind of infection *necrotizing fasciitis*, an infirmity that attacks like a two-headed snake. First, the infection itself produces inflammation, muscular damage, and progressive swelling of the deeper tissues. Then, as the encased structures expand, the overlying and inelastic fascia exerts pressure, further squeezing the muscles and shutting off circulation. This combination of factors proves deadly, preventing the antibiotics from reaching their destination, rendering the body unable to fight the infection.

Like neurotoxic venom, necrotizing fasciitis kills its victims quickly. If this was the underlying process, saving Kathy's life would require urgent surgery. Actually, necrotizing fasciitis requires that surgery be both urgent *and* radical. The latter required that I make a long incision up and down the length of Kathy's arm, flaying her skin and exposing muscle from wrist to axilla. Having unsheathed the infection and decompressed the underlying structures, I would then need to excise, piece by piece, any muscle and adjacent tissue that was no longer viable.

All surgeons have their favorite procedures, the ones they enjoy performing most. No physician would put this one on the list.

In gentle but clear terms, I explained the potential causes and courses of treatment to the family. I told them the odds of it being necrotizing fasciitis were similar to the odds of cellulitis, about fifty-fifty. Unfortunately, in that era, before sophisticated radiological imaging techniques (which today can peer below the surface and discern the depth of infection), there was no way to be certain in Kathy's case. The risk of operating was comparable to the risk of waiting. Either decision could kill her.

"What would you like me to do?" I asked the mother and father, need-ing parental consent to operate. They stood silently for a moment. They looked at each other. They looked at Kathy, whose vacant expression only worsened the anxiety we all felt. The parents looked at each other again. The *drip, drip, drip* of antibiotic fluid grew louder and louder, pulsating through the room like a telltale heart. Kathy's father broke the silence.

"What would you do if this were your child, Dr. Pearl?"

It was a logical question, as neither parent had the medical expertise to make the decision alone. And yet it caught me completely off guard. My lower back shivered and stiffened. My mind flooded with doubt and fear. Keeping her on antibiotics and waiting could be a deadly choice. Mangling the girl's arm for a slightly better chance of survival could prove equally lethal. I didn't have the luxury of time. A decision had to be made.

There are times when the greatest service a doctor can provide is pure and unfiltered truth. And the painful truth in this situation was that I had no idea what to do. But to say those words aloud seemed unconscio-nable. "I don't know" was not the solution these parents needed at this critical juncture. I owed them an answer on which they could hang their hopes. Someone in this situation needed to not only make a choice but bear the burden of blame should something go wrong. They couldn't do it. I couldn't make them do it. And so, standing across from Kathy's mom and dad, I summoned an answer and delivered my suggestion with con-fidence, knowing any expression of fear would poison their spirits. It was in this moment that the physician culture came to my rescue. All those years of training had filled me with a kind of assuredness that defied the facts of Kathy's situation.

"I would operate," I said without hesitation.

Medical culture does not endow doctors with all the answers. But it does lend, on occasion, a sense of omnipotence, allowing physicians to repress their anxiety and doubt, leaving them with the unflinching self-confidence necessary to act decisively. That was exactly what Kathy's parents deserved.

They immediately consented to the procedure. I rushed Kathy to the operating room and incised through her skin and subcutaneous tissues, down to the underlying fascia. There it was, as I had both suspected and feared: necrotizing fasciitis. What should have been a beautiful network of healthy white strands and glistening connective tissues had turned purulent, necrotic, and slimy. Bacteria were on the attack, melting away the poorly vascularized fascia and destroying the muscle below.

For the next hour and a half, the operative team and I extended the incision the length of Kathy's arm, removing the dead tissue and opening the deep fascia. By the end, raw muscle bulged through the gruesome slash down her pale, frail arm.

We packed the open wounds with wet dressings. With the procedure complete, we changed our masks and gowns, put on new sterile gloves, wheeled Kathy back to her room, and ordered the most potent antibiotics her delicate body could tolerate. Then we waited. The pediatric intensive care team monitored the girl throughout the night and into Sunday morning. I checked on Kathy regularly and always found at least one of her parents by her side.

Midafternoon Monday, some fifty hours after I first met Kathy, I was stat-paged from my clinic downstairs. I took the elevator up to the seventh floor and rushed to her room. The infection was now raging throughout her entire body. She was unconscious and motionless. Her pulse flickering away, her blood pressure plummeting. Within minutes of my arrival, her heart stopped.

A code red rang over the loudspeaker. The pediatric critical care team rushed in to resuscitate her and restore a normal heartbeat. The monitor over her bed showed the electrical activity in her heart to be consistent with ventricular fibrillation; its two lower chambers weren't contracting. They couldn't pump blood, hushing the heart's normal *lub-dub lub-dub* rhythm.

"Paddles, clear, shock." The team passed an endotracheal tube through Kathy's mouth, down her trachea, and into her lungs, filling them with oxygen while they compressed her chest and heart during CPR.

"Increase the voltage. Clear, shock." They worked feverishly to get a response, any kind of response whatsoever, any reason not to give up hope.

"Again! Clear, shock." They did everything they could.

I glanced at the clock on the wall. The hour hand pointed to four. The minute hand stood upright. The pediatric intensivist turned to the nurse: "Time of death, four p.m."

As the physicians exited the room, I stared at Kathy's lifeless body. I took off my contaminated gown, removed my gloves, and knew what I had to do next. I stood in the corner of the room for what seemed like hours. Under my breath, I recited the impossible mantra.

Please sit down. I have terrible news. Kathy died this afternoon. We did everything we could. I am so sorry.

Please sit down. I have terrible news. Kathy died this afternoon. We did everything we could. I am so sorry.

Kathy's mother and father joined me in a quiet room near the waiting area. I looked them in the eye, asked them to please sit down, and confirmed their worst fears.

We sat in silence as tears flowed down their cheeks. Years of learning to repress and deny emotion gave me the strength to keep my cheeks dry, just as years of repressing and denying doubt gave me the ability to pick up a knife, cut open the full length of a child's arm, and remove every strand of disease and decay I could find. The psychological defenses I had used to give Kathy the best chance of survival were the same ones that left me feeling detached from the horror of losing a ten-year-old child to a horrific disease.

When her parents were ready to speak, I answered their questions as best I could.

"Her white-cell count never recovered."

"She received the strongest antibiotics possible."

"Her body couldn't fight off the infection."

"Kathy experienced no pain. I am so sorry."

I wanted them to understand there was nothing more they could have done. I needed them to understand there was nothing more I could have done. And I desperately wanted them to forgive me for failing to save their only child.

When there were no more questions left to answer and nothing more to say, I sat with the parents some more. I gave them my home phone number and told them to call me if they wanted any more information or if there was anything I could do to help. Despite my best efforts to comfort them, I knew they wouldn't sleep for days.

As doctors, we are given a sacred trust. We are expected to preserve life. It is our highest duty. Losing a patient like Kathy carries the crushing weight of defeat. It always does. And in those moments, doctors find that the physician culture possesses curative, restorative properties as well. It instills in them the ability to move forward.

I tossed and turned in bed that night, replaying everything that transpired over the previous days. But when morning came, I had to get out of bed. I couldn't afford to take any more time to mourn Kathy's death. Back at the hospital, two parents were waiting for me to repair their daughter's cleft lip. That child deserved my full attention.

In conclusion, ladies and gentlemen of the jury, I ask for your compassion and understanding. I don't deny the problems that physician culture creates or the pain it inflicts. But please, don't overlook its grace and beauty. Medicine takes a massive toll on the doctor's sense of normalcy and humanity. Physician culture gives the doctor an invisible source of strength, making it possible to perform terrifying acts in the name of healing. It gives physicians the determination to move forward in defeat. It can save the lives of patients and doctors alike. Please be merciful in your final judgment.

In the American legal system, it does not matter whether the lawyer believes the defendant is guilty or innocent. Everyone deserves, and has the right to, counsel. Exiting the courtroom of my imagination, I'm left with two competing thoughts. First, it would be wrong to reject and discard the physician culture entirely. Second, it would be a mistake not to evolve it.

PART TWO

THE PHYSICIAN'S PAIN

DID WE KILL ONE OF OUR OWN?

With every day, and from both sides of my intelligence, the moral and the intellectual, I thus drew steadily nearer to the truth, by whose partial discovery I have been doomed to such a dreadful shipwreck: that man is not truly one, but truly two.

—*Robert Louis Stevenson*

FOR THE OVERWHELMING MAJORITY OF its history, physician culture was a constructive and productive force in medicine, giving doctors the confidence to heal, the compassion to comfort the sick, and a righteous sense of mission and purpose. Those were the defining elements of the culture's storied past.

Medical practice today feels far removed from the mission-driven spirit of yesteryear. Though scientific and technological changes have advanced the diagnostic and therapeutic skills of physicians, they've also turned the doctor's world upside down, challenging their beliefs and norms like never before. No longer do the doctor's intuition, experience, and independent judgment matter most in medicine. Instead, these cultural virtues of the past are being replaced as patients, insurers, and administrators exercise greater authority in determining how medical care should be delivered. Physicians are now struggling to cope in a world where everything is changing quickly except their culture. Once a respected profession, even a calling, medicine has become just a job for many—one that half of all doctors wouldn't recommend as a career. This shift is important to understand because the attitudes and feelings of doctors bear directly on the way they treat patients.

As with any job, doctors can be made better or worse by their prevailing attitudes, beliefs, and norms. The stories in this part of the book concern how doctors relate to one another and are influenced by their own culture, often in ways they themselves don't recognize. These chapters will help you understand how physician culture shapes the thoughts and feelings of the people who provide you with healthcare.

In what ways does culture support doctors and bring out their best? In what ways does it undermine their good intentions and stifle their love of medicine? Most important, how do physicians view you, the patient, and how do they perceive (or misperceive) your problems?

As in Robert Louis Stevenson's gothic novella *The Strange Case of Dr. Jekyll and Mr. Hyde*, it is possible that one person—or in this case, one culture—can be both a virtuous force and an equally destructive influence.

———

In 1998, I WAS SELECTED to serve as the fourth CEO of the Permanente Medical Group, the half of Kaiser Permanente (KP) in charge of delivering medical care. In that position, I led ten thousand physicians and thirty-eight thousand staff, and I was responsible for the health of five million KP members on both coasts.

When I stepped into the role, the organization was in deep trouble, hemorrhaging hundreds of millions of dollars annually. We found ourselves with just two days of cash on hand, needing to borrow a third day's worth just to meet state insurance requirements. This "near death" experience left physicians afraid and distrustful of the organization, its leaders, and one another. It was my job, in partnership with our health plan CEO, to lead Kaiser Permanente through an uncertain time.

Unlike my predecessor, who spent most of his time at headquarters, I wanted to hear directly from doctors. So I made a commitment to visit each of the nineteen medical centers twice a year, a practice I continued throughout my eighteen-year tenure. On these visits, I marveled at how each facility had carved out its own unique culture and personality.

At one of the older KP medical centers, the facility in San Francisco, physicians were proudly elitist. Doctors bragged about the number of peer-reviewed articles they published in the previous year and demanded "proof of concept," based on research, for every change our medical group was considering. By contrast, physicians in Modesto, a midsized medical center in the Central Valley, reflected the values of the farmers they served. The doctors were thankful for the jobs they had and prided themselves on never going home until all the day's tasks were completed. In San Rafael, a facility located in wealthy Marin County, physicians wore sport coats and made a habit of comparing their salaries with other doctors in the upscale community around them. And in Santa Clara, the largest medical center in Silicon Valley, MDs prided themselves on their technological savvy. They would try to dazzle me with beautiful presentations, highlighting the dozens of innovations being piloted throughout their clinical departments. Regardless of their geographic or personality differences, all medical centers had one thing in common. They believed their doctors were the best around.

I began my daylong visits with a tour of the facility, followed by a lunchtime session. The audience usually numbered four hundred to five hundred physicians in person and via teleconference. The first half of my presentation updated doctors on our organization, overall, and the quality and service provided in their local medical center. During the second half, I'd open the floor and listen to what was on people's minds.

If you've ever attended a town-hall-style meeting, you've probably observed this phenomenon: The speaker ends the formal presentation, asks if anyone has a question, and no one raises their hand or approaches the microphone. Then, after a few awkward moments, one brave soul steps forward to the relief of everyone else. It takes guts to be that person.

By my third cycle through the nineteen medical centers, I realized it was often the same person who broke the ice in each location. At one of my favorite midsized facilities in Northern California, Sam was that brave soul. (Out of respect for his privacy, and that of his colleagues, I have changed his name, blurred the location, and altered some personal information.)

If you were a patient lucky enough to call him your doctor—or a doctor lucky enough to call him your colleague—you never doubted Sam's ability, dedication, or excellence. He was what physicians refer to as a "doctor's doctor," the kind of clinician they'd want to care for their own family members. He arrived at the office an hour before the first patient and stayed an extra hour after everyone else had left. On vacations, he checked his email each morning and again at night to make sure all his patients were doing well.

Because Sam's work ethic and good standing preceded him, I was surprised by the nature of his questions. They almost always centered on the monthly performance reports our medical group compiled and distributed to physicians. You may recall from Part One that most doctors despise these comparative reports, which put their clinical performance under the microscope. Sam, despite his reputation as an excellent clinician, was one of their most vocal critics.

He wasn't shy about confrontation either. Since I was the newly selected leader, most of the medical centers accorded me a honeymoon phase during my first few visits. Having steered the organization out of bankruptcy, I was enjoying what felt like a lovefest. For that reason, I will never forget the first time Sam took the opportunity to ask me a question.

"Why have you unblinded the monthly reports we receive?" he asked, wanting to know why I insisted on listing the scores for each physician in each report rather than hiding their names as my predecessor did. At the time, this felt less like a question than an accusation.

I'd included people's names on the reports for two reasons, I explained. First, I believed we owed it to our patients to confront the truth about our clinical outcomes, especially when we lagged the competition. Second, in order to improve, I thought it best to identify those doctors who were achieving superior results, so that their colleagues could consult them and learn from their successes. Of course, most doctors preferred the old way because it aligned with their cultural assumptions that the MD in their title implies excellence and that it is taboo to embarrass a fellow physician by pointing out flaws or "areas for improvement."

When I returned six months later, Sam was again first to the microphone. Bypassing any pleasantries, he got right to the point. "Why are there so many metrics in these reports?" he asked.

My honeymoon period was over. Dozens of heads in the audience nodded along as Sam listed off a seemingly endless litany of measurements by which he and his fellow primary care physicians were compared: four for diabetes control; six more for cardiovascular disease prevention; ten for various areas of cancer prevention, osteoporosis (bone strength), blood pressure, and asthma; four for a combination of patient satisfaction and resource utilization. Twenty-four metrics in all.

Sam was concerned no one could excel in all of them. He was correct. But as I explained to the group, KP had millions of members who experienced a multitude of problems. It didn't make sense to focus on one problem, like diabetes, while ignoring others, like cancer and heart disease. I pointed out that all these measures correlate with lives saved. Indeed, studies show that the organizations scoring at the top of the national quality reports have fewer patients who die from heart attack, sepsis, stroke, and certain cancers such as those of the colon and lung. I worried that any medical problem excluded from the monthly reports would not get the attention it deserved within our medical group.

All around the country doctors like Sam bemoan performance metrics for a variety of reasons. Making the data available for all doctors to see is perceived by some as threatening. Doctors who score in the lower half of their departments feel a sense of shame and failure. Others simply feel that American medicine is complicated enough as it is. Still some doctors say these measures don't adequately quantify excellence. Finally, many just find the length of the list overwhelming. To that end, Don Berwick, the former head of the Centers for Medicare & Medicaid Services and CEO of the Institute for Healthcare Improvement, proposed putting American healthcare on a "measurement diet."

Though there is more than one justifiable reason to attack these reports, not all the complaints stem from a desire to simplify, improve, or streamline American medicine. The antipathy doctors express toward them has deep cultural underpinnings as well.

For one, doctors reject the notion that anyone who is not a practicing physician is qualified to evaluate their performance. The National Committee for Quality Assurance, an independent accrediting body that developed and maintains HEDIS, the Healthcare Effectiveness Data and Information Set, is one such outsider. The organization's widely used data-benchmarking tool is used to compare the quality of health plans and their clinical outcomes, and has drawn the ire of many doctors. That's because these measurements feel detached from doctors' daily practices. They find the information hard to assemble and the submission process overly bureaucratic.

Individual doctors take umbrage with the data for yet another reason. These performance reports undermine the cultural assumption that doctors are individually superb and consistently high performers. Of course, they can't all be at the top of their practice. The data confirm it. If NBA players weren't measured by various statistics like points, rebounds, and assists, every individual in a jersey might conclude that he was an All-Star. In medicine, as in professional sports, comparative performance metrics matter.

Nowhere is medicine's individual performance gap more apparent than in the field of primary care, Sam's specialty. The issue isn't that primary care doctors perform worse than physicians in other specialties; it's that they care for the broadest range of medical problems and therefore are accountable for the most performance measures. By contrast, specialties (like cardiology) address only one organ system and others (like oncology) treat only one disease. Primary care is responsible for all of them. And, without question, the constant barrage of data used to rank them from best to worst contributes to primary care's high rate of professional dissatisfaction and fatigue.

By the time I set out for my biannual medical center visits in the spring of 2014, I had made close to two dozen trips to each facility and knew what to expect. As soon as I finished my remarks at the facility where Sam worked, I joked, "Sam, do you want to ask the first question?"

True to form, Sam's question hit hard. "Do you really believe that the physicians who score highest in the monthly performance reports are the best doctors in our medical group?"

Though it smacked of a gotcha question, I now understand that his intention wasn't to stir the pot. Coming from him, every question was an honest query and deserved an honest answer. Sam wanted to know whether I believed the value of a doctor could be determined by numerical indicators alone. I replied that the data offered valuable insights into each doctor's performance and allowed our medical group to become a national leader in clinical outcomes. At the same time, I acknowledged that numbers, alone, fail to account for other equally important qualities in a physician, such as collegiality, ethics, integrity, and professional judgment.

When I returned to my office the next day, I thought a lot about Sam and wondered whether his questions came out of concern for his colleagues or concern for himself. I logged into my computer and opened up his most recent report. I was relieved to confirm Sam's performance matched his excellent reputation. Almost every score was well above average. In fact, he ranked in the top 10 percent of primary care physicians in several important clinical areas, such as diabetes management, high blood pressure treatment, cancer prevention, and even patient satisfaction. Of course, among the twenty-four measurements included, there were a few for which he was average and one, related to immunization rates, for which he scored below the mean. But overall, Sam's outcomes were stellar.

Having satisfied my concerns about his performance, I didn't think about Sam during the rest of my medical center travels that year. Ten months later, I learned there was much more to Sam's story than I had imagined. And much more than the data indicated.

Sam's life took a turn for the worse over the intervening summer. While his wife and kids were visiting with family in New Jersey, Sam stayed behind to provide patient care, agreeing to work additional nights and weekends beyond his regular schedule. It wasn't the first summer he had skipped a family vacation, but it would be the last time he'd have the opportunity to do so. When his family returned to California that August, Sam's wife informed him she was filing for divorce. Shortly after the New Year, she took the kids back East to live with her parents.

In February, while alone in his home, Sam swallowed a handful of self-prescribed antidepressants, which suppressed his breathing and ended his suffering. He didn't leave a note.

Sam's death rocked the department. Nobody saw it coming. He hadn't told any of his colleagues that his wife was leaving him or that she was taking their kids three thousand miles away. No one suspected Sam was depressed or potentially suicidal. And frankly, how could they have known? None of Sam's colleagues had inquired about his mental health. No one had asked *why* he volunteered to work so many nights and weekends. They were just grateful they had more time to be at home with their families.

———————

I'M SITTING ON A PLASTIC folding chair in the carpeted living room of a recently remodeled midcentury ranch house. The scent of deviled eggs carries from the kitchen. It's a Sunday, late afternoon, a few days after Sam's burial. I'm surrounded by his colleagues, nearly all of them primary care doctors from his department. They've gathered to honor his memory.

I'm the only one in the room who didn't have a day-to-day working relationship with the deceased. John, the chief of the primary care department where Sam worked, is hosting this memorial service. He had called me days earlier, asking if I'd come by to say a few words. It would mean a lot to the doctors in the department, he said. In American culture, having a CEO in attendance at any event signals its importance. At a memorial service, it sends the message that the person who died was exceptional and cherished. Indeed, Sam was.

At the front of the room, against a wall of blue curtains covering a large plate-glass window, four doctors speak. One after another, they offer remembrances of their departed colleague. They're effusive in their praise. Their words are filled with emotion. Their grief is sincere.

Sam's wife isn't here. No one has heard from her either. Also absent are Sam's patients, save for the colleagues he treated. This is not an uncommon occurrence when a practicing physician dies. Rather, it's indicative of a rarely spoken truth: the doctor-patient relationship isn't meant to be a balanced one. Whereas doctors expect to be notified when their patients die—and will, on occasion, attend the funeral to pay their respects—patients are not granted the same opportunity when their doctor passes.

This imbalance exists not just in times of mourning but every day in the doctor's office, where an imaginary line runs right down the middle of every exam room, creating a clinical confession booth of sorts. Patients sit on one side. Their bodies, minds, symptoms, and secrets are all fully exposed. On the other side of the line stands the doctor, ever ready to advise and heal. Doctors are permitted to ask deeply personal questions about patients' bowel habits, mental health, and sexual activities. But the personal elements of these interactions are always unidirectional. Patients rarely ask how the physician is doing, and even less often will the doctor volunteer that information.

To do the best job possible, doctors believe they must remain detached and unemotional. They learn early in their training that disclosing any personal matters to patients is unprofessional and strictly forbidden. They believe that demonstrating emotion is an unacceptable sign of weakness.

Doctors survive medical school and residency by accepting the myth of their own invincibility. But like many professionals, physicians live with secret insecurities and anxieties about their abilities. They're ever concerned about being exposed as a fraud. When afraid, they rarely admit it. Thus, when they're overwhelmed or at their limit, they're taught to suck it up and not ask for help.

I once knew a doctor who returned to work on Wednesday after receiving a terminal diagnosis on Tuesday. Her patients were none the wiser. I have seen doctors practicing medicine with immaculate poise in the middle of a malpractice suit that threatened to topple their careers. Even during the coronavirus pandemic, when doctors had reached their breaking points—exhausted and on the verge of tears—they held it together in front of their patients and colleagues. As a nation, we have come a long way toward encouraging people to let down their guard, embrace vulnerability, and become comfortable with being uncomfortable. But not in medicine.

Hiding emotions and denying vulnerability allow physicians to muster the courage to take on daunting challenges and accomplish remarkable outcomes. For doing so, they pay a steep price. Defense mechanisms protect our egos and sense of self-worth, but they are more like fine-grained sieves than solid-steel pots. They allow us to keep most of the psychological discomfort inside, but not all of it. There's always leakage. And though this leakage doesn't prevent physicians from doing their jobs, it does compromise their psychological health, producing high levels of anxiety and distress.

Listening to Sam's colleagues eulogize him, I'm acutely aware that large chunks of his story have been omitted from their remarks. Nobody acknowledges the pain Sam must have felt. For that matter, there is no indication that his death was self-inflicted. Most important, there is no recognition or mention, whatsoever, that every single one of us in the room shares at least some of the blame for Sam's suicide.

We'll never know whether his death was the result of his marital dissolution, untreated depression, professional struggles, or some combination of these factors. We can't be sure whether encouraging him to get psychological help would have made any difference. But all of us could have done more to spot the warning signs and offer help. As we gather together in mourning, we can only imagine what Sam would have said if one of us had asked how he was feeling. We can only wish one of us had the courage to break down the emotional walls that he and all of us constructed around ourselves.

I'm the final speaker on the program. I, too, extol Sam's virtues and sanctify his life. I focus on what I know: his inspiring dedication to his colleagues and patients. I highlight the positive impact he had on the more than two thousand people who trusted him with their lives and health. Near the end, I say, "He was always there for his patients. The only time he ever disappointed them was by dying."

I can see the physicians in the room tensing with discomfort, bracing themselves for the possibility that I might say the unspeakable word: *suicide*. I take a deep breath to steady my voice. I want to. If anyone should, it's me. But I can't bring myself to acknowledge the truth. Instead, I conclude, "We will all miss him."

Like everyone else in this room, I am a coward. I said nothing of the pain Sam must have felt. I said nothing of our collective failure to reach out. I didn't discuss the long hours Sam spent alone in his office, away from his wife and kids. I didn't mention the many times he walked to the microphone to complain about the comparative performance reports.

Had any of the primary care colleagues gathered here been asked about Sam's well-being in the weeks leading up to his death, they would have told you he was fit as a fiddle. Had he scheduled a checkup with any of them, they would have begun by taking his vital signs and recording them as "normal." With two clicks of the electronic health record, Sam's doctor would use a dot phrase to enter the following: "42 Y.O. white male in good health."

If asked whether he was experiencing any pain or discomfort, Sam would have replied, "Nope, just fine," completely ignoring the psychological distress he felt. After an unremarkable physical exam, the doctor would have ordered routine laboratory studies. When the blood and urine results came back normal the next day, the physician would have sent Sam a secure email message with a personal note, reminding him to get a flu shot and congratulating him on being "healthy."

As I scan the crowd one last time, I see a room of mourners deep in thought. I can imagine what is going through their minds. Some are flooded with memories of the last time they spoke with Sam. Others are shrouded in the kind of personal sadness that penetrates the marrow. Many of them are comparing themselves to Sam, wondering how different their lives really are from his.

I wonder how many patients over the years came to talk with Sam about their personal lives, their own depression or distress, while he himself was battling suicidal thoughts. I wonder—or rather, I know—what he would have said had a patient or colleague asked him, sincerely, how he was doing. Sam would have responded that he was doing just fine. But of course he wasn't fine. Doctors act in accordance with the norms of their culture. They deny and repress their personal struggles, pretending that nothing is wrong. It is what's expected of them. But how can any culture that denies the very existence of human emotion be labeled "healthy"?

After Sam's death, his patients received a letter in the mail informing them that he would no longer be available to see them. They were encouraged to select a new doctor. To my knowledge, none of them ever knew why.

THE RISE OF BURNOUT, THE REBIRTH OF MORAL INJURY

I N THE SEVEN YEARS BETWEEN Sam's death and the publication of this book, nearly three thousand American physicians died by suicide. Based on national studies, doctors are twice as likely to take their own lives as the general population. Roughly 15 percent of physicians struggle with depression; 20 percent report having had suicidal thoughts.

To anyone outside medicine, these statistics may seem surprising and counterintuitive considering all doctors have going for them. For one, physicians are very well paid. Doctors take home an average annual income of over $300,000, which puts them in the top 5 percent of American earners. Medical practice is a highly reputable profession as well. More than 90 percent of parents in the United States would encourage their children to become doctors (a career that's second only in parental approval to engineering). Within Gallup's top five "most trusted" professions, doctors join engineers, nurses, pharmacists, and dentists as the professionals held in highest esteem by the general public.

What's more, doctors now benefit from the availability of sophisticated medications, rapid access to information technology, and new treatments for diseases that were at one time automatic killers. With medical innovation and achievement at all-time highs, this ought to be the Golden Age of physician fulfillment, not its nadir.

Yet for anyone working inside the healthcare system today, the declining satisfaction of doctors is no surprise. Reconciling this disparity between how doctors perceive their profession and how outsiders view it requires a deep dive into the work, lives, and cultural expectations of physicians. Patients may be largely unaware of the issues their doctors are facing, but they are no less affected.

Let's begin with how doctors feel about their professional lives. Half report a troubling constellation of symptoms, which includes exhaustion, dissatisfaction, and a sense of failure. Research concludes these physicians are twice as likely to commit a serious medical error, be sued for malpractice, and report difficulties maintaining healthy interpersonal relationships.

These physical and psychological difficulties have been labeled "burnout," a term first described more than half a century ago by the psychologist Herbert Freudenberger. He noted that burnout most commonly affects people in helping professions who carry high ideals and experience extreme stress.

Today, burnout is a big and burgeoning problem in practically every profession. Among the general population, it affects 28 percent of working Americans. But when we zoom in on physicians, the burnout rate balloons to 44 percent (and even as high as 54 percent in one study).

According to a recent Harvard report, physician burnout is "a public health crisis that urgently demands action." Experts predict that if left unaddressed, it will further erode the mental health of doctors and radically undermine patient care.

When asked about the causes of their unhappiness, nearly all doctors agree on the source of the problem. Burnout, they say, has a single etiology: It is the product of America's broken healthcare system. In a 2020 survey, physicians pointed at "too many bureaucratic tasks," "too many hours at work," "increasing computerization," and "insufficient compensation" as the causes of their distress.

Indeed, multiple studies find that physicians dedicate nearly twice as much time to completing administrative tasks and filling out insurance forms as they spend with their patients. Doctors and staff devote fifteen hours each week to obtaining "prior authorizations" from insurance

What Contributes Most to Burnout?

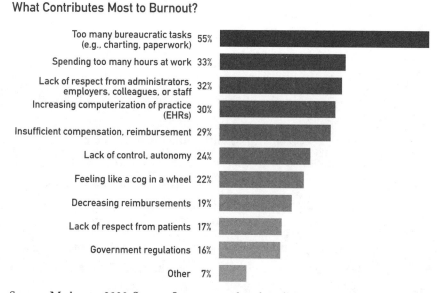

Source: Medscape 2020 Survey. Image reproduced with permission from Medscape (www.medscape.com), Medscape National Physician Burnout & Suicide Report 2020: The Generational Divide, 2020, online at www.medscape.com/slideshow/2020-lifestyle-burnout-6012460.

companies. Walk into any doctor's office nowadays, and you'll find as many people working on billing, claims, and collections as you'll find people providing care. Since 2011, the cost of managing the finances of primary care practices has shot up 74 percent. All this time, energy, and investment are being wrested from doctors and patients and put into the business side of healthcare. Even the computers stationed in the exam room are programmed to aid with insurance company approvals and billing much more than to improve medical treatment. All these distractions from medical care serve to slow the physician down, adding even more administrative toil to the doctor's busy clinical day.

Amid these barriers to better care, physicians feel overwhelmed, unfairly treated, and isolated. They focus their frustration on the usual parties: meddling insurers, manufacturers of clunky computer systems, and callous hospital administrators. All these complaints by doctors are valid to some degree, and each is indeed a by-product of a broken American healthcare system.

Doctors long to spend their days as they once did: focused solely on providing high-quality care, not jumping through bureaucratic hoops. In their minds, the high price of American healthcare ($3.8 trillion annually) could be cured by eliminating administrative complexities, reducing regulatory burdens, and trusting doctors to provide the best medical care for their patients.

Insurers see the problems differently. They look at themselves as the industry's financial stewards, concerned primarily with the growing unaffordability of healthcare for American families and businesses. They know that one-third of all healthcare dollars are wasted on redundant and unnecessary services (tests, treatments, and interventions). They are concerned about the high rates of medical error and the avoidable complications of chronic disease running rampant in the United States. In their minds, they impose all these requirements and restrictions not to frustrate doctors but, rather, to slow down reckless spending, improve the value of care provided, and prevent excessive testing and procedures.

Herein lies the struggle. The "white coats" see the problem as a failure of an overly regulated healthcare system. The "suits" see the problem as a failure of the care-delivery system, led by self-serving doctors who try to earn more money by driving up volume, regardless of whether the tests are required, the procedures needed, or the overall care effective.

Because each side sees a different problem, their solutions conflict as well. Doctors believe patient care will improve if they have more support staff, less paperwork, and fewer restrictions. Health insurers believe these changes will lead to even more wasteful spending.

If they were freed from the limitations of paperwork and prior authorizations, doctors are convinced patients would become healthier and costs would go down. Insurers don't believe them. As "financial stewards," they feel they must safeguard the integrity of each healthcare dollar, treating it as if it were their own money.

At the heart of this clash between doctors and their healthcare-system counterparts is a deep-seated and mutual distrust, which further fuels the anxiety and dissatisfaction doctors feel. Perceived insensitivity to the plight of physicians has led some doctors to reject the word "burnout" as both insulting and insufficient in describing their pain. In the minds of many physicians, to label their intense suffering as "burnout" is akin to blaming the victims (doctors) for feeling exhausted, cynical, and fatigued. They believe the word "burnout" implies a lack of resilience and resourcefulness on the part of doctors. And by placing the blame on physicians, all of us are either ignoring or forgiving the true perpetrator: the healthcare system.

According to the co-authors of a widely cited op-ed on the subject, "Physicians are smart, tough, durable, resourceful people. If there was a way to MacGyver themselves out of this situation by working harder, smarter, or differently, they would have done it already."

In place of burnout, a growing group of physicians now embrace the term "moral injury," a nod to the first principle of physician culture: *primum non nocere*, or "first, do no harm."

The moral injury argument goes like this: when the demands and requirements of today's healthcare system conflict with the doctor's duty to heal—that is, when the system prevents doctors from doing what's right, thereby forcing them to inflict harm on patients—physicians themselves experience a form of injury.

The imperative to do no harm, a pledge that dates back to Hippocrates and supersedes all other medical priorities, is sacred to physicians. Doctors have kept their end of this promise for millennia. But now physicians feel the promise to do no harm is being broken—not by themselves but by a greedy, corrupt, and dysfunctional healthcare system, led by a racket of insurance executives, regulatory bureaucrats, and hospital administrators. With all their excessive rules and red tape, these healthcare system players are forcing doctors into an endless loop of lose-lose situations that result in unavoidable harm being inflicted on their patients. Against these powerful forces, physicians feel they are unable to protect their patients. This is, to doctors, morally indefensible. It is an injury of the soul.

The term "moral injury" was first used to describe the psychological distress of combat soldiers who, in times of battle, were required to inflict harm on other human beings.

"The moral injury of healthcare is not the offense of killing another human in the context of war," according to the popular op-ed penned by Dr. Simon Talbot, a reconstructive plastic surgeon at Brigham and Women's

Hospital, and Dr. Wendy Dean, a psychiatrist and senior medical officer at a foundation for the advancement of military medicine. "It is being unable to provide high-quality care and healing in the context of healthcare."

This argument reasons that the healthcare system—with all its rules, limitations, and red tape—creates ethical conflicts for doctors, which produce in them emotional and moral exhaustion. However, one problem with labeling the doctor's experience as moral injury is it places them on an ethical high ground, above any personal or professional responsibility for the failures of US healthcare. This contradicts extensive research on the patient experience. There are in fact many situations when physicians themselves cause harm to patients, be it financial, physical, or psychological. These situations are not the result of external forces or systemic constraints. They are directly within the doctor's control.

Let's start with an example of financial harm. When a patient with a neurological abnormality complains to a doctor, "I'm having the worst headache of my life," all medical experts agree that a brain scan is a necessary and worthwhile expense. Among these patients, brain scans often reveal a ruptured intracranial blood vessel requiring immediate and aggressive intervention.

But when a patient complains of a mild, chronic headache, the probability of it being a major problem (one that requires brain surgery) is extremely low, occurring in less than 1 percent of cases. It's not zero, but the chances of it being a ruptured intracranial blood vessel or brain tumor are exceedingly slim.

In all, mild, chronic headaches send ten to fifteen million Americans to the doctor each year. And when it comes to ordering brain scans for this population, doctors are all over the place with their recommendations. Research presented to the Council of Accountable Physician Practices found the frequency with which physicians order these studies varies by a factor of four or more. That's a tremendous difference between those on the high and low ends with no measurable difference in clinical outcomes. As a result of the profession's inconsistent approach and resistance to evidence-based guidelines, US headache sufferers receive $1 billion worth of MRI and CT scans each year. That's a "conservative estimate" according to a research study from the University of Michigan. So the question remains: Is all this testing worth it?

"Guidelines say we shouldn't do this," says Dr. Brian Callaghan, the neurologist who led the study. "Yet we still do it, a lot. This is a source of tremendous cost in healthcare without a lot of evidence to justify the cost. There's solid research showing that the number of times you find serious issues on these scans in headache patients is about the same as that for a randomly chosen group of non-headache patients."

To put it even more simply, the value of these excessive scans is nil. If all doctors could just agree to (and follow) existing radiological and neurological guidelines for ordering brain scans, hundreds of millions of dollars spent on unnecessary tests each year could be invested in lowering healthcare premiums or improving preventive care and chronic disease management. Such efforts would preserve far more lives than overtesting ever could.

Unnecessary medical tests and interventions inflict financial harm, but there are times when doctors' own actions cause direct, *physical* harm to patients. Take, for example, the forty-seven million antibiotic prescriptions written each year. One study published in the *Journal of the American Medical Association* found that one in three antibiotics prescribed in the United States is unnecessary and inappropriate based on the patient's medical needs. This practice of overprescribing creates a real and immediate danger for people, putting them at risk for distressing side effects that range from nausea to kidney failure, along with life-threatening allergic reactions. In addition, the uptick in antibiotic prescriptions is contributing to the emergence of bacterial resistance. As a result, patients in hospitals and nursing homes are increasingly threatened by impossible-to-treat infections caused by new, drug-resistant "superbugs." Speaking to this threat, the former director of the Centers for Disease Control and Prevention cautioned, "If we continue down the road of inappropriate use, we'll lose the most powerful tool we have to fight life-threatening infections."

Beyond excessive prescribing, doctors harm patients through unnecessary and potentially unsafe procedures. As an example, they often recommend surgery for chronic lower back pain even when more conservative, less-risky treatments prove equally effective.

One study found that patients who underwent surgery for spinal stenosis (a painful back condition associated with aging) saw no significant difference in pain, functioning, or disability after eight years compared to patients who had received physical therapy and began an exercise program instead. And having undergone surgery, these patients risked serious infection, nerve damage, and, in rare cases, death. Still, orthopedic surgeons and neurosurgeons continue to steer patients toward the more dangerous option. Since 2001, spinal fusion procedures (the most complex and risky treatments for back pain) have increased by 70 percent.

Elsewhere in this book, you'll find even harsher examples of wrongdoing within the physician culture, including those that lead to serious medical errors, patient bankruptcies, and needless deaths. For now, it's important to acknowledge that doctors who decry the system as the sole cause of their burnout or moral grievances are making three costly mistakes: they imply they're helpless victims, assume they're faultless, and fail to take the steps needed to remedy the problem.

It's true that physicians face an overly restrictive set of systemic requirements, but they will get no relief by merely pointing out the shortcomings of the healthcare system or drawing attention to their moral injuries. Until doctors eliminate wasteful and medically ineffective services, and until they take responsibility for unnecessary medical errors and rising medical costs, the problems that plague American healthcare will grow along with the restrictions placed on physician freedom. As a consequence, burnout among doctors will only get worse.

In their quest for a solution, doctors will need to identify and address *all* the problems contributing to their burnout, not just the systemic ones. Doing so will require them to look in the mirror and acknowledge how their own cultural norms conflict with their vow of doing no harm. The origins of these troubling norms can often be traced back to medical school and residency.

Although incoming medical students report rates of depression similar to the general population, studies show that their incidences of psychological distress and depression begin to spike after just a year of classroom instruction. But how can this be? After all, in these preclinical years, medical students are not exposed to the "systemic" travails of practicing medicine. In year one, students don't provide medical care to patients, haggle with insurance company clerks, or spend hours entering data into an electronic health record. In essence, medical students show worrisome symptoms before they perform any of the tasks that practicing doctors blame for burnout.

Moreover, the norms that lead to excess costs are also learned early in training. Through their actions, senior residents and attending physicians teach young doctors what is valued and what is verboten. Students and junior residents carry these cultural lessons into their own practices and, years later, pass them on to the next generation. They are taught that surgical intervention is better for patients than "watchful waiting" or physical therapy, even when research studies show otherwise. They hear clinical faculty members refer to checklists as a "waste of time," not as a means for ensuring patient safety. They notice that no doctor ever considers (or even knows) the cost of treatments or tests when making clinical decisions.

After more than a decade of training, physicians have internalized, embraced, and reflexively follow these problematic values, beliefs, and norms. Generation after generation, the culture remains consistent, helping doctors overlook any internal conflict, concern, or guilt they may have about their conduct. When it comes to physicians' questionable behaviors, there is safety and justification in culture. Doctors conclude that if everyone is acting the same way, the behaviors they learned must be both acceptable and valuable for patients. Doctors do experience moral injury, but they also inflict injury without the help of insurers and bureaucrats. And in the process, they not only harm others, but they hurt themselves as well.

THE PROBLEM WITH PRESTIGE

A T THE END OF A long table covered with hors d'oeuvres and a birth-day cake, I struck up a conversation with three primary care physi-cians working in Washington, DC. It was 2019, and I was deeply involved in researching the consequences of burnout on doctors and their patients.

Our conversation centered on published data that indicated a high and growing rate of burnout in primary care. Asked for their views, one doc-tor described the pain he and his colleagues experience as acute and vis-ceral. "As painful as passing a kidney stone," he added, to which another doctor said, "It's more like chronic pain, a condition you deal with every day even when other people can't see it or even imagine it."

I thanked them for their insights and set my glass on the kitchen counter. Turning back, I asked, "Do you think your surgical colleagues are equally burned-out?" They looked around at one another for a mo-ment. "Doubtful," said one of the physicians. "Far less than in primary care," said another. The third guessed that maybe 10 percent of specialists suffer burnout. I knew they were all wrong but didn't argue. I had read the annual polling data on this topic and planned to send them copies of the research when I got home.

According to a Medscape survey of fifteen thousand doctors, all physi-cian specialties report a burnout rate above 29 percent. If you look at the bottom of the list, where burnout rates are lowest, you'll find several sur-gical specialties. They include ophthalmologists (30 percent), orthopedists

(34 percent), and otolaryngologists (35 percent). Strangely, you also find a couple of surgical specialties near the top of the list too. In fact, urologists experience the highest rate of burnout among all doctors (54 percent), a far higher percentage than any primary care specialty, including internal medicine (44 percent) and family medicine (46 percent).

While the Medscape survey demonstrates that burnout isn't just a primary care problem, it also raises an interesting question: Why do burnout rates vary so greatly across surgical specialties?

Recall from the surveys on burnout causes that doctors complain most about working too many hours at the office, logging too many clicks on their computers, and performing too many bureaucratic tasks without enough pay. Look closer, and you'll see these complaints don't adequately explain the dramatic variation in rates of burnout from one specialty to the next.

For example, look at pay. Urologists earn an above-average salary of $408,000, which is $42,000 more than the average ophthalmologist. Yet urology is the specialty with the highest burnout rate, 24 percent higher than in ophthalmology. This suggests that income is not as much of a burnout factor as physicians think. The fact that urologists earn nearly twice as much as pediatricians—while experiencing a 15 percent higher rate of burnout than their pediatric colleagues—confirms it.

What about the commonly held belief among physicians that spending "too many hours" at the office causes burnout? According to the Medscape poll, "the percentage of physicians who are burned out rises with the number of hours they work each week." That's true *overall*, but when you compare specialty to specialty, there are multiple exceptions. As an example, orthopedists put in more hours at work than three-quarters of the specialists surveyed, and yet they are among the profession's least burned-out doctors.

Finally, what about the bureaucratic impositions that physicians face? Once again, this is an aspect of the healthcare system that doctors detest, but it fails to account for the variation in burnout rates by specialty. All surgical specialties use similar electronic health record systems, and each must obtain prior authorization from insurers for the procedures they perform. When it comes to the number of computer clicks and annoy-ing administrative tasks, urologists have it no different than orthopedists, ophthalmologists, or otolaryngologists.

If variations in burnout among different specialties can't be explained by money, work hours, or bureaucratic paperwork, what else is there? The answer lies in the illogical and perverse obsession doctors have with pres-tige and status, two of the strongest influences in physician culture.

———

SIR MICHAEL MARMOT, A BRITISH epidemiologist and chair of the World Health Organization's commission on social determinants of health, is renowned the world over for his Whitehall studies. Through his groundbreaking research on health inequalities, Marmot found a strong association between the occupational rank of British civil servants and their chances of dying.

Men with jobs at the bottom, he found, were four times more likely to die than the men in charge, even when adjusting for the usual social-class killers like smoking, drinking, and poor diet. His findings transformed the establishment's thinking on the link between hierarchy and health.

Marmot was among the first to point out that social and professional status have a tremendous influence over a person's mental and physical well-being. Specifically, he found that our real or perceived rank—at work, among friends, or in society—greatly affects our stress levels and self-esteem.

Importantly, numerous psychological studies confirm that the *loss* of social or professional status produces the same symptoms we associate with burnout: anxiety, fatigue, and depression. This is the missing link. Physicians, having spent most of their youth competing for academic honors, are acutely aware of their standing and the importance of hier-archy in medicine. Yet they seem mostly unaware of the correlation be-tween their status and risk of becoming burned-out.

To understand this association, let's examine two different specialties that have undergone significant upticks in burnout and major declines in status.

The clearest example is urology. The number of hours urologists work and the income they earn are similar to other surgical specialties and relatively unchanged from the past. Neither factor adequately explains the high level of dissatisfaction they report. What's unusual about urology is that a few years ago, the burnout rate was relatively low. What changed?

In the first decade of the twenty-first century, medical school graduates flocked to urology for the prestige and the opportunity to perform *robotic prostatectomy*, a "cool" (video-game-like) procedure for men diagnosed with localized prostate cancer. During that time, the number of patients choosing this surgical option rose, as testing for prostate cancer became standard and these multimillion-dollar robots became available in every hospital. But starting around 2010, all of that changed.

The number of prostatectomies being performed in the United States began to decline as a result of research studies that found testing all men over the age of fifty for elevated levels of prostate specific antigen (PSA) resulted in overdiagnosis and overtreatment. Men with high PSA levels were being biopsied more than necessary, leading to painful and problematic complications one-third of the time. These included bleeding, urinary obstruction, and infection. Because of this, the US Preventive Services Task Force recommended in 2012 that men and their doctors rethink PSA testing. In subsequent years, additional studies found that "watchful waiting," during which the malignancy is carefully monitored but not treated, proves just as effective as operating. What's more, waiting helps patients avoid the risks of surgery, which include lifelong impotence and incontinence.

With the total volume of cases shrinking and with an increasing percentage of patients choosing to get their surgeries done at high-volume "centers of excellence," most community urologists have been left with fewer opportunities to perform the very procedure that attracted them to the specialty in the first place. And with lower surgical volumes, many have been forced by hospital credentialing authorities to remove the procedure entirely from their clinical practices. These setbacks have devastated the field's prestige, bumping urology down near the bottom of the healthcare hierarchy, helping to explain the specialty's high incidence of burnout.

General surgery is another specialty that has seen a growing burnout rate in recent years. One especially troubling report recently demonstrated signs and symptoms of burnout (75 percent) and depression (40
percent) among general surgery residents. This growing dissatisfaction
reflects the changes in surgical scope and, more important, a reduction in
their relative status compared to surgeons in other specialties.

General surgeons, like my uncle Herb, used to be kings of the healthcare hill. They delighted in mastering an array of complex procedures,
operating on nearly every area of the body. In some practice settings,
particularly in rural areas and underserved communities, the general
surgeon's scope of practice remains broad. But in densely populated areas, the most "interesting" (high-profile) operations are being referred to
subspecialists who have completed fellowship training and can provide
deeper levels of expertise.

For example, surgeries performed on the most complex cancers of the
liver and pancreas go to hepatobiliary surgeons. Their intensive training, combined with a narrowed scope of practice and greater experience,
helps them achieve superior clinical outcomes with fewer complications.
Endocrine surgeons, likewise, have laid claim to thyroidectomies and ad-
renalectomies. Even mastectomies, once under the domain of all general
surgeons, are being done by a smaller subset of physicians who focus their
entire practices on treating breast cancer.

As a result, many general surgeons now find their practice limited to
the most mundane medical problems: hernias, gallbladder disease, and
hemorrhoids.

———————

AMONG PHYSICIANS, STATUS IS JUST as important as money. That's why
the specialties with the highest rates of burnout today aren't the ones with
the lowest incomes. They're the specialties known for doing the fewest
high-status procedures while performing the highest percentage of me-
nial tasks.

The desire for elevated esteem and importance in the medical profession explains why many doctors take jobs in academic medical centers
after residency. They're willing to accept a lower salary in return for a

university affiliation, a prestigious title, and guaranteed referrals of complex cases. Patients who require more sophisticated care are led to think that doctors in university hospitals are on the cutting edge of clinical practice—despite no definitive evidence that those who choose academics over private practice are diagnostically or technically superior. For specialists, it's not "all about the money." For many, it's also about the prestige.

Medicine's imagined order may be news to some patients, but it is well known to every doctor in the profession. And it influences everything from a specialty's perceived value to a doctor's feelings of self-worth to, ultimately, the quality of care patients receive. Because the doctor's place in this hierarchy is so culturally important, physicians are unlikely to admit to patients when they lack experience in the areas of greatest clinical and technical complexity. And they're likely to keep on performing procedures that boost their relative status—regardless if they're the best physician for the job or if a more conservative approach might yield better results.

In physician culture, those who sit at the top are the specialists who perform the most emergent life-saving procedures. They include cardiac surgeons and neurosurgeons. Next are the physicians who do the most complex procedures. They include transplant, cancer, and trauma surgeons. Below them are the doctors from the more general interventional specialties, including gastroenterologists and orthopedists. The next level down features the upper tier of primary care, which includes OB-GYN and pediatrics, each with a specific domain (women and children). At the bottom: outpatient internal medicine and family medicine.

As a result of sitting at the bottom of the list, the doctor you rely on for routine and ongoing medical care is likely to be experiencing professional fatigue and frustration. If he or she is distracted or seemingly uninterested in your issues, the reason may be completely outside your control.

Within this unofficial ranking system, there are exceptions and historical anomalies. For instance, plastic surgeons rarely do the types of complex, life-saving procedures associated with elevated status, but patients accord them respect because of the technically demanding requirements of their craft and our country's fascination with physical beauty.

Another exception to the rule in medicine is dermatology. The procedures dermatologists perform are less complex and emergent than other high-status specialists, but these physicians benefit greatly from the laws of supply and demand. A couple decades ago, when the specialty was limping along, the national dermatology residency directors decided to cut the number of training positions in half. The sudden "shortage" caused an unexpected supply-demand imbalance, sending the salaries of dermatologists through the roof while driving broad interest among medical students. Physicians in dermatology now work among the shortest hours of any specialty, making the field an appealing choice for those seeking both a generous income and a better work-life balance. The relatively high demand for dermatologic services will continue to increase with America's aging population and rising rates of skin cancer. Consequently, for each newly trained dermatologist, there are on average two open positions being actively recruited.

Exceptions notwithstanding, the healthcare hierarchy remains a powerful force in determining the mental health and overall happiness of physicians. And it will continue to influence the future of healthcare. Every medical student understands this relative value system. When planning their careers, they run the numbers and figure out what test scores they need to earn an elite residency spot toward the top of the list. As you examine the order of healthcare's hierarchy, it's easy to see what it is that physicians value most.

Those who care for patients with urgent, life-threatening problems are more valuable than those who help prevent patient diseases in the first place. Surgeons who hold the scalpel matter far more than those who wear stethoscopes around their necks. And those with expertise in a single organ system are accorded higher esteem than those physicians capable of caring for your entire body.

ALTHOUGH EVERYONE IN MEDICINE KNOWS which jobs carry most the prestige and which specialties are "second class," nobody talks about these distinctions overtly. Instead, classism in medicine is expressed through covert language that serves to maintain the existing hierarchy without having to debate or defend the status quo. I'll give you an example I recently observed.

Two dozen departmental chiefs from a prestigious medical center in California crammed themselves into a cozy conference room on a breezy spring day in 2018. The topic at hand: the organization's quality improvement plan.

The event organizer, a thin man with closely cropped hair, served as the institution's chief of quality. He began the session by presenting data on the facility's prior-year performance across a number of national quality outcome measures. The care-delivery report card was good in many areas, including hypertension control, cancer prevention, and the frequency of catheter infections (a measure of medical error). In other areas, however, the academic medical center lagged behind other leading medical groups in the state. Most concerning were the results when broken down by specialty. Several departments at this prestigious institution had fallen below the national mean in key areas of performance.

Before the quality chief could finish his presentation and describe his quality-improvement plan, the chief of nephrology (kidney medicine) shot up from his seat.

"Why are you talking to us about hypertension and urinary catheter infections?" he demanded to know. A tall and rotund physician wearing a pinstripe suit, the nephrology chief had taken the posture of a man with every intention of causing a scene. "How dare you defame our department? Our doctors are the best in the country. We are a national leader in successful kidney transplants. You should be praising us and telling the world about all the lives we save."

Having spent time in a variety of intimate conference settings like this one, I can attest to two incontrovertible truths about department chiefs. The first is that each and every one of them believes their doctors are the best. Second, most of them are wrong.

The department chief's values and beliefs, and most likely those of the physicians in his department, were apparent to all. Saving a life through transplantation was more important than saving many lives by controlling diabetes and hypertension (the two leading causes of kidney failure). Clearly, he viewed prevention and intervention as competing—rather than complementary—forms of treatment.

Though it might be tempting to dismiss the department head as an egoist with a myopic view of what really matters in medicine, it's important to point out that insurers, patients, and popular culture share his distorted perceptions. Reimbursement models in the US reward intervention far more than prevention. American patients subscribe to the belief that more care and more complex treatments are better than preventive care or conservative management. American society worships the MVP cardiac surgeon and undervalues the team players in primary care.

Before the chief of quality could respond, the nephrology department head added one more thing. "It's not hard to be good at these office-based measures," he said, waving his hand as if casually swatting a fly. "Any physician can do that stuff." He was wrong, but nobody corrected him. Any further argument would have been futile.

American doctors and patients are hurting, in part, because they focus on only part of the problem. Every physician is aware of the healthcare system's weaknesses, which compromise medical care and increase physician burnout. What they overlook, however, is how physician culture contributes to the unhappiness doctors experience. Physicians have divided themselves into high- and low-value specialties that conform to a clear cultural hierarchy, the way high school students segment themselves by clique. This artificial ranking system frustrates doctors at the bottom, undermines their self-worth, and distorts the perceptions of patients.

HOW THE MIGHTY FELL

I N AN ARTICLE THAT SHOCKED the US healthcare industry, the *International Journal of Health Services* published an incendiary research study titled, "Primary Care, Specialty Care, and Life Chances."

Using multiple regression analysis, the researchers concluded that "primary care is by far the most significant variable related to better health status." They found that having more primary care physicians in a given geography correlated with lower mortality, fewer deaths from heart disease and cancer, and a host of other beneficial health outcomes. By contrast, the researchers calculated that "the number of specialty physicians [i.e., surgeons, cardiologists, orthopedists, etc.] is positively and significantly related to total mortality, deaths due to heart diseases and cancer, shorter life expectancy." In other words, the more specialty physicians in a given area, the greater the probability of patients dying sooner.

Based on these stunning revelations, the authors of the study laid out a clear and convincing path for the future of healthcare delivery. This is how the paper described it: "From a policy perspective, a likely implication is to reorient the medical profession from its current expensive, clinically based, treatment-focused practice to a more cost-effective, prevention-oriented primary care system."

Aside from these radical reform recommendations, the most surprising thing about this research on the high value of primary care was the study's publication date: July 1, 1994.

A quarter of a century after the study and its recommendations were published, little has changed. Instead of acknowledging the facts and heeding the conclusions of the research, the primary care problem is now worse. More and more, specialists look at primary care physicians as referral sources, not as medical equals.

It has not always been this way. Until the last quarter of the twentieth century, all the nation's top medical students were drawn to primary care. They craved the excitement of learning to make difficult diagnoses while unraveling medical mysteries. Mastering these skills required an intricate blend of deductive reasoning, intuition, and experience. That is why primary care sat atop the physician hierarchy for most of the 1900s.

As it was with urology and general surgery, primary care's reputational nosedive resulted from major changes occurring outside the clinical specialty.

The first event was the diagnostic technology boom of the 1970s and '80s. These decades saw the invention and commercialization of MRIs and CT scanners, along with improvements in the image quality of ultrasounds. These tools improved clinical outcomes but rendered the diagnostic skill of primary care doctors increasingly irrelevant. By the 1990s, these technologies had become ubiquitous, lessening the need for brilliant diagnosticians and deductive thinkers. Today, sophisticated imaging proves superior to even the most sensitive human hand and sharpest mind.

Alongside the development of new diagnostic technologies, medicine was also undergoing a research renaissance. The use of randomized controlled trials became the "gold standard" of medical investigation by the end of the twentieth century. They gave doctors a deep understanding of the origin, prevention, and treatment of diseases, from heart attacks to strokes to kidney failure. These insights were turned into science-based protocols that physicians were expected to follow rigorously and consistently. This shifted the job expectations of primary care and jolted morale. Almost overnight, doctors who once enjoyed unbridled autonomy were no longer looked at as brilliant artists but rather assembly-line workers.

While the research explosion and resulting scientific advances diminished the status of primary care, a reputational renaissance was underway for specialists. Using scientific insights and new protocols, cardiac surgeons could now perform successful open-heart operations with low, single-digit mortality rates. Interventional cardiologists were passing catheters through blood vessels in the groin up to the heart and reversing myocardial infarctions. Meanwhile, orthopedic surgeons could reliably replace hip and knee joints with space-age implants, helping people who'd been severely disabled by joint pain return to the activities they loved.

In the heat of this surgical uprising, primary care physicians were bumped aside. Patients who once came to them for medications for joint pain were now demanding orthopedic referrals. And rather than nursing patients back to health after a heart attack, primary care doctors were getting cut out of the picture—the cardiologist was now the hero upon whom gratitude and kudos were heaped. Primary care doctors could still be helpers. But in this new order of medicine, specialists ruled.

The final event, which brought an end to primary care's glory days, was the managed care movement of the 1990s. For-profit insurance companies entered the healthcare market and turned medicine into a major moneymaker. Prior to this period, insurance companies defined their role as actuarial intermediaries. That is, they simply projected the cost of future healthcare and set a premium price to cover the expenses, plus a small administrative overhead. Becoming for-profit companies altered the calculus, giving insurers a strong financial imperative to cut costs.

To do so, they placed restrictions on the physician's decision-making authority, reduced the patient's access to medical services, and limited (or denied) coverage for people with pre-existing medical problems—until the Affordable Care Act made that approach illegal in 2009.

Primary care was central to the profitability of this new business model. The tactics insurers used were two-pronged: First, they turned many primary care physicians into gatekeepers, with reimbursement tactics that financially penalized them for ordering sophisticated tests or sending patients to specialists and hospitals. Second, insurers started requiring prior authorization, demanding doctors call them during restricted hours for approval to schedule tests or obtain specialty expertise. These changes were cataclysmal, making primary care physicians responsible for both the financial repercussions and the medical care of patients. To the detriment of medical ethics, the wall separating the doctor's income and the patient's best interest had been breached.

In response, physician groups ran aggressive TV advertising, and patients voiced their displeasure at this heavy-handed approach. The overreach of the managed care movement receded some, but nevertheless, the die had been cast. The hierarchical pyramid had been turned upside down. Primary care, once the hallowed sancta where the most interesting and complicated patients were sent, now served as the dumping ground for problems specialists didn't want to treat. From alphas to omegas, no other medical specialty has fallen further in medicine's power structure.

I've overheard specialists warning medical students to avoid primary care like the plague. "You'll burn out before you pay off your student loans," they caution. And in what some would consider an ironic twist, I heard an orthopedic surgeon tell a superb medical student, "You're too smart to become a primary care doctor." Just a generation ago, orthopedic surgery was labeled a safety net for medicine's "dumb jocks."

Some medical students heed the advice to avoid primary care for financial reasons. The most recent physician compensation report shows primary care doctors earn an average salary of $223,000, whereas specialists make an average of $329,000. Money, however, is not the only reason students steer clear of primary care. After all, applications for pediatrics, a specialty with an even lower average salary than adult primary care, have held steady. No, the main deterrent is the nature of the work itself. Nowadays, primary care physicians complain that their job feels robotic, uninspiring, and transactional—a far cry from the exciting and prestigious line of work it once was. It's no wonder these doctors are among medicine's most burned-out.

And because primary care has fallen so far from grace, Americans are living shorter, unhealthier lives. The latest study to analyze the untapped and underused value of primary care was published in 2019 in *JAMA Internal Medicine*. It not only confirms decades of prior research but also spotlights troubling trends in workforce planning, physician reimbursement, and residency training.

The study's research team, a Harvard-Stanford collaboration led by Dr. Sanjay Basu, examined life expectancy rates in the United States from 2005 to 2015. The team found that adding ten primary care physicians to a population of a hundred thousand people was associated with an average life expectancy increase of 51.5 days. That's compared to a modest 19.2-day increase for an equal number of specialists.

In other words, adding ten primary care physicians has a 250 percent greater influence on life expectancy than an equivalent bump in specialists. Nevertheless, the research also found this concerning fact: within the overall US population, the density of primary care physicians declined by 11 percent between 2005 and 2015, falling from 46.6 to 41.4 per 100,000 people.

In a press release, Basu predicted that "despite the clear correlation between better health and primary care, the number of primary care physicians is likely to continue to decline." He's absolutely right. Policy experts and medical professionals understand the valuable contributions primary care doctors make, yet the healthcare system continues to invest in training more and more specialists. In the United States, primary care is like healthy food. We all know it's good for us, but we keep ordering the burger on the menu anyway.

So here's a suggestion. The next time your friend raves about the cardiologist who unblocked his coronary artery, send a thank-you card to the primary care physician who keeps your heart healthy and your body off the cardiologist's operating table.

DOCTORS AND SELF-DETERMINATION THEORY

Y ALE PROFESSOR LAURIE SANTOS EARNED her stripes in the academic world by researching the animal kingdom. Her PhD thesis and much of her early research centered on monkeys and how their behaviors differ from (and often mirror) those of humans. She found that primates and humans share many of the same predictable irrationalities: both species are guilty of making biased decisions, taking unnecessary risks, and coming up with harebrained ideas that seem destined to fail.

Today Dr. Santos is best known for teaching a class at Yale called "The Science of Well-Being," which delves into the mysterious subject of happiness. It is the most popular course in the university's history, with one in four undergraduates enrolled and more than three hundred thousand people participating online. Throughout the ten-lecture series, Santos presents dozens of research studies that demonstrate how wrong we are about what we assume makes us happy. For example, nearly all Americans carry in their subconscious a central thesis that goes something like this: *Once I get the things I want, I will be happy and stay happy.*

Based on that rough mental model, people conclude that the more income they earn, and the more possessions they have, the happier they will be. These widely held beliefs cause an entire profession of doctors to associate their unhappiness and lack of fulfillment with an insufficient level of pay. As a result, they spend more time in their offices, seeing more patients, trying to generate higher incomes. Professor Santos notes that happiness does, indeed, correspond with more money but *only to a point*. Using Gallup polling data, psychologist and researcher Ed Diener calculated that point to be $75,000. Beyond that, he says, people experience no incremental increases in joy or fulfillment.

Doctors today are constantly comparing their incomes with those around them, driving themselves mad in the process. The median physician salary in the United States, regardless of specialty, is $313,000. No specialty earns less than $200,000 on average. Even when we account for inflation, variations in cost of living, and rising medical school tuitions, doctors in every specialty earn far more than the research-validated threshold for happiness.

The relationship between income and satisfaction has been studied dozens of times, and, consistently, experimenters reach the same conclusion: money doesn't buy happiness.

But our misperceptions about personal contentment are not limited to our personal wealth. Duke University researcher Peter Ubel ran an experiment to understand the gap between the kind of work we think we will enjoy and what we actually feel satisfied doing. He and his team asked business school students to choose between two jobs. Either they could get paid $2.50 to do nothing for five minutes, or they could elect to spend those five minutes solving word puzzles. Ubel said that most students thought they'd be happier doing nothing. Instead, as he explained on the NPR show *Hidden Brain*, "The people solving the word puzzles enjoyed the five minutes significantly more."

Applied to physicians, Ubel's research, as well as Diener's findings on money and happiness, suggests that doctors are unhappy not because they're paid too little but because the work they do has become unstimulating, uninteresting, and unfulfilling.

These insights on the tasks that satisfy us are nothing new. Researchers discovered them over a half century ago. Harry F. Harlow, like Laurie Santos, was a psychology professor with a primate fascination. At the University of Wisconsin, he established one of the world's first laboratories for studying animal behavior. It was in this field of study that Harlow's most enduring contributions to American psychological research arose. In the 1950s, Harlow coined the term "intrinsic motivation," a result of research that found the joy of the task is a reward in and of itself.

Through his research, Harlow identified that motivation and pleasure stem from feeling challenged and mastering new skills. Picking up where Harlow left off was Edward Deci, a psychology professor at the University of Rochester in New York.

He along with others pioneered the self-determination theory of motivation in the 1970s and '80s. This theory toppled the prevailing notion that financial rewards are the best way to incentivize or reinforce human behavior. Contrary to what most people believe, Deci found that extrinsic rewards and penalties, like large sums of money, undermine intrinsic motivation and diminish workplace performance. He and his colleagues identified three basic needs that serve as the basis for self-motivation and psychological well-being: autonomy, competence, and relatedness.

Deci describes *autonomy* as "the desire to be causal agents of one's own life and act in harmony with one's integrated self," *competence* as the ability to gain mastery of tasks and learn new skills, and *relatedness* as a sense of belonging—feeling connected to and being able to care for others.

Indeed, this triad is a staple of medical practice. All three motivators are tightly linked to the values of physician culture. But they are under attack, some say. In a *New England Journal of Medicine* perspective titled "Physician Burnout, Interrupted," a pair of Harvard physicians note that all three pillars of motivation "have been stripped away as a direct result of the restructuring of the healthcare system," adding, "radical alterations in the healthcare system that were supposed to make physicians more efficient and productive, and thus more satisfied, have made them profoundly alienated and disillusioned."

Looking at each of these motivators in greater detail helps shed light on the painful losses and dwindling joys doctors have experienced.

Autonomy, in Deci's self-determination theory, means acting with a sense of volition—that is, the freedom to make decisions and apply sound judgment without restriction. But rather than being given carte blanche to practice as they please, doctors of the twenty-first century have lost that ability. They are expected to follow clearly defined, evidence-based guidelines. And rather than practicing as they prefer, doctors must request authorization for just about any complex test or treatment. Albeit best for patients when physicians follow scientific protocols, doctors find that practicing medicine without freedom is far less rewarding.

Physicians have long heralded variation in medical practice as a key to innovation, allowing all clinicians to chart their own course toward the best patient care. But in this century, data on clinical outcomes has turned variation into the bogeyman of evidence-based medical practice. The desire of doctors to do as they wish clashes with attempts to institute "operational improvements" (efforts to make care delivery more efficient and effective). Scientific analysis *alone* defines the best way to provide medical care.

The old assumption that "the doctor knows best" is becoming a relic of the past. To physicians, every action feels closely monitored. It's as if someone from the healthcare system is constantly looking over their shoulder, ready to criticize even the slightest deviation from what is expected or acceptable.

Like an elk surrounded by hungry wolves, the doctor's sense of autonomy is being threatened from all sides. Insurance companies demand doctors document the treatment they provide and fill out paperwork precisely if they wish to be paid. Proponents of evidence-based approaches insist doctors follow guidelines, checklists, and medical algorithms. And with the rise of online information, even patients are feeling empowered to question their physician's judgment. They're treating the doctor-patient relationship more like a waiter-customer relationship, listening to the doctor's recommendations but without any sense of obligation to follow them. As the science of medicine becomes more sophisticated, the days of unchecked physician autonomy are ending.

Competence, according to Deci, is key to feeling intrinsically motivated. For doctors, competence means being capable of performing all the procedures of their specialty. This demands practice and repetition, which over time produce expertise and create a sense of accomplishment. The opportunity to maintain this breadth of excellence is disappearing from medical practice today. Doctors, who love to dabble, have long held tight to the expectation that they should be allowed to perform a wide variety of different procedures, regardless of whether they have the experience or ability to deliver excellent (rather than just acceptable) results. For a growing number of patients and purchasers of healthcare services, this historical standard of competence is outdated and inadequate.

As in professional sports, being good at a technical skill isn't good enough. Recall basketball's greatest superstar, Michael Jordan, who after winning three NBA championships traded in his Air Jordans for a pair of baseball cleats. Though his motivations were personal and laudable (many felt the decision was a tribute to his late father, who loved baseball), the outcome was predictable. His foray into minor league baseball lasted just thirteen months. To the delight of Chicago Bulls fans, Jordan returned to win another three NBA championships before retiring. The lesson: not even superstars can excel at everything. Doctors who like to dabble may think they can be exceptional at all things. But there's a huge gap between good and great. As a result, physicians are finding their practices narrowing.

Countless studies confirm that higher surgical volumes (with a narrower range of procedures) lead to the best outcomes for patients. Medicine's migration away from generalists toward specialists and subspecialists has created friction within physician culture, wearing away the doctor's sense of fulfillment.

Although doctors like being associated with words like "expertise," "experience," and "excellence," they push back against these optimal volume requirements. This might look hypocritical, but doctors believe that practicing medicine is their right. Having learned how to do a procedure, they believe they have the requisite expertise to continue performing it throughout their career.

Further, they reject the notion that insurers and patients are worthy arbiters of excellence. The privilege to make such judgments should be reserved only for colleagues who have completed the same training, share the same medical knowledge, and perform the same types of procedures. But as with autonomy, the doctor's desired definition of competence is losing favor.

In the past, when patients needed a procedure, they'd have no choice but to ask their personal physician, "Who's the best doctor for this?" The answer was never based on scientifically validated research or even direct observation. More often than not, referrals were based on the specialist's personal friendship with the referring doctor.

Today, patients use the internet to screen physicians and are increasingly being directed to centers of excellence where highly experienced specialists generate objectively better outcomes. These physicians have achieved not just competence but true mastery. And because the majority of doctors have not achieved this level of excellence, the specialists who dabble feel devalued and left behind.

Finally, relatedness (also called connection) is the feeling that one is meaningfully connected to other people and to one's own culture. Through his research, Deci concluded that "people need to have a sense of belonging and connectedness with others" to feel satisfied and to sustain intrinsic motivation.

Medicine, unfortunately, has lost its sense of community and camaraderie. Physicians nearing the end of their careers mourn the loss of the hospital as it once was. They remember a time when every community doctor rounded on patients in the morning and every surgery was performed in one of the hospital's main operating rooms. Times, like hospitals, have changed.

Today, two-thirds of surgeries are performed in surgicenters, where patients are discharged within one hour of the procedure and doctors rarely interact with colleagues. Even with an ever-growing and aging US population, the number of people hospitalized each year is declining. Inpatient stays are becoming a thing of the past. Common operations like gallbladder removal, total-joint replacement, and appendectomy are now routinely done on an outpatient basis. New mothers, who once spent a week recovering in the hospital after childbirth, go home within a day or two. Simultaneously, the role of the rounding doctor has been largely replaced by the hospitalist, who provides inpatient care in place of a primary care doctor. In fact, less than a third of hospital-based care is provided by the patient's personal physician nowadays.

Although long hospital stays may not seem like an experience worthy of nostalgia, today's more efficient and effective treatments have fundamentally altered the way physicians in the community relate to patients and to one another: Doctors today feel lonely and detached. To the outsider, it might be hard to conceive of doctors as lonely professionals. Physicians are continually surrounded by patients and office staff. But despite being in the constant company of others, 25 percent of doctors report feeling isolated.

For them, what's missing is *meaningful* contact with colleagues. Rather than consulting face-to-face in the hospital with doctors in other specialties, most collegial interactions now take place by phone or email. Instead of performing procedures in an inpatient setting, specialists are working in outpatient venues where they rarely encounter their peers. And rather than bumping into dozens of fellow physicians during morning rounds, today's primary care physicians drive straight to their offices.

A friend of mine who practiced in the community twenty-plus years ago emailed me the following memory of the doctors' dining room. Now extinct, these communal gathering spots of yore remind us why today's physicians feel so distant from one another:

> I remember very clearly the physician dining room. It had paneled walls, like a restaurant. The room was very pretty with white tablecloths and small, intimate tables for four or six people. Sometimes, you would see doctors chatting over X-rays, seeking a friend's opinion. There was a staff of servers that stood at attention around the room in white starched uniforms. There were flowers on the table. The atmosphere was very calm and pleasant, the tones were hushed. I remember what a treat it was. I loved operating at that facility.

On one hand, such a facility can be viewed as an obscene extravagance in the context of rising healthcare costs. On the other hand, these places served a powerful purpose, one that has been lost to the detriment of all. To borrow a phrase from sociologist Ray Oldenburg, the hospital dining room was akin to the doctor's "third place": a spot unlike home (the first place) or work (the second), where like-minded people could gather, build relationships, and exchange ideas.

The physician's dining room or lounge served as a place where doctors of every rank and station would connect and collaborate. In that way, it took on the same cultural significance as the local coffee shop, neighborhood pub, or community church. In these dining rooms, physicians discussed not only what they saw on radiographs (X-rays) but what was happening in their personal lives and in the ever-changing landscape of medical practice. The doctors' dining space also had cultural currency, signaling to physicians that hospital leaders appreciated and respected the years they sacrificed to gain medical knowledge and expertise.

What my friend really missed about the dining room wasn't the free meal but the loss of relatedness: the opportunity to share ideas, hopes, and concerns with colleagues. In that way, the doctor's "third place" was the antithesis of (and possible antidote to) professional loneliness and emotional isolation. Anyone who has tried during the coronavirus pandemic to replace the experience of family gatherings with a Skype or Zoom call understands the emotional voltage drop that occurs when people are physically apart.

These losses have knocked the wind out of doctors. Connectedness at work has an outsized influence on their overall happiness: Seventy percent of doctors who say they have "many" friends at work indicate feeling highly satisfied with their lives. That's nearly two times greater than the number of satisfied doctors who report having no friends at work. More concerning is the correlation between increased isolation and higher rates of burnout. A poll by athenahealth shows that the more often doctors feel isolated at work, the more burnout they experience. In the most severe case, 84 percent of doctors report symptoms of burnout when they feel isolated every day. This link between loneliness and burnout isn't just bad for doctors. Studies demonstrate that isolation among physicians leads to poorer quality of care for patients. Isolation also is associated with more frequent displays of hostility and a greater risk that doctors will make poor decisions that lead to medical errors.

During my tenure as CEO, I often said, "Good things happen when two physicians talk." I still believe that to be true. But it's happening less and less in American medicine today.

―――――――

PUTTING THESE THREE PIECES TOGETHER, it's clear doctors today feel systematically sapped of their autonomy, sense of competence, and feelings of relatedness. As such, their lack of joy, fulfillment, and motivation is predictable. That's why Drs. Pamela Hartzband and Jerome Groopman, the two Harvard physicians who authored the article "Physician Burnout, Interrupted," argue that the healthcare system needs to bend and conform to the doctor's definition of (and desire for) each. They write:

> The problem of burnout will not be solved without addressing the issues of autonomy, competence, and relatedness. Evidence from the meta-analysis of controlled interventions supports the restoration of autonomy; giving doctors flexibility in their schedule to allow for individual styles of practice and patient interaction was one of the few system solutions that reduced burnout. . . . Competency can be restored by purging the system of meaningless metrics while maintaining a core of evidence-based measures, allowing for clinical judgment, and honoring individual patient preferences. Relatedness should be authentic, aligning the system's values with those of physicians, nurses, and other health care professionals who chose their careers out of altruism. Restoring these three pillars will support the return of intrinsic motivation.

I applaud their desire to restore the three pillars of intrinsic motivation to medical practice. Doctors are doubtless suffering from all that they've lost. And from that perspective, it's a wonder more physicians aren't burned-out. But no matter how loud doctors yell for help or how long they wait, relief isn't coming. The old normal is never returning.

After the coronavirus pandemic, financial stresses and strains on the US economy will render any solution that involves higher spending a nonstarter. The science of medicine has advanced too much to tolerate the historical variation in performance that results from giving doctors untethered autonomy, particularly when a third of the care they provide has been demonstrated to add little or no value. Of course, fewer metrics and reduced volume standards would make doctors feel more competent, but data-based performance measures, combined with higher levels of experience, undoubtedly lead to better approaches, more consistent care, and superior health outcomes for patients. Meanwhile, the loss of the

American hospital as a central gathering place has left doctors feeling even less connected to their colleagues and their profession. In the future, doctors will need to find connectedness through a common mission rather than a shared building. Whether doctors lead the way—or whether future changes will be imposed on them—remains to be seen.

BORED STIFF

I N THE FALL OF 2013, I attended the Permanente Medical Group's annual "Decades of Physician Excellence" celebration in Monterey, California. This two-day event honors the contributions of those who've spent ten, twenty, thirty, and even forty years with the group. Saturday night of this event was always the showstopper, as buses transported participants to a mansion about thirty minutes outside town.

Each room inside the stunning estate featured a different global cuisine and lively conversation. The largest room, with its soaring cathedral ceiling, was reserved for dancing. An eight-piece rock band was strumming a Motown favorite of mine when I spotted a good friend and colleague whom I hadn't seen in months. I'll call him Bill. He waved at me and made his way over. Hand in hand, he introduced me to his dance partner, an equally eye-catching physician whom I'll refer to as Sarah. The two worked in the same ER and shared a love for adventure, having recently returned from a backpacking trip through South America, where they hiked the mountain passes of the Andes.

I knew my friend had separated from his wife a couple years ago. To my knowledge, he hadn't been in a serious relationship since. He and Sarah told me they had been dating for about eight months, and they seemed very happy. The three of us talked about getting together after the New Year.

My phone rang late one evening in mid-January. It was the physician-in-chief (PIC) from the medical center where Bill worked. Unexpected phone calls from my direct reports after ten p.m. never brought good news. The PIC explained that a nurse had found one of the ER doctors unconscious in an exam room a little less than an hour ago. He couldn't be sure, but based on what they knew so far, the doctor had ordered a large dose of powerful narcotics, administered only a small amount to the patient, and, soon after, self-injected the remaining contents.

My first priority was making sure both the patient and the doctor were physically okay. The PIC confirmed that the patient was fine, and the doctor, having received a narcotic antagonist medication (Naloxone), was going to be all right as well. Next priority: dealing with the fallout. The chief confirmed that the doctor involved had been suspended, effective immediately, and was being evaluated by the on-call psychiatrist. The only remaining step was to contact our legal department in the morning since the medical center would need to fill out paperwork for the state licensing board.

I thanked my colleague for his quick and thorough handling of the unfortunate situation and told him to contact me anytime, day or night, if he needed any help.

"We've got things under control," he assured me. As I was about to hang up, I asked him, "By the way, what's the doctor's name?"

My stomach sank when he told me it was Sarah. My head swirled, first with confusion—*why, how, really, her?*—and then rage: *How could she be so stupid? How dare she endanger a patient like that?*

Within a few days, Sarah had enrolled in a state-run drug diversion program, which allows eligible defendants to avoid jail time by completing treatment and education courses. After that, she'd begin mandatory random drug testing and ongoing counseling. She would not be returning to medicine for a long time.

I called Bill shortly after Sarah started treatment. He was devastated by what had happened. He felt blindsided by her addiction and the series of lies she had told each time she used. Saddened by their breakup, he wondered if he was foolish not to have noticed the problem. I tried reassuring him that she was probably very good at hiding her addiction. He shouldn't blame himself, I said. In all likelihood, there was nothing he could have done.

Before we said our goodbyes, I asked if he thought Sarah would be willing to talk with me after she completed her rehab. He thought it would be okay but urged me to be gentle. I could tell he still loved her.

I called Sarah about a month later and asked how she was doing. "Under the circumstances, okay," she replied. I then inquired whether she was getting the psychological support she needed, and she assured me she was. Next, I asked why she did it. Her reply was not what I would have predicted.

"I was getting no joy out of work," she said, plainly. "It was the same thing every day. The excitement I felt earlier in my career was gone. I guess I was bored."

I knew what she meant. After a decade of practice, ER doctors start seeing the same medical problems, doing the same workups, and prescribing the same medications. Early in her career, the problems were challenging, and her growing expertise felt rewarding. Now each shift seemed repetitive, routine, never-ending.

I remember a mentor in medical school telling me that medicine starts out as a job, then becomes a career, and ends as a calling. But for Sarah, and for many doctors, it now goes in the opposite order.

"Had you discussed these feelings with your colleagues?" I asked.

"No, I couldn't," she replied. "How could I tell them I was bored when they were constantly saying how busy they were?" She hesitated for a second, then added, "I know they work hard. During flu season, nobody has even five minutes to eat or go to the bathroom. But most of the time, we're just doing the same steps over and over. It's like we're trapped in our routines."

After we said our goodbyes, I let Sarah's words sink in. The idea that doctors could be bored and feeling "trapped in the routine" contrasted with scores of physician surveys and studies that suggested the opposite: that doctors were completely overwhelmed by the pace and demands of their work.

Trying to make sense of this incongruity triggered a memory from a few years earlier, during my biannual visits to the medical centers. In the afternoons, I always set aside time to meet with doctors one-on-one and confidentially. Over the years, the tone of these conversations shifted noticeably from concerns about the long-term viability of Kaiser Permanente to more immediate, day-to-day matters. Starting in 2010, one complaint began to dominate these private discussions: workload.

I wasn't surprised by this. Each year, we raised the bar on our medical group's performance. We kept expanding access to care while increasing the quality of our outcomes. It was hard work that paid off. We had moved from the top 10 percent of programs, into the top 5 percent, and eventually earned the top spot in the National Committee for Quality Assurance rankings. Our successes required everyone to make sacrifices of their time and energy. However, as more physicians came knocking on my door, I worried the pace of change was too rapid.

"I'm seeing a new patient every fifteen minutes," one doctor told me, echoing the concerns I'd heard from dozens of others. "It's not sustainable."

I agreed. At that clip, every doctor would be seeing thirty patients a day. Thirty! Maybe that number would work in an urgent care center, which caters to people with straightforward problems like colds, headaches, and rashes. But given how many of our patients suffered multiple chronic diseases, fifteen minutes wasn't nearly enough time to ensure excellent medical care.

To get a better handle on the situation, I asked our data analytics division to check the patient registration system for the exact number of patients being seen per day, both by department and by medical center. I was stunned by the results. With only rare exceptions, the true average turned out to be fifteen or sixteen patients per doctor each day—half of what I was hearing from the physicians.

What was going on here? I recognized these were averages and that some of our ten thousand doctors did, in fact, see twenty or more patients a day. But if the average were fifteen or sixteen, that would also mean that some doctors were seeing as few as ten or twelve each day. I had no doubt the physicians who met with me were being honest about their workload concerns, but why were all their estimates so far off? That question went unanswered for years until I talked to Sarah. Her insight felt like an epiphany.

If she was right and the practice of medicine had become tedious, unstimulating, even boring, then it's possible that seeing fifteen patients each day could cause the same mental exhaustion as seeing thirty patients a day. Boredom had distorted the doctors' sense of time and skewed in their minds the number of tasks they thought they'd completed.

For people who feel as if there's never enough time in the day, boredom might seem like heaven. But in practice, it's hell. A year after Sarah's overdose in the ER, I came across a study featured in *Science* that helped me understand what she and many physicians might be going through. In it, researchers placed paid volunteers in a room and instructed them to sit there for fifteen minutes in order to earn the promised payment.

At each desk was a machine that generated a safe but painful electric shock. As the minutes ticked by, more and more of the subjects began to press the button. This wasn't mere curiosity driving their behavior. In all, nearly two-thirds of participants jolted themselves with electricity, and many of the subjects did so more than once—some as many as a dozen times. If just fifteen minutes of boredom could result in such self-destructive behavior, it's not difficult to understand Sarah's actions. Days, weeks, and months of tedium and repetition made time stand still, producing in her and others the fatigue and dissatisfaction we call "burnout."

Not long ago, a retired physician from Kaiser Santa Clara emailed me his "recollections of internship" (see next page). The hastily jotted entry, dated July 1, 1959, chronicles a professional life teeming with patients and filled with long, difficult days on the job.

It tells of a challenging occupation with an "endless flow of surgical admits," "no air conditioning," and "sunrise sometimes from the OR." But make no mistake: These were not complaints. This was a love poem, an ode to a career that felt far more engaging and exciting than the job most doctors find themselves in today.

As one primary care doctor told me recently, "I feel like a rat in a Skinner Box. Practicing today is more like operant conditioning than creative puzzle solving."

It would be wrong to reinstate the trying conditions of residency training as it was decades ago. Our world has evolved too much for that. It also would be an error to redesign the healthcare system around the preferences of doctors and the values of physician culture. The world has changed too much for that as well.

Recollections of Internship

J. Richard Gaskill, MD

July 1st, '59, Dallas
Parkland Memorial Hospital
Before copiers and pagers
Concerns about smoking
ICUS and Medicare
Lee Harvey Oswald and JFK.

Segregated wards oppressive
With no air conditioning
All-white medical staff
Nurses' starched uniforms and caps
Page operator's seductive voice
Often disappointing in person.

Dozens of multip deliveries
Workups, IVs, and scut
On call every other or 3rd
Sleep deprivation the norm
Call rooms a-whirr with fans
Staff lounge a welcome refuge.

Alphabetic array of disease
On crowded Medicine floors
Ascites, Bacteremia, Cirrhosis
Diabetes, Emphysema, FUOs …
Sickle cell children on Peds
Anemia, jaundice, and crises.

Variety of problems in the ER
From trauma to rare and weird
Fatal tetanus after abortion
Women with "fallin'-out spells"
Dehydrated infants, barely alive
Sunken fontanelles restored with clay.

Endless flow of surgical admits
Outpatient surgery unknown
Long cases as second assistant
Abdominal retractor in hand
Sunrise sometimes from the OR
Never again after the 30th of June.

Suddenly three years later
In the news familiar names
Mac Perry, Charlie Baxter
Pepper Jenkins, Kemp Clark
And the death of the president
In Trauma Room One.

HELPING OR HARMING PATIENTS?

QUALITY ISN'T A GIVEN

Some people see the glass half full. Others see it half empty. I see a glass that's twice as big as it needs to be.

—George Carlin

AMERICANS ARE OF TWO MINDS when it comes to healthcare. They think very highly of their physicians, yet they have extremely negative views of the healthcare system.

Like their doctors, patients subscribe to the narrative that the system is to blame for the majority of the nation's health problems. In fact, seven in ten US adults say the system is in "a state of crisis," giving it poor marks for its high costs, limited access, and pointless complexities. These widely held beliefs feed into an easily digestible storyline: doctors are the heroes who help us, and the healthcare system is the villain that hurts us.

Of course, the real-life version of events is not so simplistic. Patients fail to realize the central role *physician culture* plays in the difficulties they experience with their healthcare.

The stories and information featured in this section of the book demonstrate that the culture of doctors and the problems of the healthcare system are deeply intertwined. Although the norms, values, and beliefs that define physician culture have led to incredible medical advancements over the last half century, they also have contributed significantly to the unaffordable, inaccessible, and unsafe healthcare-delivery system we have today.

To begin to show how the physician culture fails to meet the needs of patients, consider the word "quality." Compared to patients, doctors prefer a vastly different (and far narrower) definition of the word.

In 2001, the National Academy of Medicine, an independent non-profit organization formerly called the Institute of Medicine, defined the six dimensions of high-quality medical care as "safe, effective, patient-centered, timely, efficient, and equitable."

From the perspective of patients, this is exactly what healthcare ought to be. Whether their problem is routine or life-threatening, they value convenient, affordable, and rapid access to care. Furthermore, they want to be treated fairly, safely, and with respect. Though "quality" is a tough word to pin down in any industry, visit any of the online physician review sites like Healthgrades, RateMDs, or Vitals, and you'll see just how broadly patients define it. Visitors to these webpages provide reviews and ratings on everything from the doctor's punctuality to the staff's helpfulness to their likelihood of recommending the physician to family and friends.

In this sense, patients judge the quality of their healthcare experiences in much the same way they'd critique a restaurant, retail outlet, or hotel visit. That is, they focus on what they can observe. In healthcare, that includes things like timely access, customer service, and congeniality.

This is modern consumerism 101. Patrons who see an unclean dining area at a restaurant or an unkempt hotel lobby will take their business elsewhere (and encourage others to do the same). After all, if things look untidy in the "front of the house," just imagine how mismanaged things must be behind closed doors. The same thinking applies to medicine. If a doctor is rude, or late, or if a waiting area is overflowing with displeased patients, then how probable is it that the doctor will deliver exceptional *clinical* quality?

Doctors sneer at online ratings and exclude these consumer criteria from their definition of quality. Physicians believe no patient has the expertise (or the right) to evaluate or cast judgment on their work. In their eyes, it's one thing for a customer to critique a chef's abilities. After all, some customers know how to cook. It's another thing entirely for a patient who has never been to medical school to evaluate the expertise of a cardiologist or orthopedic surgeon.

Physicians rail against the notion that a patient's satisfaction, happiness, or time spent in the waiting room has any bearing on the quality of care provided. In fact, many look down on doctors with high satisfaction ratings, accusing them of "smiling and selling."

In the service industry, the customer is always right. In medicine, doctors are never wrong. These divergent outlooks on who's right and who's wrong produce two vastly different interpretations of what it takes to deliver "healthcare quality."

Doctors wish to be judged solely on their medical responsibilities. They see their job as diagnosing illness, ordering tests, performing procedures, recommending treatment plans, and helping patients avoid disease. Physicians were taught in their training that the measures of quality that truly matter are specific to the function and purpose of *medicine*. In the eyes of the doctor, quality has nothing to do with whether the medical care is speedy, convenient, pleasing to patients, or equitable.

Physicians would rather just treat patients as they were taught and not bother with the full six-pronged framework for quality. Doctors believe people should simply trust that they are in the best of hands and be grateful for the medical care they receive.

Thus, when it comes to the meaning of "quality," the discrepancy between patients and doctors is far more than definitional. Patients embrace a multitude of quality dimensions. They favor more inputs, more data, and more transparency than exist today. Doctors, by contrast, maintain a constricted view of this term and are convinced that the quality evaluation process has gotten out of hand.

Doctors in the United States often say, "Quality is a given," implying that physicians and the treatments they provide are consistently excellent and beyond reproach. They point with supreme verve at the multimillion-dollar robots in their operating rooms and the sophisticated diagnostic machines stationed throughout their hospitals. They proudly list the prestigious institutions where they received top-notch specialty training and brag about the complexity of the surgical procedures they perform. With these indicators of "quality," American doctors are confident they provide the best care in the world.

But when we look at the data, it's clear the quality of healthcare delivered in the United States is anything but "a given." Indeed, American healthcare leads the world in medical technologies and spending on prescription medications. But the US ranks ninety-seventh in "access to quality healthcare" and forty-first in life expectancy—statistics that are on par with much poorer nations like Chile, Jordan, and Albania. Among the world's most developed countries, the United States has the lowest life expectancy, highest infant and maternal mortality rates, and most preventable deaths per capita. In studies that assess a broader definition of quality, the United States consistently ranks last in overall healthcare performance among the world's wealthiest nations.

In a culture that embraces pricey medical technologies but rejects information technology—while demanding decision-making authority as it bemoans evidence-based approaches—it should be no surprise that doctors fail to deliver the safest or most consistent treatments. And in a culture that considers it taboo to make medical decisions based on costs, doctors can't and don't provide the most efficient or equitable care possible. And as members of a culture that sneers at online patient reviews about satisfaction and service, doctors also fail to deliver timely, patient-centered care.

The perceptions and priorities of doctors today play a powerful albeit unrecognized role in our nation's lagging health and weakened economy. In the postcoronavirus world, the problems created by physician culture will worsen and prove untenable. As our nation struggles to dig itself out of the economic hole COVID-19 created, the norms and values doctors hold dear will prevent patients from obtaining the high-quality medical care they desire and deserve.

A TALE OF TWO EMERGENCIES

IT IS THE BEST OF cultures; it is the worst of cultures; it is the culture of wisdom; it is the culture of foolishness; it has saved countless lives; it has killed millions; it births heroes; it makes doctors oblivious to their faults; it instills hope; it brings despair.

Physicians say, and genuinely believe, they always put patients first. Sometimes they do. Often they don't.

As the sun began its descent over San Bruno, California, on a mild September day in 2010, a thirty-inch pipeline belonging to Pacific Gas and Electric exploded beneath a quiet residential neighborhood. So powerful was the blast that the US Geological Survey registered a 1.1 magnitude earthquake. Eyewitnesses said the explosion kicked up a wall of fire over one thousand feet high. As blazes spread from home to home, paramedics rushed in to rescue the wounded. Within the hour, every local TV and radio station had turned their cameras and mics toward the chaos unfolding in the streets.

It happened just after six o'clock that evening. The timing couldn't have been worse. It was "end of day" at most hospitals, including the facility nearest the blast, the Kaiser Permanente medical center in South San Francisco. The majority of doctors in the Bay Area were in their cars, on the freeway, starting the trek home after a long day's work, which, for many, began well before sunrise.

I, too, was heading home from the KP regional headquarters in Oakland when the story broke on one of the local AM stations: "A massive explosion in San Mateo County, dozens injured, and possibly dead." I phoned the emergency department at the South San Francisco facility and asked to speak with the chief. I was prepared to activate the phone tree and mobilize doctors from Kaiser Permanente hospitals across the region. I pictured the ED already overwhelmed and understaffed with just a skeleton crew handling what could be fifty or one hundred critically injured victims. I knew patients would be arriving by ambulance with broken bones, concussions, missing limbs, ruptured ear drums, internal bleeding, and severe burns. When the chief picked up, he sounded calm.

"You don't need to send anyone, Robbie," he said. "We have it well under control."

Without having to call a single doctor at home, two dozen physicians from the South San Francisco facility had returned to work. They, too, had been listening to their car radios, heard about the explosion, and took the nearest exit. And though they were under no contractual obligation to do so, and wouldn't get paid for their time, dozens of other physicians from nearby Kaiser Permanente hospitals weaved through rush-hour traffic toward the South San Francisco medical center as well. Only eight people died that evening in one of the most horrific pipeline explosions in our nation's history. Many lives were saved thanks to the selfless doctors who voluntarily and proactively turned their cars around.

The next day, I called the homes of those who came to the aid of their colleagues and patients. To each I offered my sincerest gratitude. All of them had the same sort of response: "It was a duty/honor/privilege to help people in need." I could tell they meant it. That night, they'd shown the world the physician culture at its absolute best.

A decade after the San Bruno pipeline explosion, in the midst of the coronavirus pandemic, I'm still reminded of that evening. When I speak with friends and former colleagues in different KP medical centers across Northern California, they tell stories of their heroic and selfless colleagues who've worked around the clock to meet the critical needs of patients stricken with the virus.

When medical disasters strike, all doctors respond the same way. They do whatever it takes to save lives. Under the most challenging of circumstances, they rush in, roll up their sleeves, and rescue people in need. With dedication, bravery, and tenacity, physicians step forward and live up to the core cultural values that inspired them to become doctors in the first place. In times of crisis, doctors undeniably put patients first. Other times, however, they don't.

EVERY FORTY SECONDS, SOMEONE IN the United States has a heart attack. It's a terrifying and all too common occurrence. Heart disease affects 121 million adults and is the nation's number one cause of death. It took the life of my grandfather, and it kills more than 600,000 Americans each year.

With those facts in mind, think back to last weekend. What activities did you do? Perhaps you were outside gardening, enjoying brunch with your family, or catching up on household chores. Now imagine that in the middle of one of these activities, you suddenly felt intense discomfort in the center of your chest. Though the squeezing sensation you experienced seemed to go away after a minute or two, it returns later, stronger.

The paramedics arrive and whisk you to the nearest emergency department. The doctors tell you they need to run some tests to figure out exactly what is wrong. From that point, there are a number of ways your situation could unfold.

It's possible your pain stems from stomach acid, regurgitating up into your esophagus, burning its delicate lining. Though it is uncomfortable, it's not deadly. After an EKG and cardiac enzyme tests (troponins) prove normal, you go home with an antacid and a list of instructions on how to avoid heartburn (also called gastroesophageal reflux disease or GERD) in the future.

In a second scenario, your worst fears are realized. The EKG shows ST-segment elevation, which is diagnostic for "a serious heart attack." With damage to your heart muscle progressing, you need immediate medical intervention. The ER doctor telephones the on-call interventional cardiologist, who immediately ceases his or her weekend activity and races straight to the ER. A team of doctors and nurses rush to the catheterization lab, unblock your occluded vessel (coronary artery), and insert a stent to keep it "patent" (open and unobstructed). Had this procedure been around in my grandfather's time, he likely would have survived and lived another decade or so. In fact, thanks to the incredible advances of modern medical science, more than 90 percent of people now survive a myocardial infarction.

Between these two extremes, there's yet another scenario to consider, sort of an intermediate option. Here your chest pain results from a partially, not fully, occluded coronary artery. In other words, there's enough blood getting to the heart muscle to keep it alive but not a sufficient quantity for you to, say, walk up a flight of stairs or endure a stressful situation. Your EKG doesn't reveal the telltale ST-segment elevation, and your cardiac enzymes are normal.

You're not having a heart attack. However, with diminished blood flow and damage to the vessel walls, your risk of a sudden and complete blockage increases. And if that were to happen, you would experience a heart attack and possibly die.

Recall that earlier, during your activity, the chest pain you experienced went away and then came back. Given that your second episode was brought on without exercise, the consulting cardiologist diagnoses *unstable angina* and admits you to the hospital. You will be scheduled for an angiogram and stent placement to prevent this problem from happening in the future.

You're frightened but relieved that the doctors recognized the problem before anything more serious happened. You ask the physician when you'll be going in for your procedure. The answer surprises you.

Had you been admitted on a weekday rather than a weekend, the interventional cardiology team would already be in the cath lab doing routine scheduled procedures. They would have added you to the patient list and placed the stent before the end of the day. Since it's a Saturday, however, there's a good chance you will wait in your hospital bed until Monday morning.

If you ask cardiologists about the discrepancy between their weekday sense of urgency and weekend tolerance for delays, the explanations seem reasonable: "We don't have enough staff in the cath lab on weekends," and besides "staffing it every day would be too expensive," and "cardiologists are only on call for emergencies over the weekend." They add: "If physicians had to come in every Saturday and Sunday for these non-emergent cases, they'd be exhausted all week, and that wouldn't be safe." Besides, "a hospital is the safest place for a patient to be."

Though all of these excuses sound defensible, they ignore an important clinical reality. Unnecessary delays put the patient's life at risk. So why risk the delay? Is there no other option?

In fact, there are safer approaches that could alleviate the risk to the patient without exhausting the staff or raising costs. They're just not solutions that doctors would embrace.

For example, here's one alternative to closing the cath lab for the whole weekend: In hospitals with low patient volume, why not make the "emergency only" days Wednesday and Sunday? That way, patients never have to wait more than twenty-four hours for treatment during these "intermediate" situations. And in larger hospitals that run more than one interventional cardiology room on weekdays, why not spread the scheduled procedures out over all seven days? With this approach, doctors, nurses, and staff would work an occasional Saturday or Sunday, taking a normally scheduled weekday as a day off.

This wouldn't be much of an intrusion on the lives of cardiologists. With thirty-two thousand of them in the United States, even if every hospital did cardiac procedures (which they don't), there'd be five cardiologists for each of the nation's six thousand inpatient facilities. That means every cardiologist would have to work one weekend day every three weeks while getting an equal number of weekdays off.

I've tried pitching this idea to cardiologists who work in one of these restrictive weekend facilities. The usual reply is a non sequitur: "That's not necessary. We're always available for emergencies."

Therein lies the real issue. Just as doctors and patients have contrasting thoughts on the meaning of "quality," they also differ when it comes to defining a medical "emergency."

Both groups agree that major injuries caused by a disaster (a pipeline explosion), severe heart attacks (ST-segment elevation with abnormal cardiac enzymes), and life-threatening pneumonia caused by a viral pandemic (the coronavirus) qualify as emergencies that demand immediate medical care. But if you're one of the thousands of patients unlucky enough to experience a potentially life-threatening heart problem on a weekend, well, what you define as a "medical emergency" is something many doctors define as a problem that can "safely" wait until Monday morning.

Ultimately, the line between an emergency and an inconvenience blurs when a patient's problem threatens to disrupt the doctor's weekend. Make no mistake, doctors work hard and deserve time off. And if there wasn't a solution that allowed them to relax and refresh, then we might have to accept that delays in treatment are the only option. But there are alternatives to the status quo. Logic dictates that it is possible for patients to receive necessary care on the weekends both safely and efficiently. Doctors disagree with that logic, refusing to consider any substitute for the way things are done in their facilities now. Physicians believe they always put patients first. Sometimes they do. Often they don't.

PART THREE | CHAPTER THREE

HUMAN SHIELDS

IN THE LATE-NINETEENTH CENTURY, PRIOR to the ubiquity of hospitals and health insurance, doctors and patients handled payments discreetly, one-on-one. This usually involved some sort of in-kind arrangement: a trade of medical services for produce, poultry, or other goods found in and around the patient's home.

These were different times in America. Doctors lived in the same small community as their patients, and all were on a first-name basis. They made house calls, even on weekends, and sometimes stayed for dinner. These were also cheaper times in American medicine. With no expensive prescription drugs or pricey overnight hospital stays, families spent hardly a fraction of their annual income on medical care. By 1900, the average American paid just $5 a year for healthcare services (about $100 in today's money). Few people needed insurance for something so inexpensive.

Medicine at the time was an unsophisticated trade with few reliable or effective treatment options. But while the local physician might not have been able to cure your pneumonia or cancer, he treated you kindly and was careful not to overcharge you for what services he could provide. This homespun style of care delivery was both intimate and personal, which made trust an essential part of every transaction.

Even when it came to the kind of "big ticket items" doctors depended on to pay their bills (childbirth, trauma care, and surgery), the quality and quantity of care provided remained the same, regardless of the patient's ability to pay.

In fact, the American Medical Association's first recorded code of ethics in 1847 made no mention of "money," "insurance," "payment," or "price," or any other allusion to the cost of care. That's because treating patients who couldn't afford to pay was an expectation accepted by all.

My uncle Herb (Alan's father), who practiced from the 1940s to the 1980s, once told me that 10 percent of his patients paid him absolutely nothing. He said this neither to boast nor to whine. My uncle would never have considered telling one of his indigent patients to go elsewhere. They paid what they could afford, and that was good enough for him. Treating a patient in need was simply a cultural given that he and his colleagues held throughout their careers—an expectation that held true until very recently.

Healthcare today is big business. The average annual price tag for a person's medical care in the United States is $10,224. That number reflects the total spent on each patient's tests, treatments, hospital stays, prescription drugs, insurance, and all other medical services. That sum is far more than any of the next-highest-spending nations: Switzerland ($8,009), Germany ($5,728), and Sweden ($5,511). As a national line item, US healthcare is racing toward an annual cost of $4 trillion, more than the entire gross domestic product (GDP) of Germany, the largest economy in all of Europe.

A century ago, patients feared a bad diagnosis because it meant having to endure physical pain and suffering. Today, a bad diagnosis often results in a different kind of suffering: financial ruin. Half of all US patients say that one large medical bill would force them to borrow money, sell their home, or declare bankruptcy. With the average family deductible currently over $3,000, studies show most people don't have enough savings to cover their out-of-pocket expenses should they experience a serious or prolonged illness. And as a result of ever-rising prices, the typical US family now spends $8,200 of its own income each year on healthcare (through insurance premiums and out-of-pocket costs). These annual expenses keep rising despite the fact that eight in ten Americans live paycheck to paycheck. As a result, the unaffordability of healthcare is killing the American dream and putting patients in harm's way.

How we got from then ($5-a-year healthcare in 1900) to now involves a complex web of political, economic, and cultural events that have transformed the macroeconomics of medicine.

———————

UP UNTIL THE MIDWAY POINT of then and now, around 1960, cost inflation of healthcare stayed relatively flat. Then, the annual cost of providing medical care to the average person was just $147. As a result, healthcare accounted for around 5 percent of the nation's GDP for much of the 1960s.

Across that decade, however, three major changes turned healthcare spending on its head. The first was an American business boom that gave unions greater bargaining power. Threatening strikes, labor leaders demanded and got expanded healthcare coverage for their members. The second shift was that businesses began to take advantage of tax incentives, which made it less expensive to give employees better medical benefits than to increase wages. Finally, there was the Kennedy-Johnson administration, which worked with Congress to ratify Medicare, a federally funded program to provide healthcare to the elderly, and Medicaid, a program for Americans living in poverty.

Thanks to these political and economic shifts, nearly 70 percent of all Americans had some form of health insurance by 1965. And with their newfound coverage, patients sought more medical services than ever before. Consequently, spending on medical care began to increase.

The relatively calm trajectory of healthcare inflation had given way to a vicious, swirling tornado of consumption and cost. Over the next several decades, expanded coverage drove increased demand for services, which fed the need for more medical care, which meant that Americans required more doctors, hospitals, emergency rooms, medications, medical equipment, and nursing homes, all of which drove up demand and prices. Amid this frenzy, the cultural norms of doctors began to change.

Fast-forward half a century to early 2021: medical costs consume 18 percent of the nation's GDP, more than three times the percentage of the 1960s. Recognizing something has to give, insurance companies are trying to tame the storm and drive down prices. Their money-saving methods involve playing hardball with doctors when negotiating their annual contracts and reimbursement rates. Physicians have answered in ways my uncle, and earlier generations of doctors, would have deemed unforgivable.

———————

In our quiet suburban neighborhood, the blare of an ambulance siren is unusual, drawing people out of their homes and into the street. On one such occasion, a rainy night in early 2010, I looked out my window to see a rig pull up to a house halfway down the block. There was Jason, a tech company executive, being wheeled out on a stretcher by two paramedics. The grimace on his face told onlookers he was in serious pain. Ten days later, while returning from my Saturday morning run, I was relieved to see Jason out and about, mowing his lawn.

He waved me over. "Just appendicitis," he said. "You docs do a great job."

A couple months after that, he called to see if I could take a look at the medical bills he'd received. I told him to stop by that evening after supper, and he arrived with a huge stack of documents.

As we dove into the material, we separated the bills by provider. The one from the hospital was several pages long and scrupulously itemized: from the electrocardiogram to the postoperative narcotics to the bandages and discharge medications. Separate from that bill was one from the ambulance company and another from the home health nurse who came to Jason's house after discharge. Finally, there were multiple bills from different doctors, including a list of charges from the ER physician, the anesthesiologist, and the surgeon. At the bottom of these documents was a three-line summary: the total sum billed, the dollars that would be paid by the insurance company, and the amount Jason owed.

The grand total for the ER, OR, ambulance ride, hospital stay, and three doctors was almost $23,000. After adding up the summaries at the bottom of each bill, Jason owed $8,250. That's what had him so confused. He knew he was on the hook for a large deductible. His company-sponsored health plan required employees to foot the first $3,000 and pay a small percentage of the professional and medication fees beyond that.

Since it was early in the year, Jason had not used any medical care. He therefore recognized he would need to pay somewhere between $3,000 and $4,000. But what, exactly, accounted for the nearly $5,000 difference? After about an hour of probing the printouts and fine print, we had narrowed the discrepancy down to two of the bills. One was from the ER doctor with charges close to $4,000. Insurance was covering only $1,200 of it. The other, from the anesthesiologist, was for $2,500. Insurance would pay $650 from that bill. The unexpected total, $4,650, needed to come out of Jason's own pocket. That didn't seem right.

"There has to be a mistake," I said, and recommended Jason call the insurance company to ask for clarification.

Monday night, Jason called to tell me it wasn't a clerical error. The thousands he owed were the result of "out-of-network" charges, better known today as "surprise medical bills." By 2010, I was aware of this pernicious billing concept but hadn't met anyone affected by it. I shared in Jason's frustration.

After all, these weren't frivolous medical services or cosmetic extravagances that would normally fall outside one's coverage. This was a life-essential intervention. Jason didn't want emergency abdominal surgery; he needed it. And this required the participation of an ER doctor and anesthesiologist.

Jason was both infuriated and baffled by his situation. Most patients don't realize it, but even when hospitals are "in-network," the doctors who practice there don't have to be. As my neighbor later discovered, the hospital he was taken to by ambulance was part of the network covered by his insurance company; however, the two doctors who'd sent him sizable bills were not. They had refused to sign on with Jason's insurer. And because they were unbound by the hospital's insurance contract, they were free to charge whatever they chose. Jason also learned that all of the emergency department doctors and anesthesiologists in the area had banded together into single specialty groups, so the hospital had no choice but to keep them on staff.

Without knowing it, Jason and many patients like him have been thrust into the middle of an intense and ongoing financial battle between doctors and insurance companies. In simplest terms, insurers are always looking for ways to pay doctors and hospitals less, while physicians believe the reimbursement rates are unfairly low. In response, they refuse to join the insurance network, thus allowing them to bill patients the difference between what the insurer covers and what doctors believe they're entitled to be paid. Few physicians see anything wrong with this tactic.

The approach is reminiscent of what sometimes happens in war. One side will bring civilians closer to military targets, hoping the other side will refrain from attacking the zone. Those who employ this dangerous trick justify it as a way to prevent further violence. Of course, when it fails, innocent people get hurt. The same is true for out-of-network billing.

Doctors hope that sending patients surprise bills will force insurance companies to pay the extra charges. Physicians see this as the only way to get insurers to raise their payments. They don't see it for what it is: using patients as human shields.

What started for doctors as a desperate negotiating maneuver has more and more become a billing "best practice." These days, physician groups are being bought up by for-profit practice management companies that specialize in finding out-of-network billing opportunities. The success of these companies has turned surprise billing into the single largest per-dollar burden for patients with commercial insurance.

Today, one in five emergency department visits result in a surprise medical bill. The two most common out-of-network charges come from anesthesiologists ($1,219 on average) and assistant surgeons ($3,633), both of whom greet patients only minutes before their procedure. Thus, unsuspecting folks like Jason have no way of knowing whether these doctors are in or out of network. Few patients in these situations would think to inquire, and those who do find that the information does them little good. It's not as if they're going to cancel the emergency procedure.

Sometimes, the surprise costs are affordable. Other times, not so much. In the past two years, a New York woman with a head cold got an out-of-network throat swab that cost her $28,400, while an English professor from California went to her dermatologist with a skin rash and, after three days of testing, came home to a bill totaling $48,330.

How do physicians justify these egregious price tags? Rather than categorizing out-of-network billing under the rubric of "moral injury," applying the term to the kind inflicted *by* the doctor, not *on* the doctor, physicians employ self-protective metaphors. Out-of-network billing is like surgery, they say: "you must inflict some pain to cure the underlying disease." As doctors see it, the insurance company is the disease.

Pushing back against unfair reimbursement is a necessary defense, according to doctors—the only way to keep the quality of patient care from eroding further. But in the end, it's patients who get caught in the middle of this dispute between physicians and payers. Soldiers in combat situations have a term for harm caused to innocent civilians: "collateral damage." It is the seemingly unavoidable consequence of what they believe to be righteous action. Doctors see out-of-network billing as serving the same function. To win the war against the insurance companies, surprise medical bills—and the financial devastation they cause patients—are unfortunate but unavoidable consequences.

———

EVERY CULTURE HAS ITS HEROES: people who represent the highest virtues and ideals. In physician culture, doctors are the heroes, always willing to sacrifice for the greater good.

But what happens when physicians don't behave like heroes? Rather than admit to their faults, they tell stories to preserve their heroic identities, portraying themselves as honorable in both deed and motivation.

For example, visit the website of the American College of Emergency Physicians (ACEP), and you'll find a page dedicated to the organization's mission and values. ACEP bills itself as "the leading advocate for emergency physicians, their patients, and the public" and claims that "quality emergency care is a fundamental right" that "should be available to all patients."

These are inspirational words. However, they contradict the organization's actions. For years, ACEP and its physicians have aggressively lobbied lawmakers to keep their out-of-network dollars flowing. Backed by private-equity groups, the physician organizations that represent ER doctors, anesthesiologists, radiologists, and other specialists have funneled millions of dollars to members of Congress in an effort to derail out-of-network billing reforms.

The language of physicians helps to obscure the differences between their words and actions, thus safeguarding the profession's esteem and goodwill while maintaining the perks of the practice. Rather than doctors feeling embarrassed or hypocritical when they say one thing and do another, culture is there to protect them. Physician culture excuses doctors who look away when collections agents go after their patients over unpaid medical bills. Culture is the invisible force that allows doctors to deny any wrongdoing, even when lawyers from their practice management firm sue (and garnish the wages of) their patients—people who never expected to receive an out-of-network bill to begin with.

This is the self-preserving power of physician culture. It reinforces the sanctity of doctors by instilling in them a potent set of defense mechanisms: repression, denial, and projection. And with these cultural protectors in place, doctors don't see the financial harm they cause to the very people who entrust them with their lives. Drive by any ER entrance, and you won't find a sign that says, "We Sue Patients." Instead the banner reads, "Heroes Work Here."

There are dozens of explanations for why healthcare has become so expensive in the United States. Out-of-network billing is just one of them.

You might expect doctors to be embarrassed and apologetic about their role in the excessive costs of healthcare and its flagging quality. Instead they remain convinced their actions are appropriate, their care the best in the world, and their services a value no matter the price. Physician culture distorts their perceptions, providing doctors with an effective shield from the truth.

Author's note: In late 2020, Congress approved legislation to protect patients from surprise medical bills starting in 2022. Though the law was touted as a win for consumers, it was an equally large victory for doctors, hospitals, and their private equity investors. The bill, rather than abolishing the practice or reducing exorbitantly high medical prices, merely shifts more of the financial accountability over to the insurance companies.

THE REAL PRICE OF Rx

IN 2018, NIRMAL MULYE, CEO of a Missouri-based drug company called Nostrum Laboratories, was asked by the *Financial Times* why he raised the price of a decades-old antibiotic by more than 400 percent, from under $500 to over $2,000. The drug in question, nitrofurantoin, is used to treat bladder infections and sits on the World Health Organization's list of essential medications.

It was a tough but fair question that put Mulye in the difficult position of having to defend not just his company but the entire pharmaceutical industry. CEOs in this sector of the economy typically try to avoid the spotlight, especially with their companies under growing scrutiny from both patients and lawmakers over the rapidly rising price of Rx.

I thought I had a good sense for how the CEO would reply. Leaders of companies like his are carefully coached by PR teams and legal counsel to control the interview and give nonanswers to hard questions. Watch enough of these Q&As, and you'll easily spot the tricks of the trade. There's bridging: "We can't discuss X, but what I can tell you is Y." There's flagging: "The most important point is X." And then there's polite avoidance: "I can appreciate X is of interest right now. We are carefully assessing it and will get back to you real soon."

Reading the article, the last thing I expected was a straight answer from Mulye. That's why I was surprised by the quote he gave. "I think it's a moral requirement to make money when you can . . . to sell the product for the highest price."

According to this drug industry executive, quadrupling the price of a life-essential medication is a *moral requirement*. Mulye went on to compare his pricing strategy to that of an art dealer who, as he put it, "sells a painting for half a billion dollars." Presumably referencing the Leonardo da Vinci work *Salvator Mundi*, which fetched a record $450.3 million at auction, Mulye's comparison left readers stunned.

I don't know anyone who has spent hundreds of millions of dollars on a piece of art, but I do know the types of people who purchase his company's antibiotic. Most are families with sick children who must make difficult financial sacrifices in order to afford a $2,000 bottle of pills. As one would predict, Mulye received immense criticism for his honest answer and for admitting that his company put greed above the needs of patients.

The way US drugmakers price their products is both legal and lucrative for shareholders, but it is not moral or compassionate. Drug companies have earned the criticisms they get for our nation's high and rising pharmaceutical prices. But the same criticisms over greed could also be applied to doctors.

Each year American physicians accept more than $12 billion from the pharmaceutical industry in the form of gifts, meals, vacations, consulting arrangements, direct payments, and honoraria for promotional talks. Outside the healthcare-industry press, these payments have gone largely unnoticed, especially by patients. But in recent years, as healthcare costs continued to rise, these once-secretive payments have become a national concern. So much, in fact, that in 2010 Congress passed legislation called the Physician Payments Sunshine Act, requiring physicians and drug companies to make information about these payments publicly available. The results have been fascinating.

Per the most recent data, more than half of all physicians (57 percent) admitted to accepting meals or payments from a drug- or device maker over the past year. Overall, those who do are fewer in number compared to data from 2014, when the government started publicly reporting the names of physicians who accepted cash from the drug industry. However, doctors who accept financial payments are receiving larger and larger sums than ever before. In one year alone, seven hundred US doctors took more than $1 million from the pharmaceutical industry.

These payments lie at the center of major scandals that have erupted inside prestigious institutions. Both Harvard University and Brigham and Women's Hospital in Boston came forward in 2018 with information that Piero Anversa, a respected cardiac stem-cell researcher, had falsified data in at least thirty-one medical journal publications. As director of the Brigham Center of Regenerative Medicine, Anversa manipulated photos and lied about the efficacy of cardiac stem cells as a treatment for patients with heart failure. That's *after* he and his laboratory received millions of dollars in grants and established themselves as global authorities in this area.

Shortly after that, a *New York Times* investigation into the prestigious Memorial Sloan Kettering Cancer Center in New York turned up a series of "insider deals among hospital officials" along with "undisclosed industry relationships" between physician leaders and drug companies. A month before the exposé, the center's chief medical officer, Dr. José Baselga, stepped down after failing to disclose serious conflicts of interest. Among them, Baselga had, to quote the *Times*, "put a positive spin on the results of two Roche-sponsored clinical trials that many others considered disappointments, without disclosing his relationship to the company." In essence, he provided overly favorable reviews of the Swiss drug giant's medications while failing to disclose $3 million in direct payments from the company since 2014.

In describing the fallout at Sloan Kettering, I wrote in *Forbes* that Baselga, along with the center's executive physician Dr. Craig B. Thompson, had been encouraged to step down from their posts for their involvement in the scandals. The institution's crisis communications team leapt into action that day, noting, "It is misleading to write that Dr. Thompson 'was forced to resign.' As is clear from his letter, Dr. Thompson chose to resign," adding, "Dr. Baselga resigned. He was not fired."

The institution didn't deny the allegations against these men. No one from the cancer center attempted to defend the doctors' actions, and none of the Sloan Kettering executives were willing to comment on the events that transpired.

In my leadership roles, I've learned to decode what organizations mean when someone leaves a high-paying position for "personal reasons" or suddenly decides to resign from a high-profile job. Healthcare leaders treat these unexpected exits with great skepticism. For instance, when it comes to licensing or obtaining hospital privileges, quitting while under investigation is treated the same as being terminated. Every physician in this circumstance must disclose the accusations on their applications or risk having their privileges rescinded when they are discovered.

Of course, it is obvious why doctors don't turn away drug company money or perks. The offers are too good to refuse. Imagine getting invited and paid to attend a conference at a beautiful resort in exchange for your participation in a one-hour panel discussion. Or imagine earning $1,000 to serve on an "advisory group" that meets once a year by phone for two hours. It's not just easy money. It's also an incredible ego boost. Doctors are told, and tell themselves, they're receiving these payments in exchange for their clinical expertise and their role in advancing scientific knowledge. They believe their time and insights are incredibly valuable and that these payments prove it. In practice, drug companies select doctors based on their prescription patterns—inviting those who prescribe the company's most expensive and profitable medications most frequently.

Ask doctors about their involvement with drugmakers, and they will loudly deny any wrongdoing, insisting there's "no relationship" between the perks they get and the medications they prescribe. Doctors genuinely believe this. In fact, one opinion survey found more than 60 percent of physicians insist that drug industry payments have no meaningful influence on their practice. Over 70 percent deny that complimentary meals influenced their actions.

Research on the topic reveals the truth. A study in *JAMA Internal Medicine* looked at the prescribing habits of physicians after attending industry-sponsored dinners. Compared to their colleagues, these doctors were far more likely to prescribe the brand-name drug touted at the dinner over a less expensive generic. That is why attendees of these promotional functions are awarded no continuing medical education (CME) credits. Of course, the dinners and events and advisory boards aren't really about education. They're about reciprocation. Like airline-rewards members with platinum status, doctors know what they need to do to keep the perks coming. This unspoken arrangement propels pharmaceutical industry profits, as it has for nearly a century.

Dating as far back as the 1930s, Indianapolis-based drug giant Eli Lilly & Company bestowed upon all medical students a handsome black bag with the recipient's name embossed in gold on one side and "Lilly" stamped on the other. Inside were a variety of tools, which over the years included items such as a stethoscope, reflex hammer, and combined oto-ophthalmoscope. To the medical students of the day, the bag and its contents were appreciated for their cultural cachet as much as the free clinical hardware. This gift, which they'd carry whenever and wherever they provided medical care, was a power symbol and a source of great pride for aspiring physicians.

It wasn't until the 1960s that these gifts came under attack for their obvious ulterior motive. Congress held hearings where generational battles broke out among physicians. On one side stood the prior generation of doctors, who saw no foul play. They trusted these gifts represented nothing more than the largesse of a kindly midwestern pharmaceutical company. And on the other side, an emerging counterculture of doctors saw nothing more than a series of bribes, meant to contaminate and corrupt the recipients. Medical students from the University of California San Francisco recognized that Eli Lilly and other drugmakers gave out black bags solely for the purposes of creating a reciprocal relationship with physicians. Once doctors accepted the bag, they would never refuse a meeting with the company's sales reps. Some fifty years later, the bags are no longer given out, but the manipulative tactics of drug and device manufacturers remain largely the same.

When I speak to CEOs and CFOs at business conferences and ask whether direct payments or free meals given to someone in their purchasing department would impact their decision making, nearly all say yes. In fact, an attendee sitting in the front row once yelled out, "Why else would you give someone a free meal?"

When I pose this same question to doctors, they get defensive: "We'd never do anything to harm a patient!" Of course, that's the physician culture speaking. Doctors truly believe they can't be manipulated. It's a false belief that only greases the wheels for drugmakers. Pharmaceutical representatives are trained in the art of taking advantage of the doctor's moral naivete.

To anyone outside the medical profession, the sales tactics used by drug companies seem too conspicuous to overlook. For example, a popular approach involves sending a personable and sprightly drug ambassador to the doctor's office once a month, always bearing gifts: donuts, coffee, branded mugs, pens, and samples of their most profitable medications. These not-so-innocent offerings are the product of a careful calculation by pharmaceutical sales teams, showing a deep understanding of human psychology. The drug rep and the manufacturer both understand that these "freebies" create an unspoken, unconscious quid pro quo arrangement whereby the doctor feels culturally obligated to reciprocate.

To see this process in action for yourself, go to the airport, and watch the Hare Krishna volunteers at work. First, these berobed devotees give travelers flowers or handmade beads, and *then* they ask for donations. Once the unwitting travelers accept the "gift," they feel culturally obligated to respond with a "donation."

In the pharmaceutical sales world, the return on these small "gifts" is humongous. Researchers estimate drug companies earn $10 of added revenue for each dollar spent on "detailing" (marketing) to doctors. That's an even better ROI for Rx makers than direct-to-consumer advertising, according to one study.

Ultimately, physicians don't intend to cause harm by reciprocating the perks and payments of drug and device companies. But they do cause harm. When doctors accept freebies from for-profit entities, the harm is not experienced by patients in the exam room or medical office. Rather, it hits them later, at the drugstore in the form of rising out-of-pocket prices. It affects them when they're forced to pay higher insurance premiums year after year. It reaches into their pocketbooks when employers try to offset rising healthcare costs by flattening workers' wages. The physician culture shields doctors from the damage they inflict through their prescribing actions. Physicians conclude that they're not doing anything wrong.

In addition to suffering financial harm, patients also pay a physical price when their doctors fall under the influence of drug companies. If you need proof that there's no such thing as a victimless conflict of interest in healthcare, consider the opioid crisis, which began in the first decade of the twenty-first century. By 2015, opioid overdoses were rising at a rate of 28 percent per year. In rural states like West Virginia, one in five babies were born addicted to these dangerous narcotics and underwent painful withdrawals during the first two weeks of their lives. Amid the drug epidemic, overdoses became the second leading cause of death for young adults ages eighteen to thirty.

As we now know, most people begin their journey toward addiction with prescription medications, such as oxycodone. Once firmly in the grip of dependency, they find it cheaper and easier to purchase heroin, frequently cut with fentanyl or unusual agents, including snake venom. As a result of growing addiction, more than sixty thousand Americans from all socioeconomic strata die unnecessarily from drug overdoses each year. These deaths were never the intent of the physicians who prescribed the pain medications. Rather, they were the result of the doctors' cultural inclination to look the other way, refusing to acknowledge the reality of their relationship with the pharmaceutical industry.

Drug companies in the 1990s and 2000s set about influencing doctors to prescribe more and more of these addicting and potentially lethal medications. And they were successful beyond their wildest dreams. They wined and dined physicians and brought in "experts" to tout the safety of these medications to their peers. Of course, the experts selected to present and promote these products were the doctors most willing to prescribe them (and tell others they should too). Like in a Ponzi scheme, everyone happily pretended there were no losers. And many were paid well for their efforts.

In 2017, one Rhode Island physician received a four-year prison sentence for receiving $188,000 in kickbacks from the drugmaker Insys. The doctor and company's actions cost Rhode Island insurers over $750,000, according to his plea agreement. But the true degree of deception came into focus during the testimony of a patient who, at the sentencing, said that her doctor "made me a junkie" and refused to act when she came to him with concerns about addiction.

Physician culture portrays its members as moral agents who always put their patients first. This belief shields doctors from feeling guilty when they accept drug company money. It keeps them from having to see the harm they inflict on patients.

A GREAT INCONVENIENCE

CUSTOMER SATISFACTION IS A PILLAR of practically every money-making venture on earth. Look at retail—the industry that coined the phrases "the customer is always right" and "give the lady what she wants."

These days, businesses are competing for more than customer loyalty. They're competing for survival. The coronavirus pandemic has left the US economy in tatters, with many retail shops, restaurants, and other businesses now circling the financial drain. Following several stops, starts, and resurgences of COVID-19 throughout 2020, more and more temporary store closures have become permanent. Thousands of mom-and-pop shops have shuttered forever, while those still standing must compete harder than ever to keep customers.

Organizations are bending over backward to please their patrons, not just in-person but online too. Shoppers today have come to expect the sorts of comforts and conveniences that past generations could've only imagined. With a swipe or a tap on their phones, Americans can order new shoes, get groceries delivered to their doorstep, and comparison shop for cars.

It seems there's no limit to how far sellers will go to make the lives of buyers easier. But there are some obvious exceptions to the normative rules of customer satisfaction, such as the DMV and discount airliners. Then there's one massive exception: the medical profession. Few patients would use words like "convenience," "comfort," or "satisfaction" in the context of their healthcare experiences. It's not that doctors are incapable of delivering great service. It's that service is not something physician culture prioritizes or even values.

People are slowly noticing the craterous customer-service gap that exists in the doctor's office. It seems everything is made harder in medicine than it has to be. After all, if people can check their bank statements from their phones 24/7, why can't they get that same level of safe and secure access to their medical information? Twenty-plus years after Y2K, less than 30 percent of patients are able to access their medical records, laboratory results, or a list of their medications, according to a 2020 survey.

Likewise, scheduling a medical appointment not only takes time but also requires a lot of patience. Rather than booking it online, 85 percent of Americans still have to schedule their visits over the phone, calling the doctor's office during "normal business hours." For people trying to find a new primary care doctor, this process can take hours or days. Contrast that with the experience offered by popular travel websites, which allow customers to book an entire two-week vacation (including flights, hotels, and rental car) all online and in less than an hour.

And what about price comparisons? In other industries, it has become standard practice to offer total transparency. Through Amazon and dozens of ecommerce sites, people can compare the price and reviews for any item they wish to purchase. Healthcare remains an outlier. A 2020 study found that 91 percent of Americans want clear pricing information in healthcare, but nearly all are disappointed.

Transparency of any kind is a rarity in medicine. Take, for example, the Open Notes rule slated to go into effect nationwide spring 2021. If you're a patient, you may not be aware of it, but it's one of the most significant medical-transparency achievements in history. Part of the 21st Century Cures Act, Open Notes gives all patients in the United States the right to immediate digital access of their medical charts, including their test results, pathology reports, and even their doctor's written, clinical notes. As you might have guessed, physicians fought this forced-transparency requirement tooth and nail. Doctors warned the federal mandate could confuse and frighten patients who wouldn't be able to understand their diagnosis or know how to process bad news without a physician present.

But that's not what really had doctors worried. Their concerns had more to do with the shifting power dynamics this rule would bring about. Physicians want to keep control of the information so as to maintain power in the doctor-patient relationship. This new law creates a power-sharing situation doctors despise. Patients would be allowed to decide for themselves when or if to discuss a diagnosis and whom they'd want to treat their problem.

Just as men in previous generations portrayed women as the weaker sex, unable to handle life's difficulties, doctors wish to have power and control over patients. However, in today's world, this patriarchal attitude is no longer viable. Patients have proven time and again that they can handle difficult medical information that's emotionally painful to process. It's doctors who struggle to deal with change.

Before the era of modern information technology, previous generations of patients had no choice but to accept the limitations and inconveniences of the healthcare they received. Today they're less forgiving. A 2018 study by the Virginia Commonwealth University Health System indicates that 61 percent of patients would switch doctors right now for the ability to get an appointment quickly, 52 percent would switch to get an appointment at a convenient location, and 51 percent would jump ship for better service.

Indeed, there is mounting evidence that patients of the twenty-first century are growing tired of "business as usual" at the doctor's office. In one study, researchers examined more than thirty-five thousand consumer reviews of physicians posted on Google. They wanted to identify the words most commonly associated with patients' experiences. When people left negative reviews, researchers found that only 4 percent of the complaints were explicitly tied to the medical treatment they received. The other 96 percent focused on issues related to "customer service."

Patients feel disrespected by long wait times, short visits, and poor communication. They don't get why doctors leave them hanging for days before answering simple, nonurgent questions. They wonder why physicians aren't willing to communicate with them via text or email. And with more and more healthcare dollars coming out of the patient's own pocket, why is it so hard to figure out what something will cost? The answer doesn't just reside in the healthcare system. It also resides in physician culture.

As doctors dismiss the virtues of customer satisfaction, more and more patients are "voting with their feet"—taking their business to alternative care venues and leaving the doctor's office in the dust.

One survey found that 34 percent of millennials reported visiting a retail clinic for care in the last year. As younger patients see it, all primary care providers are relatively equal in their ability to treat day-to-day problems, so why go back to the same doctor you saw last time if they aren't immediately available? Why not use an online app to find a nearby doctor who can see you today? Or why not drive to whatever retail or urgent care site is most conveniently located, be it near home or work, with the guarantee of being seen in fifteen minutes or fewer?

Millennials seem to have started a trend that is causing great angst inside traditional healthcare venues. A study in the *Annals of Internal Medicine* found that visits to a primary care physician have declined nationwide by more than 24 percent in the past decade. Meanwhile, the proportion of patients without a personal physician rose from 38 percent in 2008 to 46 percent in 2016.

For today's busy patients, convenience trumps loyalty. Doctors are perplexed and disturbed by this trend. In a 2019 survey, physicians said that gratitude from, and relationships with, patients are the most rewarding aspects of medical practice (at least for them). In other words, doctors want their relationships with patients to be "exclusive" (and permanent). For patients, however, the relationship status reads: "it's complicated."

On one hand, patients continue to describe their doctors as both wonderful people and excellent practitioners. A marketing study from 2019 affirmed just how much people trust and treasure doctors. When asked to select the companies, institutions, or individuals they trust to do the right thing, respondents selected their "primary doctor" as number one from a list of more than two thousand options, which included Oprah, Amazon, teachers, Tom Hanks, the military, Google, and the police.

On the other hand, it's clear the relationship is fraying. Patients are losing patience, describing their healthcare experiences as annoying, frustrating, and at times infuriating. They wish healthcare was easier, more convenient, and user-friendly. Instead, doctors want everything to happen on *their* terms. They expect patients to accept medical care when and where it is most convenient for clinicians. Physicians don't want to play by the rules of retail, bending over backward to please people. They want to practice by the rules of physician culture.

The widening disconnect between patients and doctors is rooted in a set of diverging values and expectations. Patients think excellent customer service and greater convenience are especially important. Doctors don't. In fact, 60 percent of physicians feel *too much* emphasis is being placed on "patient satisfaction."

Add "service" and "satisfaction" to the list of words that patients and physicians define differently right alongside "quality" and "emergency."

Doctors assume that any *service* they provide that leads to an accurate diagnosis and proper treatment should bring the patient great *satisfaction*. If there's nothing more important than your health, then shouldn't all patients be extremely happy when their health improves? To doctors, the qualities that are increasingly important to patients—convenient access, compassionate care, and excellent service—pale in comparison to the value of a doctor's technical skill and clinical knowledge.

What we have here is a broadening gap between physician culture and consumer culture. And because doctors are reluctant to adapt to the changing expectations of patients, more Americans are ending their exclusive relationships with doctors and starting to "play the field." Like a jilted dating partner, doctors assume it will only be a matter of time before patients realize that drugstore clinics and urgent care centers are no match for their unique expertise. *Then* they'll come crawling back, right? Right? Once again, doctors are wrong.

Physician culture is notoriously stubborn and resistant to change. To give you an example, consider that video-based platforms have been connecting people safely and reliably since 2003, and yet, as recently as 2020, only 8 percent of Americans had experienced a "telehealth" (video) visit with a doctor.

Of course, all that changed during the coronavirus pandemic, when video visits replaced in-office appointments for millions of patients. And they've loved it. Telehealth saves Americans time and money. From a customer satisfaction standpoint, telemedicine combines easy access with high-quality care.

Over the past year, patients have taken to social media to ask why the option of telemedicine wasn't made available to them years ago. There are two reasons, one systemic and one cultural.

The systemic roadblock involved the Centers for Medicare & Medicaid Services (CMS). The agency's strict billing requirements limited payments to doctors who offered video visits. Meanwhile, HIPAA guidelines tightly regulated the use of telemedicine. Both of those restrictions were relaxed during the pandemic without incident.

The cultural causation tied into doctors' belief that excellent care can only be provided in a hospital or an exam room in the physician's office. There was no research or scientific evidence to validate this assumption, just long-standing norms and preferences. But as soon as physicians had no choice but to offer video visits for routine care, they could quickly see the benefits for themselves and their patients firsthand.

In 2013, I predicted virtual visits would someday replace 30 percent of all medical services provided in a doctor's office. Given the nation's experience during the coronavirus pandemic, that number could be 40 percent or more without any sacrifice in overall quality. Once patients get used to the conveniences of virtual medicine, they won't accept a return to the old normal ever again. As such, the pandemic will continue to alter the expectations of patients even after the virus is controlled, whether doctors like it or not.

PART THREE | CHAPTER SIX

THE LANGUAGE BARRIER

THERE ARE NEARLY TWO HUNDRED thousand medical terms in the physician's vernacular. Most are polysyllabic tongue twisters of Latin or Greek origin, in addition to an alphabet soup of acronyms. Most are used to define diseases, describe treatments, order tests, or identify body parts.

The beauty of this lexicon is in its specificity and scientific universality. Meaning, whether you're a nurse, neurologist, or laboratory scientist, you know that *corpus callosum* is what connects the left side of the brain to the right. And you can use that term without any modification, qualification, or further description. It carries the exact same meaning among chemists, biologists, anatomists, and geneticists. It connects them all.

Linguists call this type of language usage *informative*, meant to communicate essential facts and data. And because doctors employ this function of language to protect and save lives, each word must communicate an accurate and exact medical detail. There is no room for ambiguity or misinterpretation.

Precision and correctness are the keys to avoiding confusion and inflicting harm. For example, it's not enough to say that a patient's pain is abdominal. Physicians need to clarify whether it is *epi*gastric (above the stomach) or *hypo*gastric (below it). Any error in identifying the exact location can result in the wrong differential diagnosis and treatment.

In most aspects of life, being 99 percent correct is "close enough" to perfect. In medicine, being 1 percent off can cause a deadly medical error.

Because the wrong drug name or anatomic location or even a mispro-
nounced syllable can spell disaster for patients, medical students spend
every waking hour memorizing and gaining mastery over these terms.
And because they do, patients all over the country are safer.

There is, however, a downside to this extremely complicated web of
words. Even though doctors understand each other perfectly, "medical
speak" is a strange tongue to most patients. One study published in the
American Journal of Health Behavior found that 81 percent of physician-
patient encounters contain at least one unclarified medical term, meaning
patients are likely to misinterpret what the doctor says. Another study
found that only half of patients who go to a doctor with a problem leave
the office with a good understanding of their condition. When doctors
use these scientific terms and medical acronyms with people who aren't
clinicians, they sound like they are speaking a foreign language.

―――――――――

Misunderstood medical verbiage is not the only reason patients fail
to grasp what physicians say. Doctors also use words and phrases to cloak
the truth and comfort patients, like a parent hiding an unpleasant reality
from a child. For example, if a treatment carries a one in one thousand
likelihood of curing you, your physician might say something rosy, like
"anything is possible." That sounds a lot better and more promising than
"there's virtually no chance."

There are other times when doctors use language to communicate their
values, beliefs, norms, and subjective judgments with colleagues. We can
think of this use of language as *cultural*. It works to preserve physician
identity, bringing doctors closer together. But it also serves another purpose. Sometimes, it is used to draw an exclusionary line between those
who are inside physician culture and those who are outside.

In the book *The Secret Language of Doctors*, Dr. Brian Goldman describes in great detail his introduction to hospital slang as a resident. It
was in that inpatient setting where he became acquainted with the exclusionary language of his fellow colleagues. Visit Dr. Goldman's website,
and you'll find a page of comic-strip renderings dedicated to the uncom-
plimentary terms that healthcare professionals use with one another to

label patients and their problems. There the differences between informative and cultural uses of language are made clear as day.

Any physician who has worked long hours under stressful circumstances (in other words, all physicians) knows it's easy to get annoyed, even angry, with patients who make the job difficult. In high-pressure situations, language can provide levity, allowing doctors to express their frustrations without directly confronting the patient or acknowledging their own emotions. The following are some examples of the doctor's argot in action.

In medical school, physicians learn that *primipara* is the technical term for a woman giving birth for the first time. In hospital slang, a first-time mother who frets over every little cramp and contraction has a different, less-flattering name. She is a "whiny primey." In residency, doctors are frequently jostled out of bed to care for patients in need. It's part of the job. However, physicians have little patience for those who abuse the medical system. In hospital slang, patients who continually come to the ER seeking admission to the hospital, even when nothing major is wrong, are termed "frequent flyers."

Goldman says there are two avenues of thought when it comes to hospital slang. "To use those coded words and phrases—and to share them with my colleagues—made me feel a great kinship to my band of brothers and sisters," he says, acknowledging the bond that language builds between physicians. But he also acknowledges its other intended use, admitting that unflattering slang words "helped me cope with unpleasant situations and the unspeakable human tragedies health professionals experience as part of the job."

This dual function raises important points about the use of humor in medicine. Not only does it signify membership and foster closer connections within the culture, but it also gives physicians an acceptable way to cope with the psychologically painful aspects of their work.

Humor is commonly associated with the helping professions, especially those jobs where workers are constantly reminded of life's fragility. It's no coincidence that cops and hospital workers use slang and humor similarly. Both have a "code brown," referring to bodily functions. And both use insensitive terms to describe vulnerable people in danger or distress. In cop speak a drunk person passed out in public is jokingly labeled a "sidewalk inspector." In medicine a frail, elderly patient with dementia for whom little can be done may be referred to as a "GOMER." The abbreviation (made popular by the 1978 satirical novel *The House of God*) is short for "get out of my emergency room."

Humor helps cops and doctors alike repress their discomfort and relieve their tension. For example, most people outside medical culture would be startled by the scene inside an OR, mid-surgery. As doctors slice through skin and muscle, rock music blares from speakers. Idle gossip and off-color jokes circulate. Although this environment has all the crassness and crudity of a fraternity mixer, these surgeons are intently focused.

They're obviously aware of the hazards of their work. Surgeons know they are capable of committing hundreds of different technical errors that could kill a patient. For most, however, having to work in an eerily quiet operating room filled with nothing but beeping machinery would only serve to amplify the pressure they feel, reminding them of all that could go wrong. This is why physicians in high-pressure specialties have long relied on a lively atmosphere and gallows humor to dull their fears and calm the jitters.

———————

SLANG AND HUMOR UNITE DOCTORS and ease their apprehensions, but these cultural uses of language can also dehumanize the very people doctors promise to protect. The coded language of medicine's "in group" creates a vertical relationship: putting the physician *above* the patient.

Early on, junior residents soak in this relative value structure through observation and experience. A senior resident, for example, will instruct them to "go see the diabetic" in the emergency department. The intent might not be to demean the patient, but that's exactly what happens. Rather than saying, "Go evaluate the person in the ED with diabetes," the doctor reduces the individual to nothing more than his or her disease. Similarly, one colleague might say to another, "Let me tell you about a case I had," implying that the medical details are what's interesting, not the person with the problem. In both instances, the message is clear: no need to waste your time getting to know someone's life story or focus on the human side of the doctor-patient relationship. Physician culture minimizes the importance of both.

Though doctors use insensitive language when talking about patients, they are overly sensitive when it comes to the language used to describe themselves. If you want to drive doctors mad, call them "providers" instead of physicians. Technically, a physician is just that: someone who provides medical care. But the term elicits outrage from those who see it as an insult to their many years of education, extensive training, and acquired expertise.

The origin of the word in healthcare can be traced back to a 1993 federal law that defines a provider as "a doctor of medicine or osteopathy, podiatrist, dentist, chiropractor, clinical psychologist, optometrist, nurse practitioner, nurse-midwife, or a clinical social worker who is authorized to practice by the state and performing within the scope of their practice as defined by State law." In other words, here's a lengthy list of clinicians in which a doctor is but one.

Physicians detest the term "provider" because it flattens the healthcare hierarchy, failing to distinguish doctors from midwives or social workers. The word eats away at the very notion of physician exceptionalism. It challenges the cultural assumption that doctors are entitled to special privileges. "Provider" is like medical gerrymandering: it redraws the boundaries of the cultural circle, allowing a flood of others into the doctors' elite club.

That's why the term "physician" is preferred. It leaves no doubt as to where doctors rank within the medical hierarchy. In surveys, 65 percent of physicians report feeling disrespected by the term "provider." Not surprisingly, only 25 percent of nurses find the term undesirable. That said, many nurse practitioners and physician assistants object to being called "mid-level providers," a common label they feel is outdated and offensive. Nearly all prefer the term "advanced practice provider." Every culture tries to elevate the status of its members.

Everywhere you look in healthcare, the doctor's time and preferences are prioritized above the patient's. No matter the healthcare setting, language is used to affirm whose time matters most.

Consider the waiting room. The term itself evokes images of antechambers in medieval castles where villagers sat patiently, hats in hand, for his or her royal majesty to arrive. Of course, doctors don't talk about waiting rooms in this elitist way, but they also never speak of the inconveniences their patients must endure while waiting. Instead, physicians talk up the importance of "maximal efficiency," making sure none of their own time is wasted waiting on patients. Doctors tell patients to check in fifteen minutes before their scheduled appointment. And just as they're told, patients quietly sit in a room dedicated to the activity of waiting on their doctor. Then, once the doctor is with a patient, another type of language barrier emerges: that is, patients often have a difficult time getting a word in. Research indicates that doctors spend an average of only eleven seconds listening to a patient before interrupting. Doctors don't hijack these conversations with the intent to be rude. They simply believe taking control allows them to diagnose and solve problems faster.

Having taken exams for much of their lives, doctors approach medical care as they might a calculus quiz: They try to find the right answer in the fewest steps possible. The language physicians use when discussing their own time management reflects this mentality: "greater efficiency," "faster diagnosis," and "time-effective." How patients feel about these "time-effective" interactions is unimportant to the doctor. Physicians are taught that the patient's role is to answer questions promptly and follow the doctor's recommendations precisely.

Though they love to say they put the needs of patients ahead of their own, their actions—and their use of language—show these words are often hollow. But why do doctors behave this way? Do they prioritize their own time because the burdensome healthcare system forces them to rush patients in and out? Or do they cut patients off and hurry them out of the exam room because it is culturally acceptable to do so? The most accurate answer is *yes*.

IMPERSONALIZED MEDICINE

ALL HER LIFE, MY AUNT Ruthie was remarkably energetic and resilient. When she lost her hearing in her seventies, she taught herself lip-reading. Even well into her nineties, she stayed spry and mentally sharp. She was, in every way, her mother's daughter: proud and determined. Her mom, my grandmother, was responsible for the operations of a large network of parking garages in New York—a role she *began* in her eighties. In her seventies, my grandmother helped publish and distribute what she called "movie star magazines," forerunners to *People* and *Us Weekly*.

With her mom as her role model, Ruthie refused to let advancing age slow her down or let anyone tell her what to do. Living in a retirement facility was out of the question. Instead she kept her apartment in Lower Manhattan, spending her days exploring the South Street Seaport and people-watching along the waterfront. On nice days, she'd hit the pavement with her walker, bopping from one park bench to the next until around noon, when she'd find a cozy or trendy new place to dine. Whenever I was in New York, she'd take me to her favorite lunch spots, always insisting it was her treat.

One beautiful spring day, with blue skies above and a light breeze on our faces, Ruthie and I popped into a charming deli, where we dined on matzo ball soup and pastrami sandwiches. Afterward, I walked her back to her apartment and asked to use the restroom. On the bathroom floor was a trash bag filled with dozens and dozens of plastic pill bottles. On my way out, I asked who'd prescribed all those medications. From memory, my aunt provided the names of six or seven different physicians.

Looking closer at the bottles, I realized many of the drugs had been initially prescribed years ago. I asked if she still needed them. She didn't know for sure, but she assumed she did since her doctors kept renewing them.

I urged my aunt to make an appointment with a physician who could review, evaluate, and coordinate her medical care. She agreed and scheduled a visit with a gerontologist I recommended in the Village. A few months later, when I was back in Manhattan, we met again for a nice walk and some lunch, this time at a cute little bistro with a flowery, fenced-in courtyard area. Her treat, as always. After we caught up on life and family news, I was eager to hear what the gerontologist told her.

"He said I could keep taking the medications if I wanted to, but only one of them makes much of a difference at my age," she replied.

"What did you decide to do?" I asked.

"I went to the pharmacy and dumped the whole bag in a disposable container," she said with sparkling laughter. She was relieved to have reclaimed all that extra space on her bathroom floor.

Physician's note: The advice Ruthie received would not have been appropriate for a patient with serious medical issues, like heart failure or asthma. But it was the right thing for my aunt, and it was long overdue. A few weeks after she dumped the pills, she noticed most of the distressing side effects from her old medications were gone.

My aunt lived another eight years, passing away a few months shy of her one hundredth birthday. Looking back, Aunt Ruthie was the perfect patient: She always kept up with her appointments, followed physicians' recommendations, and took all medications as prescribed. And as a result of being the ideal patient, she wound up with a trash bag filled with medications, nearly all of which were unnecessary.

Each of her physicians was well trained, competent, and highly respected. Yet the care my aunt received was fragmented, uncoordinated, and potentially dangerous. This discontinuity in American medicine is ubiquitous and cultural, demonstrating how the beliefs and norms of doctors don't always align with what's best for patients.

Physicians approach the needs of patients using a two-part recipe: one part science and one part culture. The result is a system of care that's technically excellent, but imprecise and impersonalized. To understand why, it's essential to see patients and their problems the way doctors do. Physicians know that, biologically, patients are more alike than different. Despite the billions of people on this planet, all human DNA is 99.5 percent identical. This means that regardless of one's race, gender, or place of origin, a person's medical needs and treatments can almost always be determined reflexively based on laboratory results. If a biometric number is too high, the doctor's job is to lower it. Too low, the doctor raises it. Once a patient's lab results are within a normal range, doctors keep prescribing whatever medications got them there and will help keep them there. Success is measured by whether follow-up studies are normal, not whether the care provided makes a person happier or more fulfilled. In no medical textbook will a doctor in training receive the following advice: *If a ninety-year-old woman's greatest pleasure is walking along the waterfront, then do not prescribe a medication that causes light-headedness and puts her at risk of falling, even if it offers a small chance of extending her life by a few months.*

Doctors are trained to make "the right medical decision," not to spend the time finding out what matters to a patient so that, together, they can select the right option for that particular individual. This approach exists partly because finding out what matters most to a patient is difficult. Filling in the blanks of people's lives—discovering their unique desires, expectations, and preferences—takes a lot of time and evaluation. And time, for doctors, is more limited now than ever. As a result, physicians embrace a one-size-fits-all approach that can effectively treat disease but often ignores a more humanistic truth: what's best for one patient may not be optimal for another, even if they do share similar DNA.

This view that all patients are identical leads to another cultural misconception: *If all doctors focus on their own specialty and do their jobs correctly, there's rarely a need to touch base, collaborate, or look over one another's shoulders.* This belief is widespread and the reason doctors fail to coordinate care. They see their jobs as specialty specific. If you are a cardiologist, only the heart matters. If you are a gastroenterologist, you focus solely on the food passage and the associated organs. If you are a hematologist, it's all about the blood.

Renowned surgeon and author Atul Gawande summarized it well in the *New Yorker*: "The public's experience is that we have amazing clinicians and technologies but little consistent sense that they come together to provide an actual system of care, from start to finish, for people. We train, hire, and pay doctors to be cowboys. But it's pit crews people need."

Indeed, physician culture, like American culture, worships heroes and superstars. The heroes are those who focus on, and master the treatment of, one organ (like the heart or kidneys) or one specific disease (cancer or arthritis). Physicians undervalue the generalist, the doctor who connects all the pieces. As a result, rarely does any one doctor take responsibility for the totality of a person's medical care.

Within physician culture, the best medical care results when each specialist corrects every abnormality identified within their narrow specialty. The overriding assumption is that all the pieces will somehow fit together. It is a poor assumption.

———

IN 2019, MY SISTER KAREN and her husband, Steve, found themselves living through a real-life medical nightmare. When Steve was admitted to a local hospital in Westchester County, New York, he and Karen began a journey of near-constant anxiety, confusion, and fear.

Before his hospitalization, Steve had lived a rich and full life. He was many things to many people. When he was young in his career, Steve mentored kids at the Washington Heights YMCA in New York City. When he grew a little older, he was a taxi driver for a short while and a dean at a community college for a long while. He was the founder of Systems and Solutions Group, which, in partnership with Steve Jobs, helped to install and integrate thousands of computers across the New York City school system. Steve played guitar in a local band, took up woodworking, and was quite the home handyman. He was also an excellent writer and a legendary storyteller, known to hold court for hours around the dinner table with friends and family, musing about the state of the world, enchanting guests with anecdotes, and telling jokes ("Sometimes even new ones," Karen liked to remind him). And, in addition to all these things, Steve was a smoker—a heavy smoker.

By the time he turned seventy-three, his lungs were tarred from decades of noxious smoke and chemical irritants. That's what landed him in the hospital in 2019. But it was physician culture more than anything else that caused Steve and Karen to endure months of torment and frustration as they navigated our nation's complex and confusing system of medical care.

Though Steve's smoking had produced years of health problems, physicians at the hospital couldn't be *exactly* sure what was causing his 102-degree fever, severe dehydration, and pneumonia. Perhaps it was a simple virus, one that his immune system would ultimately overcome. Perhaps the cause was a bacterium that antibiotics would eventually eradicate. Or perhaps the underlying etiology was something more serious like cancer with secondary infection. The radiology studies were inconclusive.

Doctors started Steve on antibiotics to fight the most common bacteria that cause pneumonia. Once his fever broke, his breathing stabilized. He was discharged with a referral to see a pulmonologist, who couldn't solve the mystery of Steve's infection either. For months, his lung problems waxed and waned. The pulmonologist consulted an infectious disease expert, who prescribed three different drugs, one of which required Steve to visit an infusion center every Friday for an intravenous medication.

Despite all that care and attention, his X-rays never improved, and his health continued to deteriorate. Steve was fatigued and constantly lethargic.

Karen put on a brave face and comforted her husband, but she couldn't be sure what to do or how to help. This was a foreign feeling for my sister, who is one of the most intelligent and confident people I know. Today she is the CEO of a massive food and health nonprofit in New York called God's Love We Deliver. Before that, she was CEO of a Planned Parenthood. She is accustomed to dealing with complex issues, engaging in difficult conversations, and finding solutions when none seem to exist. But with her husband's life hanging in the balance, Karen didn't know where to turn or what to do.

Every morning, she felt as though she was waking up to a more challenging, more frustrating day than the one before. With each new problem came a new question for which she didn't have an answer: *Do I call the doctor because Steve is more tired? Should I take him to the emergency department because his breathing seems more labored? Does Steve have cancer? How worried should I be?*

My sister was running herself ragged. She had to connect and coordinate Steve's care with each of the treating physicians while keeping up with the particulars of his progressive illness.

Growing up in a family of medical professionals—and with two brothers who are physicians—Karen had more access to clinical expertise than most. Though she wanted to respect Steve's privacy (and not overshare his problems with her brothers), she had reached her wits' end and reached out for advice.

From the information Karen had given me, I saw more than a few red flags. Though I'm not an expert in pneumonia or lung cancer, I assumed his doctors would have performed a bronchoscopy. They hadn't. This particular exam, which involves passing a scope into the lung to obtain cultures and perform biopsies, would have allowed Steve's doctors to search for that elusive diagnosis. And given how many uncertainties plagued his condition, I figured they would have suggested Steve visit one of the academic medical centers in New York City. Again, they hadn't.

Karen would later find out that Steve's physician didn't perform the bronchoscopy for a reason he'd never disclosed. It turned out the doctor didn't have the hospital privileges needed to schedule the procedure. Why he didn't have them remains as unclear to me as why he failed to tell the family. In any case, why not refer Steve to a colleague who did have privileges? Why not suggest that Steve be transferred to an academic center in New York City? Physicians are quick to refer patients to doctors in other specialties because doing so implies they're all on the same excellent team. But when a referral speaks to a doctor's limitations within their own specialty, they may be reluctant to admit it. The reason is, of course, cultural.

As Steve's weight and vigor waned, Karen had to rely more and more on his doctors for advice and medical care. Soon she was coordinating communications with more medical professionals than she could keep track of. Hearing my sister describe her frustrations led me to resent the doctors' lack of responsiveness and the inconsistency of their care.

On weekdays, during normal business hours, physicians would insist that Steve come into the office immediately when his breathing problems flared up. But on weekends or evenings after five o'clock, they'd tell him to go to the emergency department for evaluation. There he'd be treated by doctors he never met. Each time he'd have to repeat his entire medical history from the beginning—answering the same questions time and again.

Four months into his treatment, and seven months from his first hospitalization, Steve's health plummeted. Dehydration and fever sapped his strength. New cultures of his phlegm and sputum were sent to a lab, showing the presence of an additional infectious agent. This one required a more powerful, multidrug cocktail that overwhelmed Steve's fragile body. Day after day, hour by hour, Karen watched her husband disappear into the bed sheets. He became frail, gaunt, and lethargic. Even walking a few steps to the bathroom sucked the breath from his lungs.

Late one night, Karen had no choice but to bring him back to the hospital. Steve's kidneys were failing. As he teetered between life and death, the intensivist in the ICU suggested intubation. Karen asked whether he might ever come off the machine once he was placed on it. The doctor said, "Probably not, but you never know. There's always hope." By then, she knew the end had come. Steve died before the sun came up.

As I think back on this raw and emotional time in Karen's life, I know much of the pain and frustration was unavoidable. Steve's medical issues were complicated, his diagnosis difficult to establish, and his health compromised by his two-pack-a-day habit.

I also know that Karen and Steve had to deal with a bureaucratic, uncoordinated, and grossly outdated healthcare system. They had to battle the insurance company for approval during each and every round of diagnostic tests. They had to fill out endless forms and explain Steve's history and medical condition to each new doctor they met. And despite the abundance of multimillion-dollar medical machines available to diagnose Steve's problem, probe his body, and pump him full of medicines, there was one piece of technology conspicuously absent. None of the physicians nor the hospital shared a comprehensive electronic health record that would have enabled all clinicians to access and update Steve's medical information.

Beyond all that, Karen and Steve had to tolerate a physician culture that continually served the needs of the doctors more than theirs. As a doctor, I can forgive the physicians for losing their battle to Steve's enigmatic and complicated disease. No matter what they did, the outcome would likely have been the same. Moreover, I'm empathetic to the time pressures his doctors faced, and the insurance distractions, and the frustrations they encounter in their daily work. But as Karen's brother, I can't excuse what I saw as a lack of empathy or compassion that left Steve and Karen feeling abandoned.

Based on the values, beliefs, and norms that Steve's doctors learned throughout their training, I doubt any of them felt as though they harmed their patient or gave him anything short of exceptional treatment. They were providing care exactly as they had seen their mentors do it. Unfortunately, because the culture of medicine celebrates the cowboy but does not value care coordination, convenience, or personalization, Karen and Steve's frustrating experience remains the rule, not the exception, in the US today.

THE TRUTH IS COMPLICATED

My mother, Lillian, telephoned on a Sunday night in early December 1998 with great enthusiasm in her voice. She had just won a local golf tournament down in Florida, besting every woman in her retirement community, many of them "several years younger," she told me. The trophy was heavy, stood more than a foot tall, and was topped with a gold-plated female figure in mid-backswing.

"That's fantastic news," I said. I looked forward to seeing the trophy on my next visit from California. She made quick with her goodbyes, wanting to update my brother and sister as well.

My mother was born in Brooklyn and grew up far from the sunny golf resorts of Florida. Her parents raised their four kids to appreciate every bit of good fortune that came their way. Times were tough. As her parents struggled to keep a roof over their heads and put food on the table, my mother cherished the little things in life. As a child, her most prized possession was a doll my grandmother had fashioned out of rags, twisted and tied up with a piece of red ribbon. Back then, *buying* a doll wasn't even a consideration.

What they lacked in money and possessions, my grandparents made up for with love, kind attention, and the desire to give my mom every opportunity the US educational system afforded. She took full advantage. At age fifteen, she graduated high school at the top of her class, skipping three grades along the way. After earning outstanding scores on the state regent exams, she received a full academic scholarship to Brooklyn College, the only way she could afford to attend. Along the way, she mastered three foreign languages while excelling at history and mathematics.

My mother was a petite woman, barely five foot one, with long and luxuriously dark black hair. Everyone she met was enamored by her beauty and intelligence. She was a soaring figure in my life. My brother, sister, and I could not have asked for a better mother or role model.

We always looked forward to our Sunday evening phone calls with Mom and Dad, a tradition held over from decades ago, when long distance calls were cheaper on that day than any other. Telephoning on a weekday was an extravagance our mother would not condone.

That's why I knew something was off when my dad called me two weeks after my mom's big golf tournament, *on a Friday*. With his voice trembling, he said that Mom was in the hospital with a stroke. Two years earlier, doctors had diagnosed her with chronic leukemia. She was now experiencing a "blast crisis" of white blood cells, rising to thirty times the normal number. Despite the high count, the cells were immature and unable to fight infection. Pneumonia began to overwhelm her body's defenses a few days later.

My siblings and I flew to Florida as quickly as possible to be with our parents. Though we could see that our mother's life was nearing the end, my father, overcome with grief, pleaded with doctors, nurses, and God to save her. Plaintive tears filled his eyes as he bargained for more time, telling anyone who would listen that he would trade his entire life savings for just a few more days with her. In those final moments, he could not accept the inevitability of her death. When a loved one is dying, a couple more days together seems priceless.

In the end, and out of love, my father consented to place his wife in hospice care. He knew she would not want to spend her last hours hooked up to a breathing machine, unable to share her final thoughts with the people she loved most.

Every day, patients and their families are forced to make excruciating medical decisions like these. They turn to their physicians, hoping they will help them through this difficult process with compassion, honesty, and support. Standing in the way are the doctor's time pressures, training, and cultural norms. The combination too often leaves patients to fend for themselves.

Although doctors rarely lie to their patients, they often fail to tell the whole truth when life's end is near. Instead they offer hope, even when hope contradicts reality. Doctors worry the full facts will be too much for patients to handle, so they omit the details, like the patient's chances of surviving or the odds that an experimental medication will be successful.

In early 2020, a friend of mine was diagnosed with an aggressive ovarian cancer that rapidly spread to her liver, lung, and brain. While delivering the news, her doctor was quick to add, "It's not a death sentence."

I have no idea why he would have said that. If he was implying that a cure was possible, then he was being sadistic, not compassionate. The next day, I found myself having to explain to her, as she lay in her hospital bed, the detailed reality of her situation. She deserved the truth, so that she could say goodbye to the people she loved. She called each of them, and they all came to visit. She passed away three days later. Her family and friends cherished the last hugs they gave and the goodbyes they would otherwise have missed.

―――――――

NOBODY ENTERS MEDICAL SCHOOL HOPING to learn how to carefully craft half-truths for dying patients. And yet, by the time doctors finish their training, all are well versed in walking that fine line between fact and fiction.

A seasoned surgeon will tell a patient, "Operating is your best chance," when in fact he means, "Nothing I do will cure you, but I feel as though I have to try something." Admitting defeat is another thing doctors are never taught in medical school. Thus, when a patient's odds of survival are essentially zero, oncologists will insist, "You never can be sure," and "I've seen miracles happen."

In the culture of oncologists, these words of hope disguise an ugly truth, one that was revealed in the 2014 report "Unintended Consequences of Expensive Cancer Therapeutics." The authors of the paper looked at the results of more than seventy chemotherapy agents that received FDA approval. On average, they found the treatments extended life by only 2.1 months, time that the patients often spent in pain, isolated from friends and family. The profits of these drugs totaled more than $100 billion, which hardly seems commensurate with the results. And here's the ugliest part: most patients have no idea that the doctors who administer chemotherapy are paid a percentage of the drug's price, usually around 6 percent, whether the infusion helps or harms.

Residents learn to manipulate the truth by watching attending physicians as they talk with families. They are taught never to show reluctance to treat, since doing so communicates that the doctor is giving up. They hear senior physicians telling sensational stories of long-shot cures, pumping patients and their families full of false hope. Doctors urge patients to "battle" cancer, to "win" the war against their disease. Implicit in these words is a clear disdain for anyone who succumbs without fighting.

In 2018, Arizona senator John McCain, then eighty-one years old, decided to forgo additional treatment for an aggressive form of brain cancer. When the news broke, I heard cable TV stations consistently claim, "An American hero is giving up his fight against cancer." Giving up? Nothing could have been further from the truth.

John McCain understood what too many people, including physicians, do not. It takes tremendous courage to accept death as a part of life. It is a sign of strength, not weakness. Military commanders who knowingly lead their troops into battles they can't win are not brave. They are foolhardy. Senator McCain had simply admitted the truth to himself. He knew that what he valued most was spending his last days with the people he loved.

In these terrifying moments when death is near, what people want are candor and clarity. To the chagrin of many patients, their desires conflict with the doctor's fundamental belief that intervening is superior to inaction. As such, truth gets twisted and replaced with stories about the theoretical patient who survived, that one-in-a-thousand aberration.

This isn't what patients or their families really want or deserve. People desire the facts, not platitudes, deceptions, or empty promises. The truth, even the worst truth, gives patients control and removes the fear of uncertainty that can cloud their judgment and worsen their anxieties. Seventy percent of patients report wanting to spend their last days with their families at home. Less than half get that chance. Doctors believe they should prolong life at any cost, even if there's little more that medicine can do but bring further pain. They tell themselves that patients can't handle the truth about their prognosis. In reality, it's doctors who struggle to accept their own limitations.

Having treated hundreds of terminally ill patients, I know the biggest fear they face is being abandoned by their physician in their final hours. They worry the person they've trusted for months or years will walk out on them if they forgo further treatment. Every patient nearing the end deserves support, compassion, and presence. Most doctors can't (because doing so is too uncomfortable for them) or won't (because it isn't a priority).

———————

ONE OF MY JOBS AS a junior resident was covering the surgical ICU, a unit with a dozen or so extremely sick patients all lying in their beds, many waiting to die. My shift lasted for twelve hours, starting at either six in the morning or six at night. It was there and then, early in my surgical career, that I learned to ignore the lingering and persistent presence of death, pretending it was something other than an inevitability.

Despite the horrific prognosis for most of the ICU patients, their deaths were always treated by senior physicians as unexpected and abject failures. It was as if my co-residents and I were expected to provide them with some kind of life-extending elixir, the way doves brought ambrosia and nectar to Zeus each day, thereby conferring immortality. Of course, we possessed no such elixir.

When a patient died during one of our assigned half days, we were expected to explain what happened at the department's next monthly mortality and morbidity (M&M) conference. There we'd recount what went wrong while defending our actions.

In theory, these sessions served educational purposes, placing the patient's care in the context of the medical literature or focusing on alternative procedures that might have been considered. On some days, these sessions were fairly benign, with discussion and debate confined to the medical particulars involved. More often, they were unnerving and bombastic, more like an inquisition than a forum for improvement. Although I didn't realize it at the time, these conferences served as funnels to force-feed physician culture to impressionable residents like me.

In front of a dozen or more white-coated surgeons, including the department chair, a resident would be expected to review the pertinent history of the deceased patient, describe the operative procedure, and explain the cause of death. By the end of the discussion, you knew that someone had to be blamed. And you knew you didn't want that someone to be you.

Like parochial school nuns wielding twelve-inch rulers, the doctors presiding over these M&M conferences struck almighty fear into the presenting resident. From their chairs, the physicians fired a barrage of questions: Why didn't you give this medication? Why didn't you order this laboratory test? Why did you administer too much or too little fluid? What were you thinking?

In these high-pressure situations, residents endured harsh criticism and, sometimes, public humiliation. Every word spoken carried either the risk of self-incrimination or, worse, the possibility of throwing another resident under the bus. Fair or not, you had no choice but to "take it like a man." Excuses and finger-pointing were culturally unacceptable.

After witnessing my first M&M, I understood that I had only one job during my ICU rotation: keep the patients alive, including the hopeless ones, until the end of my twelve hours on duty. After that, any patient who died was the other resident's responsibility. Each day, as the sun was rising or setting, I'd arrive at the unit and receive "sign out," which included a quick exchange of information with the outgoing resident about any tasks left to do or any pertinent updates on what had transpired over the past twelve hours.

I remember the visceral fear I felt when someone on the verge of death was admitted right before my shift began. I can also recall the sense of elation I experienced when I would sign out and transfer accountability for that patient's care back to my colleague. Like a twisted game of hot potato, you never wanted to be the one holding the responsibility for the death of a patient. Although it's difficult to admit, at a preconscious level, I sometimes rooted against my colleague. Of course, I didn't want someone's life to end unnecessarily. But if they were going to die, I secretly hoped it would happen before or after my shift. I wish I could say my desire was to see the patient relieved of suffering. In reality, my desire was to avoid any blame for their death.

———

Music has its one-name icons: Madonna, Sting, and Prince. Medicine has the Whipple, an operation for patients with cancer in the head of the pancreas. Named after Allan Whipple, the first surgeon to perform it, the operation is incredibly complex, very risky, and highly coveted. In fact, it's one of the most prestigious operations a general surgeon can perform. Doing one successfully is the stuff of legends. As such, chief residents are always on the lookout for an opportunity to schedule the great and powerful Whipple.

These opportunities are exceedingly uncommon. The problem with most pancreatic cancers is that their symptoms are too vague to diagnose until it's too late to intervene. The Whipple is reserved for those rarest of occasions when the pancreatic cancer is diagnosed at a curable stage. The best clue for identifying an eligible Whipple candidate can be found in patients who are experiencing painless jaundice. This symptom may be an indication that the pancreatic cancer is still in an early stage and treatable. By contrast, patients with advanced pancreatic malignancies tend to experience an excruciatingly painful type of jaundice, indicating it's too late for the Whipple.

I'll never forget the first time I came face-to-face with one such candidate. During my first year of residency, I went to see an elderly gentleman with distinctly yellow eyes and skin hued like straw. After examining him and reviewing the X-rays, I called the chief resident, a wily character named Archie, to discuss the patient's medical problem.

Archie was short and thin. He had the competitive streak of a college wrestler, which he had been. When I told him about the patient, I could hear the excitement in his voice. Archie had chosen general surgery because he loved trauma. He believed the bigger the operation, the better. This was Archie's chance to strut his stuff in the operating room.

Prior to the era of sophisticated diagnostic machinery, surgeons couldn't be sure the extent of a pancreatic tumor's spread or its exact location. Often, the only way to find out was to operate. Once inside the abdominal cavity, the surgeon would dissect in the area of the pancreatic tumor. If the cancer was encasing the major abdominal blood vessels, the tumor was too advanced, and the procedure would need to be abandoned.

The radiological studies we ordered on the elderly patient looked ominous. It appeared the cancer was already too large and too advanced for us to proceed with surgery. I brought the films to Archie and dejectedly asked him whether he wanted me to tell the family that a cure wasn't possible. Archie, like a wrestler executing a two-point reversal, went on the attack and took control.

"Hell no," he responded. "We're doing the surgery."

I was taken aback. Based on everything I had read, there was a 99.9 percent chance the surgery would fail. Not wanting to embarrass him, I leaned closer and asked why, hoping he'd educate me about some obscure article I had missed or a brilliant new maneuver he had figured out. Instead, he let physician culture do the talking for him.

"A chance to cut is a chance to cure," he said.

After cutting the patient open, exposing the cancer, and assessing the spread, the look on Archie's face said it all. A complete resection was indeed impossible. Archie wasn't perfect, but he taught me a lot. From him I learned many operative tricks and maneuvers that I used throughout my surgical career. He also taught me how to behave if I wanted to be a "badass surgeon," as he called it.

In my career, I have heard the mantra many times: "a chance to cut is a chance to cure." Always spoken resolutely and with confidence, it gives surgeons permission to operate even when they shouldn't. It is yet another way that physician culture inhibits medical excellence.

THE DOCTOR'S DOUBLE STANDARD

In November 1999, the Institute of Medicine (now the National Academy of Medicine) issued a damning report on American healthcare titled, "To Err Is Human." Citing multiple studies, the paper claimed that as many as one hundred thousand patients died each year as the result of preventable medical errors. That estimate ballooned to two hundred thousand the following decade and then to two hundred fifty thousand plus, as new research found failures in patient safety to be even more widespread than previously thought.

Though the information included in the report wasn't altogether new, it left medical professionals with an unshakable image: deaths from medical errors in the United States were equal in number to a fully booked 747 jetliner falling out of the sky—every single day of the year.

When the report first circulated, I remember the feeling that sweeping changes were in the air. With a new century upon us, it felt like the right moment to make quality, preventive medicine and patient safety our nation's top healthcare priorities. Combined, they could reduce premature deaths by half a million annually in the United States alone.

Having recently been appointed CEO, I believed Kaiser Permanente had an incredible opportunity to lead the way. Going in, I knew that merely following the basics of patient safety and quality management would not be enough to reach the apex of medical groups. After all, the healthcare organizations in the upper quartile of the rankings were already doing what was expected. They were avoiding unnecessary infections by using impeccable antiseptic technique when inserting plastic catheters. They were preventing pneumonia by elevating the head of the bed and ambulating intubated patients. They were double-checking every time to make sure they didn't administer the wrong drug or the wrong dose to the wrong patient. And they all were trying to maximize prevention and minimize complications from chronic diseases.

If we were going to become number one, we would need to go above and beyond what others were doing and accomplish something most others couldn't. We would need to change the cultural values, beliefs, and norms that prevent doctors from putting patients first.

For starters, we needed to address the well-documented norm of circling the wagons and protecting fellow doctors whenever an error is made. As with the "blue wall of silence" in law enforcement—the unwritten rule that cops don't report fellow officers' errors, misconducts, or crimes—physician culture has its own rules governing mistakes. Doctors hope that "if I don't criticize your errors, you won't come after me when I mess up."

At Kaiser Permanente, there was no way we could become the national leader in quality and safety if our physicians tolerated mediocrity and covered up one another's medical errors, no matter the circumstances. I knew I'd need to make some unpopular decisions. Unlike my predecessor (and his predecessor before him) who left the names of doctors off monthly performance reports, I decided to unblind the data so that every physician could view their own scores and everyone else's. If we were going to start putting patients first, we needed to stop worrying so much about whether individual physicians would be embarrassed by their performance scores.

When it came to boosting patient safety, I decided we needed more data. We also needed to investigate medical errors in real time. We came up with a plan to address each need.

At the time, doctors were expected to submit a report to their departmental quality leader following any medical error or clinical omission. In practice, few doctors did, at least not in a timely manner. As a result, the data proved unreliable and incomplete. To solve that problem, we created a unique telephone number in each medical center and asked everyone, including doctors, nurses, and staff, to immediately report an error or even a potential error (a seminal event or "near miss") directly to the medical center's physician-in-chief. Over time, reporting medical errors and near misses became the new normal. These changes sent the message that protecting patients from errors is more important than protecting colleagues who commit them.

Finally, to achieve nation-leading surgical results, we challenged the cultural belief that performing surgery is a right rather than a privilege. You might recall from a previous chapter that doctors love to dabble, believing it's possible to be a master of all surgical procedures.

This error in thinking was uncovered around the turn of the twenty-first century when multiple studies began to demonstrate what seems so obvious now: The more a surgical specialist performs a particular procedure, the better the outcomes and the lower the complication rate. Most national specialty societies publish *minimal* volume standards that surgeons must fulfill to keep their hospital operating privileges. These thresholds are exceptionally low, meant to define basic competency. Our goal had to be *optimal* volume standards.

Going forward, we would determine the number of procedures a doctor had to perform annually to achieve superior, not average, clinical outcomes for the most complex and risky operations. And to become the best in the nation these standards needed to be implemented in every department in all KP medical centers. We knew putting these measures in place would be difficult. In each specialty department, surgeons would need to divide up the types of cases done so that every physician would have a narrower area of specialization than in the past. And for some of the more uncommon and complex operations (the precious gemstones of the surgical world), we'd need to greatly restrict the number of physicians allowed to perform them.

Implementing these new rules was going to be especially difficult in our obstetrics and gynecology departments. At my regular quarterly meeting with the OB-GYN chiefs, I had prepared myself for resistance but hoped they would embrace what was clearly best for patients.

At ten in the morning, on the sixteenth floor of the regional Oakland offices, I stood in the mouth of a large U-shaped conference table and began my presentation. I was surrounded by the department chiefs: seventeen women and two men. I began by laying out a vision for the future: Kaiser Permanente would become the national quality and safety leader in every clinical area.

To help us get there, I needed three things from this group. First, we'd need to become number one in screening for cervical and breast cancer. Because routine screening was and remains an evidence-based approach that all physicians in OB-GYN value, the chiefs nodded in agreement. Second, we needed to achieve the lowest maternal death rate in the country. In order to set the national standard in this measure, I described a plan to fund and hire additional perinatologists, a subspecialized physician trained in both obstetrics and pediatrics. The chiefs again nodded with approval because doctors always welcome additional resources and expertise, provided no one's income is negatively impacted.

Finally, I told the chiefs that we needed to achieve the lowest operative complication rate of any hospital system in the country. To accomplish that, I presented an opportunity that I was confident would improve patient safety and reduce complications.

The plan involved the hysterectomy, a nearly two-hundred-year-old procedure that remains the most common gynecological operation performed today. The traditional method for removing the uterus begins with the surgeon making a long abdominal incision, which requires the patient to spend several days in the hospital and endure six weeks of recovery.

In 1989, a new and more effective technique emerged. The laparoscopic approach to hysterectomy requires a surgeon to make only a small incision in the belly button, insert a tiny camera, and perform the operation while watching the internal anatomy through a TV monitor. The method is minimally invasive and enables patients to go home the same day, returning to normal activity in just a week.

Published data confirm that, in skilled hands, a hysterectomy done laparoscopically is appropriate for around 80 percent of patients. However, the procedure carries a higher risk of complication than the "open approach" because of the surgeon's limited visibility. As a result, the best outcomes are achieved by more experienced (fellowship-trained) surgeons with a high annual volume of procedures.

So I proposed that only surgeons doing a high (optimal) volume of laparoscopic hysterectomy procedures would be assigned to the operating room. Anticipating that these changes would raise fears among the chiefs, I explained that all OB-GYN physicians would keep their jobs, and no one's salary would be cut, even if they no longer operated. I thought I had effectively addressed all the systemic concerns the chiefs might have, including money and job security. Yet the moment the proposal left my lips, the heads in the room stopped nodding, and all the smiles turned flat.

Based on the reaction, it was clear I'd crossed a cultural line. Taking away a gynecologist's "right" to perform hysterectomies was a clear violation of a well-established norm. I tried to explain the benefits.

"If each OB-GYN physician focuses either on the operating room or on the delivery area, everyone will be exceptional in one area rather than being just good or average in both." From a quality and patient-safety perspective, it seemed an excellent option. The chiefs in the room didn't see it that way.

There's a reason "obstetrics" and "gynecology" are hyphenated. Physicians in this specialty pride themselves on the breadth of their expertise. Doing a little bit of everything, from surgery to labor and delivery, is the reason many graduating medical students choose OB-GYN for their training. My plan to cleave the specialty in two violated the group's core identity.

Despite the negative reaction in the room, I knew this plan was the right thing for our patients. So rather than backing down, I asked the chiefs, "If *you* were undergoing a laparoscopic hysterectomy, how many procedures would the surgeon have needed to do last year in order for you to feel safe?"

I wasn't asking whom they'd pick for the surgery but, rather, how many cases they felt were necessary before they'd give their consent. The answers varied, but the range was thirty-five to fifty per year (about three or four each month). Naturally, my next question: "What is the current, minimal volume requirement at your medical center for laparoscopic hysterectomies?"

The answers varied from twelve to eighteen cases per year, less than half the number of procedures the doctors in the room would demand themselves. Shockingly, these low-ball numbers were *much higher* than the national average. At the time, about half the laparoscopic procedures in the United States were completed by OB-GYN physicians who did fewer than ten per year.

My final question: "Why would you set lower standards for your patients than for you yourselves?" No one had an answer.

Of course I knew the reason. No doctor will admit it, but nearly all physicians feel entitled to advantages they would not extend to their patients. When doctors need to see a primary care physician for a routine problem, they don't wait an average of twenty-four days for an appointment like the rest of the country's patients. They call their colleague directly and get the visit scheduled before the week is over. And when it comes to having surgery, be it for themselves or a loved one, physicians demand superior standards.

Eventually, the OB-GYN chiefs agreed to raise surgical volume requirements, along with other quality and safety improvements. At the start of this process, Kaiser Permanente was ranked above average by the National Committee for Quality Assurance, but not exceptional. By the end, our medical group was ranked as the nation's best.

———

IN 1717, A DUTCH PHYSICIAN and chemist named Herman Boerhaave was handed a medical device so spectacularly brilliant and transformative that he would go on to describe its inventor as "the most ingenious artist in mechanics." Excitedly, the doctor told all his colleagues about Daniel Fahrenheit's incredible thermometer, which could measure internal body temperature.

He boasted that physicians could now quantify the degree of a patient's fever more precisely than ever before. And given the scarcity of medical expertise in the eighteenth century, one might wonder, "What doctor *wouldn't* want one?" The answer, it turned out, was almost all of them. The idea that a device made of metal, glass, and mercury could rival (no less surpass) the value of the doctor's touch in assessing fever was preposterous. Respected physicians of the era would sooner cut off their hands than trust a gadget to do the doctoring.

It was not until 134 years after Dr. Boerhaave's initial enthusiasm that a German physician named Carl Reinhold Wunderlich started to change the minds of physicians. Looking at the results of more than a hundred thousand clinical observations, Dr. Wunderlich published research demonstrating that normal human body temperatures range from 37 to 38 degrees centigrade. Using these insights, fever no longer was graded as minimal, moderate, or extreme. Deviation from normal had an *exact* number. Any reading above that level was a symptom of disease that the clinician needed to investigate, diagnose, and treat. Only upon the discovery of temperature's direct correlation with severity of illness did the device begin to take hold in medicine.

According to medical historians, nearly 170 years elapsed between the thermometer's introduction in medical practice to the tool's widespread use among physicians.

Though the first thermometers were comically large and slow to equilibrate, the reluctance of scientists to embrace the instrument had nothing to do with its awkward engineering or with faulty science. The limiting factor wasn't the device at all. It was the physician culture's stubborn resistance to change. In the eyes of doctors, the thermometer devalued the importance of human touch and human intuition, two staples of medical practice. And, by implication, any tool that devalued human skill also devalued the human using it.

Though major scientific advancements are adopted much faster nowadays, studies confirm it still takes an average of *seventeen* long years for a superior medical innovation to make its way into routine patient care. These delays are excessive, unnecessary, and inexcusable. They prove that physician culture continues to triumph over the needs of patients. Centuries after Semmelweis and Boerhaave, any clinical advancement or medical opportunity that threatens the beliefs, values, or prestige of physicians still faces an uphill battle in becoming standard procedure.

PART FOUR

THE SOCIAL LADDER

PART FOUR | CHAPTER ONE

A CULTURE WITHOUT ANSWERS

This isn't just my lane. It's my f***ing highway.

—*Dr. Judy Melinek on Twitter, November 9, 2018*

A S A CHILD, I DREADED going to the pediatrician's office for my annual checkup. Inside that spartan, squat, red brick building in Queens, I sat quietly on a vinyl seat with my head down and pulse racing. My nostrils filled with the smell of disinfectant. Those yearly visits always started the same way. The nurse called me in and measured my height and weight. When the physician entered, he listened to my heart and palpated my abdomen. Then he'd go into his office with the forms my parents brought for the upcoming school year. This was the moment I learned to dread.

Upon returning to the exam room, the doctor would be carrying either just the forms or the forms along with a metal bowl containing a syringe, which would be filled with the recommended vaccine for my age that year. My heart sank every time it was the latter. The memory of it remains a sore spot from my childhood. In fact, these episodic injections had such a lasting impact on me that even as a practicing physician, I had to look away anytime the nurse gave a shot to one of our patients. As a plastic surgeon, I barely notice the blood that wells up when the scalpel transects and splits the skin. And yet, I am still uncomfortable watching someone get an intramuscular injection.

Going to the doctor is a nerve-wracking experience for the majority of Americans. From children to adults, more than half of all patients say they're afraid of visiting their family physician.

Fear of the unknown can haunt patients for days leading up to a medical appointment. When they schedule a visit for an unexpected health problem, patients fret over what the doctor will find. They're concerned the diagnosis will be cancer or a medical problem that will require surgery. And even when there's no obvious reason to be afraid, patients often feel uneasy right up until the moment they exit the medical building. For many people, anxiety is the conjoined twin of medical care, impossible to separate.

Not so with doctors. It's striking how differently physicians experience their environment and their interactions with patients. Be it in a medical office or hospital, physicians feel right at home, moving about with efficient and effortless grace. On rounds or in an exam room, the doctor's routine makes perfect sense. Like priests at Mass, physicians know exactly what to say, what to do, which rituals to follow. Whether working in the ICU, the ER, or the operating room, even the most gruesome and intrusive aspects of medicine never bother doctors.

They can plunge a knife into a patient's body and amputate a limb, all without a hint of hesitation. With no sign of embarrassment, doctors ask patients a litany of invasive questions. They inquire about a person's excrement and vomit as comfortably as they would discuss the weather or sports.

To doctors, there's nothing personal about getting personal. Questions that would embarrass people in any other setting are, in the doctor's office, merely a clinical means to reach a curative end. For example, asking "Is the blood *in* the stool or only on the *outside*?" helps to separate cancer from hemorrhoids. The answer to "Was the vomitus green or clear?" places the blockage in either the stomach or the small intestine. It's all just part of the physician's job.

Doctors feel well trained and comfortable in dealing with just about anything that might come up in the course of their day-to-day. At least, that's how things were for most of the twentieth century.

Today, the doctor's peace of mind is under attack. As we've seen, one source of discomfort comes from the scientific advancements of the twentieth century and modern information technologies that, together, challenge the doctor's autonomy and high status. Then there are the endless demands from purchasers, insurers, and the government, which saddle doctors with hours of mindless paperwork, necessitating thousands of computer clicks.

There's yet a third set of modern invaders, banging loudly on the exam room door, demanding to be let inside. Doctors experience them as societal attacks on their sense of comfort. Whereas physicians once dealt with purely medical problems (those deriving from diseases of the heart, lung, brain, etc.), they must now help patients deal with the health effects of social and political problems: immigration policy, gun violence, global warming, gender inequality, racial inequity, socioeconomic imbalances, changing sexual norms, suicide, and so much more. As a result, the physician's scope of work is rapidly expanding to include a whole host of issues not traditionally taught in the medical school curricula or talked about in hospital cafeterias.

These intrusions defy the customary role of physicians as first defined in the Hippocratic Corpus, a collection of about sixty texts from the fifth century BCE. The material contained titles such as "On Regimen in Acute Diseases" and "On Fractures, on Joints, on Injuries of the Head." None of these tomes discussed or even identified a doctor's responsibilities in matters of politics, personal relationships, or the plight of society. For most of medical history, these texts delineated the physician's duties as curing diseases and treating injuries. Nowadays, "everything else" is in scope, which means that every patient is a potential Trojan horse, bringing something new and troubling from the outside world into the doctor's once-safe lair.

Don't misunderstand. Societal change has been a constant throughout history. From the Revolutionary War to the sexual revolution to the digital revolution, physicians have lived through and been cognizant about every major social movement in this nation's past. What's different is that these types of topics now routinely invade the doctor's professional space. Physicians feel extremely uncomfortable broaching these strange subjects—the way patients feel when discussing constipation or erectile dysfunction. In the minds of physicians, their offices and exam rooms have ceased to be sanctums of inner peace.

Doctors, already overwhelmed with their daily duties, feel as though society's problems are sucking the last bit of oxygen out of the air. Neither their medical training nor culture has prepared them to take on these new tasks. They would like to keep society's ills and ethical concerns where they feel they belong, outside their clinical practices. They just don't know how.

ON DEATH AND DYING

THE MYTHS OF ANCIENT CIVILIZATIONS reveal that people have always been fearful of death and fascinated by the thought of immortality. In one ageless example, *Hymn to Aphrodite* tells of the human quest for eternal life. The Homeric poem introduces us to Tithonus, prince of Troy. He has taken a lover, Eos, the goddess of dawn. They make a handsome couple. Each morning, Eos glimmers with beauty. Her lover is himself a sight to behold: Trojan royalty with a warrior's passion. And yet their love is cosmically unnatural. For a goddess, dating mere mortals is prohibited under divine Greco law.

So what's a mythological couple to do? Eos, hopelessly in love, vows to do everything in her power to ensure that her relationship with Tithonus lasts forever. She whisks him away to her celestial palace, and there, with tears in her eyes, she pleads with Zeus, god of gods, to grant him immortality. Seeing that Eos truly loves Tithonus, Zeus agrees. But in her passionate haste, Eos commits an epic error. She asks that Tithonus be granted eternal life but forgets to request eternal *youth* for her lover as well. As a consequence, the prince does indeed live forever, but his existence is marred by this grand mistake:

> She nourished him, keeping him in her palace with grain and ambrosia. And she gave him beautiful clothes. But when hateful old age was pressing hard on him, with all its might, and he couldn't move his limbs, much less lift them up, then in her *thûmos* [roughly translated: heart, mind, and

will] she thought up this plan, a very good one indeed: she put him in her
chamber, and she closed the shining doors over him. From there, his voice
pours out—it seems never to end—and he has no strength at all, the kind
he used to have in his limbs when they could still bend.

Our hearts go out to Tithonus for his suffering. An eternity of infirmity:
Could anything be more tragic? Though we might struggle to imagine
the misery of living forever—unable to get out of bed or walk around
freely—this ancient Greek tale is not purely mythical. The curse of Tithonus has been resurrected in modern times: not through the hubris of
gods but through the actions of doctors.

The twenty-first century has granted humans access to medications and
procedures that can extend life almost indefinitely. Ventilators can breathe
for us, intravenous tubes and pumps can nourish us, and hemodialysis machines can filter wastes and excess water from our blood, all but replacing
healthy kidneys. These present-day miracles, paired with around-the-clock
nursing care, can turn any of us into Tithonus, alive but damned.

—————

UNTIL THE SECOND HALF OF the twentieth century, the overwhelming
majority of critically ill patients suffered from acute and urgent problems. Pneumonia and perforated intestines were far more common than
chronic diseases. Although many people admitted to critical care units
died, those who survived often recovered fully and lived normal, fulfilling lives.

Times have changed. Walk into any ICU, and you'll find the majority of beds filled with frail, incapacitated patients in their eighties and
nineties. Most will never be able to live without constant medical care.
Many will never eat, breathe, or urinate again without machines. They're
too weak to get in or out of bed without assistance. Once discharged,
they will languish and deteriorate, requiring hospital readmission within
months if not weeks. Few if any will ever return to a vibrant life.

Helplessly, these patients lie in their beds as physicians, nurses, and
technicians poke them with needles, drawing blood out and pushing
medications in. They writhe in pain by day and endure sleepless nights.
They tug at the plastic tubes extending from their mouths to their lungs

and from their nose to their stomach. They are restrained and sedated. They suffer delirium, growing confused and paranoid. In the ever-distressing, noise-polluted, sick-care environment of today's hospital, it's not clear whether these patients are being treated or tortured. Doctors today are struggling to confront the reality that medicine can simultaneously preserve life while inflicting hell on earth.

The fact that humans can survive under such dire circumstances—or, rather, that medicine can extend their lives almost indefinitely—is considered by many to be a great scientific achievement. But like so many tragic protagonists of yore, doctors feel beset by the gifts they've been given. Physicians now wrestle with an ethical quandary that didn't exist a generation ago. What should they do for patients who survive past the point that life is worth living? Indeed, modern medicine has advanced the medical frontier so far and so fast that the most pressing question isn't whether we have the ability to keep every patient alive. Rather, the concern haunting physicians is, "Should we?"

For doctors seeking answers, the clearest (and most culturally supported) guidance on how to care for people in their final act of life comes from the American Medical Association's *Code of Medical Ethics*. Here's "Opinion 5.7":

> It is understandable, though tragic, that some patients in extreme duress—such as those suffering from a terminal, painful, debilitating illness—may come to decide that death is preferable to life. However, permitting physicians to engage in assisted suicide would ultimately cause more harm than good. Physician-assisted suicide is fundamentally incompatible with the physician's role as healer, would be difficult or impossible to control, and would pose serious societal risks.

As if etched on a silver platter, these edicts prove more decorative than practical. Doctors are instructed to "save a life at any cost" and "first, do no harm," but what should they do when these actions simply prolong pain and contradict the desires of patients?

In opposition to the rigid proscriptions of doctors who lead the AMA and other medical organizations, elected officials in several states have passed Death with Dignity laws, which legalize certain forms of medically assisted death. One in five Americans now resides in a geography that allows terminally ill patients to end their lives with medical aid.

In California, such a law went into effect June 9, 2016, making it legal for physicians to prescribe life-ending medications to patients who meet strict qualifications. The person must have a terminal illness with death expected in fewer than six months. Two doctors must concur the patient is of sound mind. And these individuals seeking eternal peace are required to administer their own life-ending medication without assistance from doctors or loved ones.

The week that this legislation was enacted, I received dozens of emails from physicians in our medical group. None of them wrote to ask for details on how to proceed. Rather, all of them wanted to be sure they would not be required to prescribe life-ending sedatives for their patients.

The reaction reminded me of other medical-ethical issues from the past, such as performing abortions and prescribing medical marijuana under state law. For a few doctors, these actions violated personal or religious beliefs, and they felt morally bound to refuse. Most, however, just didn't want to be directly involved. Doing so felt messy, time-consuming, and sullied. So it is with medical aid in dying.

Although it is now legal in numerous states for patients to shorten their suffering, people who are terminally ill often encounter difficulty finding a doctor willing to assist. A survey of 270 California hospitals, conducted eighteen months after implementation of the state's End of Life Option Act, found that six in ten inpatient facilities had a policy *forbidding* physicians from participating, even though doctors who prescribe an aid-in-dying drug in accordance with state law are not subject to legal liability or professional retaliation of any kind. These hospital policies, which contradict state policies, leave doctors in ethically compromised positions. They must either stand idly by and watch their patients suffer or choose to challenge the rules of their hospital and the norms of physician culture. Either proves emotionally draining for doctors. They would rather not deal with these "messy" issues at all.

In the past, dying was simpler for both doctors and patients. Most people didn't survive long enough to suffer slow, horrific deaths. Those who did expected nothing more from physicians than compassionate care on their way to salvation. Today's doctors have difficulty knowing what's best for their patients. And as such, it shouldn't surprise anyone that burnout rates among critical-care specialists have soared in recent years.

THE DECISION TO END A patient's life isn't always uncomfortable. To explain, I want to introduce David, a physician, colleague, and friend.

David graduated from Yale Medical School six classes ahead of me. He stayed on the East Coast for his residency in orthopedics while I ventured to Stanford University to train in plastic and reconstructive surgery. We both eventually accepted positions in the Permanente Medical Group in California, and that is where our paths first crossed. David's office was in the orthopedic wing of the medical center, situated across the parking lot from the hospital's surgery department, where I spent my days. I planned to operate on an eighteen-year-old patient with a complex hand fracture and wanted a second opinion about whether to immobilize it with a rigid plate or just insert a couple of metal wires. So I walked over to David's office. With the door propped open, I found him sitting behind his desk, leaning back in his chair, holding a patient's chart above his face. From the doorway, I could see only his beard—full, rich, and rusty. I knocked. Without looking to see who was there, David stood up and began making his way over. Tall and handsome, his eyes met mine, and he welcomed me into his office with a toothsome smile. As he walked around the desk to shake my hand, I observed his right side dipping with an obvious limp. His leg swung in a circular motion like the side rod of an old steam locomotive. I did my best to pretend I hadn't noticed. As a fellow physician, I could have asked him about it. In fact, it would have been natural for me to inquire, doctor to doctor. But there was something about David's confidence and ease that made his imperfections seem somehow off-limits. As colleagues in different specialties, we didn't work together often, but eight years into my practice, I suddenly became dependent on David's surgical skill.

Early one fall, I led a team of plastic surgeons, anesthesiologists, and nurses from Kaiser Permanente to Mexico to operate on children with cleft lips and palates. Together, we procured supplies, packed them in cardboard boxes, and flew south with a pair of volunteer pilots. On our second day in the small town, I met up with an anesthesia colleague for our morning run. As we reached the main road, the sun edged up over the horizon, smearing the sky with oranges and reds. We must have been two miles from where we began, running against traffic along the shoulder of a narrow two-lane highway, when it happened. I didn't see the truck shift into the passing lane behind me, but I heard it a split second before the driver-side mirror crashed into my right arm, fracturing it in multiple places just above the elbow.

In a panic, my running partner sprinted back to town for help. Forty minutes later, I was being helped into an airplane. The pilot hastily explained my options. Stanford University Hospital was only a couple of miles from the airport in Palo Alto he liked to use, but the University of San Diego was even closer. I shook my head at both suggestions and asked him to radio ahead for an ambulance to drive me to the Kaiser medical center where David worked. I wanted him to do my surgery.

I called from the plane and described the situation. At the emergency department entrance, David greeted me with yet another toothsome smile, one that exuded warmth and confidence. His demeanor was that of an experienced and well-trained physician, someone not easily rattled by a hideous and potentially career-ending injury like mine. He examined my arm, talked me through the procedure, ordered some X-rays.

Before he left, he said something I'll never forget: "Today is a wonderful day!" It seemed an odd choice of words, considering I was minutes away from major surgery with my arm severely fractured, my bone exposed, and my face contorted in pain. At first, I couldn't tell if he was being sarcastic or glib or delusional. As I would come to find out over the next fifteen years, this was simply David's outlook on life—captured in a mantra that his colleagues came to expect in delightful daily pronouncements. Like most of his patients, I found David's optimism oddly reassuring, even contagious. I felt at ease under his care, a feeling that proved well-founded.

Two weeks after my cast was removed, I was back in the operating room, assisting with surgery. From that day forward, I smiled whenever I heard David's full-throated laugh, and I never again doubted his rosy declaration that "today is a wonderful day."

Throughout his career, David was regarded as a gifted surgeon and an effective physician leader with talent and ambition to spare. By the time he decided to retire, he had achieved more than most, even though he had chosen to call it quits at the relatively young age of sixty. At his retirement party, David told the crowd that he'd made two great decisions in his career. The first was going into medicine. The second was leaving it.

He relished the thought of having time to focus on two of his other passions. David was both a skilled craftsman and an animal lover. He held equal space in his heart for vintage furniture and the untamed beasts of the Serengeti. And, true to David's demeanor, he combined his passions with exuberant creativity. Within a year of his retirement, David's home in Santa Cruz brimmed with wild, wood-trimmed treasures. In the foyer was a Georgian armchair with the hand-chiseled feet and face of a Nile crocodile. In the living room, sat a vintage bench bordered by two elephant tusks carved out of oak. In the dining room, at both heads of the table, the faces of two perfectly textured lions emerged from the chairbacks, looking quite hungry.

After David's retirement, we stayed in touch through mutual friends. In the years that followed, I enjoyed hearing about his growing acclaim as a woodworker and artisan. In 2017, nearly a decade after he left the medical group, I got a call from a colleague and close friend. Her voice cracked as she asked whether I'd heard the news about David. I confessed I hadn't.

"I'm so sorry to tell you this," she said, bracing me. "David is dead."

She explained that he had taken his own life, passing away inside his home three days after the New Year. It felt oxymoronic at first blush: David choosing death. He was one of the liveliest and most optimistic people I'd ever met. He had the gravitational pull of Jupiter. Everyone wanted to be close to him. He radiated joyfulness and energy. David had a delightful family and a satisfying avocation. He'd enjoyed a productive medical career, followed by eight years of artistic and commercial success. Throughout his life, he garnered the near-universal respect of everyone he met.

As a fellow physician, I recognized that everyone dies eventually. But if there was anyone I would have thought incapable of choosing death over life, it was David. Seven months later, I reached out to his widow, Carol. I hoped the passage of time had dulled the pain of her loss, at least enough to explain what happened. A week later, we were sitting together in the living room of her home overlooking the ocean, talking about David's love of both furniture and untamed creatures. We laughed as she remembered the time David boxed up a mahogany armoire (which resembled a black rhino in both shape and size) before shipping it cross-country as an unsolicited anniversary gift for old friends. He never once contemplated the possibility that they'd have neither the space nor taste for this quarter-ton creation.

Thinking back to the first time I met David, I asked Carol if she'd be comfortable telling me about the sole imperfection I had seen but failed to ask about: his limp. She graciously agreed, starting the story at the beginning.

As an incoming freshman at Dartmouth College in New Hampshire, David stood six-foot-three. While waiting in line to register for his classes—his head poking several inches above those of his fellow classmates—David was approached by several members of his dorm's intramural football team. Though he hadn't played in high school, he was flattered and looked forward to making new friends. His innate competitiveness and athleticism made him a natural, earning him a nickname: the Bearded Brawler. When fraternity rush came, all the houses on campus hoped he would pledge.

But early one March day during his senior year, David's life and body were turned upside down. All his life, David loved to ski. Having grown up in Vermont, David chose Dartmouth in part for its proximity to the mountains. During a coed ski trip to the White Mountains, David lost control coming off an icy cornice, crashing headlong into a grove of white pines. In this pre-helmet era, he not only fractured his pelvis but also suffered a major head injury. He was rushed to the nearest hospital, where he lay in a coma for two weeks.

Carol had met David just six months before the accident. He was beginning his final year of college, hoping to go to medical school at Yale, just a few hours south of Dartmouth. She was a sophomore, trying to figure out her future. She remembered their first date, a blind date, the kind of setup destined to send both singles home feeling disappointed. But the night defied all expectations. She recalls the magic of it. They agreed to meet at a campus library just north of the Dartmouth Green. Carol was walking down a long staircase from a second-floor reading room when she saw him waiting below. Carol was taken by how attractive he was. David would later confess that he fell in love as he watched her descend the stairs.

But now, seeing David in his hospital bed, Carol wasn't sure he was going to make it. Even if he did, she worried he would be cognitively impaired for the rest of his life. Doctors put him in a refrigerated bed to keep his brain from swelling. She remembers that he had frost on his mouth and on his eyebrows. It was a terrible sight. Half a year into their relationship, their love was like a flower in full bloom. When he received his acceptance letter from Yale, they dreamed of long weekends in New Haven and talked of their future together. Being that it was love at first sight, you can imagine how difficult it was for Carol to see David lying in a hospital bed, fighting for his life, just months after they met. She remembers seeing him in a full-body cast, in traction, unconscious. Sadness weighed on her day after day.

Looking back, Carol could've bailed right then. They were a new couple. Nobody would've blamed her. Besides, it was college. She was smart, attractive, and eager to embrace the fullness of her twenties. She could have had her pick of boyfriends.

Perhaps David's mom suspected as much. At the hospital, she encouraged Carol to stop visiting her son. "Move on with your life," she insisted. But Carol wasn't going to be told what to do or whom to love. She decided to stay. Every afternoon, she'd return to the hospital. At David's bedside, she would run her fingers through his hair, stroke his rusty beard, and whisper words of encouragement while he slept.

Slowly, David began to emerge from the coma with retrograde amnesia. He could hardly remember anything. But whenever Carol went to see him in the ICU, she insists that David's pulse sped up, something everyone in the room could see on the heart rate monitor. At first, David couldn't even remember her name. To help jog his memory, Carol told him that they were together and in love. Still unable to recall, David looked around the room, then at Carol, then at the nurse adjusting his IV, and then he whispered to his girlfriend, "Have we slept together?"

Carol blushingly replied, "I'm not going to say. Let's see if you remember."

David gradually got his memory back. He remembered seeing Carol at the top of the staircase and falling in love with her as she walked toward him that first night. He eventually remembered almost everything, except the accident itself. He even remembered the answer to the embarrassing question he had asked Carol in the hospital. In the months that followed, he learned to read and write again. Over the next two years, David underwent five surgeries, spending weeks at a time in a hospital bed, encased in plaster.

Carol stayed by his side through it all—through the cognitive rehabilitation, and the bed rest, and the infection that nearly cost David his leg. She cheered him on as Yale allowed him to matriculate. In recognition of his ongoing medical needs, the school provided accommodations to help him to master the basic science material in anatomy, physiology, and pharmacology, all from his hospital bed. And it was in that same hospital room that David proposed to Carol, more than fifty years before his death.

Sitting beside her, I could see Carol's eyes welling up. They had only grown closer as time went by, she said. In their early years as a couple, she celebrated the wildness in her husband. He adored her in return. Carol was quite often the only stabilizing force in his life, keeping him close to earth even when his world seemed to be spinning out of orbit. She had accepted the challenges life handed him. She understood what he needed to get past the accident and through his surgeries. In the years that followed, she was the rock that helped David survive a string of hardships: various illnesses, career challenges, and a drinking problem that nearly ended their marriage. Decades after that, she helped him cope with age-related arthritis that limited David's ability to create the furniture he dearly loved.

But of all the scares, bumps, and bruises, Carol remembered one incident in 2011 as a turning point, the moment their world started to fall apart. David was in the changing room at the gym when he started feeling dizzy. Next he felt pains in his chest, and he called out for help. An ambulance took him to a nearby hospital. There, in the emergency room, doctors came in and out, giving Carol bits of information at a time. When the medical team finally let her enter the curtained-off area, she wasn't prepared for what she saw.

David's skin was waxy, his eyes were rolling in the back of his head. Doctors couldn't get a pulse. He was dying. Carol yelled into his ear, "David! David! Hold on, David! Hold on! Don't let go! David, baby! Don't let go!"

He didn't respond immediately, but a few minutes later, David opened his eyes. He took a moment, looked around the room, found Carol standing there, and winked at her. With David resuscitated, Carol watched as the doctors wheeled him to the catheter lab. There, they unblocked and stented the occluded blood vessel, restoring the full flow of blood to his heart.

I smiled at this image of David, a big cat with nine lives. Time and again, he seemed to snap back to life—either literally or figuratively—at the sound of Carol yelling in his ear. So often it seemed David's survival wasn't the product of mere luck, or providence shining brightly upon him. With each close call, as he neared the edge, Carol was there to yank him back to safety and surer footing. She was his ballast against the storms, against his own demons. For half a century, he filled her life with love and endless adventure. In return, she grounded and protected him.

After the heart attack, David's cardiologist ordered him to enroll in a rehabilitation program. Carol would accompany him as often as possible, and that's when she noticed something odd. While walking through the parking lot on the way to the clinic in 2014, Carol noticed her husband scuffing his foot. She assumed David, ever the daydreamer, was lost in his thoughts, lazily shuffling along, perhaps planning his next beastly creation.

But perhaps it was more than that. David was getting older. Time, disease, and surgeries had taken a toll on his limbs. Carol could usually ignore these limitations, accepting them as nothing more than old scars. But this problem seemed different, more troublesome. It wasn't long before David could barely clear the stairs with his bad leg. He took a few nasty tumbles. Then a few more. Within a month, he was falling all the time. Carol scheduled a visit for David with his primary care physician, Dr. Samuelson, and took a day off work to accompany her husband. She wanted to hear what the doctor had to say.

Dr. Samuelson, cognizant of David's prior heart attack and his arthritis, put his stethoscope to the patient's chest and inspected his hands. The doctor asked if David was having any trouble climbing stairs, and he said "no." He then inquired if the anti-inflammatory meds were working, and David replied, "Yes, doctor." Like good physicians do, Dr. Samuelson asked if there was anything else bothering him. "No, doctor," David said, choosing not to mention his difficulty walking, the falls, or the fuzziness in his head.

Frustrated and fearful, Carol jumped into the conversation. With tears streaming down her cheeks, she told the doctor there was something terribly wrong with her husband. She explained what was going on: the scuffs, the falls, everything. Carol pleaded for help.

With eyebrows raised, the physician returned his gaze to the patient. "Okay, David, let me see you walk down the hall." Sure enough, David struggled to lift his uninjured leg, so Dr. Samuelson ordered a battery of diagnostic tests.

The root problem, it turned out, was not easy to pin down. For an abnormal gait, the differential diagnosis (the totality of conditions that share similar signs or symptoms) is massive, filling entire sections of textbooks. David's brain scans and nerve conduction tests were inconclusive. Physical therapy and a trial of high-dose steroids didn't help either. His physicians tested for myasthenia gravis, then multiple sclerosis, and a host of other potential causes. They couldn't identify the problem, nor could they rule out the worst. Over the next few months, the falls became more frequent. David's ability to walk diminished. Soon he was forced to use a motorized scooter.

As Carol told me this, I was reminded of the paradoxes of aging: how quickly our world expands when we are little and how fast it contracts when we grow old. As newborns, our universe is measured by the size of our crib and then the length of the living room. As we grow, our domain expands. We discover the block surrounding our house. We ride bikes to new neighborhoods, drive to new towns, fly across the country, and then around the world. In our youth, each day is a new adventure, exhilarating and mind-opening. But by 2015, David's world was closing in on him, sucking him in toward a dark and constricting unknown. Soon he would be confined to his house, then a room, and then finally a bed.

Neurological diseases can wreak havoc on the mind and body, but they torture their victims in different ways. Polio, for example, is compassionate.

Though it can be devastating, physically, its severity doesn't progress after the initial assault. Alzheimer's is gentler too. As the mental deterioration progresses, the patient is spared knowledge of its impact.

In contrast to these neurological conditions, there are a few that prove more sadistic. They completely spare cognition while progressively destroying all motor function. One such disease, amyotrophic lateral sclerosis (ALS), is a neurodegenerative condition that destroys nerve cells in the brain and the spinal cord. With it, weakness slowly grips the body, ascending the legs first, then the arms, and, finally, the diaphragm and chest muscles, ultimately choking its victims to death. It has been compared to sitting in a bathtub, motionless, as water slowly rises to your neck, then your lower lip, and to your nose. The only way to escape suffocation is by inserting a tracheostomy tube in the throat, making it impossible for the person to speak or breathe on their own. It's a living hell.

David had long suspected that ALS was destroying his body, but he kept that concern to himself. Carol, normally the only one in the relationship willing to confront painful truths, wore blinders as well as refusing to acknowledge the probability, even to herself.

Neither confessed their fears aloud. Both hoped they were wrong. In February 2016, David and Carol got their answer. As the doctor read the results from David's chart, Carol climbed into her husband's lap and wept. Though his arms were too weak to hold her, David did his best to comfort his wife, returning to her the emotional support she'd given him for half a century.

They both knew what the ALS diagnosis meant but hoped David might have anywhere from to two to three years left. It ended up being less than one. As the truth of his condition pressed on him, David bargained for whatever meaningful time he could get. Until that point, despite his physical challenges, he controlled his own destiny. Now that was longer possible.

Living with ALS means accepting progressive losses, followed by a series of retreats, then a few hard choices, each with the potential to be the last. In the months after his diagnosis, when he could no longer walk, David told himself that it would be a wonderful day if he could propel his own wheelchair. And when he couldn't do that or make it out to his woodworking shop or even past the threshold of his bedroom without assistance, David was determined to make his last days on earth as wonderful as they could be.

It was early winter 2016. Normal seasonal illnesses were making the rounds, infecting neighbors and friends. They all recovered as healthy people do. But a chest cold hit David full force, knocking the wind and the spirit right out of him. Unable to cough or clear his throat, he was drowning in his own phlegm. He gasped for air with every word he spoke. Carol and David both knew the end was near.

David had stretched his point of no return beyond its logical limits. There were two remaining boundaries he refused to cross. First, he would not, under any circumstances, die in a hospital. He made it clear he was going to die at home. Second, he wouldn't consent to having a tracheostomy tube placed in his throat. He couldn't tolerate the thought of depending on a machine to breathe for him.

By early January, David had lost everything he was willing to lose. He was now left with a pair of final choices: how and when he wanted to die. In a way, luck was on David's side. California's End of Life Option Act had gone into effect the previous summer. Thus, two nights after New Year's Day, David became one of the first California residents to sign his final papers, exercising his legal end-of-life option.

The next morning, he awoke in good spirits. As those closest to him arrived at the house, one by one, David looked out his bedroom door at the wooden treasures that filled his home. There was the crocodile armchair, the elephant bench set in oak, and the hungry lions poking out from the dining room—dear friends he would never see again. He was proud to have given life to these majestic creatures. They would live on long after he departed.

Friends and family took turns visiting David in his room, holding his hand, and saying their permanent goodbyes. David smiled widely at each of them and said, "I'm going home."

A mixture of secobarbital capsules and applesauce was David's final meal. Carol opened a nice bottle of Cabernet Sauvignon while the record player hummed songs from their youth. She toasted to incredible memories, to a life filled with joy, to more friends and wonderful experiences than most people could dream of.

As David closed his eyes, Carol ran her fingers through his hair, just as she did when they were college sweethearts. This time, there would be no yelling him awake. And for the first time in her life, Carol accepted there was nothing more she could do for David. She leaned over and whispered in her husband's ear, "You can go now, baby. We will be okay."

David died in his bed, surrounded by candles and family and dear friends. In the hours that followed, his wrinkles began to unfurrow as peace settled across his face. There was no more pain.

David went out the way he lived, on his own terms. And when he knew there was no way of making tomorrow a wonderful day, he decided to make the fourth day in January of 2017 his last.

How doctors view death hasn't evolved or kept up with the changing beliefs and values of their patients. In a survey of more than one thousand Americans, people were asked what they thought should be the most important thing at the end of life. They were given two options. Seventy-one percent chose "helping people die without pain, discomfort, and stress." Only 19 percent selected the other: "preventing death and extending life as long as possible." These findings suggest most of us would choose to follow David's example if given the option. Doctors can't decide whether patients should have the choice.

At the request of David's survivors, the names, locations, and identifying details included in this story have been modified. But my gratitude for David's surgical skill and his friendship are both authentic and eternal. May he rest in peace.

THE YOUNG AND THE BREATHLESS

E ACH SEMESTER AT THE STANFORD University School of Medicine, Dr. Abraham Verghese begins his first lecture on physical diagnosis with a painting from 1887. On a large projector screen, new medical students gaze upon *The Doctor* by Sir Luke Fildes. The exquisite oil on canvas depicts a Victorian-era physician sitting beside a sick child, her limp body draped across two kitchen chairs.

Verghese, a brilliant physician and the best-selling author of *Cutting for Stone*, is as well versed in the history of this iconic painting as any art critic or museum docent. Looking up at the masterpiece, students observe the doctor's attentive regard for this sick child. His worried and sympathetic countenance is unmistakable. It is a look that encapsulates the purest ideals of physician culture: empathy, concern, and dedication.

The professor explains that the painting was inspired by an actual physician who cared for Fildes's own son, a touching tribute to a doctor who did everything he could but was unable to save the young boy's life. With this insight in mind, the students in the classroom observe another attribute of the doctor. The physician is clearly stumped, his efforts to preserve life shrouded in futility. There's nothing more he can do to alter the child's fate. Knowing this, he offers all he has left to give: his caring commitment, genuine compassion, and full attention.

This painting is about the physician and also about the patient. It symbolizes a central desire we all share when seeking medical help. To quote

Verghese, *The Doctor* captures "our desire to be cared for with the kind of single-minded attentiveness of the physician seated to the left of the child." That aspiration remains strong for patients today. Yet the commitment and dedication of doctors have waned.

In lectures, Verghese laments that medical care has lost touch with these traditional ideals. The advances of modern medicine represent a "deal with the devil" of sorts. Doctors have been granted full access to the wonders of science, and in exchange they have given up many of the virtues and values depicted in the painting.

Trying to explain this strange evolution, Verghese criticizes today's doctors for being too reliant on, and subservient to, technology. With medical facilities now overflowing with high-tech machinery, doctors have lost their grip on the healing power of touch, and they have lost the mindful attentiveness required to earn the patient's trust.

Art captures moments in time, serving as an everlasting reference point for the past. Fildes's masterpiece documents a different era in healthcare. From our present reality, this painting tells the story of how far medical treatment has progressed and how much has been lost along the way, including much of the doctor's compassion and many of medicine's highest ideals.

When looking at the forlorn face of *The Doctor*, we can intuit how painful the end-of-life conversations must have been during that era of medicine—a time when physicians were powerless to alter the course of disease. The pain that doctors feel today is different but equally intense. They now possess the powers of science and speed of modern technology. And with unprecedented ability to heal the dying, one might expect twenty-first-century doctors to be comfortable, confident, and content. Instead, they feel anxious, exhausted, and paradoxically powerless. Nowhere is this incongruity more evident than when treating a critically ill child.

To explain this baffling dilemma and what it means for the future of medicine, I offer the following stories. Fair warning: Whether you're a patient or a doctor, this chapter may make you uncomfortable. That is, in part, the point.

In summer 2017, I spoke at an event that brought together physicians and the parents of sick children with a hope that both groups would learn from each other. This conference focused on a specific pediatric disease called hydrocephalus, a word with Greek origins that translates to "water on the brain."

Sitting in the back of the ballroom, I listened intently as one mother detailed the frustration and pain she felt as her child underwent a seemingly endless barrage of life-threatening surgeries. Next, a father took the stage. In words filled with emotion and stripped of pretense, he described the dire helplessness he felt watching his daughter endure dozens of operations, each as torturous as the next. One mother talked through her tears about the nonstop pain her child experienced and, in turn, the pain it caused her family. Every speaker who took the stage had paid a terrible price. And all of them had concluded through their experiences that unconditional love in the face of unimaginable hardship had given their lives deeper meaning.

The last set of speakers was a husband and wife named Stephen and Cindy. They approached the stage holding hands and stood together at the podium. Taking turns, they described their newborn son, Charley.

He was their fourth child, behind two girls and a boy. Stephen and Cindy couldn't wait to bring him home from the hospital, and their two oldest daughters, ages six and eight, couldn't wait to meet him. Unfortunately, the introductions had to wait. Charley had been born extremely premature, weighing less than a pound at birth following just twenty-two weeks of gestation. Stephen and Cindy told their kids that Charley needed to stay in the hospital for a couple of months to get stronger. They rearranged their schedules to be sure one of them could be near their son at all times.

In addition to his prematurity, Charley had a genetic abnormality that would limit his intelligence and muscle function. A few days after birth, he experienced bleeding in the fluid-filled spaces inside his brain (ventricles). The consulting neurosurgeon and the neonatology team sat down with Stephen and Cindy in a small conference room at one end of the ICU. They told the parents that Charley's problem was common in very premature babies. Because his blood vessels were not fully mature, they remained fragile. The leaking blood was partially blocking the normal passageway of cerebral spinal fluid out of the head. The doctors warned that if the blockage worsened, pressure would build and compress the child's brain. They recommended inserting a device through one of the soft spots in Charley's skull to measure the intracranial pressure. The parents consented.

A few days later, the team of specialists called Stephen and Cindy in for an emergency meeting. Indeed, pressure was rapidly building inside Charley's head. They told the parents that their son had hydrocephalus and needed an operation to relieve it. The neurosurgeon planned to place a long plastic shunt to divert the fluid from the brain to the abdominal cavity. The operation, if successful, would relieve the pressure.

There were risks, of course. The neurosurgeon explained that all shunts eventually fail. And since the distance from the child's head to the abdomen would lengthen as he grew, the system would need to be extended, even if the shunt stayed patent (open).

The pediatricians explained the future was unpredictable, noting a number of long-term consequences. Hydrocephalus can produce excruciating headaches and diminished intelligence and result in major disability. Further, with Charley's genetic abnormality the doctors couldn't promise he would ever walk or lead a normal life. However, they stressed to the parents that if the pressure were not relieved, their son would soon die.

The neurosurgeon handed the parents a consent form, which would grant him permission to move forward with surgery. The pediatric team encouraged the parents to sign it. But rather than saying yes right away, Cindy and Stephen wanted a little time to digest and discuss what they had learned. It was a lot to take in, they said. The doctors told the parents to make it quick, reminding them that Charley would die if nothing were done.

The next few hours were the hardest of Stephen and Cindy's lives. In one of the hospital's meditation and prayer rooms, the couple sat on a sofa. They told each other how much they loved their newborn son and all their kids. They didn't know if they could stand watching Charley suffer. They worried about the impact his problems would have on their entire family. They knew it was possible, even likely, that Charley would never live independently. They feared he would endure endless pain and frustration.

Stephen and Cindy then told the audience at the conference that they decided not to sign the consent form. As they said this, an audible gasp filled the ballroom. By refusing to consent to surgery, the parents knew the infant would die that night or the next day. Looking at Stephen and Cindy's faces, and listening to them choke on their words, everyone understood the unbearable anguish this decision inflicted. The couple never told their other children about the choice to let Charley die, and I've modified enough details in this story so that they won't find out.

On the day Stephen and Cindy refused to consent to surgery, the neurosurgeons and neonatologists were relentless in trying to change their minds. Over and over, they repeated, "You do understand that Charley will die? Time is running out." These constant appeals continued through the next day. Only when Charley died did the doctors cease their urgings.

From the stage, Stephen and Cindy acknowledged that nearly all the parents in the room would likely disapprove of their decision, just as the doctors did. As Charley's parents, they, too, would question their decision forever, but they continued to feel it was the best of two horrific options.

When the audience settled down, Stephen added: "We wish Charley would have been born thirty years ago, when no one could have saved his life, or thirty years in the future, when we pray that genetic abnormalities and hydrocephalus will be curable problems. No parent should have to make this kind of decision."

Cindy offered a concluding thought to the physicians in the room: "It's easy for doctors to condemn parents like us. But they aren't the ones who have to live every day with the consequences. They don't have to watch the child struggle through life. They don't have to watch their other children suffer. They don't have to live with constant pain."

Charley's life reminds us how much more complicated medicine is now than at any other time in history. When I tell David's story to physicians, they understand and respect the choice he made, even if they would have made a different one. The thought of extending David's life by a couple of suffocating days feels inhumane. When I tell Charley's story, however, few physicians express sympathy or support for the parents. They can't imagine making the same choice. From the point of view of the values and beliefs of physicians, Stephen and Cindy's decision is inexcusable.

I first met Hunter at an event in Washington, DC. Though barely out of high school, she was composed, articulate, and mature beyond her years. Speaking to hundreds of policy experts and physicians about her experience as a patient didn't seem to faze her in the least.

Bubbly and precocious, Hunter was every parent's dream kid and every teacher's ideal student. By age fourteen, she had already enrolled in classes at the local college to augment her regular course schedule. She played soccer, softball, and basketball and started running track in high school. She was on the swim team. She even tried cheerleading.

"But that wasn't your cup of tea," says Maria, her mother, to which Hunter replies, "Yeah, dance—I hated that."

I'm sitting across from the two of them inside a cramped library nook on the campus of Marywood University in Scranton, Pennsylvania, not far from Hunter's home. We're no more than a few minutes into our discussion when it becomes clear to me that Maria is Hunter's biggest cheerleader, a lifelong supporter of her daughter's dreams.

Maria is perpetually celebrating Hunter's scholastic accomplishments, both in high school and now at Marywood. She cheers on her sporting triumphs, her keen sense of style, and, lest I forget, her volunteering efforts. Maria lists off Hunter's numerous charitable endeavors like ingredients in a beloved family recipe: Cinderella's Closet, Marley's Mission, Jog for Jude, and Big Brothers, Big Sisters. The mother points out that while most teenage girls are hanging out with friends or surfing social media, Hunter spends almost every free moment helping others.

She describes her daughter with words like "amazing" and "beautiful" and "unstoppable." And to fully appreciate the significance of this mother's adoration, you have to understand what the two of them have been through.

In September 2015, Hunter helped organize a blood drive at her high school. The program was sponsored by Geisinger Health, a highly respected hospital system with facilities across western Pennsylvania. Lots of students showed up to donate, including Hunter. It was her first time giving blood, and she, like me, was nervous of needles. At the prescreening, Hunter winced as a nurse pricked her finger. The woman checked the reading and told Hunter that she couldn't give blood, at least not that day. Another nurse handed her a brochure and sent her off.

The next morning, when Maria asked about the blood drive, Hunter replied, "I don't know. They pricked my finger—something was a six. They gave me this stupid brochure," presenting a pamphlet on iron deficiency anemia.

"Wait," Maria said, "was it your hemoglobin? Your hemoglobin is a six? That's not normal."

As a nurse herself, Maria knew that anemia in teenage girls is most often the result of menstruation or poor diet, but Hunter's hemoglobin reading was less than half a normal measurement. Not knowing what to make of it, Maria drove her daughter to their primary care doctor for further testing. He did a full evaluation, including checking her stool for blood.

"That's how we found out about the colon cancer," says Hunter. It wasn't the last of the bad news either. As part of her preoperative evaluation, the doctors uncovered another health problem. Maria got a call the next day while driving.

"The pediatric neurosurgeon told me I needed to pull over to the side of the road. I thought, *Oh God, no. This is not good.* And that's when he told me she's got a second tumor. She's got a brain tumor. I just remember screaming and crying outside the car. I didn't know how I was going to tell Hunter."

That night, the mother and daughter sat down on Hunter's bed, held each other, and cried. But only for a moment. With stunning resolve and acceptance, Hunter got up off the mattress, got in the shower, got a bag packed, and got in the car with her mother, heading to the Geisinger hospital in Danville. There a neurosurgeon would drill a hole through Hunter's skull to determine whether the tumor was malignant. It was.

Maria remembers thinking in that moment that she was so proud of her fearless daughter. She is also deeply thankful for her Hunter's love. "You know, Hunter said to me early on, very early on, before the brain tumor was even discovered, she said, 'You know, Mom, there's nothing we can't do if we do it together. We can get through this, no matter what.'"

For the next two years, Maria put most of her life on hold to take care of her daughter. They spent nights on the bathroom floor when Hunter was sick from chemotherapy. They made every medical appointment together. Maria kept the house looking impeccable while making sure there was always a home-cooked meal on the table. She even went on a liquid diet with Hunter whenever she was due for another colonoscopy. They were brave for each other and unbreakable together.

Despite their courage, the surgeries Hunter needed all carried incredibly high risks. The brain surgery, if she chose to go forward with it, would last more than seven hours and was rife with possible side effects, including paralysis and severe cognitive damage. Hunter, the multisport athlete and A student, was in danger of losing all motor function and regressing to the mental state of a child.

At the hospital, the neurosurgeon, Dr. Marco, was keen to put the mother and daughter at ease. "This is easy peasy," he assured them, pointing at Hunter's brain MRI. "I'm going to crack the bony plate right here, peel it back, and pluck that tumor right out."

Walking out of the surgeon's office, Maria's sister turned to her and Hunter and said, "I don't know if I like this doctor." Maria disagreed: "I love him. I want somebody with that kind of confidence operating on my child."

This kind of bravado is not only common but essential for surgeons, particularly neurosurgeons. They know that the slightest error can cause disability or death. Confidence is required to go forward, even when the odds are long. The alternative, doubt, leads to mistakes.

For Hunter and her mom, the surgeon's confidence lifted their spirits and, fortunately, proved well-earned. After seven hours of intensive surgery, out came Hunter's brain tumor. Next, a different set of doctors set their sights on the young woman's colon cancer.

Here the decisions involved were just as complex. Based on her colonoscopy, Hunter had hundreds of polyps (overgrowths in the lining of the large intestine). The polyps extended from the intersection of her small and large intestine up, across, and down her colon, then throughout the rectum. These overgrowths lined her entire large intestine, each of them at risk of becoming cancerous. With high odds that one or more of them would become malignant, the best treatment was removing the entire large intestine, all the way to the end.

The problem with this course of treatment was that it would leave Hunter with an ileostomy. That is, the end of her small intestine would be sewn to her skin. For the rest of her life, she would need to wear a bag to collect her feces and periodically empty its contents into a toilet. The alternative, leaving in the rectum, put Hunter at risk of developing an aggressive malignant cancer, capable of spreading throughout the rest of her body, killing her. Without hesitation or doubt, the physicians encouraged her to proceed with a complete resection.

As doctors see it, having an ileostomy bag isn't a big deal. In fact, compared to the heightened risk of dying from colon cancer, there's only one right answer. But that's not how seventeen-year-old Hunter saw it. In her eyes, the "right answer" involved going to college and meeting boys without an ileostomy bag in tow. Hunter decided the doctors would need to leave her rectum intact.

"How did they respond?" I asked.

"My doctors agreed with me," she replied. "They were fine with it."

Maria interjects with a minor correction, "You didn't give them an option."

"Yeah, I guess I didn't really," Hunter says as the two share a laugh.

So with Hunter's mind made up and with Maria's reluctant support, the surgeon performed a colectomy, preserving the rectum to maintain bowel continence. "Just enough so that I wouldn't have to have a bag," Hunter adds.

Maria explains Hunter's decision by telling me about her great-aunt, who, at the age of ninety-two, was diagnosed with ovarian cancer. The malignancy was discovered because of a bowel obstruction. After surgery, the elderly woman walked around the house with her colostomy bag visible, collecting her feces until it was full.

If you were to search Google Images for "colostomy bag," you might be surprised by what you find: a collection of photos featuring fit and attractive people proudly displaying colostomy pouches on their waists. This "ostomy awareness" movement is meant to destigmatize the bags. But as Hunter sat across from her physicians, listening to them explain both the recommended surgery and the resulting ileostomy, she wasn't thinking about becoming the internet's next body-positive model. She was thinking about her great-aunt's colostomy bag and how it would be perceived by future men in her life. Though she understood the dangers of a partial procedure, an ileostomy wasn't an outcome she could accept.

"Believe me, we talked about it," Maria says. "The doctors begged and pleaded. But Hunter never wavered. She just said, 'Nope, I'm not doing it. I will not do it.'"

I'm both charmed and stricken by this young woman's decisiveness. And I am certain that her surgeon would disagree with Hunter's account of the story. I doubt any of the doctors were "fine" with her decision. Most physicians would call her choice "poor" if they were being polite and "stupid" if they were being honest.

A generation or two ago, the parents and the surgeon would have agreed to do what was best, medically, without regard for the child's preference. No one would have asked about Hunter's wishes or considered how the procedure might affect her social life. And after the procedure, when the pathologist declared all the polyps benign, everyone would agree the procedure was a great success.

Many surgeons still believe such a decision shouldn't be left up to a seventeen-year-old girl. But the days of "the doctor knows best" are disappearing from view. Patients today, especially younger ones like Hunter, feel emboldened to question and challenge their doctor's judgment. Rather than having to *comply* with a treatment plan, they feel they have the right to decide whether or not to *adhere* to the physician's recommendations. Patients expect more control and the right to make "stupid" decisions. The role of the physician is, therefore, being reshaped from that of absolute authority to more of a healthcare partner, someone who serves as a helpful source of information but is not the ultimate decider. This reflects a massive change in societal expectations. Patients now realize they're the ones taking all the clinical risk and they're the ones who have to live with the complications.

In physician culture, decisions like Hunter's are cause for concern. Doing only a portion of the recommended surgery not only puts the patient at risk of harm but puts the surgeon at risk too. Hunter's unilateral choice forced her doctors to practice what they believed to be "bad medicine." Had she consented to the surgery they recommended, the physicians would no longer have to worry about the polyps becoming malignant and spreading. But by leaving the rectum intact, the doctor would be criticized should Hunter later be diagnosed with cancer. Legally, the final decision is always the patient's. Culturally, however, it's considered the doctor's duty to steer people toward the right conclusion. When patients choose wrong, it's seen as the physician's failure.

For now, it seems Hunter made the right choice for her. At the time of this book's publication, she has been in remission for nearly four years. At eighteen, she created her own nonprofit, the Hope for Hunter Fund, to give "Chemo Cozy" jackets to pediatric oncology patients going through chemotherapy. She graduated from Marywood University with two bachelor's degrees, majoring in information security and computer science as well as minoring in mathematics and Spanish—all in just three and a half years.

Following college, she got an internship at Geisinger as a data analyst and visited often with the doctors who helped her through her illnesses. Hunter began graduate school in the fall of 2020. Her mother, Maria, remains her daughter's biggest fan.

———

LIKE A SHADOW, DEATH ACCOMPANIES doctors everywhere they go. It is a constant companion, looming over every choice they make and every patient they treat. A decade of training teaches physicians to repress and deny their fears, but death is never fully out of the doctor's sight or mind. For the oncologist and the pathologist, death is an ever-present player, always commanding the spotlight. The radiologist sees death around every corner—worrying that a seemingly innocuous spot on a mammogram might, in fact, be malignant. For psychiatrists, death peers from behind the curtain at night, casting doubt as to whether a patient seen today might die from suicide tomorrow.

I met death on my first day as a medical student. Inside the laboratory for Anatomy 101, my lab partner and I stood nervously above a cadaver who, in the weeks ahead, would teach us the organs, bones, muscles, blood vessels, and nerves of the human body. I can still remember the smell of formaldehyde piercing my nostrils and lungs as we dissected the corpse.

All medical students participate in this ritual and get to know this odor well. It is their first exposure to the smell of death. During my clinical years, I learned to detect the other odors of death, including the ammonia-like aroma of liver failure and the ironically sweet stink of diabetes with its associated ketoacidosis. Each new whiff expanded my olfactory abilities. Professors teach their pupils to identify these smells, so they can diagnose the problem, intervene sooner, and prevent further harm. Doctors vow to battle and ward off death's rank and rotting odor for as long as possible. Like the Knights of the Round Table, their quest is valiant and true, but, alas, death comes for all of us.

Physician culture is nothing if not consistent when it comes to matters of life and death. It provides a two-dimensional view of the world. For centuries, doctors have upheld their oath to sustain life no matter the price. There's crispness and cleanliness to this mindset that has, for centuries, allowed doctors to bypass any moral or ethical ambiguity about what to do for patients who are nearing the end. When it is your job to save a life at any cost, medical decisions are relatively easy. You don't hesitate to slash open the throat to establish an airway or crack open a chest and reach inside to massage an idle heart. The stories of David, Hunter, and Cindy and Stephen teach us that the relationship between the doctor and death has become impossibly complex.

Physicians feel overwhelmed. Emotion-filled conversations with patients and their families compete for time with piles of paperwork and administrative demands. Physicians find it hard enough to accurately

diagnose problems and prescribe effective treatments. Having to contemplate medicine's mounting ethical gray areas on top of it all feels
impossible.

Doctors are ill prepared for the newest challenges presented by life
and death: They weren't taught to help a sick patient die peacefully. They
never learned to stand idly by while a child perishes or to let a teenager
put her own life at risk. As doctors face a crisis of uncertainty, the physician culture they inherited offers little help.

PART FOUR | CHAPTER FOUR

COLORBLIND

L OVE FOR AND FEAR OF others are two of life's most powerful emotions. The latter—being afraid of those who are different—can cause
great discomfort and stoke terrible suspicions. It can fuel hatred, man-
ifested by discrimination, hostility, and aggression. It leads members
of a culture's ingroup to view those in the outgroup as inferior. And in
physician culture, a culture dominated by white men for all of American
history, fear and disdain have led doctors to harm, exploit, and abuse patients of color. It is a contagious and shared fear, one that has stained and
contaminated the whole of American healthcare.

Take, for example, the unfortunate legacy of Henrietta Lacks. Back
in the early 1950s, Ms. Lacks went to Johns Hopkins Hospital to have
a tumor removed. During surgery, doctors took her cells without her
knowledge or permission and cloned them for generations of research
projects. Since she was Black, Ms. Lacks's physicians didn't even consider
the possibility she was entitled to ownership of her own cells. Today, vials
of her cell line are sold for up to $10,000. Her family continues to fight
for ownership.

Go back two decades further, and you'll find an abuse of Black patients
even more egregious and indefensible. In 1932, the US Public Health
Service, in conjunction with the Tuskegee Institute, began the Tuskegee
Study of Untreated Syphilis in the Negro Male.

The initial study involved six hundred Black male sharecroppers
(about two-thirds of whom had syphilis). The doctors involved wanted

to understand the natural history of untreated syphilis. Thus, none of the men were told about their disease or the true nature of the study, which was conducted without the consent of the patients. As a result, the men thought they were getting medical care. Instead, they received intentionally ineffective treatments and suffered severe health consequences, including blindness, deafness, mental illness, heart disease, bone deterioration, and death. Though the patients were told the study was to last only six months, it was extended for forty years. During this time, none of the participants were injected with penicillin, even when the antibiotic became a standard and highly effective treatment for syphilis in the 1940s. Other forms of abuse on Black patients persisted throughout the twentieth century. Most of them went unnoticed.

When I was a first-year medical student, we honed our diagnostic skills by meeting once a week with an attending physician on rounds. He'd present a case (a patient) and demonstrate the key findings (abnormalities) upon physical exam.

One week, the physician instructor took me and two of my classmates to see a thin Black woman in her early twenties. She had come to the ER with pain in her left knee and lower abdomen. I expected the attending physician would have us listen to the woman's bowel sounds and then check to see whether there was any rebound tenderness—that is, pain that becomes more intense after pushing into the area and letting go, indicative of irritation in the lining around the intestines.

Instead, he told the nurse to place the patient in stirrups for a pelvic exam. This seemed odd. A pelvic exam is part of the evaluation of abdominal pain but is rarely where the analysis begins. With a grin, the doctor turned to us and said he was about to demonstrate the "chandelier sign."

I had never read about this diagnostic maneuver, and eagerly leaned over his shoulder as he picked up the vaginal speculum (a metal tool, hinged like a duck's bill). I watched as the doctor used it to expose the patient's internal anatomy. Next, he reached in with his index finger and, with a flicking motion, struck the woman's cervix, moving it abruptly to one side.

The woman cried out in pain and her arms shot up in the air, reflexively, as if reaching for the ceiling (chandelier). Much to the doctor's satisfaction, the cause of her swollen and inflamed knee had been confirmed: gonorrhea with spread to the knee joint.

I was appalled at what I had just seen. If the physician had suspected the woman had gonorrhea, there were a number of other ways to make the diagnosis. He could have gently swabbed the discharge from the cervix to obtain the culture. And while awaiting the lab results, he could have preemptively started the patient on an antibiotic. If he didn't believe the inflamed knee joint was related to the abdominal pain, he could have used a local anesthetic, inserted a needle into the joint, aspirated the fluid, and examined it under the microscope. Any of these methods would have been more compassionate and less humiliating for the patient.

I know that if this were his daughter, the physician would not have demonstrated the "chandelier sign." But in his mind, the fact that she was Black and poor with a sexually transmitted disease made it all right to inflict pain for the edification and "amusement" of the three medical students.

History has taught us that these were not isolated examples of racist or sadistic doctors who delighted in harming people they saw as "other." Rather, these were overt expressions of the same underlying prejudices that exist in American healthcare today.

———————

IN 2020, ONE OF THE most chaotic strings of events in US history occurred in just a matter of months. As the coronavirus pandemic ravaged homes and hospitals, and as communities and businesses began to feel unprecedented economic pressure, and as a contentious presidential election loomed, and as the push for racial justice in America intensified, the cracks in the country's foundation grew wider and more visible.

As one online commentator put it, "Imagine living through the Spanish Flu, the Great Depression, and the Civil Rights Movement . . . all at once."

During the mass demonstrations that followed the police killing of George Floyd, politicians and TV pundits voiced concerns that large gatherings of mostly unmasked people could lead to further outbreaks of the coronavirus. Health experts like Dr. Anthony Fauci, one of the nation's leading immunologists, agreed: "When you get congregations like we saw with the demonstrations, that's taking a risk." Even the World Health Organization weighed in, supporting the protests while asking demonstrators to exercise caution by wearing masks.

There was, in that moment, a strange convergence of seemingly unrelated events: A global pandemic, which was affecting the health of millions of people, was suddenly sharing airtime with protests against the unequal treatment of African Americans. And as the two biggest storylines of 2020 briefly overlapped, one of the greatest medical threats to human life at the time was being ignored.

The connective tissue, which bound the pandemic with the protests, was institutional racism. Contrary to what commentators chose to discuss, marches against inequality did not threaten the African American community's health nearly as much as the inequality that already existed in US medicine. Consider the disparities of the disease in question. African Americans comprise 13 percent of the US population but accounted for a quarter of the country's COVID-19 deaths, according to the CDC. In fact, when corrected for discrepancies in age, the mortality rate for Black people was more than double that of their white counterparts.

Present these data to doctors, and their first response is to blame socioeconomic factors like income and education, elements that exist outside the purview of their offices and medical practices. No doubt, social and economic undercurrents help explain higher rates of coronavirus deaths among African Americans. Racial minority groups are more likely to work essential (frontline) jobs, live in more congested neighborhoods, and have unequal health insurance coverage. Indeed, all these factors contribute to poorer health outcomes.

Dive a level deeper, however, and it becomes clear that Black patients also suffer higher rates of prejudice and mistreatment in US hospitals, clinics, and physician offices, driving up their risk of death. As an example, billing data showed that African American patients who came to the emergency room with symptoms of COVID-19 (including cough and fever) were far less likely to be tested than white patients with similar symptoms. This doesn't make any sense. With Black patients twice as likely to die from the disease, the logical response would be for doctors to test African American individuals more, not less. But when faced with a shortage of COVID-19 testing kits, a disproportionate number were used on white patients. In the early days of the pandemic, when emergency rooms had to ration testing kits, doctors could perform only two or three tests per eight-hour shift. In the frenzy, and amid the fear of losing a truly sick patient, doctors saved those kits for the candidates they deemed most deserving. This quick-fire deciding process played out at a subconscious level, and, more often than not, the patients tested were the ones who looked most like their doctors.

In the culture of medicine, doctors believe they treat all patients the same. The data indicate otherwise. When presented with evidence of racial bias, physicians point to flaws in society as the reason Black patients experience poorer health. They insist that social determinants (where people are born and raised, work, play, and socialize) along with social dynamics (such as racial segregation, poverty, and educational barriers) are to blame—not doctors.

As in so much of American healthcare, the systemic and cultural issues are intertwined. In this century, expressions of racism in medicine have become less obvious, and more statistical, but no less prevalent.

For example, one reason African Americans have died at twice the rate of white patients from COVID-19 is that Black people have statistically higher rates of diabetes, hypertension, and heart disease than other groups. When not properly controlled, these are three of the medical problems shown to worsen the severity of COVID-19 and increase a patient's chances of dying. The prevalence of these chronic diseases can be attributed, in part, to diet and stress, but much of the problem results from poorer medical care provided by doctors. Overall, the average Black patient receives $1,800 less per year in total medical care than a white person with the same set of health problems. As a consequence, African Americans experience 30 to 40 percent worse health outcomes than white Americans, according to a report by the Robert Wood Johnson Foundation, the nation's largest philanthropy dedicated to health. And that's a reflection of how doctors practice.

Childbirth is another example. Black mothers die at four times the rate of white mothers, according to the CDC, while the mortality rates for their unborn children are twice as high. Doctors view this as a systemic failure, but the research contradicts this conclusion. When the treating physician is African American, not white, this discrepancy evaporates.

Consider, also, the death rate from breast cancer for Black women is 50 percent higher than for white women. One reason is that only 60 percent of low-income women are screened for breast cancer versus 80 percent of high-income women. But even within the same economic stratum, white women have higher screening rates than African Americans. What's more, Black women are less likely to be offered breast reconstruction after mastectomy, something that is directly under the physician's control.

Heart attack and stroke data are equally concerning. Not only do 25 percent of African Americans have elevated blood pressure, compared to 10 percent of white Americans, but Black patients are also 10 percent less likely to be screened for elevated cholesterol than white people. The result is a higher rate of heart failure and stroke for African Americans. Doctors are aware that Black individuals may be genetically more prone to elevated blood pressure. Knowing that, physicians should pay added attention to various risk factors for cardiovascular disease like elevated cholesterol. Instead, as the data show, they tend to skip over these life-saving practices when the patient they are treating is Black.

In a culture that believes all patients are treated equally, white physicians fail to recognize how often Black patients are treated as other. A powerful example occurs when Black patients go to the doctor in pain. Research shows that, compared to white patients, Black patients are 40 percent less likely to receive medication to ease their discomfort after surgery.

As Dr. Uché Blackstock, the founder of Advancing Health Equity, explained in a conversation with *Forbes* contributor Maryann Reid: "Black patients' pain is routinely underrated and undertreated by clinicians. The undertreatment of pain has significant deleterious consequences, such as lost wages, decline in mental and emotional health, self-medication with counterfeit medications and chronic stress. One of the promises in the Hippocratic Oath is 'do no harm,' however, clinicians have routinely caused Black patients more harm by undertreating their pain."

The most flattering explanation for this discrepancy is ignorance. And there's evidence to suggest that it is part of the reason Black patients receive less pain medication. A 2016 survey found that half of white medical students and residents hold false beliefs about the biological differences between Black and white people. Among those misperceptions: Black people have thicker skin and less sensitive nerve endings. Knowing this, we might blame our nation's educational system for this failure. However, I believe there's a far likelier reason that white doctors underprescribe pain medication to Black patients. That reason is cultural.

In a profession of mostly white men, physicians fail to empathize with the suffering of those they see as other. Put plainly, white doctors literally don't feel the pain of their Black patients—at least not as strongly as for patients with similar skin color and overall appearance. No one wants to see themselves as biased. But attributing these problems to external factors or biological falsehoods alone is a clear-cut expression of prejudice. And these excuses prevent doctors from confronting the basic psychological and cultural patterns that lead to poorer outcomes.

Taken together, the data confirm that the color of people's skin determines both the quantity and the quality of healthcare doctors provide. Black patients get fewer pain medications, less screening, and inequitable attention from doctors—even when the data are adjusted for systemic barriers like underinsurance, educational inequities, and the geographic availability of hospitals and clinics.

Dr. Darrell Gray, a gastroenterologist at The Ohio State University and medical director for the National African American Male Wellness Initiative, thinks doctors need to come to grips with the prejudices they may not even know they have.

"I think there are patients who experience the detrimental impacts of implicit bias, meaning those unconscious kind of stereotypes that influence someone's care," he said in a news interview from 2020. "If a patient comes in and looks a certain way or talks a certain way, there may be bias and that could impact their treatment."

Dr. Gray's reference to "implicit bias" is a crucial component to understand the incongruity between doctors' words and actions. Decades of psychological and neurological testing show that even when we are certain that we're being fair to everyone, our decisions often reflect hidden preconceptions. Implicit bias connects our societal realities with medicine's cultural norms, leading to disparities in clinical care.

In one notable study called the Implicit Association Test, participants are asked to look at a combination of facial expressions and words on a computer screen, rating each as either good or bad with the touch of a key. The self-administered test, which you can take online, is capable of identifying even a millisecond's delay when assigning positive or negative attributes to people of different races. Consistently, white test takers associate white faces with "good" attributes and Black faces with "bad" ones. Although doctors are certain they treat all patients the same, regardless of race, the data indicate something different. Harvard researchers found that two out of three clinicians have an implicit bias against African Americans, despite the majority of doctors in the study denying any racial prejudices during the self-evaluation phase of the test.

THE HEALTHCARE PROFESSION HAS, FOR centuries, tilted toward white men. The homogeneity of American physician culture has, therefore, made doctors oblivious to their own biases. But the problems extend beyond the exam room. When white clinicians interview medical school applicants, their implicit biases lead them to prefer students who look like them, talk like them, share the same interests, and come from similar backgrounds. But unrecognized bias alone does not explain the insufficient number of Black doctors in healthcare today compared to the patient population served.

If you want to understand the origins of racial discrimination in American physician culture, a good place to start is with the largest physician membership organization in the United States. Since the early 1900s, the American Medical Association has served as an accrediting body for more than one hundred of the nation's medical schools and has therefore played a decisive role in who gets trained to be a doctor and who is eligible for state licensure. Historical records show that for most of the twentieth century, the AMA used its tremendous power to deny membership to African American physicians.

The depth of racism within the medical profession can best be understood against the backdrop of that century's most significant integration milestones. Consider that it wasn't until 1964 that the American Medical Association forced its state chapters to integrate and to stop excluding Black physicians from membership. That was ten years after the US Supreme Court ruled in *Brown v. Board of Education of Topeka* that racial segregation in public schools was unconstitutional. It was sixteen years after an executive order desegregated the US armed forces. And it was seventeen years after Jackie Robinson famously broke the color barrier in Major League Baseball by joining the Brooklyn Dodgers.

Fast-forward to 2008. Forty-four years after it repealed its discriminatory rules against Black doctors, the AMA finally acknowledged "its past history of racial inequality toward African American physicians" and publicly apologized for decades of racist policies and actions.

Medicine's troubling history, during which it lagged the nation's path toward integration, helps explain why nearly 90 percent of graduates from US medical schools were either white or Asian from 1978 to 2008. Combined, Black and Hispanic people make up less than 10 percent of current practicing physicians.

Ask white doctors whether they think this is a problem, and most will assert that you don't need to be Black to effectively treat Black patients. Research on clinical outcomes suggests otherwise. A study published in the *Proceedings of the National Academy of Sciences* found that Black babies were three times more likely to die in the hospital than white newborns when cared for by white doctors. When Black doctors cared for Black babies, the mortality rate was cut in half.

Similar findings came from a study out of Stanford in which researchers randomly assigned Black and non-Black male doctors to a group of over 1,300 Black men in Oakland, California. They found that patients treated by Black doctors were more likely to seek preventive services than those treated by non-Black doctors. The effect was particularly pronounced for invasive tests. Black patients with Black doctors were 47 percent more likely to get diabetes screening and 72 percent more likely to get cholesterol tests than ones with white physicians. They were also more likely to discuss personal health issues with doctors of the same race. The study concluded that increasing the number of Black doctors "could help reduce cardiovascular mortality by 16 deaths per 100,000 per year" among Black men.

———

Months of protests following the killing of George Floyd, combined with the rise of the Black Lives Matter movement across the country, have pushed the issue of race into the doctor's office. It's something physicians can't ignore anymore. It wasn't that racial disparities were completely unknown in healthcare before. It was that physicians didn't see themselves as contributing to the problem. With all the pressures weighing on doctors today, the thought of trying to overcome institutional racism seems like too great a burden. Therefore, rather than acknowledging their implicit biases or double-checking their decisions when caring for Black patients, doctors continue to tell themselves they treat all patients the same, despite growing data to the contrary.

The long-hidden problem of racism in healthcare won't be seen, let alone addressed, until the US trains and hires a more diverse physician workforce. Individuals from different backgrounds see problems and opportunities differently. In general, they are more likely to notice problems that affect people similar to themselves.

Consider, for example, who would be the first to notice higher rates of COVID-19 mortality among Black patients, a white doctor or an African American physician? Who would be the first to hear about the issue of doctors underprescribing pain medications to Black patients? Finally, who would be more concerned about omissions in prevention, doctors whose friends and families are given superior medical care or ones whose communities experience excessive chronic illnesses?

To be clear, white physicians do not consciously decide to give Black patients substandard care. Yet it is also true that solving institutional racism is not their highest priority—especially not when they feel overwhelmed by other workplace demands and systemic pressures. If you doubt that these facts prevent racial equality in American medicine, just ask yourself this question: Who would be more likely to challenge the biases embedded in physician culture, the doctors who benefit from those biases or the doctors who are discriminated against?

DOES SEX MATTER?

Iː 1865, ᴛʜᴇ ꜱᴀᴍᴇ ʏᴇᴀʀ that antiseptic pioneer Ignaz Semmelweis died in a mental hospital in Vienna, a decorated surgeon named James Barry died from dysentery in London. Though their deaths and contributions to medicine have little in common, their legacies offer an important reminder: physician culture strongly defends the actions of doctors and stubbornly resists any forces that might conspire to change those behaviors.

Barry, born in 1789 to a humble family of grocers, was a bright child who quickly outgrew his hometown of Cork, Ireland. At age seventeen, he followed his mother to London to live with an uncle, an aristocratic member of the Royal Academy.

With access to fine mentors and excellent teachers, Barry was accepted at Edinburgh, one of the top medical schools in Europe. Once there, however, the young man had a tough time fitting in. Standing just five feet tall, Barry wore a long overcoat, even in the summer, along with a pair of three-inch shoe inserts. Fellow classmates teased his short stature, high-pitched voice, and baby-smooth skin. Some of the medical students accused him of being a child, perhaps as young as twelve. So suspicious were Barry's peers and professors that the medical school tried to ban him from sitting for his exams. It took the help and intervention of a wealthy family friend to ensure Barry could complete his training.

By 1812, Barry had earned his medical degree and quickly gained a reputation as a hot-tempered and ill-mannered surgeon. He was known to shout and curse at patients, often smashing medicine bottles in frustration. Barry was also accused of being a womanizer, paying "improper attentions" to the wives of other men. He was labeled, among other things, a homosexual, allegedly "buggering" the governor of colonial South Africa while traveling as a surgeon with the British armed forces.

And yet, despite all the allegations of impropriety, Barry was regarded throughout his medical career as an excellent surgeon. He was the first doctor to successfully perform a C-section. And in 1857, he was named inspector general, a post that put him in charge of all military hospitals. In the later years of his career, Barry advocated for cleaner water in Cape Town and ensured that every patient who came to a hospital was treated, including slaves and the poor. On several occasions, Barry was both arrested and demoted for his forceful insistence on equal treatment of vulnerable populations.

The life of James Barry was as public, eventful, and controversial as that of any physician then or now. But when the renowned surgeon died at the age of seventy, a postmortem discovery would challenge everything his contemporaries thought they knew about him.

James Barry, it turned out, was anatomically female. Shocking to all, this discovery spread like wildfire throughout the British Empire.

Barry had been named Margaret Bulkley at birth. When his aristocratic uncle died, Barry took both his name and identity. For nearly fifty years, Dr. James Barry successfully hid his biological sex from the world, talking, dressing, and presenting himself as a man.

Victorians of the era, and historians of today, have speculated why the exceptional physician concealed the truth. Most suggest Barry only adopted a male persona because women were banned from British medical schools. They note that Edinburgh didn't *knowingly* grant its first medical degree to a female doctor until 1894, more than eighty years after it graduated Dr. James Barry.

Regardless of the exact reason, Barry no doubt fared better professionally as a man than he would have as a woman. In modern academic medicine, the same holds true. Men continue to receive professional advantages.

Of course, discrimination based on gender is more nuanced now than in Barry's time. And yet it is the experience of many women that political correctness only forces inappropriate behaviors into the shadows. The same problems and prejudices that seem to have compelled Barry to dress and comport as a heterosexual man continue today for women of all orientations and the majority of lesbian, gay, bisexual, and transgender individuals. Physician culture has evolved its views on sexuality and gender since the nineteenth century, but not nearly at the same rapid pace that society's views have changed. As a result, bias and harassment remain problematic in medicine.

AS MEDICAL STUDENTS, RESIDENTS, AND junior faculty learn the rules of the profession, they pick up on certain beliefs and behavioral scripts about men and women. These beliefs reveal an important truth, left over from the past.

In my first year of residency, I heard a story that took place more than a decade before I began my training at Stanford. Cardiovascular surgery had advanced rapidly throughout the 1960s and '70s. Once-hazardous procedures had become viable patient options. So, to communicate the institution's prowess in these areas, the department at Stanford decided to host a teleconference, live from the medical center's operating room. Various heart surgeons were eager to demonstrate the success of their cutting-edge procedures.

As the surgeons planned out the event, they brainstormed ways to keep viewers entertained during the transition from one OR procedure to the next. The all-male attending staff came up with an idea they uniformly agreed would be "good, harmless fun." To pull it off, they convinced one of the few female surgical residents to dress up in a cheerleader's outfit and dance across the screen with pompoms in hand. I heard about the famous "halftime show" often during my training, usually with a combination of pride and admiration for the ingenuity of it all.

The men behind the skit didn't intend for the performance to be defamatory or hurtful toward women, but of course it was. Female medical students who were interested in surgery at the time possessed very few options or opportunities. This stunt revealed an important truth about American medicine and sent a message that has been difficult to shake in the decades since: women could be selected into a surgical residency, but they would never achieve the same level of status or respect as their male counterparts.

There were, needless to say, no formal or written rules for maintaining discrimination in medicine. Then again, there was no need to spell it out. The absence of women in the field, combined with the sexist treatment of those who attempted to break the glass ceiling, proved to be effective deterrents on their own. Even now, decades later, fewer than 10 percent of cardiovascular surgeons in the United States are women.

THROUGHOUT THE HISTORY OF MEDICINE, few individuals have spoken out against covert or overt forms of sexism in the workplace. A notable exception was Dr. Frances Conley, one of my professors at Stanford.

When I met her, she had already achieved high status and esteem as the nation's first female tenured professor of neurosurgery. In the early 1990s, as the number of women physicians slowly began to increase, Dr. Conley made headline news when she resigned from her post at Stanford to protest the medical school's brazen gender discrimination.

Her book, *Walking Out on the Boys*, first published in 1998, describes the world of academic medicine as a place where women are considered inferior and treated as such. She noted that as of 1993, two years after her resignation, women accounted for fewer than 10 percent of full-time professors in academic centers across the United States.

"The fact that much of the academic world is closed to women (and minorities) means medical school is and remains an institution of rigid hierarchies—almost an archetypal patriarchal society," Dr. Conley wrote.

Her book provides clear insights into the influence physician culture has over both individual actions and the entire profession. Dr. Conley was one of the most talented and hardworking doctors I've ever met. She was a great teacher: demanding but supportive, and wholly intolerant of the smallest deviation from excellence. She was quick to confront those she felt were giving anything less than superb medical care. She was not afraid of anything or anyone. And yet when surgical colleagues made demeaning comments or directed inappropriate sexual suggestions toward her, she routinely let them slide. She understood that when you have limited power, you must decide which battles to fight.

In the end, when she "walked out on the boys," Dr. Conley's conflict wasn't limited to a single faculty member, administrator, or school policy. Rather, she opted to pick a fight with "a medical culture that condoned stereotypic thinking, outdated behavior, and an arrogant superiorist ideology coupled with a stubborn resistance to change."

After her resignation, and the wild publicity firestorm it kicked up, Stanford officials promised to make sweeping policy changes and asked her to return. She agreed to rescind her resignation and rejoined the faculty. In 1997, she was named chair of the Stanford University Academic Council.

Against the backdrop of this century's #MeToo movement, these events from the 1990s seem at once shocking and all too familiar. Recall that in 1991, the same year Conley resigned, more than one hundred marine and navy aviators sexually assaulted dozens of women at a conference in Las Vegas during what became known as the Tailhook Scandal. A month later, law professor Anita Hill gave public testimony against Supreme Court nominee Clarence Thomas, accusing him of sexual harassment. That same year, William Kennedy Smith, a physician and member of the prominent Kennedy family, went on trial for rape. In addition to the primary accuser, three other women came forward, willing to testify that Smith had sexually assaulted them in the 1980s. It took the jury a little more than an hour to find him "not guilty."

Today, ongoing accounts of brazen sexual misconduct and gender discrimination continue to plague our country and the field of medicine. A recent survey from the *New England Journal of Medicine* shows that more than 65 percent of female medical students report gender discrimination, and nearly 20 percent say they've experienced sexual harassment. Overall, harassment in medicine may be less overt than in the past, but today's physician culture still condones inequitable practices that put women at a professional disadvantage.

Thirty years after Dr. Conley publicly resigned in protest, just 5 percent of physicians in her chosen specialty are women. In fact, although women account for half of all medical students, only 12 percent of current neurosurgical residents are female. Meanwhile, two-thirds of all the most competitive surgical residency positions are matched to men.

Defenders of the status quo point to forces outside physician culture that contribute to these discrepancies. Societal expectations, for example, still pin women in caregiving and child-rearing roles. Therefore, as the thinking goes, any woman hoping to start a family would need to think twice about entering a lengthy surgical residency with late hours and onerous night calls. Still unacknowledged is just how often male physicians play direct and indirect roles in steering away women who wish to pursue these opportunities.

A female medical student who expressed interest in becoming a pediatric surgeon recently told me that the chairman of surgery at her university had discouraged her from spending time on research. Though he may not have known what her career plans were, he knew for certain that the door to a high-quality surgical residency would be closed to any student who failed to publish multiple research papers.

Even in specialties like pediatrics, which comprise large numbers of female physicians, women experience more obstacles than their male counterparts when it comes to getting ahead. Consider a 2019 American Board of Pediatrics ruling on the path to certification for a new subspecialty called pediatric hospitalist medicine. The board's decision allowed pediatricians who have practiced inpatient pediatrics for four consecutive years (between 2015 and 2023) to get certified without having to complete additional fellowship training. However, it denied that privilege to doctors when a "practice gap" prevented the physician from completing four consecutive years. The ruling made it clear that this would be enforced *even when the gap occurred during maternity leave.* Consider the implications of this ruling for any woman who finished her pediatric training during this period and wanted to have a family. Though she might have practiced for a *combined* eight years during that nine-year period, if her decision to have a child fell in the middle of that stretch, she most likely would fail to meet the requirements for joining this prestigious pediatric subspecialty.

In almost any medical environment, signs of discrimination by senior physicians aren't hard to find. Female residents lament how often they're referred to by their first names on rounds, while male residents are repeatedly called "doctor" by attending physicians. And even as recently as a decade ago, female medical students were frequently asked about their family plans and desire for children—questions never posed to the male medical students holding the retractor on the other side of the OR table. Although this behavior happens less frequently today because of a heightened awareness of the legal risks, the mindset remains.

Those at the top of the culture who engaged in "good harmless fun" decades ago are still in charge (or, if not them, their hand-chosen successors are). Medicine remains a hierarchical profession, one that for centuries was all-male and that continues to resist inclusion now.

In every culture, those with power and privilege are slow to cede either. In physician culture, attempts to implement change encounter stiff resistance. Academic centers view themselves as meritocracies, believing they train the most qualified applicants and promote only the best faculty members. In practice, medicine's history of discrimination repeats itself.

Behind closed doors, the chairmen of departments in elite specialties, which might accept only a few residents a year, worry aloud about matching too many female residents—for fear they will require a monthlong maternity leave. Once graduated and practicing medicine, their male counterparts have an easier time getting research published and securing academic promotions. As a result, men continue to dominate as department chairs, making it difficult for women to ascend the physician hierarchy. It's hard enough caring for patients, publishing papers, teaching the next generation of physicians, and serving on hospital and educational committees. Doing so with one hand tied behind your back makes it almost impossible. The results are predictable: professional dissatisfaction, personal unhappiness, and increasing rates of burnout.

DISCOMFORT WITH DIFFERENCE

I N THE SOUTHWESTERN CORNER OF Brooklyn, along the banks of the Hudson River, there once stood a magnificent wall. Densely constructed with brick and stone, it was erected by army engineers not long after the War of 1812.

By order of Congress, soldiers lined the wall with two tiers of cannon and called it Fort Hamilton after the American military hero and statesman. This wall, and many like it along the Eastern Seaboard, guarded against the naval fleets of foreign enemies. It served its purpose well— so well, in fact, that as wars came and went, the fleets of enemy ships never arrived, never even dared to test the wall. By the twentieth century, wars were being fought in the skies, and the thick armored wall along the Hudson River no longer served as a barrier against this next generation of threats. Before long, Fort Hamilton was turned into a processing center for troops shipping out to Europe.

Today the wall serves no military function at all. Instead it serves as a guardian of history. Every day at ten a.m., its heavy wooden doors swing open, inviting people into New York City's only military museum. Inside visitors move about freely, exploring the cavernous exhibits, learning about the antiquity of our nation's harbor defenses. Some walls come down, and some walls stay standing. This wall, which once kept enemies out, now welcomes everyone in.

Now picture another kind of wall, only this one you've built around yourself. Like Fort Hamilton in its heyday, your wall is so imposing, heavily guarded, and densely constructed that no one from the outside world would dare attempt to enter or attack it. This wall keeps you safe. It guards your secrets.

Although this wall you've constructed for safety and security protects you from judgment and shame, it simultaneously holds you prisoner, damning you to a life of isolation. The only safe way to venture beyond the wall is by leaving your true identity at the gates. Outside, your personality, mannerisms, opinions, and interests are false, designed to hide who you really are. Day after day, your disguised self grows lonelier and more exhausted. How long do you think you could keep this up? How many days, weeks, months, or years could you pretend to be someone you are not?

For Dr. Judy Lively, the answer was forty years. Four decades of living a double life, hiding her truth from nearly all her friends, family, physicians, and love interests. Judy lived most of her life in pain and discomfort behind a wall so impenetrable that nobody was allowed inside. This is the story of how she opened the gates to her world—it is a journey that contains lessons for us all.

It's midmorning, early August. Sunlight enters through the sliding glass doors behind me, slowly filling the room. The walls and furniture, richly decked in dark tones, are steadily waking up to the light. Judy and I sit across from each other in my friend's living room in Lafayette, California, near Mount Diablo. The charming hillside house isn't far from the Kaiser Permanente Medical Center in Walnut Creek, where Judy worked for over twenty years as a surgeon and physician leader.

Judy crosses her legs and folds her palms across her knee. Seated next to her is her partner, soul mate, and spouse—the love of her life.

Two months before Judy agreed to sit down with me, she retired as physician-in-chief (PIC) of the Diablo service area (DSA). PIC is the most senior leadership position throughout the vast DSA with its four-hundred-square-mile catchment, three hospitals, and more than a dozen large medical office complexes. As PIC Judy was responsible for the medical care of nearly five hundred thousand Kaiser Permanente members.

Under Judy's leadership, the service area became a national leader in quality and patient satisfaction. The gap between the mess she inherited and what she achieved was so massive that few objective observers would have predicted such a high degree of success, despite her impressive resumé. Trained at Johns Hopkins, Judy experienced a meteoric rise through the leadership ranks, first as chief of surgery, then assistant physician-in-chief, and ultimately PIC.

One of my first responsibilities when I was selected as the medical group's CEO in 1998 was to choose the PIC for the DSA. Choosing Judy was one of the best decisions I ever made.

"Do you remember why I selected you for the job?" I ask her.

She seems caught off guard by the question. Judy leans back against the sofa, arms folded, and tells me she assumes it was because she was the most qualified candidate. That is true. But my choice was a bit more complicated than that.

"When I interviewed you, do you recall that I asked you a really inappropriate question?"

Once again, Judy appears unprepared for this line of inquiry—and now looks a bit worried too. "No, I do not," she replies. "No."

"I asked you a question I had never asked anyone before, and one I've never asked again. Of course, in retrospect, it was inappropriate and illegal for me to ask it, but I was new at my job." Judy is shaking her head, flummoxed. I hesitate briefly, then plunge ahead. The question was this: "If you had to choose between your job and your spouse, which would you pick?"

Judy laughs, uncomfortably. Her spouse is sitting beside her and scanning Judy's eyes intently, waiting for a response. "Well, what did I say?" Judy implores, never once breaking eye contact with me.

"You told me that you would choose your job," I reply. "I've thought about this often, Judy, for nearly twenty years. I've replayed it a hundred times in my mind. Why did I make you answer this very personal question?"

One logical answer would have been my own insecurity. I was a new CEO in charge of saving a sinking ship, and I didn't have much time to turn the organization's performance around. I knew it would take commitment and courage to fix what was broken, and I couldn't afford to select a leader who was anything short of "all-in." That reasoning led me to a second question. Why did I worry about this with Judy, but not the other leaders I selected at other medical centers around the same time?

"I had every confidence that you could do the job," I say. "But I needed to know if you wanted it. I needed a leader who was willing to sacrifice everything. I think I sensed something was happening in your life that could get in the way."

Before I can say another word, Judy offers me forgiveness. "I get it," she says. "You had a problem to solve. You had an impossible job, and you needed someone who was willing to sacrifice everything to get the job done. That's what I did."

Judy is merciful with me, and her forgiveness is generous. My question could have resulted in real harm—both to the organization (had Judy chosen her spouse and I hadn't chosen her) but also to Judy. Even raising the issue could have caused her to doubt herself as a leader, doubt herself as a partner in marriage, and doubt that the organization she loved truly had her back. Time seems to have healed any resentment I might have caused. Even if I experienced a little beginner's luck as CEO, I'm thankful my question didn't leave any permanent scars.

By the time Judy's first term as PIC ended in 2004, she was confident I would support her reappointment. She was right. In fact, I considered her my eventual successor. I was grooming her to become the next CEO of the Permanente Medical Group.

But the year following her reappointment, Judy's ascent up the career ladder ended abruptly. She decided the time had come to blaze her own trail, one that others could follow. Her hope to provide a path for people in similar circumstances is the reason she is letting me share her story with you.

———————

JUDY'S DAD WAS A CAREER military officer and a Southern Baptist minister. Accordingly, her family moved every couple of years.

"My mom was the classic army wife," Judy recalls. "She lived at home, and her job was to be my dad's counterpart in the military world as he ascended the hierarchy of the chaplaincy. She was brought up in the Deep South. She's your classic Southern belle. Everything is proper. I think she's still annoyed that I don't wear dresses."

Theirs was the traditional military family in most ways but not all. Judy says her story begins to "congeal" in the fourth grade, when her family moved to Fort Hamilton in New York. Yes, *that* Fort Hamilton, the site of the wall. There, just outside the active-duty military base, Judy recalls an experience she had in the basement of the housing complex with a group of similarly aged girls and boys, an experience that began to change how she saw herself.

"So we're all together in the basement, and we were prepubescent, so there wasn't any sexual stuff. It was literally just 'what do *you* got?' I refer to this experience as 'you show me yours, and I'll show you mine.' Prior to that experience, I didn't realize anatomy was different, that people were built differently."

Growing up, Judy was an only child who saw only herself in the mirror. She lived in a God-fearing home where most questions about below-the-waist anatomy were strictly off-limits. And this is where Judy's lifelong secret begins to take shape. It's where she first acquired a coping mechanism to deal with the fact that she wasn't like the other children.

Judy was a girl living in a boy's body. She had male parts and was given a male birthname, Judson, Judd for short. But she felt no other genuine connection to her biological sex. She didn't *feel* like a boy. She had an interest in dolls, her mother's clothes, and hanging out with other girls.

At the same time, Judy also had a feeling, or more like a fear, that God was always watching and judging her. "When you're a boy growing up in a religious family, you're expected to be a boy. And so I remember getting to a point where I decided that my adaptive response was going to be a wall. I constructed a Medieval castle wall, multiple feet thick, and really tall. I was on one side, everyone else was on the other side, and the people on the other side were never going to know what I knew on my side of the wall."

That's how young Judy's life of secrecy began. Throughout childhood and adolescence, she took on a very convincing male persona. It is common in the world of transgender females to adopt the normative concept of masculinity and to run with it full speed.

"In addition to high school athletics and playing varsity sports, I would go sky diving, parachuting, whitewater rafting; combat handguns and knife fighting, martial arts, you name it. In college, I was a varsity fencer back in the days before girls were allowed to compete. I had a series of activities that allowed me to return to school and recount the very macho thing I had just done that weekend."

In those days, Judy was simply doing her best to live up to everyone's expectations. She used a male front for protection, hoping it would prevent anyone from ever imagining the truth.

Even now, as I sit across from Judy, with her makeup tastefully applied, components of her male persona remain firmly intact. She doesn't deny it. Having lived as a man for so long, Judy is now an amalgamation of gender identities. The role of Judd remains an indelible part of her.

As I think back to that 1998 job interview and the inappropriate question I asked Judy (whom I knew as Judd at the time), I believe I sensed something beyond her impressive resumé. Something didn't seem to fit. I'm convinced now that I observed a "softer side," one that contrasted with her very aggressive, macho persona. At the time, I believed I needed a stop-at-nothing, take-no-prisoners candidate who wouldn't quit when the going got tough. I knew the going would get tough.

If my confusion about Judy was any indication, I can only imagine how difficult it must have been for her to be transgender in the 1970s and '80s. Back then, talking about her feelings wasn't an option. Coming out at a school filled with army brats wouldn't have been considered an act of bravery or vulnerability. It would have been suicide.

Although she was aware that something didn't feel right about her body in middle school, Judy didn't explore her feelings until high school. She remembers one afternoon sneaking off to the mall after class and buying a pair of high heels under the guise of a love-struck boy shopping for his girlfriend. She tossed the shoes in the car, drove out to a field, and tried them on.

"That stuff was so dangerous," she tells me, "and only done when I was 100 percent sure I could keep it private." That afternoon, alone in an empty field, Judy glanced down and admired the bright red pumps on her feet. She found a sturdy patch of dirt to walk about. She wobbled uncontrollably with each step. Nevertheless, she felt strong. She loved the way the shoes fit and how they looked. She felt pretty and tall. After a few more struts up and down the dirt patch, Judy recalls undoing the straps, grabbing the heels off her feet one at a time, and throwing them as far as she could into the tall grass. She put her tennis shoes back on, drove home to a family that greeted her as Judd, and went to bed with her secret.

Throughout high school, Judy continued to earn top grades and varsity letters. Performing as Judd, she succeeded academically and athletically during undergrad at William & Mary too. Then it came time to choose a medical school.

Judy says she chose Johns Hopkins because it had a fast-track option that shortened the academic requirements by a year. It was only a coincidence, she tells me, that Johns Hopkins Hospital was the first institution in the United States to perform sex reassignment surgery.

This groundbreaking medical work began in the early 1960s, years before the Stonewall riots in New York City sparked this country's LGBT rights movement. And because this work was so innovative and interesting, the pioneers of the surgical program at Hopkins often made their way out West to speak at plastic surgery meetings in San Francisco. Physicians from Stanford regularly hosted these doctors for departmental dinners in Palo Alto, where they'd discuss the newest procedures, surgical innovations, and (after a few drinks) the psychological challenges of their work.

Doctors who had grown up wholly assured of their cisgender identity described to colleagues the shock of examining a beautiful female patient only to discover she had a penis and testicles. To doctors of this era, all of them raised in a heteronormative society, the confusion was too much to bear. They each told stories about colleagues who suffered erectile dysfunction and intimacy problems as a consequence of these clinical interactions, even though no physician would admit to having such a problem himself.

To Judy, a person experiencing gender dysphoria firsthand, there had never been an outlet for her feelings: no peers to share in or validate her confusion and no reliable sources of information to which she could turn. She felt completely alone. All that changed during her second year of medical school. Fortunately for her, transgender patients regularly flowed in and out of the Hopkins medical system.

"The resident running the clinical service thought it would be funny to subject me, the medical student, to doing a history and physical on a gender-reassigned patient," Judy says, noting she had no idea about the patient's gender identity. "So the first physical exam I ever did turned out to have been on a post-op male-to-female transsexual. Prior to that point, I didn't really know words like 'transsexual.' I had no concept of the terminology. But after that physical exam, the words came to mean something to me."

Take a moment to appreciate the significance of this event for Judy. Beyond the sophomoric cruelty exhibited by the resident in charge, Judy was suddenly thrust into a moment of inner awakening. Coming out of that experience, she had not only the words but also the power to understand and describe herself.

This is language that American physicians are only now, slowly and uneasily, beginning to learn and apply in medical practice. Most physicians, like most Americans, were raised with simplistic ideas about sex and gender. They were taught to recognize two sexes, male and female, which align with two genders, man and woman.

These traditional views remain wired into the physician culture through the medical terminology all doctors use. From the moment they turn on their computers, physicians encounter traditional gender norms and labels. For example, all typed entries into a patient's medical record begin with a basic rundown of the person's age, race/ethnicity, and sex. A male patient's chart might begin: "John Doe is a 44-year-old white male who presents with a chief complaint of—" leaving little room for twenty-first-century nuance. In creating that preamble, the doctor would document the patient's sex by clicking either "male" or "female" from a pulldown menu. And that action has the power to generate another set of problems.

Consider, for example, the EHR quagmire that can occur when physicians click "female." With that selection, doctors are expected to enter information on menstrual history or *LMP* (last menstrual period) for any patient over the age of twelve. Now let's assume the patient is an adult who happened to have testes prior to undergoing gender reassignment surgery. Clearly, that person would never have had a period. However, that's not something the computer—or physician culture—is prepared to recognize. This is evidenced by the next set of computer prompts, which includes a series of urgent alerts. The algorithm was created with the assumption that a premenopausal woman without a period must have either an unrecognized congenital abnormality or some potentially life-threatening disease that requires further testing.

Doctors of generations past could not have imagined a medical record or a professional discourse that included terms like "transgender," "gender nonconforming," or "nonbinary." Back in the day, when physicians entered the exam room to provide medical care for a Susan Smith or a John Johnson, they were able to make assumptions about the types of diseases they might treat and the type of language they could use. But many of today's physicians are literally at a loss for words. Medicine's training model, record-keeping templates, and long-standing binary views leave doctors feeling confused, uncomfortable, and unprepared to care for patients who don't conform to yesterday's norms.

Try to imagine how Judy must have felt, not just as a medical student but as a patient going in for medical care. Nothing the doctor told her about her changing body matched her lived experience or how she felt about herself. Long before there were books on gender-neutral parenting or bathroom debates in the halls of Congress or psychological discussions about the dangers of putting artificial limitations on gender, Judy had to figure it all out on her own.

———

AFTER JOHNS HOPKINS, JUDY, STILL going by her male name and identity, was accepted into surgical residency at Case Western Reserve University in Cleveland, Ohio. There, during a rotation in the burn unit of the metro hospital, the hotshot-macho-surgeon-in-the-making met a woman unlike any other she had ever known.

"She was the head nurse of the operating room," Judy says, turning to the woman beside her on the sofa. Karen reaches for Judy's hand with a gentle grin as she recalls the "man" she first met in 1984.

"Even as a resident, he was the one that the doctors brought their families to, to be operated on. His skills were top of the line. He was a well-respected doctor. And he was handsome too," Karen says, giggling. "So I asked him out."

The two fell quickly in love and were married a year later. With residency completed, they packed up and moved to Texas, where Judy entered the US Army. It was there, in October, that she made the hardest and riskiest decision of her life. After living for twenty-eight years inside a protective barrier, Judy stepped out from behind the wall and revealed her true self to Karen. It was a moment that would challenge Karen's outlook on her marriage and her life.

That night, Karen came to a series of difficult realizations: that her husband had been keeping a lifelong secret, that her husband was a woman, and that they were suddenly in a same-sex relationship. Karen could have understandably bolted right then and there. She had fallen in love with a macho man. And without warning, a woman stood before her, asking to be loved.

Remembering back on that uncertain time, Karen explains, "It was confusing and difficult, and we cried a lot. We fought sometimes. There were times when I just wanted my husband back. It was a raw, emotional time."

It was also a scary time. They were in Texas. Judy was active-duty military. "I was worried for his safety," Karen says. "I was worried about what would happen to his job and to us. So the first decision we made was that Texas was not the right place for us."

By 1988, after moving around to several locations, the couple made their way to California. The Bay Area proved a much a better place to build a new life, together, accepting that their love was greater than the sum of their body parts. Karen and Judy were welcomed immediately into San Francisco's LGBT community. They began meeting other transgender people and establishing a support system made up of other couples whose stories resembled their own.

But for Judy, life as a doctor remained a daily challenge. From the time she left the house in the morning until she returned home at night, she had to be Judd, the masculine surgeon and rising physician leader. Those ongoing deceptions were more difficult than one might think.

"Imagine you're walking down the hall and you need to go to the bathroom," Judy tells me. "You see the men's and the women's signs next to each other. Before you reach for one door or the other, you have to consciously remember which persona you are. I eventually got very good at knowing where all the unisex stalls were."

Think about that for a second. Every time you have to urinate at work, you must solve an intellectual puzzle. You must be vigilant and conscious of even your most instinctive thoughts while in front of your colleagues. Then, driving home at the end of the day, you must shift from one frame of mind to another. Driving back to work the next morning, you must pivot and switch back into your macho personality once again. Think of all the energy that goes into switching personas, back and forth, every day, multiple times a day. For Judy, it was exhausting.

Doctors are trained to consider the impact of stress on their patients' lives. They understand certain events can trigger anxiety: the death of a family member or the loss of a job. They compile facts about patients to reach the right medical diagnoses. But even if Judy's doctors had known about her struggles with gender identity, they could not have imagined the depth of distress it caused her.

In a medical culture that can only see black and white, the gray areas of Judy's life were invisible to her colleagues. She remained dedicated to her career and kept her persona intact. All this left her with little time to stabilize a shaky marriage. Karen was distraught, fearing what the pace and demands of Judy's work would mean both for their relationship and for the professional happiness of the person she loved, the doctor everyone still knew as Judd.

At the time, Judy was hell-bent on climbing the career ladder at any cost. She obtained an MBA knowing it would make her a better physician leader. She worked overtime wanting to prove herself to her colleagues.

Karen thinks Judy's career aspirations were motivated by inauthentic desires: "It was his persona deciding for him. It was him wanting to prove once again that 'I am the ultimate macho male.' And his path toward being a leader created a lot of problems for us. I really hated that he was continuing this farce. And I felt that at least if he stayed with surgery and decided to come out to his colleagues that he could remain a surgeon and avoid the public eye. But being in a high-level position would risk everything."

Nevertheless, Judy continued in the role that Karen didn't want her to pursue and played the role that Karen didn't want her to play. As a result, she worked extremely hard to achieve the impossible in the Diablo service area and succeeded year after year.

In hospitals, everyone respects someone like Judd, the confident surgeon with exacting standards and great clinical instincts. They trust him and readily follow his lead. Physician culture is rife with this archetype. As CEO, I loved Judd, the fearless and tireless leader. What Judd couldn't be sure of was how people would respond to Judy if they ever met her.

In 2002, Judy began visiting a therapist who confirmed she was transgender, something Judy had known since she first learned the term in medical school. Then, with Karen's support and encouragement, Judy began taking female hormones. At the time, that was the extent of Judy's transition.

Clinics dedicated to performing surgery for male-to-female patients require them to live as a woman, openly, for an entire year before scheduling the procedure. The reasoning is twofold. First, since the operation is irreversible, doctors want the person to be 100 percent certain about proceeding (the same is true about the irreversibility of cosmetic surgery, yet physicians have no qualms about moving forward quickly). The second reason they impose this requirement reflects the beliefs of physician culture. Doctors experience cognitive dissonance when the amputation of a penis isn't a matter of necessity but choice. In the absence of cancer or gangrene or a life-threatening illness, doctors are reluctant to remove what they perceive to be "normal" anatomy. Physicians believe patients must be protected from their emotions, spared from making a rash and illogical decision. They have difficulty understanding why someone would undergo the surgery and worry they will regret it unless given time to reconsider.

This sense of cultural unease spills over in the operating room, where I've heard attending physicians and assisting surgical residents wryly comment, "It's a waste to have to throw out a completely good penis." These attempts at humor, even unfunny ones, reveal the depths of discomfort physicians experience when addressing increasingly complicated issues surrounding sex and gender.

Before proceeding with her transition, there was one more task Judy needed to complete: informing the person to whom she reported. That was me.

One day in 2005, we took the elevator from the second-floor boardroom to my office on the nineteenth and sat down as evening dawned in Oakland. I listened as Judy described to me in detail the facts of her gender identity and her plan to undergo gender affirmation surgery. She assured me she could still do the job as PIC, and do it well, but she would be willing to resign if that were my preference.

I told her that keeping her in the role was a high priority for me. I was confident her colleagues and patients would accept her decision. She was equally optimistic but then told me one more thing about her future at Kaiser Permanente.

"I didn't want to go any further up the ladder," Judy remembers. "I didn't want to take the chance that somebody would discount or dismiss the organization because of my gender transition. I was worried that if I were ever to become the face of the organization that I might hurt KP. And it was a very conscious decision. I didn't want to do anything that would ever hurt KP."

Though I understood her rationale, the news came as a shock. My respect for her expertise and all she had accomplished had made me oblivious to some basic truths about physician culture and American society's views on sexuality and gender identity. Having trained in the Bay Area and taken care of dozens of patients undergoing gender reassignment surgery during my residency, I was more comfortable with Judy's decision than most.

Today, six in ten Americans say they have become more supportive toward transgender rights compared to their views five years ago. Fifteen years back, acceptance was much harder to come by. And besides, it's one thing to profess acceptance and another to act in ways different from your implicit biases and internal emotional reactions. Judy's physical appearance, voice, and mannerisms would be foreign to her colleagues and potentially problematic for many.

I told Judy that I disagreed with her decision to halt her career ascent because I had never once seen her fail. I knew she would be a remarkably successful CEO, despite how some people might respond. I also knew I wasn't going to be successful in reversing her decision.

We then talked about the process by which she would tell others, both inside and outside Kaiser Permanente. Judy had planned meticulously for every possible reaction and contingency, something she felt was necessary to protect the organization. Her preference was to inform her colleagues and the world with Karen by her side. I supported her plan. Here's how the *San Francisco Chronicle* described Judy's announcement in 2005:

> Dr. Judson Lively, a surgeon and one of Kaiser Permanente's leading Bay Area administrators, stood nervously before 100 colleagues in a Walnut Creek conference room Tuesday and told them it was no accident there were butterflies on his black tie. Lively told them a fable that was in essence the story of his life, of being trapped inside the body of another, yearning for a transformation to be set free. "I stand here before you today to inform you of something that I have kept hidden from the world and virtually everyone else, with the exception of my family, for my entire life," Lively, flanked by his wife and daughter, told the hushed crowd. "I'm 48 years old. For over 40 years I have known that I am a transsexual woman. My heart and soul really are those of a woman."

Nearly all Judy's colleagues and patients took the news in stride. "I sent seven hundred letters to coworkers before the announcement," Judy says. "I reached out to one hundred patients, to all the people I was following post-op, peri-op, or pre-op. Patients for whom I was actively involved in their care. I went to their homes and had private conversations in their living rooms to tell them. And if they wanted . . . I would transition their care to another physician who I would handpick for clinical excellence. Zero patients chose to bail. Zero."

Unsure whether the hard part was really over, Judy prepared those around her in the Diablo service area for what might become a public spectacle. She held meetings with all the staff at her medical center. She brought in a panel of experts to describe the process of transition and answer questions. She made sure the nurses and receptionists in the surgery department were comfortable talking about the decision and could answer any questions that patients might have.

Throughout 2005, Judy continued to provide care as a surgeon while performing her duties as physician-in-chief. She underwent her surgical transition in 2006.

"I suspect the average male gets some kind of weird heebie-jeebies when he thinks about castration, you know, losing a penis or testes, but I never had that anxiety," Judy explains. "They were never mine to begin with. So I went into surgery not remotely worried that I was going to somehow experience a sense of loss because I never felt they were a part of me anyway."

After Judy's announcement and surgery, she returned to work, having shed the male persona she'd worked so hard to cultivate. She didn't return to her clinical and leadership roles as a totally new person, rather as the person she'd kept hidden behind the wall her entire life. Judy's work-life balance improved, as did her relationship with Karen. There were the big-picture benefits of finding acceptance and gaining the support of her colleagues. After her wall came down, Judy no longer dreaded that her secret would be discovered. There were also the smaller, but no less important, benefits that many people might take for granted. For starters, Judy began using the women's bathroom without a second thought. In time, she and Karen settled into their new lives together, more confident in their love and surer of the future. Judy remained physician-in-chief for a third term, leading the medical center to even higher levels of quality and service performance. When Judy retired in 2017, the physicians in her medical center threw a massive gala in her honor. That year, she and Karen moved to a beautiful, quiet home on the western slope of the Sierra foothills.

THE LAST STRAW

B Y THE START OF THE CIVIL WAR, American inventors had fashioned a number of useful devices for helping battlefield surgeons remove all sorts of lead projectiles and foreign matter from the body. The *Manual of Military Surgery*, along with the *Illustrated Manual of Operative Surgery and Surgical Anatomy* (both published in 1861), offers clear specifications on the surgical tools of the trade and their uses on soldiers harmed during conflict.

Some of these instruments feature impressive engineering, both sleek and sophisticated in their design. A pair of long and slender bullet forceps, for example, combine smooth scissor-like handles on one end with a dainty pair of melon-ballers on the other, allowing the doctor to clamp firmly on, and rapidly extract, a bullet. Curved-saw scissors cut tough tissues, while metal probes located metal fragments buried in wounds (just listen for the clang of metal on metal).

In some cases, doctors used the same tools on patients to remove bullets that soldiers used to unjam their guns. Take the 0.69 caliber musket-ball puller, also known as a bullet worm. This device included two overlapping corkscrews capable of extracting a ball from a gun or from the human body.

Sometimes plucking a bullet from tissue or bone wasn't enough to save the body part in which it was lodged. In those cases, a combination of tourniquet, bone saw, and amputation knife worked effectively to detach gangrenous and decaying limbs.

Since the invention of guns, there has been an ongoing race between firearm designs and advances in surgery. At the height of the Civil War, the slow-moving Minié (or minnie) bullet was introduced as a revolution in wartime weaponry. The projectile caused catastrophic injuries that rarely lent themselves to successful surgical repair. With a capability to kill at a distance of over one thousand yards, this soft but heavy lead shell produced large, gaping holes in the flesh of its victims. A single shot created an entrance wound the size of a thumb and an exit wound the size of a fist. It destroyed muscles, arteries, and tissues beyond any possible repair. When it hit bone, the bullet stopped, expanded, and flattened on impact. Those struck by a Minié through the abdomen, thorax, or head never stood a chance.

For those Civil War soldiers who could be saved, surgeons used murky water, bare hands, and dirty rags to clean out wounds before administering chloroform to quiet and still the patient for amputation. With the patient insensate, the surgeon would make a scalpel incision through the muscle and skin, down to the bone. Next he'd transect the bone above the incision level, leaving a flap of tissue in front and a second one behind the remaining bony stump. The surgeon would then tie off the arteries with either horsehair, silk, or cotton threads before using a rasp to scrape the ends and edges of the bone smooth, so that it would not work its way back through the skin. The two remaining flaps of skin left by the surgeon would be pulled and sewn closed, leaving a small drainage hole on one or both sides. The stump would then be covered with isinglass plaster and bandaged up. The soldier would wake up hours later, thirsty and in excruciating pain.

Walt Whitman, the American poet who wrote *Leaves of Grass*, scribbled some notes in his diary about a scene from Virginia in the winter of 1862, following the Battle of Fredericksburg:

Spent a good part of the day in a large brick mansion on the banks of the Rappahannock, used as a hospital since the battle—seems to have received only the worst cases. Outdoors, at the foot of a tree, I notice a heap of amputated feet, legs, arms, hands, etc., a full load for a one-horse cart.

These unpleasant images of war didn't just harm the sensitive souls of poets. Physicians, too, bore emotional wounds. Daniel Holt, a surgeon of the 121st New York Infantry, wrote in his diary, "The wounded as they come to the rear, make a person feel sad." As the war wound down in 1864, James Moore, a Maine surgeon, lamented the groans of the wounded upon which he performed "any quantity of amputations" in what looked like "a big slaughterhouse." Another surgeon, Isaac Kay of the 110th Pennsylvania Infantry, wrote in a letter to his wife: "I cannot sleep my dear darling. . . . I must wait until I get home to tell you of the scenes through which I have passed."

The physical toll that war takes on soldiers has, in every military conflict, dropped a heavy psychological weight on physicians. During World War I, pilots with their faces blown apart haunted the surgeons who cared for them. In Vietnam, napalm burned so hot and so long that patients' flesh bubbled on the operating table.

If war is good for anything, it is a furnace for medical innovation. Over the past century and a half, great clinical advancements have emerged out of wartime necessity. The Civil War ushered in a wave of new surgical specialties and the construction of hundreds of hospitals. World War I gave us ambulances and safer anesthesia. During World War II, military surgeons invented mobile army surgical hospital (MASH) units, and in Afghanistan physicians boosted wartime survival rates with the "flying emergency room."

Nowadays, trauma medicine is so specialized and sophisticated that most present-day physicians will never have to treat a gunshot victim. And for the ER physicians and surgeons who do, the steps to follow have become rote and routinized.

As a medical student, I remember learning all about ballistics and, let me tell you, TV shows don't do the damage of a gunshot wound justice. A bullet doesn't pass through the body in a clean, linear path like an arrow. Once it penetrates the skin, the bullet spins and cracks, creating a wide path of destruction along with a secondary shock wave that further expands the radial damage. As a resident I spent long nights at the local county hospital pulling bullet fragments out of bodies. As an attending surgeon I repaired the more visible signs of gun violence: transferring skin from one part of the body to cover holes in another and filling in gaping defects with large bone grafts to the face.

Over time, caring for gunshot victims simply became part of my job. The gore, the guts, the blood—all of it became familiar, routine even. The work was never easy, but it was well circumscribed. First, I'd do my best to stem the bleeding, repair the damaged organs, and save the patient's life. Then I'd return to the operating room to reverse whatever damage remained. That is what I saw as the totality of my obligations. I never talked to patients about gun ownership rights or cautioned parents about the risks of accidental death by firearm. Yet these are increasingly the expectations placed on physicians today.

Gun control advocates have called on doctors to step up, join the debate, and protest in the streets wearing their white coats. They believe physicians need to face and fight the specter of gun violence, not just in the ER and OR, but in the community and halls of Congress as well. To underscore the imperative, activists point to the forty thousand people who die annually from gunshots, a number that is ten times higher than the next four highest GDP countries *combined*. These aren't just societal problems, they say. These are medical and ethical problems that demand action from everyone who has taken an oath to help others.

———————

In October 2018, the American College of Physicians (ACP) published a position paper in the *Annals of Internal Medicine* on gun violence, with suggested approaches to curb deaths and injuries from firearms. Among dozens of recommendations, the paper included two highly unexpected items, major deviations from past positions and traditional physician expectations:

- Physicians are encouraged to discuss with their patients the risks that may be associated with having a firearm in the home and recommend ways to mitigate such risks, including best practices to reduce injuries and deaths.
- Physicians are encouraged, individually and through their professional societies, to advocate for national, state, and local efforts to

enact legislation to implement evidence-based policies, including those recommended in this paper, to reduce the risk of preventable injuries and deaths from firearms.

The National Rifle Association (NRA), in response to what it deemed an overreach by the ACP, tweeted: "Someone should tell self-important anti-gun doctors to stay in their lane. Half of the articles in Annals of Internal Medicine are pushing for gun control. Most upsetting, however, the medical community seems to have consulted NO ONE but themselves."

The organization's timing could not have been more incendiary. The NRA posted its tweet just hours before a man shot and killed twelve people at a country music bar in Thousand Oaks, California. Incensed, doctors responded with stories of traumatic gun-related injuries and deaths witnessed under their care, posting them under the hashtag #ThisIsOurLane.

"I'll be the first to admit, National Rifle Association, that your 'stay in your lane' tweet about doctors not consulting you is correct. I did not stop to consult you the last time I had someone bleeding out from gunshot wounds on the stretcher in front of me," wrote one physician. "Treating gunshot wounds has always been our lane. Sadly, without better ways to control access to firearms, it always will be."

One of the more emotionally charged responses came from forensic pathologist Judy Melinek, who replied to the NRA's tweet: "Do you have any idea how many bullets I pull out of corpses weekly? This isn't just my lane. It's my fucking highway."

In an interview with a British newspaper, Dr. Melinek explained her comments: "We need to do something and telling doctors to stay in their own lane is not the way to do it. We're the ones who have to deal with the consequences. We're the ones who have to testify in court about the wounds. We're the ones who have to talk to the family members. It breaks my heart, and it's just another day in America."

Doctors are taught to keep their feelings in check, not wanting to let displays of emotion distort their objectivity or compromise a patient's medical care. Perhaps that's why the 2018 spat between doctors and the

NRA felt so different—and so significant. Hundreds of physicians responded online with a kind of emotional, venomous, and impatient language that has not been typical for doctors at any point in history. It signaled that an important cultural shift was under way.

The uproar on Twitter highlighted a decades-long tension between gun-lobbying groups and researchers on the topic of gun violence as a public health issue. Under intense pressure and lobbying from the NRA, Congress in 1996 effectively barred the Centers for Disease Control and Prevention from studying the public health effects of gun violence. That legislative restriction, which still exists, came three years after a landmark CDC study undercut the NRA, finding that "a gun in a home does not make everyone safer." Ever since, researchers and the NRA have been locked in battle over the right to investigate and report on the issue.

In March 2019, an approved spending bill liberalized the restriction somewhat, letting the CDC do research on the "causes" of gun violence. However, it stipulated that "none of the funds made available for injury prevention and control at the CDC may be used to advocate or promote gun control."

The ACP position paper, and all the doctors who've followed its recommendations since, were effectively stepping over that line. In doing so, they brought attention to a far bigger battle being waged inside physician culture.

How far, exactly, should doctors step outside their comfort zones to address social issues? Should the doctor's obligation to the lives of people extend past the operating room? Past the hospital entrance? Out of the parking lot and into the community? Into the living rooms of patients? Into the halls of Congress? What is inside the physician's lane and what's out?

Physician activists are screaming for doctors to widen their lanes, while traditionalists in the medical community believe the ethical responsibility of doctors belongs only to the patient in front of them. As individuals, many physicians are appalled by gun violence and hope for sensible legislation. At the same time, they can't imagine adding another accountability to their already overwhelming medical practice.

TWENTY-FIRST-CENTURY DOCTORS WORRY THAT EVERYTHING currently happening in society is becoming their responsibility: from public housing shortages to food scarcity to gun violence to immigration to climate change to gender equity to racial injustice to the entire gamut of mental health.

At a time when physicians feel stretched thin by clinical demands and bureaucratic pressures, having to engage in debates with advocates and opponents is a drain on their time and energy. It's not why they chose to become doctors.

Those who turn to physician culture for answers or protection can find some solace in the American Medical Association's *Code of Medical Ethics*, which underwent a massive makeover in 2017. The 560-page update contains a subsection titled "Physician Exercise of Conscience," which stands in firm defense of the doctor's right to avoid anything that makes them feel uncomfortable.

> For some physicians, their professional calling is imbued with their foundational beliefs as persons, and at times the expectation that physicians will put patients' needs and preferences first may be in tension with the need to sustain moral integrity and continuity across both personal and professional life. . . . Thus physicians should have considerable latitude to practice in accord with well-considered, deeply held beliefs that are central to their self-identities.

To translate: If a doctor's "deeply held beliefs" are in "tension" with a patient's needs, then the doctor should be afforded some "latitude" and be given the right to say no. This culturally supported argument is proving to be a weak defense of the status quo in clinical practice. In the old days, doctors could hide in their offices and ignore the changes happening outside their windows. But as the lines between social and medical issues continue to blur, physicians feel like bystanders in a riot: trapped and helpless with no escape. Like it or not, their lanes are widening to include a panoply of issues, including these:

Immigration. Doctors practicing near the southern border and in major cities are being forced to navigate the thorny politics of our nation's ever-intensifying immigration battle. Consider the undocumented immigrant who tests positive for COVID-19. In that scenario, the doctor is required to report the patient's medical information to the state, potentially putting the person and their family at great legal risk. Doctors must now figure out where their responsibilities begin and end when it comes to the health of refugees, undocumented immigrants, detainees, and those who might face deportation.

The opioid crisis. Doctors in rural and middle America are struggling to deal with the devastation wrought by the ongoing opioid epidemic. Many have yet to adequately acknowledge their role in creating the crisis or accept that their close ties to the pharmaceutical industry only increase the possibility of it happening again.

Narcotic prescribing habits in the United States continue to put patients at risk. The solutions require greater investments of time and energy. In their offices, it is much easier for doctors to prescribe large doses of painkillers for chronic musculoskeletal pain than it is to help their patients find safer treatment alternatives. And it is more convenient to write a single prescription for one hundred pills following an orthopedic procedure than it is to monitor the patient's progress and write a series of smaller prescriptions when needed. According to the CDC's most recent numbers, more than sixty thousand people die annually from drug overdoses. Of those deaths, almost 70 percent involve a prescription or illicitly acquired medication.

Vaccines. There is nothing more disheartening for a physician than watching a patient die from a preventable cause. And yet physicians in affluent areas like Marin County, California, are seeing vaccine-preventable diseases (once thought to be eradicated) return to their communities. Doctors are expected to intervene and persuade parents to vaccinate their children, but they worry all that effort will prove fruitless. In 2020, as major drug companies sprinted to produce an effective vaccination for COVID-19, more and more Americans expressed their hesitancy to take it, reflecting public concerns about both the science and the politics of this pandemic. Polls repeatedly showed that less than 50 percent of adults would be willing to take an FDA-approved vaccine upon initial availability. Now, helping patients overcome their concerns about the COVID-19 vaccine is yet another expectation in an already full day.

Climate change. Global warming is a growing global health issue, one that's gaining attention in medical school classrooms and in the boardrooms of some of the nation's largest healthcare organizations. Around the world, excessive heat is claiming the lives of young and old people alike. In the United States, health professionals are seeing more severe allergies, respiratory illnesses, and cardiovascular conditions resulting from increased air pollution, which already causes an estimated nine million premature deaths each year worldwide. The US healthcare industry is being labeled a major part of the problem, with hospitals contributing 8 percent of the nation's greenhouse gas emissions. With the worst consequences of global warming still ahead of us, a growing chorus of doctors is clamoring for climate-change advocacy and demanding their colleagues join them in the fight. To advocates, changing the nation's policies falls under the doctor's responsibilities. To many physicians, it is just one more to-do item for which they won't be compensated.

In each of these broad social areas, doctors feel intense pressure from activist colleagues, patients, and national organizations to widen their lanes, raise their voices, and advocate for controversial policies. Simultaneously, they face mounting time pressures, increased anxiety, and growing dissatisfaction in their clinical practices. Reminiscent of the idiom "the straw that broke the camel's back," physicians feel as though they must carry the weight of the world on their shoulders. For many, the load is already too heavy. The majority just want to practice medicine as they were trained to do. As the protective boundaries of physician culture dissolve around them, doctors don't know where to turn for help. They wish these societal issues and impositions would just go away. They will be sorely disappointed.

PART FIVE

THE EVOLUTION OF PHYSICIAN CULTURE

ECONOMIC DESPERATION

It isn't sufficient just to want. You've got to ask yourself what you are going to do to get the things you want.

—*Franklin D. Roosevelt*

THE YEAR WAS 1932, AND the United States was wading neck deep through the Great Depression. It was a hard time for almost everyone. Nearly half the banks had failed, and a quarter of the country's workers were unemployed. Even upper-middle-class professionals, including doctors and lawyers, saw their incomes drop by as much as 40 percent. Americans who had enjoyed the cultural enlightenment and economic prosperity of the Roaring Twenties found themselves living by a new motto in the 1930s: "Use it up, wear it out, make it do, or do without."

Unable to provide for their families, men of the era experienced new stresses and strains that exacted a terrible psychological toll on entire households and communities. Austerity measures sent more women into the workforce and forced everyone to do more with less. Families saved each penny and cut every corner they could.

For many, making do meant doing without healthcare services, save for the direst circumstances. Amid the Depression, most Americans could not afford even basic medical care.

That same year, 1932, a self-organized group of doctors, academics, and public health professionals issued a first-of-its-kind report on the economics and organization of medical care in the United States.

Following five years of rigorous research and analysis, the committee of experts calculated just how bad America's healthcare problem had become. The group found that the average city-dwelling family was spending $250 a year on medical care. That's about $4,500 in today's currency and a far too substantial sum, given the economic hardships of the time.

Hoping to right the ship, the so-called Committee on the Costs of Medical Care (CCMC) issued a series of landmark recommendations. First, the committee put forth a proposal to tackle the rising unafford-ability of medicine. The solution, according to the report, was for American healthcare to be "prepaid."

In today's healthcare system, prepayment is called "capitation." From the Latin *caput*, meaning head, the word refers to a "per-head fee." In practical terms, capitation involves a fixed, annual, per-patient payment, made up front for all healthcare services that will be rendered in a given year. This sum is typically calculated based on the patient's age and known diseases.

As with all insurance payment models, physicians can expect to be compensated more for treating patients who are older, sicker, and likely to need more care than those who are younger and healthier. But there's an important difference between capitation and the most common reim-bursement model in the United States today, known as "fee-for-service."

With fee-for-service (FFS), doctors receive a payment *each time* they see a patient, provide a test, or deliver a treatment. Under this arrange-ment, it's to the doctor's economic advantage to see a patient three times, even when the person's medical issues could be resolved in a single visit. And, strange as it may seem, doctors often do better, financially, in the fee-for-service model when they make their patients sicker. Physicians who cause a complication can bill twice in most FFS insurance models—once for the original procedure and then again to correct the problem. Of course, doctors would never intentionally harm a patient, and they're not happy when a problem arises. But they do benefit. Compared to capitated payments, fee-for-service incentives nudge doctors in the direction of recommending complex, pricey, and excessive services even when they add little medical value and involve greater risk to the patient.

The CCMC authors pointed out that prepayment (capitation) shifts the incentives for physicians from doing more to doing better. Instead of rewarding doctors to intervene once a problem develops, capitation propels doctors toward preventing diseases, avoiding complications, and finding more efficient ways to deliver medical treatment. With capitation, doctors theoretically *could* continue to overtest and overtreat patients, but they'd be financially responsible for the added costs.

Despite the CCMC's report on the benefits of prepayment for patients, only a fraction of physicians in the 1930s were willing to accept the financial risks involved. The reasons for that were both economic and cultural. Earning a fixed amount of money—in exchange for meeting all the medical needs of every patient for an entire year—was a frightening financial proposition for doctors who could still remember the Spanish flu that ravaged American cities from 1918 to 1920. They feared another disease outbreak or public health catastrophe would force them to provide unexpectedly high volumes of care without any additional compensation.

By contrast, fee-for-service limited the doctor's exposure to risk. Culturally, this concept of "do more, earn more" appeals to physicians because it directly connects their income with the medical care they provide. When doctors have to drive to the ER at midnight to sew a laceration, they get paid for their time and effort. When they schedule two cases in the OR, they earn twice as much as when they only do one. Rather than recasting the doctor's role as someone who helps patients avoid illness, physicians relish playing the part of hero and doing the things they value most: battling severe diseases head-on, performing complex procedures, and pulling patients from the brink of death. For all these reasons, doctors of the Depression era rejected the idea of prepayment. And they still do today.

The next recommendation from the CCMC was for the nation to adopt a higher-performing model for providing medical care. The authors concluded the problem with healthcare's delivery system was "not the system, but the lack of a system." In the 1930s, nearly all physicians worked alone. Isolated from other doctors, they failed to share best practices, learn from each other, or collaborate to provide better treatments.

The report suggested moving medical care from an industry of solo practices to a more organized and coordinated system. Its authors promoted the expansion of group practices and the formation of community medical centers. This recommendation proved overly problematic for doctors who held tight to their independence. Having their names on the front doors of their personal offices filled them with pride, whereas sharing the spotlight with others seemed unnatural. Regardless of the problems patients faced at the time, or the data-based recommendations put forth by the committee, doctors refused to redesign the delivery system.

Despite the resistance, members of the blue-ribbon committee knew the future of medical practice needed to be both more *efficient* and more *effective*. After studying every model of healthcare financing and delivery in the United States from 1927 to 1932, they concluded that providing higher-quality care at more reasonable costs required American healthcare to become *integrated* and *prepaid*.

Countless studies have since confirmed what the CCMC report recommended ninety years ago. Based on national outcome data, the healthcare organizations providing the highest quality at the lowest cost in the United States today are not the ones built around independent, fragmented physician offices. Rather, they include teams of doctors working within large multispecialty medical groups that accept capitated reimbursements.

Looking back, it is amazing how many of the CCMC recommendations during the Great Depression continue to be corroborated today by the nation's leading quality and safety organizations like the Leapfrog Group, the National Committee for Quality Assurance, and the Centers for Medicare & Medicaid Services.

But despite the promise for improvement, precious few of the recommendations from the CCMC's report have been implemented nearly a century later. Doctors in fragmented, fee-for-service practices still outnumber those in integrated and capitated organizations. Like their predecessors from ninety years ago, doctors today resent the notion of being told how to practice, how they should be paid, or with whom they should work. Physicians continue to cling to their independence. Their culture remains as strong and stubborn today as in 1932.

When the report was released, seven of the CCMC physicians broke from the official recommendations. With the support of the American Medical Association (AMA), which was then and is now the nation's largest association for physicians, they noisily fought the CCMC's plan, issuing a minority report of their own. This spin-off group felt strongly that independent practicing physicians should be in charge of any changes to the organization, delivery, and financing of medical care in the United States.

The dissenters described prepaid healthcare as "unethical" and tantamount to "Sovietism." They worried that, if enacted, the CCMC's recommendations would lead to "the destruction of private practice."

Eager to preserve the autonomy of individual physicians, the AMA mounted a fierce and targeted public relations campaign against the CCMC's majority report. It worked. The newly elected president of the United States, Franklin Delano Roosevelt, agreed to shelve the bold new recommendations and uphold the status quo. A year later, when the president again mulled the possibility of healthcare reform, the AMA restated its position, louder, asserting that "all features of medical service in any method of medical practice should be under the control of the medical profession. No other body is legally or educationally equipped to exercise such control."

By "the medical profession," the AMA wasn't referring to members of the CCMC or physicians in group practice. It stood, instead, for the majority of its members: those in their own private offices who liked things the way they were.

So instead of pushing Congress to enact a national health insurance plan as proposed in the CCMC's majority report (and as the president himself had desired to do), Roosevelt took the politically expedient path. In 1935 he signed into law an iconic piece of legislation: the Social Security Act. Few Americans today realize this bill was a negotiated compromise, allowing all workers sixty-five and older to receive continuing income after retirement in exchange for a law that omitted all language aimed at reforming US healthcare.

In the decades that followed, doctors and medical societies continued to stifle any efforts to alter the existing structure of healthcare or reduce physician reimbursements. As a result, our nation's system of medical care today is marked by outrageous costs, lagging quality outcomes, and an embarrassing patient safety record. And because of the powerful, persistent, and persuasive physician culture, American healthcare remains insulated from change.

———————

The year was 2020, and the nation came grinding to a halt. By July, the coronavirus pandemic had taken more than a hundred fifty thousand lives and forty-five million jobs. After just three months of a partial lockdown, the nation was medically, psychologically, and financially ravaged.

That year, as the virus brought the world economy to its knees, Americans were left with the kind of economic plight not experienced in generations. Signs of turmoil were all around: Unemployment filings hit record highs. The price of a barrel of West Texas oil turned negative for the first time in US history. Congress approved more than $3 trillion in emergency relief during just the first three months of the pandemic, another record high, while the next three months saw the US gross domestic product, the broadest measure of goods and services produced, fall 9.5 percent. It was the most devastating three-month collapse on record, wiping away nearly five years of economic growth.

When experts crunched the numbers—combining the federal deficit, state-tax shortfalls, and nonrecoupable business losses—the nation's financial hole looked bottomless. In fact, the nonpartisan Congressional Budget Office predicted the economic shock waves of the coronavirus pandemic would be felt for more than a decade. Other groups argued the effects would last for generations.

Economists in 2020 estimated the nation's coronavirus recession will tack an additional $8 trillion on to the national debt over the next decade, pushing the total owed by the federal government to over $41 trillion (or 128 percent of the national economy). To put all those "-illions" in perspective, consider that the national debt will be equal to every man, woman, and child in the United States owing more than $115,000 to lenders by 2030.

Given these circumstances, the International Monetary Fund joined several governmental and nongovernmental organizations in predicting the likely global decline would be the worst since the Great Depression. However, there is one key difference between the economic devastation of the 1930s and the economic desperation that's expected to last throughout the 2020s.

At the time of the Great Depression, American healthcare costs accounted for just 4 percent of the nation's total expenditures. That number has since quintupled. Healthcare now consumes nearly 20 percent of the US GDP: one out of every five dollars in the economy. Worse yet, that percentage will continue increasing. Prior to COVID-19, the Centers for Medicare & Medicaid Services estimated the average annual growth in healthcare expenditures would be 5.5 percent through 2027, taking the nation's yearly medical costs above $5 trillion by the start of the following decade.

In steadier and more prosperous times, American businesses, taxpayers, and lawmakers could tolerate the uptick in healthcare spending and afford the large annual rate increases. That's no longer the case. In a post-coronavirus era marked by economic stagnation, it will be fiscally impossible to maintain this level of spending.

Back when business was booming amid a 4 percent unemployment rate, companies didn't dare slash worker benefits. Today they have little choice. In a depressed US economy, no one will be able to pay these higher healthcare costs. The businesses most in danger of going bankrupt have already reduced operational overhead as much as possible. Now, reining in medical expenses is on every company's agenda. According to surveys, more than 80 percent of CFOs plan to implement aggressive cost containment measures in 2021 and beyond, which will include scaling back employee benefits like healthcare, making further layoffs, and accelerating automation.

Employees in this newly slack labor market will have little choice but to accept the consequences of cost containment. Stagnant wages, part-time work, and weaker health insurance options will become the new normal of the US labor force. Those who refuse to play by these new rules risk joining the tens of millions of American workers who have already become unemployed.

The federal government, which will need to pay the interest on $8 trillion of additional borrowing, will likely set its sights on cutting the costs of American healthcare. At present, government-run Medicaid and Medicare programs consume close to $1 trillion or 25 percent of total healthcare spending. With an aging population and a doubling in unemployment, those costs will continue to soar. Likewise, individual states are now confronting the reality of having to balance their budgets in the face of drastically reduced tax revenues. Lawmakers who once pursued major health-coverage expansions (e.g., Medicare for All) will have no choice but to pivot and find ways to start slashing costs.

For decades, policy experts and futurists insisted that unsustainable healthcare spending "must" be reined in and "should" be a national priority. And for decades, the relative vibrancy of the US financial system allowed our country to keep this conversation at a hypothetical level. While American leaders framed reforms in terms of "should" and "must," meaningful change stayed at a distance and the nation's problems grew worse.

Now that businesses, taxpayers, and the government can't afford to pay more for healthcare, decades of "should" have been replaced by "will." In less than a year, the coronavirus narrowed our nation's economic options down to two. We can lower healthcare costs by providing less coverage, rationing medical care, and trying to ignore the resulting health consequences. Or we can evolve the healthcare system and with it the physician culture, adopting a more efficient and effective model for care delivery. The once-popular option of talking without taking action no longer exists.

BETWEEN SCYLLA AND CHARYBDIS

ODYSSEUS, THE LEGENDARY GREEK KING of Ithaca and protagonist of Homer's epic *The Odyssey*, had been warned by the sorceress Circe of the horrors that awaited his men should they attempt to sail through the narrow Strait of Messina.

She cautions that on one side of the waters stand soaring cliffs, home to a vicious sea monster named Scylla with six terrifying heads, each filled with three rows of gnashing teeth. Were Odysseus to steer his men toward that side of the strait, the beast would be sure to emerge from its cave and consume a half dozen sailors with a collective snap of its jaws. On the other end of the strait, the men would encounter Charybdis, a smoking, gurgling, massive whirlpool that threatened to swallow the ship whole. Homer's hero, no fool, asks, "Is there some way I can get safely through, past murderous Charybdis, and protect me and my crew when Scylla moves to strike?"

Not a chance, Circe tells him. With the sacred gods standing in the way, there could be no safe passage. And so, faced with a terrible choice, Odysseus reasons, "Only a fool would risk losing all to the deep and swirling water," and he steers the ship toward what he believed to be the lesser of the two evils.

Since 1932, fourteen US presidents have had to navigate the nation's healthcare system through similarly treacherous waters. All of them faced two distinct threats. Like Odysseus, some deemed one threat or another to be the lesser of two evils and pulled the tiller hard in that direction. Others believed they could navigate past both monsters through a center path, a modern-day maneuver unavailable to Ithaca's king.

The presidents who steered toward one evil did so with the conviction that the other path was unacceptably treacherous. Some worried that rising healthcare costs and unchecked inflation threatened to sink the entire US financial structure (like the gurgling whirlpool of Charybdis). Those presidents maintained that overspending on healthcare would consume precious resources, destroying our country's global competitiveness. Others intensely feared the three-headed monster that lurked on the other side. This group of presidents felt it imperative to avoid the snapping jaws of uninsurance, underinsurance, and unavailable healthcare. To them, the health and lives of tens of millions of Americans would be put at great risk if the trio sank its teeth into our citizenry.

Steering away from Scylla. As an example of the latter group, Lyndon Johnson saw lack of health coverage as a grave threat to seniors and people living in poverty. As president, he urged Congress to expand insurance coverage and increase access for these vulnerable populations. He was counting on the vibrancy of the US economy, the low cost of medical care in the mid-1960s, and his political acumen to persuade lawmakers to act. Johnson succeeded, signing into law two Social Security Amendments in 1965, establishing the Medicare program for the elderly and Medicaid for the poor.

Eluding Charybdis. By contrast, Jimmy Carter saw a nation edging closer to the rim of economic collapse. He had taken office during a period of "stagflation," a combination of high inflation and slow economic growth. Carter urged Americans to scrimp and save. In keeping with his cost-saving agenda, he proposed restrictive and punitive legislation to lower hospital spending. Carter's plan was unpopular with everyone, including senator Ted Kennedy, who told the attendees of a 1978 Democratic Party conference in Memphis: "There are some who say we cannot afford national health insurance. They say it has become an early casualty of the war against inflation. . . . But the truth is, we cannot afford *not* to have national health insurance." Everyone knew who he meant.

Bypassing both threats. Unlike Johnson and Carter, a variety of US presidents have dared to attempt what was impossible for Odysseus: avoiding both Scylla and Charybdis. All who tried, regardless of party affiliation or political philosophy, charted their course based on the strategic approaches outlined in the CCMC's 1932 report.

In each case, our nation's commander pushed for legislation and regulatory changes that would steer the country's healthcare system toward *integration* and *prepayment*. Every time, their efforts were met with major opposition. Standing in the way was an invisible entity: not a divine force as in Odysseus's dilemma but a powerful obstacle nonetheless.

Blocking the path was the same physician culture that resisted Roosevelt's push for national healthcare reform in 1932. For the past ninety years, this powerful force has fought and driven back every presidential attempt to move the US away from its outdated, fragmented, fee-for-service model.

Take Nixon, who in the 1970s had to address stiff increases in the cost of Medicare and Medicaid. Not wanting to raise taxes or compromise coverage, the president's solution was the Health Maintenance Organization (HMO) Act of 1973. The bill, torn from the pages of the CCMC playbook, was designed to bring groups of doctors together (integration) and replace existing fee-for-service reimbursements with a prepaid, comprehensive care model (capitation). In response, private practice physicians rose up to challenge the president, depicting the very concept of HMOs as a Faustian bargain by which our nation would have to sacrifice healthcare excellence for lower costs. Though integrated-delivery groups and practice-based HMOs have done well in certain parts of the country since, doctors in most locations have resisted the model, not wanting to cede autonomy or abandon fee-for-service payments. As a result, the HMO concept has gained limited traction nationally.

Twenty years later, in 1993, Bill Clinton pushed for a "managed competition" model. Wanting to both reduce the budget deficit he inherited and expand healthcare coverage, Clinton's approach also followed the CCMC's guidance. His plan promised universal coverage, along with competition among insurance companies and government regulations to ensure cost controls. Once again, doctors subverted the proposal, fearing it would restrain their independence, reduce their incomes, and poison the doctor-patient relationship. Clinton's healthcare-reform hopes died an ugly death following a vicious and vitriolic advertising campaign from the AMA.

In 2009, Barack Obama governed alongside a Democrat-led House and Senate. Knowing that he had the votes in Congress to pass a comprehensive healthcare bill, he pushed for radical legislation aimed at expanding coverage and rewarding clinical "value" over "volume." The following year, after nearly twelve months of negotiation with leaders of both parties, he signed into law the Affordable Care Act (ACA), bringing the United States one giant step closer to universal health coverage. The bill was filled with provisions to spur integration and prepayment, once again mirroring the CCMC's recommendations.

For example, it raised payments for the highest-rated healthcare organizations in the Medicare Advantage program, a prepaid alternative to traditional (fee-for-service) Medicare. Alongside it, the law increased the national footprint of Accountable Care Organizations, which are prepaid groups of doctors who agree to join forces with one or more hospitals, all working together to lower costs and improve clinical quality.

There was something in Obamacare for everyone. There were subsidies for the poor, coverage protections for people with "pre-existing conditions," and the right for young adults to stay on their parents' insurance policy until age twenty-six. But once again doctors resisted the reforms. A Deloitte poll from 2013, a time when many Obamacare provisions were set to take effect, found the majority of physicians already unhappy with the direction of US healthcare. They complained that the law would further erode their professional independence and their income. Rather than seeing the ACA as an opportunity to work together to create integrated medical groups capable of providing better medical care at a lower price, doctors instead looked for opportunities within the law to increase their own revenue through aggressive coding and billing. As a result, the most powerful healthcare legislation in more than half a century succeeded in expanding coverage but barely moved the needle on medical care outcomes or costs.

Most recently, the Trump administration continued the historical presidential march toward capitation and integration. His election in 2016 came one year after the passage of the Medicare Access and CHIP Reauthorization Act. Shortened to MACRA, the law was designed to roll back the nation's reliance on fee-for-service and move toward a "pay-for-value" model with two alternative approaches. One plan rewarded independent doctors in fee-for-service practices who achieved superior clinical outcomes. The other focused on groups of physicians working in a capitated reimbursement model. The second plan offered even higher incentives than the first based on participants' overall quality performance. The administration, assuming doctors couldn't resist the opportunity to earn higher payments, expected physicians to do the logical thing: form Accountable Care Organizations in search of greater rewards. Though physicians supported the idea of earning added payments for improved quality, they bristled at the part of the plan that contradicted their cultural beliefs. Namely, physicians found it unfair that they could be financially penalized in a capitated system based on uncontrollable factors like whether patients follow their medical recommendations or how effectively their colleagues practice. In other words, the pay-for-value plan would make doctors' income reliant on the actions of others. Theoretically, physicians could do everything right, but if the patients don't take their medications or get their preventive screenings, all doctors in the group would take the financial hit. As in the past, the values of physician culture supersede any financial incentive. Physicians treasure their independence and dislike the thought of relying on others to get ahead. As a result, few have chosen the path most in line with the CCMC's proposal.

Over the past five decades, Americans have elected an eclectic group of presidents. Their views on economic affairs, foreign relations, social issues, immigration, and tax reform have run the gamut from liberal to conservative. And yet their healthcare ambitions, along with their chosen tactics, have been strikingly similar.

Be it HMOs under Nixon, managed competition under Clinton, ACOs under Obama, or "pay for value" under Trump, the legislative aims were identical. In each case, regardless of party, the president believed he could avoid both Scylla and Charybdis by moving American healthcare toward capitation and high-performing, integrated medical groups. Each time the US leader pushed for laws and put in place regulations meant to expand coverage without raising medical costs. But in each case, efforts fell short of expectations. While charting their healthcare course, all the presidents overlooked a sturdy and stubborn force that continues to dam the river of change.

No matter how strong the consensus for well-coordinated, prepaid healthcare, doctors and the medical societies that represent them have blocked the way. Whenever a legislative effort has threatened the cultural principles they cherish, doctors have stood their ground and voiced their displeasure. They have been unwilling to abandon their individual offices or relinquish their sovereignty over medical decisions. They've continually subscribed to their own exceptionalism, believing they reserve the right to be the final arbiter of what is best for patients. Having dedicated a decade of their lives to reaching the top of the healthcare hierarchy, they refuse to share the platform with others. They want to bill for their time and services just as they always have. They refuse to accept any approach that will make their incomes dependent on the compliance of patients or the actions of other clinicians. They relish the opportunity to be heroes. They reject the idea of being a cog in a wheel or simply another member of a medical care team. And they resent the very notion of being evaluated by anyone who is not wearing a white coat.

Physician culture, bolstered by powerful lobbying groups like the AMA and national specialty societies, has fiercely and successfully resisted nearly a century of reform efforts. As a result, our nation's healthcare is, as independent researchers and health experts often recite, "the most expensive and least effective in the developed world."

Ninety years after the CCMC report was released, the United States continues to be threatened by the gurgling drink of rising healthcare inflation *and* the snapping jaws of inaccessible medical care. We have yet to pass through healthcare's narrow Strait of Messina to the calm waters at its end. Our failure to complete the course charted by the CCMC haunts us to this day.

TWO PATHS, BOTH FRAUGHT WITH PERIL

A T THE END OF *THE ODYSSEY*, courageous Odysseus returns to Ithaca to reclaim his rightful place as king. But his presence is not welcome by all. Angry locals conspire to kill him. To resolve this conflict between the hero and the mob, Homer enlists a literary trope that has come to be known as deus ex machina. The story concludes not with people solving their own conflict, but with the gods swooping down from the heavens and saving humankind from its own self-destruction.

With the United States swept up in the greatest economic disaster since the Great Depression, divine intervention would be a welcome resolution. Unfortunately, these modern (nonmythical) times offer us no such option. Going forward, we will need to solve our own healthcare problems and face the consequences of our past inactions. This will be a painful process.

Medical costs have reached a historic apex at a time when the United States is experiencing one of its sharpest economic contractions. Economists eye an ongoing downturn, with massive job losses, business failures, and declines in spending expected to continue for years to come. As a result of the nation's immense economic struggles, one way or another, healthcare costs will come down. The only question is, how? The United States has but two options: it can constrain coverage and limit access to medical services or it can decide to steer a new course, one that reaches the long-sought destination of broadly available, prepaid, integrated, high-quality, affordable healthcare.

OPTION 1: A TWO-TIER SYSTEM OF HEALTHCARE

In the world's poorest countries, there are two types of healthcare systems. There's one for wealthier citizens who can afford private insurance and receive care at private facilities. Then there's a less attractive system of care for everyone else. The latter is publicly funded and government run with limited access and frequent delays. For underresourced nations with no viable alternatives, a two-tier system of healthcare is the only choice. I have observed its heartbreaking consequences firsthand on more than a dozen global surgical missions and visits abroad.

A few years ago, I traveled to India to meet with physicians, hospital leaders, and representatives from the Bill & Melinda Gates Foundation. The group was there to identify and solve the root causes of maternal mortality.

As we examined the data, it became quickly apparent that, for much of India's population, *coverage* was not the same thing as *access*. The constitution of India obligates the government to ensure the "right to health" for all citizens. The problem is that the nation's entire GDP is under $3 trillion (less than what Americans spend on healthcare alone), and only 2 percent of that sum is apportioned to healthcare services. In a country of 1.2 billion people, that's simply not enough. Because patients experience insufficient access to hospitals, doctors, and healthcare services, about 90 percent of childbirths in India take place at home. And because there are not enough facilities or local doctors capable of performing a cesarean section, women who experience a life-threatening obstetrical problem can't get the immediate help they need. In this underfunded healthcare system, childbirth is a deadly gamble for most families.

Overall, death rates for mothers and babies are ten times higher in India than in the world's most industrialized nations. That's not true, however, among the country's wealthier families. Patients with private insurance and convenient access to both obstetricians and operative facilities experience low complication rates, similar to those in the United States. Although India is an extreme example of a two-tier healthcare system, poor clinical outcomes are the inevitable result of any attempt to contain costs through *rationing*.

Most Americans understand the need for healthcare rationing in impoverished countries. But they have a hard time accepting the need to limit medical spending in a nation as wealthy as ours. In 1990, cash-strapped Oregon tried to implement a data-driven process to "prioritize" Medicaid services. A task force was assembled to rank medical treatments from most to least cost-effective. It then determined how many interventions in a given year the state would be able to fund. Health experts lauded the approach as a highly rational and morally correct solution, informed by a transparent process involving substantial community input. But when patients got ahold of the list of services that were excluded, the outcry was so deafening that lawmakers had no choice but to ditch the plan.

Though nobody likes healthcare rationing, the reality is that it already occurs throughout the United States. Most people don't notice it because the process happens quietly, develops slowly, and transpires far less transparently than in Oregon's failed experiment. What's more, many people don't recognize the cutbacks at all because they largely impact families living below the poverty line.

In one example of hidden rationing, studies have shown that rising deductibles and copayments have forced low-income parents to administer less insulin to their children with diabetes than pediatricians recommend. Likewise, growing evidence suggests that rising out-of-pocket expenses have forced many Americans to delay expensive tests and forgo necessary procedures, even prior to the COVID-19 outbreak.

As the United States attempts to claw its way out of a coronavirus recession, all states, even the wealthiest, are now cash-strapped. Take California, which sought to erase an unprecedented deficit under its progressive governor, Gavin Newsom. In 2020, he introduced a proposal to cut a wide array of Medi-Cal services (the state's version of Medicaid). The state legislature opposed the move and voted to avoid deep spending cuts by tapping into California's rainy day fund. But unless the state does something drastic, the deficit will grow deeper each subsequent year, just as it will in nearly all the other financially challenged states throughout the land. Sooner rather than later, elected officials will be left with no reserves to draw on. Someday in the not-too-distant future, taxpayer revenue will prove insufficient to pay for the overly expensive, fragmented, fee-for-service healthcare approaches of the past. That day is drawing near.

In 2020, tens of millions of laid-off Americans relied on temporary unemployment benefits, which Congress struggled to pass. As the economy failed to rebound and as new jobs were slow to materialize, stimulus funds dried up, leaving more and more people scrambling for relief. Economists of all stripes now expect more people to become dependent on government-subsidized healthcare coverage and unemployment benefits, which will stretch state budgets until they break. Meanwhile, small businesses, many facing bankruptcy, will have no choice but to scale back coverage options for employees or eliminate healthcare benefits altogether. Workers, in turn, will need to enroll in Medicaid or apply for federally funded exchange subsidies, further straining government budgets.

Though Congress funded economic relief packages early in the pandemic, it did so with the assumption that the virus (and economic headwinds) would be short-lived. Now reality is sinking in. Amid a protracted recession, lawmakers simply can't offset workers' lost income indefinitely. Ending the financial tailspin will require years of aggressive spending cuts at both the state and federal levels. Healthcare programs, along with other entitlements, will be first on the chopping block. Reduced healthcare coverage and restricted access may help close the gap and temporarily stop the bleeding, but it will cleave the nation, leaving it with two disproportionately served groups of Americans: the privately insured and everyone else.

Of course, our nation's "everyone else" will be better off than India's "everyone else," but Americans won't be happy with the results. With limited funds to go around, overt rationing in the United States might mean that low-income and underinsured patients are forced to wait a year or more for procedures like total-joint replacement. It might mean some people end up being excluded from certain high-cost treatments, including new and expensive drugs. It might mean that no one over the age of eighty gets heart surgery unless they pay for it themselves. It might mean shuttering dozens or hundreds of low-volume hospitals throughout much of middle America. It might lead to government-imposed restrictions on who gets MRIs or CT scans, not unlike the CDC's testing restrictions early in the pandemic, when there was a shortage of COVID-19 kits. All of these restrictions may sound extreme in a country like ours. And while it is impossible to be certain which treatments and procedures will be lost or constrained, we can be certain that rationing will be necessary when federal and state budgets dry up.

Given these risks to our nation's health, why would elected officials and business leaders even consider going down this path? The answer is simple. From an economic and political perspective, eliminating some treatments and procedures would be the easiest and most expedient solution. Whenever an organization or public entity is fighting for economic survival, people understand that concessions need to be made. Cutting healthcare coverage won't make patients happy, and such a move would never fly in stable economic times. But people will perceive it as an understandable, perhaps even a necessary, choice given the circumstances. And rather than having to make one drastic change all at once, this solution demands only minor cutbacks year after year. The long-term consequences won't be pretty or popular, but the payers, including large corporations and governments, will be largely spared from blame for the deteriorating health of their employees and constituents. Instead, the blame will get shifted to those who deliver the care, including doctors, hospitals, and public health agencies.

Don't forget, there is another option, one I am admittedly partial toward. It offers the potential to reduce costs, improve quality, and make healthcare more convenient for patients. It is not a new concept, and I cannot claim credit for inventing it. In fact, the blueprint was first sketched back in 1932.

OPTION 2: A NEW (OLD) MODEL OF EFFICIENCY

A popular science fiction trope revolves around the existence of a "multiverse" (or multiple universes) that lends itself to a fascinating subgenre of fiction called "alternate history." Here authors imagine what might have happened if, say, Lincoln skipped the theater, Napoleon avoided defeat in Russia, or the Germans claimed victory in World War II.

Were we to apply this same suppositional thinking to healthcare, we can imagine what might have been if the AMA lost the fight to the

CCMC. In this alternative version of history, President Roosevelt would have signed into law a national healthcare reform plan in 1932, anchored by a prepaid reimbursement model and a more integrated approach to care delivery.

The transition from fragmentation to integration, and from piecemeal payments to prepayment, would have fundamentally altered the way physicians treat patients. Over time it would have reshaped their values and beliefs too. A prepaid and integrated system of healthcare, formed in the 1930s, would have led generations of doctors to practice in group settings where excellent care depends on teamwork, interspecialty collaboration, and communication across the entire health system.

Rather than investing major medical resources in futile end-of-life treatments, our nation would now spend wisely on prevention. Doing so would help patients control blood pressure, lower blood lipids, and avoid cancer at a rate of over 90 percent (rather than 50 or 60 percent as is standard in fragmented, fee-for-service care settings today). As a consequence, patients would experience far fewer heart attacks, strokes, and malignant tumors than they do today. In this alternate timeline, hundreds of thousands of American lives would be spared each year from ravages of chronic disease and medical error. And when the coronavirus came ashore in 2020, fewer people would have fallen ill and died.

Had integration become the norm, the notion of celebrating a single clinician's heroics would seem strange, and likely unacceptable, to fellow doctors. Primary care would be a revered specialty, collaboration (not competition) would be the norm among specialists, and physician satisfaction would be the highest in history. Rather than rejecting new information technologies or science-based approaches, doctors would embrace them as paramount to providing superior care and lowering healthcare costs.

Likewise, if prepayment had become the standard reimbursement model in US healthcare, there would be several large HMOs and Accountable Care Organizations in every major city all striving to be the best in the areas of quality, convenience, and affordability. They'd offer patients video-based care solutions and work off comprehensive electronic health records designed to enhance care delivery rather than maximize payments. Medical care would be easy to access and inexpensive, and patients wouldn't fall through the cracks so often. There would be no need for physicians to waste hours each day on coding and billing for the services they provide. Doctors would stop overtesting, overtreating, and overcharging because there would be no incentive to do so. They'd be responsible for finding and implementing better ways to provide care, and they'd find satisfaction in upholding the traditional mission of medicine: helping those in need. And because each of these steps would give doctors a greater sense of control and purpose, burnout rates would be a fraction of what they are today.

Had these changes transpired in the 1930s, the United States would now lead the world in dozens of health measures. Americans would be living five years longer than they do presently and with fewer chronic diseases. Doctors would value prevention, collaboration, primary care, evidence-based approaches, and patient safety. Ultimately, the systemic changes, including integration and capitation, not only would have improved the medical care patients receive, but also evolved the physician culture such that the United States would be the world's role model for clinical excellence and doctor satisfaction.

Here's the important part: these types of medical outcomes aren't entirely a work of fiction. They are extrapolations of the clinical results attained by some of our nation's most *efficient* and *effective* medical groups and organizations, including several members of the Council of Accountable Physician Practices (CAPP) such as Mayo Health System, Geisinger Health, and Kaiser Permanente. These are integrated and prepaid health systems. Their cultures contrast sharply with smaller, fee-for-service practices. And though they are not mirror representations of the vision laid out previously, and though they all have performance areas in which they lag, together they provide higher-quality care, often at lower prices, than doctors in the communities around them.

Yet despite their success, these larger medical groups are exceptions to the rule of US healthcare delivery. For three-quarters of a century, the physician culture has helped doctors and our nation retain its fragmented and outdated system. And as a consequence, the United States is the only wealthy nation on the planet that has managed to steer its ship in the direction of both Scylla *and* Charybdis.

The obvious question is: If the destination is so idyllic, why don't all physicians pursue it? The answer is, once again, both systemic *and* cultural.

First, making the transition to capitation and integration is more difficult and contentious than one might presume. The path is littered with potential pitfalls: It's difficult to maintain revenue during the switch from fee-for-service. It's also difficult to rightsize the number of doctors needed in each specialty. It's hard to convince physicians to narrow their clinical focus. It's expensive to make the necessary IT purchases and train effective leaders during a period of financial uncertainty. Moreover, doctors worry that if they fail to lower the cost of care through capitation, they will find themselves with reduced income, having to tap into their savings to stay financially solvent. And if integration doesn't produce the operational efficiencies required, the transition could threaten the economic survival of every participant.

Besides the systemic impediments, there are the cultural ones as well. Times of change make people uncomfortable. It feels awkward to work in a group after working alone for so long. It is distressing to cede decision-making authority to others after playing the role of sole decider. It is highly challenging to switch from volume-based payments to value-based payments. If physicians could make these shifts through a series of small steps, they might agree to take the chance. But these changes require doctors to leap, not step, outside their cultural comfort zones. There are good reasons that most innovative business efforts die in the early phases and never reach a critical mass. Doctors who take it on themselves to create something new, hoping to avoid both Scylla and Charybdis, will struggle and likely fail unless they have the commitment and courage to stay the course. The path forward will prove painful. Addressing the cultural resistance of doctors will be as challenging as making the systemic adjustments.

The good news for physicians is that once systemic changes get under way, cultural ones follow. As the economic incentives shift, the culture evolves in response. As an example, paying physicians on a capitated basis refocuses their attention and values on things like preventive care, avoiding unnecessary errors, and helping patients manage chronic diseases. In a prepaid model, doing these things is in doctors' financial and individual interest. Likewise, bringing doctors together in a single medical group with strong physician leadership leads to new cultural norms. Within integrated care settings doctors proactively seek solutions that raise the bar for quality. They collaborate, cooperate, and embrace the technologies that enable better communication and care. Over time, each of these changes becomes part of a new, shared value system.

To be clear, physicians won't transform healthcare simply or solely because it is the right thing for their patients or the economy. If those were the key drivers, change would have happened a long time ago. Instead, doctors will embrace capitation and integration because they believe it is in their own interest. And they'll do it because, compared to rationing, it is the lesser of two evils.

Until the transition is complete, physicians immersed in the traditional culture will feel threatened, and they will fight back. Those who choose to resist change will urge groups like the AMA to step up and use their powers to battle disruption. Medical societies will lobby Congress, hoping to impose regulations that make the move over to capitation as painful as possible. Physicians in fee-for-service practices will attack the reputations of nearby doctors who defect and join prepaid, integrated care organizations. Over time, as higher-volume, higher-performing centers of excellence attract patients away from smaller community hospitals, these local institutions will rile up local leaders and residents (the way taxi drivers went after Uber and Lyft). Doctors who find themselves on the outside, still operating in the old model, will openly criticize the quality and credibility of those who are on the inside implementing the new model.

All this resistance is predictable. For decades, physician culture has insulated doctors from the financial, ethical, and clinical pressures to change. What's not clear is whether healthcare will finally evolve in response to the magnitude of the economic difficulties or if it will devolve into a two-tier system as a result of cultural inertia. But we do know with certainty that the status quo can't last in the context of the coronavirus pandemic and the economic devastation it has produced. Something will have to give.

WHO WILL LEAD THE CHANGE process and traverse the previously unnavigable strait? Will it be doctors and hospitals or another entity that forces change upon the entire healthcare system?

If physicians and hospitals refuse to take the lead, one possibility is that transformation will be led by US businesses, which currently insure half of all Americans (155 million people). In this situation, radical change will be imposed on doctors, not by them.

One example of business-driven disruption, which was reported in the *New York Times*, involved a company out of Wisconsin that offered $5,000 to employees in need of total joint replacements. The only condition: they needed to get the procedure done in Cancun, Mexico, by a company-approved orthopedic surgeon from the Mayo Clinic. The disruption in this case involved a company, not a doctor or hospital, moving toward higher-quality care at lower overall costs. Likewise, Ashley Furniture sent about 140 employees and dependents for treatments at a hospital in Costa Rica, which has saved the company $3.2 million in health costs in under three years. And to improve the quality of care domestically, Walmart has chosen a handful of US hospitals and orthopedic surgeons to perform all total joint procedures for its employees, selecting providers based on high volumes, excellent outcomes, and low prices.

Having pushed their employees to obtain medical care through a limited number of high-volume "centers of excellence" in the precoronavirus era, big businesses could further flex their muscles in the future. It's not hard to imagine a scenario where the nation's Fortune 100 companies collectively agree to pay for medical care delivered through only high-quality, technologically advanced, multispecialty medical groups and hospitals. They could then negotiate capitated rates with participating medical groups, insisting on quality and service guarantees. Individual employees might prefer the doctors they had in the past, but in a postcoronavirus era with high levels of unemployment and ultraexpensive medical costs, they'd have no option but to accept these new models.

Another potential path toward a disruptive solution involves large corporate healthcare ventures. Take Haven, a medical nonprofit formed in 2018 by the CEOs of Amazon, Berkshire Hathaway, and JPMorgan Chase. With more than 1.2 million employees among them, along with trillions of dollars in assets, companies like these have the clout to lead and dictate the terms of healthcare's transformation. Although Haven struggled to get off the ground, and eventually disbanded in 2021, some experts believe that corporations are the only American entities with enough power to someday establish a new model of care. They could replace health plans with a retail business model, replace in-person visits with virtual care, and replace today's fragmented system with a one-stop shop that puts patients at the center of everything. And with a knack for operational efficiency, the enterprising superpowers that comprise the Fortune 100 list could do it all for substantially less than healthcare costs today. If that were to happen, the switch would prove as disruptive to current healthcare providers as Amazon was to bookstores, brick-and-mortar retailers, and the entire media industry.

The US government could play a role in disruption as well. Facing difficulties of its own in funding Medicare and Medicaid, the new administration and cabinet could aid businesses in this transition by instituting a series of legislative steps that mirror those available to businesses. For example, President Joe Biden, along with Congress and state governors, could together announce that on a particular day, say in 2024, CMS and the government-run healthcare exchange plans will only pay for care delivered by integrated organizations (doctors and hospitals) through capitated payments.

Next, lawmakers might insist that all electronic health record manufacturers open their application programming interfaces (APIs) so that third-party developers could create tools to connect disparate systems. This would allow CMS and other arms of government to measure and publicly report the results of each integrated health organization in the areas of prevention, patient safety, and chronic disease management. Future payments could then reward the highest-performing medical groups, forcing those at the bottom to improve or exit the marketplace.

The only alternative to government and business-led healthcare transformation involves change from within, with doctors and hospitals acting as catalysts for reform.

Despite the criticisms I've leveled at doctors and the current physician culture, I'm bullish on their ability to achieve remarkable outcomes in the face of adversity. A shared mission and sense of purpose have motivated physicians throughout history to do that which seems impossible. When the coronavirus hit our country, doctors put the lives of patients ahead of their own rather than retreating in fear. I'm optimistic the same selfless qualities that have guided the profession for centuries can help doctors realize the extent of moral injury that would ensue should the United States devolve into a two-tier system of healthcare. I'm therefore hopeful that doctors will embrace change before change is imposed on them. And if they do, I'm confident physician culture will evolve for the betterment of all.

DENIAL, ANGER, BARGAINING, AND DEPRESSION

IN EVER-GREATER NUMBERS, PATIENTS AND doctors are waking up to a painful reality: the American healthcare system of the past is falling financially out of reach. Already more families are "doing without" healthcare during the coronavirus recession, forgoing the treatments they need but can't afford. Doctors, too, are feeling the pinch. In 2020, management consulting firm McKinsey found that 53 percent of independent physicians were worried whether their practices will survive COVID-19. In the hardest stretches of the pandemic, nearly the same number of doctors reported having less than four weeks of cash on hand. It's estimated that physicians have watched their incomes drop by as much as 50 percent on average. Many have had to lay off loyal employees and forfeit their leases.

With economic pressures continuing, physicians are eager to turn back the clock and return to the halcyon days when talks of healthcare-system reform were just that: talk. As unhappy as they might have been before the pandemic—quarreling over prior authorization forms and irritating insurance regulations—doctors would gladly trade the "new normal" for the old one. With the passage of time, the problems doctors complained about in 2019 will pale in comparison to the problems confronting them in 2021 and beyond. Medicine is becoming a profession in which the immediate past looks so much brighter than the future. Even when the coronavirus is gone, the economic wreckages left in its wake will force doctors to alter their practices and, in turn, let go of many of the cultural values they hold dear. As a consequence, physicians are soon to experience a great sense of loss.

Elisabeth Kübler-Ross's famous psychological model of grief provides a useful system for thinking about what will happen next. We can predict that every doctor will experience the first four stages: denial, anger, bargaining, and depression. What remains to be seen is how many will reach the fifth and final stage: acceptance.

Denial is the first stage of grief. In it, according to the writings of David Kessler, who co-authored two books with Kübler-Ross, life proves extremely difficult. People who are experiencing loss, or the need for change, find themselves in a state of shock. Denial helps them cope.

Psychological trauma expert Ronnie Janoff-Bulman observed that denial helps the human mind "dose" itself. Just as taking too much medicine all at once can be hazardous for the body, accepting the full flood of emotions that accompany loss can be bad for the mind. Denial is the brain's way of making sure that people don't experience too much grief before they're ready.

Indeed, denial proves healthy in moderate amounts. It allowed the oncology pioneers to advance the field of cancer research and treatment. Without denial, the pain and harm they inflicted on patients would have tormented and overwhelmed physicians, preventing medical progress.

In contrast, denial becomes unhealthy when it is prolonged, all-encompassing, and unshakeable. And in that respect doctors' ongoing denials of the need for change in healthcare over the past two decades have been destructive, preventing them from seeing their contributions to the growing unaffordability of medical care and to the declining quality of American healthcare. Their prolonged denial has hurt patients and undercut the nation's average life expectancy. It has allowed doctors to ignore the harm they cause through medical errors, out-of-network billing, ineffective medical procedures, and excessive end-of-life care. It has inflicted deep psychological damage on physicians themselves. The consequences of unhealthy denial include occupational exhaustion, dissatisfaction, and frustration. In a word: burnout.

Overcoming denial proves challenging. In the world of business, difficulty in acknowledging the need for change has been extensively studied and documented. In the book *Only the Paranoid Survive*, former Intel CEO Andy Grove recalls the glory days when his company dominated the world of memory chips. The silicon chip, once "the heart of the computer," was Intel's breadwinner. It stored data and was essential to practically every computer function. But global competitors eventually found ways to match Intel's manufacturing quality and bring down costs. Undeterred, or perhaps feeling protected by the company's proud history, Intel's long-tenured employees remained certain of their product's superiority. They loved telling tales about the company's early days and celebrating their decades of accomplishments. In their minds, they were the world's leader and would stay irreplaceable forever. In other words, they, like doctors, were in denial about the world around them and the imperative to shift direction. The lesson Grove extracted from the experience was that "we all need to expose ourselves to the winds of change." This is as true for doctors today as it was for Intel's engineers in the past.

Grove, along with company cofounder Gordon Moore, eventually redirected Intel's manufacturing from memory chips to microprocessors. This new silicon chip technology was designed not around data storage but specific operational functions that now guide cell phones, automobiles, robots, and home appliances. In essence, Grove declared that Intel's products would become the *brains* behind future technologies rather than remaining the *heart* of the computer. As logical and obvious as this transition looks in retrospect, it pained many at Intel and cost thousands of employees their jobs.

But by overcoming denial Grove and Moore helped the company avoid bankruptcy, thereby saving tens of thousands of jobs, and driving profitable growth for the next several decades. Many physicians believe it's impossible to draw comparisons between medicine and business. But when it comes to disruption, physicians and businesses are equally vulnerable.

Anger comes after denial and is a useful (albeit uncomfortable) stage in the grieving process. It is said that anger is pain turned inside out, providing an outlet for people's suffering. It serves as a conduit to externalize feelings of guilt, hurt, or fear.

As with denial, anger has been a familiar response for physicians throughout history. Whenever external forces challenged their values, beliefs, and norms, doctors have projected their fears and insecurities onto others in the form of anger. In the nineteenth century, when doctors were told they were the source of infection, they unleashed their anger on Ignaz Semmelweis. In the twenty-first century, American physicians demonstrated their anger when data-driven measurements confirmed their poor performance. Feeling that their autonomy and competence were being threatened by the evidence-based medicine movement, doctors lashed out at the healthcare leaders who demanded consistency in clinical practice and promoted scientifically derived checklists.

Today, anger remains the dominant emotion for doctors who argue that they and their colleagues are suffering from moral injury. In many online physician forums, "moral injury" has become the all-caps response to any suggestion that doctors must share in the responsibility to lower costs or change the way they practice. Physicians express anger over the hours they work, the pay they receive, the bureaucratic limitations imposed on them, and the various evils of the current healthcare system. They warn that an unhappy, burned-out physician makes more errors and leaves the profession earlier. Doctors decry their moral injury on social media, believing that once the nation understands the pain they are experiencing, and once healthcare leaders feel the wrath of their anger, the system will acknowledge its errors and acquiesce to their demands.

Like an American tourist abroad who yells louder and louder at the locals who don't speak English, physicians act as though repeating the same words at higher decibels will change the responses of insurers, hospital administrators, and electronic medical record companies. Of course, they are wrong. The problem isn't that doctors aren't being heard; it's that they are speaking a different language.

Against today's economic headwinds, any solution that depends on more dollars for doctors or fewer hours on the job will be a nonstarter. Until physicians acknowledge and accept their role in the failures of the healthcare system, little will improve, and their anger will only intensify. Though becoming angry feels cathartic, the action rarely proves effective. It won't soothe the sense of loss physicians feel or ease their emotional pain.

Bargaining is a logical next step in the grieving process. It stands to reason that if the world won't change (no matter how loudly doctors scream), perhaps it's possible to negotiate a better outcome.

Just as my father bargained for more time with my mother prior to her death, today's doctors would do or give anything for the medical profession to return to "normal." Having battled the coronavirus with valor, physicians are emerging from the fight as national heroes.

Numerous opinion polls show the pandemic boosted the public's view of doctors, but it won't result in patients or businesses or government officials cutting doctors any slack. In the context of the current economy, the "hero's welcome" comes with no added rewards for service.

Like military veterans, doctors will continue to receive praise for their sacrifices but will not be accorded special privilege and will have no added bargaining power. Americans will remain grateful for all that physicians did, but they won't be able to reach deeper into their own pockets to meet the monetary demands of doctors. Amid the financial crisis, nearly everyone is a victim of the pandemic. Save for the wealthiest corporations, most businesses can give no more. State governments can't increase Medicaid payments. Politicians from both sides of the aisle now see the futility of pushing for any healthcare plan that requires raising taxes.

As the nation looks to move past the pandemic, doctors will have no choice but to bargain alongside everyone else for what they feel they are owed. However, rather than bargaining for a bigger slice of the pie—as they did prior to the pandemic—physicians will now be bargaining for *less* of a reduction.

In medicine, as in life, what *should happen* often diverges from what *will happen*. Doctors, having been trained and immersed in the physician culture, believe they *should* be given the autonomy to practice as they please. Physicians feel they *should* be able to exercise independent judgment without having to consult a checklist. They insist the skill of a doctor *should* be measured by fellow physicians (if by anyone) and certainly not by patients or independent auditors. Most important, physicians feel the way they practice *should* be decided by fellow doctors, based on the norms created by their medical and surgical specialty organizations. But no matter how angry physicians get or how hard they bargain, the days of "should" are gone.

Depression follows failed attempts at bargaining. It pulls people from the past into the present to confront the painful reality of their situation. It is the inner nadir needed to begin one's ascent toward acceptance.

Even prior to the pandemic, doctors reported alarmingly high rates of depression. Among medical students, researchers found 27 percent experienced depressive symptoms, about three times higher than the general population. It was worse for medical residents, 29 percent of whom suffer depression. In their clinical practices, doctors experience higher rates of suicide than any other profession. According to the American Foundation of Suicide Prevention, "The suicide rate among male physicians is 1.41 times higher than the general male population. And among female physicians, the relative risk is even more pronounced—2.27 times greater than the general female population."

The causes of depression and suicide among physicians are multifactorial, deriving from workplace stresses, unhealthy coping mechanisms, and systemic issues that make the physician's job difficult to perform. Against the nation's lingering economic problems, the sources of anxiety among doctors will grow in both prevalence and severity. The heightened period of depression to come will be the most difficult and dangerous part of the grieving process for physicians.

The challenge for doctors in moving from depression to acceptance is psychological. They might lack the energy or confidence to move forward. Yet, despite those barriers, success will prove impossible for anyone who tries to take *small* steps. Unlike the other stages of grieving, acceptance is a choice. A big one. It requires commitment and, consequently, a radical leap forward. Like jumping from one rooftop to another, safely reaching the other side demands courage. Those who jump halfheartedly will find the end of the journey extraordinarily painful.

ACCEPTANCE AND THE FIVE Cs OF CULTURAL CHANGE

THREE WEARY TRAVELERS WANDERING THROUGH the desert find themselves in a desperate search for water. One of them spots a wall ahead in the distance. The men run toward it as fast as they can. Standing in front of the massive structure, stretching miles in opposite directions, they can find no way around or through it. One of the men climbs on the shoulders of his fellow travelers to see what is on the other side. He lets out a yelp of elation, hoists himself over, and disappears behind the wall. The second man follows him, scurrying over the wall with delight. The third man, with great difficulty, manages to scuttle up the wall to see what the other eager travelers have found. Looking down, he sees a cool, verdant garden with luscious fruit trees, a waterfall, and birds of different colors strolling the grounds. But instead of following his companions, the man jumps back down and begins to pace the grounds outside, waiting for other weary travelers to help over the wall.

This ancient Buddhist parable describes a bodhisattva, a person of compassion put on earth to save the suffering. This sacred role, which requires great personal sacrifice, mirrors the virtues of medical practice. As healers, doctors have traditionally put the needs of others ahead of their own. In the twenty-first century, however, physicians are focused on their own suffering. Hundreds of thousands of doctors from all specialties and backgrounds are experiencing dissatisfaction, fatigue, and unfulfillment. They feel beaten down, frustrated, and burned-out. They long for a return to the days when practicing medicine brought peace of mind and professional pride. But in today's world, they find the path to both destinations blocked.

Doctors have voiced their discontent, telling the world all about the problems they face. They've called out the individuals they believe to be responsible for harming them and their patients. They've outlined their demands, detailing how the healthcare system should change and the remedies they expect from its biggest players. They've emptied their lungs crying out for help, and they're losing patience waiting for relief. So far, no one has come to their rescue. Hanging in the air of silence is a sobering message: *Medice, cura te ipsum*. Physician, heal thyself.

After denial, anger, bargaining, and depression comes the final, massive step. Accepting the need to change, and making the commitment required to transform healthcare, will be an agonizing process. For many physicians, acceptance will feel unfair, like personal defeat. After battling the system for years, doctors are likely to find that acceptance is akin to surrendering their cultural values and beliefs to the enemy. Based on Kübler-Ross's model, however, that's the wrong mindset.

Coming to grips with healthcare's new normal does not suggest that physicians must be happy about the changes they need to make to their practice and their culture. Acceptance is not about feeling good in the face of loss. It is about acknowledging the reality and inevitability of change, and then deciding to move forward.

Physicians won't be alone in this journey. Every industry, not just medicine, will confront a new normal. For doctors, choosing acceptance will mean adopting new norms, updating expectations, and leading the transformation of medical practice, despite the discomfort. Acceptance in a postpandemic healthcare environment is not choosing today over yesterday. It is about redefining the future.

Doctors will experience this process as loss. They will need to let go of the fee-for-service reimbursement system. They will need to sacrifice some of their freedom. They will be forced to relinquish their roles as cowboys and take their place among the pit crew.

Some physicians will remain angry or depressed and, in either case, unable to let go of the past. Others will discover that the future offers them opportunities to replace what has been lost with a new identity and sense of purpose. Evidence-based practices aren't necessarily the most enjoyable way to provide medical care, but they lead to better outcomes for patients. Being part of a team isn't as special as being a solo superstar, but the camaraderie feels good. Making medical care more efficient is harder than increasing the amount of care provided, but it is the right thing to do. Physicians may regret what must be sacrificed, but those who complete this phase of the grieving process can find contentment and a renewed sense of fulfillment. With acceptance, physicians can begin to heal themselves.

Across my leadership career, I've faced the challenge of helping thousands of doctors overcome a variety of losses. Some situations involved learning to accept the need for systemic and operational improvements. Others demanded that physicians make difficult cultural adjustments. Along the way, I've achieved success at times and found failure too.

Based on these experiences, I offer the Five *C*s of Cultural Change. I wouldn't dare claim these are the only ways to evolve complex organizations or help people move forward. But for anyone uncertain how to begin, consider this a starter's guide for the perplexed. Each of the Five *C*s are anchored in healthcare, but they will prove equally useful to leaders in areas like business, education, the arts, or public service. In fact, they'll be of help to leaders in any organization needing to move its culture forward in a world turned upside down.

The Five *C*s of Cultural Change
1. Confront

The first step toward solving any problem is admitting one exists. In American medicine, cultural change will only begin when doctors acknowledge and confront their role in making US healthcare the most expensive and least effective system in the developed world.

This process proves difficult in a culture that teaches doctors to deny and repress the truth. Overcoming psychological defenses is never easy. Leaders can assist others by pointing out the difficult facts, offering support, and making sure all individuals face up to (rather than deny) reality.

Fifteen years ago, leaders in the Permanente Medical Group saw an opportunity to lead the nation in patient safety. Doing so required a combination of systemic and cultural changes. As a first step toward reducing medical errors and preventing future mistakes, we zeroed in on malpractice claims. Helping doctors *confront* their role in medical mistakes was a vital first step.

Being on the receiving end of a malpractice lawsuit is one of the worst experiences in any physician's life. It puts doctors in a dangerous psychological state. They feel personally attacked, bringing up deep-seated emotions that may include shame, insecurity, and fear. At work, they may become resentful or distracted. Either feeling can put patients at risk, exacerbating the threat of committing future medical errors.

The approach we adopted helped physicians lower their defenses, confront their role in the problem, and overcome cultural resistance to change. It began as soon as the plaintiffs' attorneys mailed notice of intent to sue. These documents were always sent to both the individual doctors and our entire medical group (the more defendants and the deeper the pockets, the greater the potential payout).

Rather than just waiting for the case to go to trial, as in the past, our medical group began a new, more proactive approach. Upon receiving notification, we reached out to all physicians named in the lawsuit and offered confidential psychological support. An important element of this outreach was making sure the physician understood that frustration and distress were normal feelings. For many, this simple acknowledgment helped legitimize the emotions involved.

As a next step toward helping people confront their role in contributing to the problem that occurred, we gathered a team of clinical experts to review the circumstances of the alleged mistake and find out if anything could be done to minimize the risks going forward. Sometimes complications arose because a single doctor lacked knowledge or technical skill. In those situations, we offered the person additional training and proctoring so as to protect future patients.

At other times, entire departments were responsible. In those cases, we hosted mandatory education sessions and put in place detailed quality-improvement programs. Prior to this process, particularly when lawsuits were resolved without going to trial, doctors and their clinical departments could deny their role in causing harm and hence fail to learn from the event or make the needed improvements. Under the new approach, they had no choice but to confront and address their shortcomings.

Although the process was painful, forcing doctors to confront the problem helped preserve the careers and well-being of dozens of physicians while preventing injury to countless patients. Combined with other medical group changes during the first five years of the program, we lowered our malpractice payments to half the state average.

In US healthcare, there are dozens of problems that doctors will need to confront going forward. They include the profession's reliance on unnecessary procedures for revenue, the worship of costly and dangerous interventions, the downplaying of preventive care, the failure to offer more convenient scheduling and telemedicine services, and the lack of coordination between specialists.

Further, doctors will need to confront the many harmful biases that have endured throughout the history of American medicine. The ugly stains of racism, sexism, and elitism are remnants of an insular culture that will have to be addressed. These forms of mistreatment have violated the doctor's promise to "first, do no harm," leaving many patients to suffer needlessly. They have resulted in the exclusion of many talented would-be physicians from the medical profession. This, too, has inflicted harm on patients.

Because two-thirds of doctors are unaware of their own implicit biases, physicians will need to look for evidence of bigotry or exclusion in their practices. Though it will be unpleasant for many proud and prominent doctors to seek out and confront these prejudices, doing so will help them earn the trust of their patients and improve the medical care they provide.

The lesson: Every industry has an invisible gorilla—a problem or challenge that people fail to see even though it's right in front of them.

In medicine, doctors call out the malfunctions of the healthcare system while never noticing an equally sizable problem staring them in the face. Physician culture causes harm to patients, burns out doctors, and has sped up the downfall of our nation's health. Until doctors recognize and confront their contributions to the failures of American medicine, physician culture will continue to inflict harm.

2. Commit

Confronting the truth is an important first step toward meaningful progress, but it means nothing without the intention to act. Firefighters can *confront* the reality that a building is on fire, but it takes *commitment* to run in and save lives. The following is an example of how doctors in our medical group committed to a risky technology project that saved and improved millions of lives.

Nowadays, physicians have a love-hate relationship with the electronic health record (EHR). These computer systems are clunky, cumbersome, and time-consuming. Yet doctors know they can't provide excellent medical care without the information they contain. EHRs give physicians fast and reliable access to patient medical histories, prescription records, and test results. They help hospitals reduce medical errors, shorten inpatient stays, and produce better clinical outcomes than the old paper records ever could.

By the 1990s, information technology was transforming practically every American industry. Healthcare was a notable holdout. One survey from 1998 showed only 2 percent of US healthcare providers had successfully implemented a fully operational computer system.

Looking back, I can understand why large healthcare organizations were reluctant to purchase an EHR system. Connecting thousands of physicians digitally is neither cheap nor easy. Kaiser Permanente was looking at a multibillion-dollar investment in an uncertain technology at a time when two-thirds of US households still didn't have an internet connection.

Had the effort fallen short of expectations, our organization might never have recovered from the financial damage. On the other hand, success would create the opportunity to dramatically improve our clinical outcomes and give patients a far more convenient healthcare experience. We decided to move forward despite the risks.

Success would require that all physicians be willing to use the same computer system and data entry protocols. Without the "all-in" commitment of our ten thousand doctors (and the clinical staff who support them) failure would have been inevitable.

As leaders, we were asking a lot of professionals who were neither digital experts nor technophiles at the start of the century. A survey from that time showed less than one-quarter of all physicians were "open-minded" about using new computer technologies. Hardly any of them owned a home computer, and even fewer had taken a typing class.

Getting physicians up to speed on the EHR system was going to take time, which there's never enough of in medicine. Doctors were going to need to master both a new technology and a new workflow while caring for a full panel of patients. The EHR would require doctors to spend more time inputting medical data, not less, at least at first. Rather than jotting a few sentences in a paper medical record as they had done before, physicians would have to abide by the software's commands. The new system required doctors to fully document patient encounters. That meant keeping track of much more information than before, mastering a litany of dropdown menus, and immediately responding to clinical alerts every time the computer identified and flagged a potential patient problem. To maximize collaboration, doctors would need to spend time in the evenings and on weekends meeting with colleagues to create shared computer shortcuts, including dot phrases and macros (single commands that would generate a series of computer actions).

We expected physicians to resist such a major operational change— one that would reduce their independence, demand greater collaboration across specialties, and require time to master something they never asked for in the first place. Earning their commitment required that leaders go the extra mile too.

Through townhall meetings, physician leaders from the regional executive staff and each of the nineteen medical centers made appeals to every doctor's heart and mind. Acknowledging that the new computer system would leach time from their workdays, leaders asked physicians to consider the benefits for patients. It would be impossible to provide excellent care without full and immediate access to comprehensive medical information, they explained. And although the data entry process would be clunky and disruptive, doctors needed to remember how many medical errors had been caused by poor communication between clinicians and by sloppy handwriting (one report from that time period indicated that 1.5 million injuries occurred each year because pharmacists or hospital workers misread a doctor's handwriting). Finally, they assured the doctors that assistance and tech support would be available 24/7.

In those sessions, regional and medical center leaders spent hours addressing concerns around data security, patient privacy, and the rollout process. What would happen if the system crashed and nobody could access medical records? What if the data got hacked? What if a patient sends an email when the doctor is out of the office?

None of these were easy questions to answer, but the leaders did a great job of listening and responding to every concern. Our medical group paid clinicians extra for the time it took to learn the new system. We brought in *locum tenens* (substitute) physicians to assist with patient care during the daytime training sessions. Then we asked for more feedback, listened carefully, and responded accordingly.

I wish I had recorded those meetings. In the room, both sides of the physician culture warred with each other for weeks. The autonomy-loving side worried that executive leaders would use the digitized information to add more metrics to the performance reports. The patient-loving side talked about the opportunity to save lives. Some doctors feared they'd become data entry clerks and lose their relative status. Others reveled in the idea of winning even more of their patients' trust. This battle pitted the desire for independence against the instinct to help those in need. The fear of uncertainty clashed with the opportunity to lead the nation in patient safety.

By the end of these sessions, nearly all physicians were committed to doing whatever was needed to achieve success. Without their commitments, the process would have undoubtedly failed.

Across the next fifteen years, the return on investment for the EHR system was undeniably huge. Kaiser Permanente's market share (the percentage of insured patients who received all their medical care through KP) rose from 34 percent to 46 percent. Superb physicians from across the nation chose to join our medical group, many of them recognizing that comprehensive patient information leads to superior clinical outcomes. Quality scores skyrocketed too: We reduced patient deaths from heart attacks, strokes, cancer, HIV/AIDS, and sepsis by more than 30 percent compared to national averages. Despite the challenges that remained with EHRs, subsequent physician surveys indicated that none of the doctors in our group would choose to abandon them and return to paper records.

In the postcoronavirus era, physicians will need to commit to change and find innovative medical solutions with fewer financial resources. It is one thing to say, "we must improve." It is quite another to take the risk and the steps needed to improve.

The lesson: Every American workforce is currently navigating some kind of major threat—be it automation, outsourcing, or economic hardship. In every industry there will be people who will try to hold on to the past, hoping the old normal will return. But that won't be possible. In each case people have to commit to new ways of working or commit to finding new work elsewhere. No matter how painful or fear-inducing it may be, successful change won't happen without an "all-in" commitment.

3. Connect

In any organization that undergoes extensive change, there are always some employees who adapt to new modes of working faster than others. Rather than punishing those who lag, there's a better approach: connect those who are struggling with those who are succeeding.

We used this concept following the implementation of the Affordable Care Act in 2010. The legislation created a surge of more than nine million newly insured Americans between 2013 and 2014 alone. During that period, Kaiser Permanente added hundreds of thousands more patients than in a typical year. To handle the higher demand for medical services, the Permanente Medical Group (TPMG) hired over two thousand recently graduated physicians in just eighteen months (three times the normal number). As residents, these doctors were used to seeing about half as many patients as experienced TPMG physicians do.

Our normal approach was to ease inexperienced doctors into the rigors of full-time practice over a two-year buffering period. But with nearly half a million new members, taking it slow wasn't an option.

To help our new physicians adapt to more intense workplace demands, we borrowed an approach from husband-and-wife philanthropists Jerry and Monique Sternin. In the 1990s, while working with the Save the Children program in Vietnam, the couple promoted the concept of *positive deviance*, an idea popularized by brothers Chip and Dan Heath in their book *Switch*.

Jerry and Monique had been assigned to help some of the poorest rice farmers in Southeast Asia reverse a troubling norm: more than 90 percent of Vietnamese children were malnourished. Their approach, in retrospect, sounds obvious, but it went against the grain of every prior attempt to address the issue. Rather than trying to solve the dozens of *problems* contributing to malnutrition—including Vietnam's shoddy infrastructure, poor education system, economic disparities, and weak crop selection—the Sternins set out to learn from the *successes* of the few families with well-nourished children.

They went from village to village and asked the mothers of the healthiest kids to explain in detail what foods they served their families. They then contrasted the diets of those children with everyone else's. In one town, parents added the green tops of local plants to their kids' meals. Moms in another village cooked with the addition of tiny crustacean-like animals that lived in the rice fields. The Sternins realized right away these mealtime enhancers were providing essential vitamins, proteins, and other nutrients to children's diets. But rather than lecturing parents on the science of proper nutrition, the Sternins simply encouraged all families to emulate those with the healthiest kids.

Everywhere the couple looked, they uncovered new and useful solutions that could be adopted by local families. Ultimately, the Sternins helped reverse decades of malnutrition in the villages—not by trying to identify and solve all the contributing problems, but by learning from the rare success stories and spreading those solutions from one mother to another.

This "positive deviance" model proved highly effective in helping new doctors in our medical group adjust to a heavier workload. Modifying the concept to fit our needs, we identified doctors who had adjusted exceptionally well to a more robust practice shortly after graduation. Somehow, through trial and error, the successful ones had discovered innovative ways to organize their clinical practice and reduce stress. To scale this approach, the medical group funded a mentorship program called Doctors Helping Doctors. The more successful physicians were given a paid half day each week to spend with their newly hired colleagues. Sitting side by side, the well-adjusted physicians would show their colleagues a variety of computer shortcuts and ways to manage their days more efficiently.

This $10 million investment proved to be financially shrewd. Physician satisfaction rose significantly, reaching levels 20 percent higher than those reported in statewide surveys. Two years following the program, 98 percent of the doctors who were newly hired at the time were still with the medical group. So rather than having to replace burned-out doctors and fill unanticipated vacancies, we ended up fully staffed with more excellent candidates applying to our group than we could possibly hire.

In the future, as physicians from solo practices join medical groups, and as doctors switch from fee-for-service to capitation, some will struggle with the transition while others will quickly achieve success. Connecting the successful doctors with their struggling colleagues will help to improve the performance of the entire medical group or organization.

The lesson: People can learn a lot from their mistakes, but they can learn a lot more from emulating the positive accomplishments of others. Regardless of the industry, look for success stories, and find ways to scale them.

4. Collaborate

Often departments within the same organization will see each other as rivals, vying for higher status and more resources. But improving organizational performance demands that professionals assume complementary, not competing, roles. Getting people to work cooperatively rather than against one another isn't easy, especially during times of rapid change and significant uncertainty. One way to promote collaboration is making sure everyone shares responsibility for the organization's wins and losses.

In medicine, doctors who work in integrated healthcare settings (with various specialties connected both physically by location and digitally through a common electronic health record) are able to accomplish what no individual physician can achieve alone. Whereas the traditional physician culture celebrates the superstar, organizations that successfully raise quality and lower costs find ways to transition from an "I" model to a "we" mentality. Regardless of whether doctors work in Accountable Care Organizations, large academic medical centers, or multispecialty medical groups, they provide more value to patients when they work together toward common goals rather than when they compete for individual recognition and rewards.

Recognizing the value of teamwork, TPMG introduced the concept of *group excellence* several years ago. Rather than pitting doctors against one another, we emphasized the value of collaborative performance: helping physicians in each specialty and in every medical center match the performance of the best.

To motivate people to help one another, we defined success based on how our medical group performed when compared to the roughly one thousand other medical groups in the United States. Importantly, we *did not* single out physicians who scored at the top, nor did we embarrass those in the lower quartile. Rather, we looked for opportunities whereby everyone could improve. To borrow a baseball analogy, we didn't try to select an MVP or a batting champion. Instead, we focused solely on what it would take for us to win the World Series.

As healthcare organizations move away from individual offices toward more integrated care-delivery models, they will benefit by emphasizing interprofessional collaboration over competition. As an added benefit, this approach reverses some of the cultural issues that contribute to physician burnout, including medicine's unhealthy obsession with status. Pitting one physician against another means that there invariably will be "winners" and "losers." In an integrated healthcare model, particularly one that's capitated, everyone can win through the success of the collective.

At the beginning of our programmatic focus on "group excellence," Kaiser Permanente was ranked above average in quality by the National Committee for Quality Assurance but was not exceptional. By the end, our medical group was rated the best in the nation. In addition, collaboration allowed our organization to earn the number one rating for customer service in both California and the mid-Atlantic states, according to J.D. Power.

The lesson: In every industry, the measurements and indicators of success used in the past won't suffice in the future. All organizations have the option of driving individuals to work harder. Successful organizations understand that the better option is working smarter through increased collaboration.

5. Contribute

Prior to COVID-19, I often heard doctors complain that the computerization of medicine had eroded their creativity and autonomy. Others told me that online rating and review sites were undermining the importance of the doctor-patient relationship. Still others lamented that the long hours and endless administrative tasks had stripped them of their passion for medicine.

Although there is some truth in each of these assertions, doctors across the nation are so angered and saddened by what has been taken from them, they rarely focus on all that they give. As a profession, medicine was built around a noble purpose: to help and heal those in need. Helping not only heals the patient; it heals the doctor as well. I have witnessed this phenomenon firsthand many times.

I saw it in a young medical student named Graham whom I met in Washington, DC. He is one of those people who seems to have been born with a desire to assist others. In grade school he'd sneak out of church services to look after the babies in the nursery downstairs. Growing up, he'd go with his parents into nursing homes and "sing with the old folks." Like many physicians I know, Graham grew up a giver.

A few summers ago, Graham gave someone the gift of a lifetime. While in between his second and third years at the George Washington University School of Medicine and Health Sciences, he donated a kidney to a complete stranger. When we spoke about it in 2018, he struggled to explain why he had done it. The idea came to him while sitting in the medical school library, reading about polycystic kidney disease.

"I turned to my friend and said, 'We should donate a kidney.'" His friend laughed, but Graham was serious. He didn't know anyone who needed one, but it was something he felt compelled to do. And so Graham consented to surgery and had his kidney removed. Minutes later, the organ was on a plane to Georgia heading toward a waiting recipient, which kicked off a chain of kidney donations to nearly a dozen others. "I donated a kidney to somebody, and their loved one donated to somebody, and then their loved one donated to somebody."

Today Graham's giving spirit continues. He and his wife foster children while he pursues a medical career that's focused on improving the health of marginalized communities. But for all the do-goodery, Graham is careful not to call his actions altruistic. "I do think that there is a self-serving aspect to my decisions," he said, adding, "I wouldn't do them if I didn't find them fulfilling and rewarding."

And that's the point: helping people in need not only heals the patient, it heals the doctor. So much of what doctors find fulfilling and rewarding about medicine is gone. That is why giving—connecting to a higher purpose, even if for self-serving reasons—can return to doctors that feeling of mission they've lost.

I saw this same desire to help in a man I met out West named Nathaniel, who goes by Nat. He was born with achromatopsia, which left him without cone cells in his retinas. With this condition, Nat can see just about as well as a person who walks out a dark movie theater and looks straight up at the sun: everything is too bright to focus on. In addition to light sensitivity, Nat also can't see color and has a reduced field of vision. All this combined makes him legally blind.

Growing up, Nat was a musician. He played guitar with bands in the Bay Area, wrote music, and even scored a small record contract. But when he realized his ambitions of making it big in the music industry weren't panning out, he turned to a field where success would prove even harder to achieve. Nat wanted to go to medical school.

The big problem, he discovered, was that medical schools aren't designed for people who are legally blind. He applied to a total of eighteen universities and was eventually accepted to UCSF. There he struggled and faced a ton of obstacles on his path to earning a medical degree. I can't imagine how difficult it must have been for him to learn physical diagnosis or complete the surgical rotations. But Nat knew if he could finish the journey, he could offer unique perspectives and mentorship to both patients and colleagues alike.

Pursuing a medical degree "was, objectively, not the smart thing to do," he said, "but you do it because you're a person who thinks there is change to be made, and I want a role in making change happen."

Nat did make change happen. After graduating from his program with the prestigious Gold-Headed Cane Award, a recognition from his classmates that Nat embodies the qualities of a true physician, he now serves as medical director for practice innovation at UCSF Health. There he developed an e-consult program, which gives primary care providers timely access to specialty expertise and gives patients the opportunity to connect with a specialist from the primary care doctor's office, thus saving on travel, missed work, and other costs.

Nat's is a story of struggle, but not one that ever led to regret or a sense of entitlement. In his quest to become a doctor, Nat found opportunity and gratitude. Like Graham, he realized that medicine not only heals the patient, it also heals the doctor.

Finally, I saw the healing power of giving in December 2004, when a devastating tsunami struck the island nation of Sri Lanka, killing tens of thousands and leaving more than a million homeless. Almost immediately, local clinics reached capacity as infectious diseases like cholera, measles, and malaria threatened much of the coastal belt. Upon hearing the news, I wrote a "send-all" email to the physicians of TPMG, offering to provide transportation and medical supplies to any doctor who was willing to travel to Sri Lanka on short notice and volunteer to provide emergency relief services.

In the interest of full disclosure, I gave the recipients of this email informed consent, explaining the risks involved in the relief effort. Doctors were likely to find contaminated water and a food shortage in the wake of the tsunami. On top of that, Sri Lanka had been tangled in civil war for decades. These were dangerous circumstances to be sure.

I hit the send button, hoping a handful of physicians would volunteer. Given that it was the December break for schoolchildren, I didn't expect a big response. But by the next morning, more than two hundred physicians had replied, many of them while on vacation with their families. I was inspired and humbled by their desire to help people who were suffering more than nine thousand miles away.

We quickly partnered with a global relief organization to coordinate the air and ground transportation as well as find housing. For the next several months we sent a succession of teams to Sri Lanka, initially to provide emergency medical care to the tsunami victims, then to address the psychological problems of families who had lost loved ones, and, finally, to treat the long-term infectious disease epidemics that ensued. In total, more than twenty thousand lives were saved by these heroic volunteers.

Other relief missions followed. In 2005, dozens of TPMG physicians provided medical assistance to the victims of Hurricane Katrina. In 2010, our doctors again volunteered, this time in Haiti after a powerful earthquake toppled buildings and left thousands of people trapped beneath the rubble.

In 2014, when the Ebola epidemic struck in West Africa, physicians risked their lives to provide medical treatment for victims of this devastating infection. On these volunteer trips, doctors worked fourteen to sixteen hours each day, often in scorching heat. In Africa, confronted with the dual threat of 120-degree temperatures and a deadly virus, doctors had to receive IV fluids to sustain hydration while wearing protective full-body suits as they provided medical care to patients. They did all this without pay or complaint.

Compared to working in hot, dirty, and underresourced environments, you'd think the American medical office—with its air-conditioning, comfortable furniture, indoor plumbing, and steady pay—would feel like a vacation. The opposite proves true.

Upon returning home from these mission trips overseas, not a single physician mentioned the travails of practicing medicine in such difficult conditions. To a person, they spoke of the camaraderie, sense of purpose, and memories they will cherish for the rest of their lives. This is physician culture at its best.

Though giving more of one's time may seem absurd to doctors who bemoan "too much work and not enough money," doing so proves an effective stepping-stone toward greater fulfillment in both medicine and life. The path to professional contentment will demand courage as doctors take unfamiliar steps toward a new set of cultural norms, values, and principles. Make no mistake. This journey will be hard and painful but ultimately rewarding.

It is said that in 1666, Christopher Wren, history's most famous architect, was commissioned to rebuild St. Paul's Church after the great London fire. Five years later, with construction under way, he is said to have encountered three bricklayers. He asked them, "What are you doing?" The first replied, "Laying bricks to feed my family." The second said, "Building a wall as contracted." The third responded, "Constructing a cathedral to God." The point, he proffered, is that a job becomes a career and ends up a calling. Nowhere is this sequence more relevant or important than in medicine.

The lesson: Helping not only enriches the lives of others but enriches the lives of those who choose to help. In a postcoronavirus world, people in every industry have the opportunity to help those in need. Those who do will add meaning to their work and to their lives.

THE VIRTUES OF BEING DIFFICULT

G IVEN THE SCARCITY OF LITERATURE and discourse on physician culture, doctors are largely unaware of the influence it exerts over their thoughts and actions. As they go about their routines, they make hundreds, even thousands, of daily decisions based on the norms and beliefs they internalized early in their training.

As a result, we know that physician culture can affect patients in big ways and small, occasionally resulting in unintended harm. As US healthcare completes its transformation toward a more efficient and effective future, Americans will need to protect themselves and their families from those aspects of physician culture that lead to poorer outcomes and higher costs.

Although patients themselves cannot transform this culture, they can influence physicians' actions. Behaviors, unlike beliefs, can be modified quickly. And that process can begin as soon as patients demand it.

This chapter contains nine sets of questions that will help protect you and your family from the negative aspects of physician culture while helping to accelerate the transformation of medical practice. The doctor-patient relationship today is an asymmetrical one, with doctors playing the part of authority figure. That's why asking these questions will feel uncomfortable for most patients: They challenge the traditional power structure. Nevertheless, every person seeking medical care has the ethical and legal right to demand answers. Don't be afraid to be a "difficult" patient. After all, it's your health at stake.

Fans of *Seinfeld* might recall one especially cringeworthy episode in which Elaine Benes, a lead character, gets caught peeking at her medical chart, something almost no patient would think about doing in the 1990s. There, written in pen, she sees the word "Difficult." Frazzled, Elaine attempts to explain herself to the physician.

"You know, I noticed that somebody wrote in my chart that I was difficult in January of '92, and I have to tell you that I remember that appointment, exactly. You see this nurse asked me to put a gown on, but there was a mole on my shoulder, and I specifically wore a tank top so I wouldn't have to put a gown on. You know they're made of paper."

Of course, Elaine's explanation only confirms that she is indeed difficult. And despite the comedic absurdity of this plotline, the episode hits on a real source of anxiety for patients. Nobody wants to be labeled "difficult." Patients worry that stating an objection or questioning the physician's expertise will compromise the care they receive. It is this fear of offending the doctor that helps explain why people tolerate long wait times, unclear medical explanations, and rudeness in the doctor's office.

But when the norms of physician culture stand in the way of excellent care, patients benefit by speaking up, asking questions, and deciding what is best for their own health. Although it takes courage to do so, once enough patients raise the questions outlined in this chapter and insist on getting honest answers, the behaviors of physicians will change. And so, too, will their culture.

Not every set of questions on the following pages will be relevant for each medical visit or individual. The first five questions will apply to the greatest number of patients and medical encounters, whereas the final four affect a narrower group of people with more complicated healthcare needs. If it helps to remember, consider taking a photo of these pages, or jot down some notes on an index card the next time you visit with a physician.

THE NINE QUESTIONS PATIENTS SHOULD ASK THEIR DOCTORS

1. What's this going to cost me?

The doctor's cultural bias: In polite society, it's rude to discuss money. In physician culture, it's similarly taboo to factor the cost of care into clinical decision making. Physicians believe their job is to treat disease and save a life at any cost, not to offer price comparisons for medications, surgeries, or diagnostic tests.

Relevant background: This thinking not only is outdated but also wastes patients' hard-earned money. Because doctors are always in a rush, they schedule procedures and write prescriptions out of habit, rarely considering the price when making these quick decisions. As a result, patients overpay for operations done in the hospital when outpatient surgicenters offer identical outcomes at lower prices. Patients also overpay for brand-name drugs even when there are chemically identical generics available. Finally, some specialists, like anesthesiologists and surgeons, use out-of-network billing as a common way to garner added income, thus hitting patients with surprise medical bills.

Related questions for the patient: Are you in my insurance network? Is the hospital you are recommending for my procedure in my insurance network? Will all the doctors (including your assistant surgeon and the anesthesiologist) be in my network? Are there less expensive medications or ways to address my problem? And if so, how will the outcome be affected (if at all)?

The desired behavior: These cost-related questions are designed to disrupt the doctor's automatic thoughts and behaviors. They force the physician to consider equally effective, lower-priced solutions. Doctors may not prefer to provide a detailed breakdown of costs and benefits for the care they recommend. But when patients take the time to ask, the care they receive proves less expensive yet no less effective.

2. Did you wash your hands?

The cultural bias: Doctors understand the dangers of not washing their hands. They can explain exactly how germs and diseases are transmitted through poor hand hygiene, and they know full well that hospital-acquired infections (HAIs) are the fourth leading cause of death in the

United States. Nevertheless, physicians fail to wash their hands as much as one-third of the time, according to clinical research studies. That's because doctors see themselves as healers—incapable of spreading disease to patients—and are therefore entitled to skip this important step.

Relevant background: Not all restaurants have the same standards of cleanliness, and the same is true of healthcare facilities. Rates of HAIs vary greatly by location, and each state has different reporting requirements, which you can find online. Patients who start there will be better armed with information on hospital cleanliness and compliance before going in for treatment.

Related questions for the patient: Will you and everyone else involved in treating me observe proper hand hygiene today? Did you wash your hands before you came into this exam room/hospital room? What is the rate of hospital-acquired infection in this facility (or in the facility you are planning to use for my procedure)? How do these numbers compare with other hospitals in the community?

The desired behavior: You want all physicians caring for you to wash their hands every time they come near you. When you ask about hospital infection rates, your doctor will probably refer you to the administrator's office. But by asking these questions, you are reminding the physician how important this step is for *your* health. The doctor is more likely to observe proper hand hygiene when you make it clear that you are paying attention. Over time asking these questions will lead to a permanent shift in physician behavior and an overall reduction in preventable hospital deaths.

3. Can I email, text, or virtually visit with you?

The cultural bias: Doctors have always assumed that the best medical care is provided in their offices and not via video or email. As a result, patients are forced to miss work and endure unnecessary inconveniences when receiving routine medical care.

Relevant background: It took a global pandemic to help doctors and patients realize the benefits of virtual care. Not only did telemedicine keep doctors and patients safer during a viral outbreak (by keeping them apart), the experience helped everyone realize how many problems could be resolved through this widely available and convenient form of technology. Whether doctors continue to offer telehealth solutions in the future will depend on two factors. One is whether Congress permanently eases regulations around the reimbursement of video visits and interstate licensing. The other is whether patients demand these services.

Related questions for the patient: Can I make future appointments online rather than by phone? Is there any way to get some of my care through video rather than in person? Can I email or text you with any questions I have? How can I check the results of my laboratory tests online? How do I access my own medical record online?

The desired behavior: Americans are busy people with overpacked schedules and overflowing to-do lists. Doctors can give their patients relief from worry and stress by offering reliable and private access to online scheduling, video visits, secure emailing, and relevant medical information. Patients can acquire these time-saving conveniences, but only by demanding them.

4. Am I going to be safe?

The cultural bias: Doctors see themselves as excellent caregivers who always put their patients first. Sometimes they do; sometimes they don't. When they don't, it's often because physicians are slow to criticize colleagues who cut corners and fail to report them when they harm patients. In physician culture, doctors protect one another's back.

Relevant background: More than two decades after the Institute of Medicine exposed the problem of patient safety in its report *To Err Is Human*, medical errors remain a huge problem in American hospitals. But it's never easy for patients to figure out whether their doctors (or the places they go for care) are as safe as they should be. That's because most hospitals don't release patient safety statistics to the public, and most physicians don't want to keep track of past complications.

Related questions for the patient: What is the rate of medical error in this hospital (or the hospital you're planning to use for my procedure)? What percentage of your patients experienced a complication after you performed this procedure last year? What percentage of your patients were extremely satisfied with the outcome? What is the worst outcome a patient has ever experienced after you did this procedure?

The desired behavior: When patients consent to a procedure, they are entering into a contract with the doctor that requires full disclosure. Any physician who fails to answer these questions honestly is taking a medical and legal risk. It's important to understand that physicians are legally obligated to disclose what *can* go wrong during a procedure. But when deciding whether to proceed with a doctor's recommendation, patients will want to know how often something *does* go wrong. This line of questioning forces the doctor to tell the whole truth about the risks of moving forward with a procedure.

5. Do you have any conflicts of interest?

The cultural bias: Doctors who accept money and gifts from drug and medical device companies believe these payments in no way affect or influence their medical decisions.

Relevant background: That belief is wrong. There is a reason every peer-reviewed medical journal in the country requires doctors and researchers to disclose potential conflicts of interest when submitting the results of a study. There's also a reason every medical conference that provides continuing medical education credits requires presenters to disclose any and all conflicts. The reason is obvious: When money and gifts exchange hands, the recipients feel obligated to reciprocate, making it impossible to remain unbiased. And yet some US physicians who accept six- and seven-figure annual payments from drugmakers insist they are uninfluenced in their prescribing habits. Multiple studies have proven this assumption false.

Related questions for the patient: Did you receive any money last year from drug or device companies? Did you attend any dinners or events sponsored by the drug company that manufactures the medication you're prescribing to me? Did you accept any gifts or other freebies from the medical device manufacturer of the surgical implant or product you're planning to use?

The desired behavior: Financial advisers who profit from the investment opportunities they recommend are expected to inform their clients of any conflict of interest. Patients are entitled to the same level of transparency and honesty from their doctors. Getting physicians to answer questions about potential conflicts can empower patients to make more informed healthcare decisions. In the end, it's the patient's life and finances that are at risk, not the doctor's.

6. Who's going to coordinate my care?

The cultural bias: Doctors assume every patient's care is well coordinated because they presume all the specialists involved will effectively handle their specific area of expertise, resulting in excellent care overall. The cardiologist will focus on the heart, the nephrologist on the kidneys, the pulmonologist on the lungs, and so on. And having covered all the organs, they believe all the components of care will seamlessly fall into place.

Relevant background: Unfortunately, that's not how well-coordinated care happens. In a medical culture that undervalues primary care doctors and preventive medicine, getting properly coordinated healthcare proves harder than it should be. When doctors work independently rather than collaboratively, patients and their problems fall through the cracks. People who require care from multiple specialists can't assume that their physicians are working closely together to coordinate treatments. The reality is that doctors regularly fail to check in with their colleagues. In our fragmented and dizzying healthcare system, patients need a quarterback: someone who can connect the dots, ward off medical errors, and make sure all physicians are on the same page. Whether patients are enrolled in an HMO, a PPO, or a traditional insurance plan, the best doctor to play quarterback is usually the personal physician.

Related questions for the patient: As my primary care physician, how closely will you work with the specialists involved in my treatment? As my specialist, how closely will you work with my primary care doctor? How will the two of you exchange clinical information to maximize my chances of a successful result? How will you coordinate my medical care with the other specialists treating me, both before and after the procedure you're recommending?

The desired behavior: Patients want all the doctors caring for them to talk frequently with one another and for one of them to be responsible for coordinating the totality of medical treatment provided. Asking questions about teamwork encourages physicians to communicate with one another, consider conflicts in treatment recommendations, and close any care gaps that might exist.

7. Is this procedure or treatment necessary?

The cultural bias: Physicians attach great importance to performing complex procedures. Those who do the most difficult surgeries or complicated interventions sit atop the physician hierarchy.

Relevant background: These perceptions can cloud the doctor's ability to judge whether an operation or treatment is appropriate or even useful. Whether it's surgery for knee pain or yet another painful round of chemotherapy, patients often undergo aggressive interventions, even when data prove they are potentially harmful or no better than a more conservative treatment. Physician culture maintains that "a chance to cut is a chance to cure." To challenge this assumption, patients need to get the facts and ask for evidence of success. If there are no existing data on the probability of success, patients should know that researchers typically only publish results of studies when the outcomes are favorable, not when the approach or treatment fails. So when asking the following questions, watch out for answers like "you can't be sure" or "the only way to know is to try."

Related questions for the patient: What evidence has been published to show that the intervention (procedure, treatment, or medication) you are recommending will work? Is there research and/or data to the contrary? Are there less invasive options that may resolve my problem? Is the probability of success 90 percent or 10 percent? On what basis is that assessment made, and for how long might the benefits last?

The desired behavior: There are no guarantees in medicine, but there are often scientific studies that can give patients a clearer indication of whether an intervention or medication is right for them. By asking these questions, patients can discover whether there is a less invasive alternative or whether the risks of a procedure outweigh the benefits. Either way, patients are better off being an active, not passive, participant in the decisions that impact their health.

8. Are you experienced?

The cultural bias: Physicians define mastery as being able to do a little bit of everything rather than doing one thing exceptionally well. This inch-deep-and-a-mile-wide interpretation of competence is not serving today's patients well.

Relevant background: Doctors find it difficult to admit when they lack the necessary experience or expertise. And they rarely volunteer the names of other doctors who are more skilled or better trained. Before you agree to undergo a major procedure with significant risks, you'll need to do a little homework. First, get a second opinion. Next, check independent research organizations like Leapfrog Group for surgical volume standards. That way you can compare the doctor's experience with the established minimums. Remember: there's no guarantee that a surgeon who performs a procedure fifty times a year is better than one who does it thirty times. But a physician who does only a handful each year is most assuredly less competent than the other two.

Related questions for the patient: How many of these procedures did you perform last year? What do you believe is the minimal number needed each year for optimal outcomes? How many procedures would a doctor need to have performed over the previous twelve months before you'd let them operate on a member of your family? Who in our area has done this operation or procedure the most?

The desired behavior: Doctors would prefer that patients not ask all these questions about their competence. They'd like people to simply trust that the MD in their title connotes excellence in all things medical. But inquiring about the specialist's experience and outcomes is the best way to know for sure how skilled an individual really is. If the answers are unsatisfactory, go elsewhere.

9. Can we talk about the end?

The cultural bias: In the United States, death and dying have become practically unmentionable words. It turns out, doctors are as uncomfortable with the topic as their patients are.

Relevant background: Physicians are trained to never let the patient lose hope, even if that means avoiding the truth about the chances of dying or living in agony. When it comes to discussing death, American culture and physician culture share similar anxieties. For physicians, saving a life is the highest virtue, while losing a patient is tantamount to failure (even when providing more care would have been futile).

Related questions for the patient: Can you tell me the full range of my end-of-life options, so I can make a fully informed decision? Will you make sure my quality-of-life preferences are added to my medical record? How will my quality of life change if I refuse further treatments? When it's clear to me that I don't want any more medical care, will you support my decision and continue to help me? Will you connect me with a hospice center or palliative care expert as soon as I'm eligible? Will I be able to spend my last days at home?

The desired behavior: The desired behavior is to get doctors to tell patients the truth when death is possible, likely, or imminent. Most people nearing death desire two things: They want their physicians to be honest, and they want assurance they won't be abandoned by their doctors regardless of the choice they make. These questions help patients achieve both.

It is said that "silence is golden." And sometimes in life it is better to remain quiet than to speak up. But in the context of being a patient, silence is risky, dangerous, and of no value whatsoever.

MEDICINE: A LOVE STORY

I NEVER MET TWO PEOPLE more in love than my parents, Jack and Lillian. Their story is quintessentially American. They met at Coney Island in the summer of 1941. On the miles-long beach peppered with people, he spotted her in a crowd. Whenever he told the story, he swore it was love at first sight.

He was in the middle of dental school, working nights as a waiter to earn tuition money. She was already a college graduate and had a job as a receptionist in a doctor's office. With so many time constraints, my mother cherished the evenings and Sundays they spent together throughout their early courtship. Life that summer and into the fall was new, exciting, and wonderful.

That winter, on December 7, 1941, Japanese pilots bombed Pearl Harbor. That was the day life changed for Jack, Lillian, their friends, their family, and the world. An oppressive weight fell on the country's collective shoulders. We were at war. Americans felt a sense of urgency amid those uncertain times, and my parents were no different. After dating my mom for only six months, my father asked for her hand in marriage. On October 18, 1942, they said, "I do." She was a beautiful bride. He was a handsome groom. After their nuptials, my father felt a sense of urgency to build a life together and start a family.

Knowing that when he graduated dental school, he would be joining the 101st Airborne and going overseas, he wanted to have a child as soon as possible. His bride, based on those same facts, said no. My mother, ever the realist, didn't know when or if he would return from war or what kind of world would exist when the fighting was over. In her mind it would be unwise to risk the possibility of having to raise a child on her own. Still she promised to wait for him and demanded he return home safely. He wrote her a letter every day they were apart—with two exceptions. On June 6, 1944, he was parachuting over the beaches of Normandy on D-Day, and on June 7, he was captured by the Germans and had to make a daring escape later that night.

When he returned to the United States in late autumn 1945, he was a decorated soldier, a war hero, and a man no less infatuated with my mother than on the first day they met. It was only then, once they were reunited, that she was willing to start a family.

For his entire life, my father was certain my mom was perfect. He said it often, and no one ever doubted that he meant it with all his heart. She, in turn, loved him deeply, as much as he loved her. She adored his starry-eyed optimism, his impetuousness, and his daredevil moxie. But my mother was a realist. She recognized he wasn't perfect.

Nevertheless, throughout their fifty-six-year marriage, my father never saw her any other way. He remained oblivious to any imperfections she might have had. Even on her deathbed, my father saw perfection. He felt as deeply in love with her then as on their wedding day. And until the day she died, my mother could not have imagined loving any man as much as she did my father. Though they loved each other in different ways, I never once doubted the sincerity or depth of their affection for one another.

From both of them I learned the meaning of love. And through their mutual admiration I came to understand that love has many sides and no two people experience it exactly the same way. Shortly after my seventeenth birthday, I began college and soon realized this lesson applied to more than just romantic relationships. Going into my freshman year of college, my plan was to become a university professor. But six months later, my mentor, a brilliant philosophy instructor, was denied tenure because of his political views. That's when I abandoned my plan and decided to embrace what I believed would be a totally apolitical profession:

medicine. As an idealistic youth, I wanted a career that was honest, mission-driven, and free of subjective biases. As a naive undergraduate, I assumed that's what medicine was.

In medical school, that's precisely what I found. My love for medicine was as pure as my father's love for my mother. I could find no flaws. Starting on my first day at Yale, I saw only beauty as I explored the anatomy and physiology of the human body. Even the diseases I encountered while studying pathology and pharmacology added depth to the relationship. In my residency training and early clinical years, medicine filled me with excitement, joy, and purpose. I cherished every moment of being a doctor. Surgery was an art; the human body a canvas. Every surgical mission abroad only served to expand my love for medicine. In my eyes, the profession was perfect. I had found true love.

Over time, however, my love for the profession evolved, becoming more like my mother's love for her husband. Though my ardor and commitment never faltered, the imperfections of medicine gradually came into focus. As a resident, I basked in the bright lights of the operating room but started to recognize the ethical compromises attending physicians made to enhance their income. Once in practice, I still enjoyed curing disease but came to realize how, with better preventive care, many patients could have avoided getting sick in the first place. As the dense fog of infatuation began to lift, I recognized flaws I hadn't before. Slowly the physician culture came into view. I saw its faults and virtues and endless contradictions. There were parts of it I embraced even tighter and parts I couldn't accept.

Across my career I've watched this culture do wonders, and I've watched it inflict harm. I've seen it destroy lives and change them for the better. I've recognized the many ways it can hoist up physicians and make them great or tear them down and hurt patients in the process.

I continue to marvel at the duality of physician culture: at all the ways it adds meaning to the lives of doctors and all the ways it saps their spirits. When a physician shows empathy and compassion to a patient, when it's just two people engaged in the ancient ritual of giving and receiving medical care, I see a culture at its best. I cherish that part of medicine's five-thousand-year history. But I also shudder at the toll it takes on both parties. It can drive doctors to put themselves ahead of their patients while denying and repressing the horrific consequences of their actions. This culture can be a faithful companion, a demanding teacher, and a destructive force all in the same day.

Unlike my parents, whose faults were minor in comparison to their virtues, the physician culture complicates my love of medicine. There are aspects of the profession I deeply admire. And there are parts I am ashamed of and hope to change. Acknowledging its problems doesn't mean I love medicine any less. In fact, I adore it as much now as I did when I first chose it. But rather than ignoring or trying to hide its failings, I've explored them and laid them bare before you. My desire in doing so isn't to castigate the culture, belabor its shortcomings, or embarrass individual doctors. Instead, my hope is to improve healthcare delivery in our nation, evolve physician culture, and restore the joys that have been stripped from the profession.

———————

IT IS A GEOLOGICAL FACT that two nearly identical raindrops, falling side by side, can land just inches apart in the watersheds of the Great Divide, high up in the Rocky Mountains, and end up in two different oceans. One drains into the Pacific, and the other flows all the way to the Atlantic, three thousand miles east.

I've seen with my own eyes how physicians who are equally skilled, passionate, and dedicated can end up on opposite sides of the profession with only the slightest shift in circumstance. To help you understand what I mean, I'd like to tell you about three doctors. One got lost in a crisis of his own creation. The others remain perfectly satisfied.

Let's begin with a colleague and friend, whom I'll call Mike. He was and still is a skilled surgeon with impeccable credentials and a profound commitment to delivering excellent patient care. Mike and I first met in 2009, five years after he completed his training and opened his office in Northern California. We became fast friends.

In our conversations, Mike confessed that while his solo practice was going well, the economic recession had drained much of the pleasure from his work. Insurance companies were squeezing his payments and threatening to cut him from their networks if he refused to accept the lower fees. He felt powerless to resist.

Mike asked whether he should abandon private practice to join a larger healthcare organization. I told him it wasn't for me to say. That's not because I didn't have a personal preference. I believe group practice to be more rewarding for both doctors and patients, but I recognize there are trade-offs to both.

Mike decided to stick it out with private practice initially, but the following year, he received more threatening letters from insurance companies with even lower proposed fees. Enough was enough. He took a job with a competitor of Kaiser Permanente. For the first couple of years, he loved working in a medical group, having colleagues to rely on (and to cover him during nights and weekends). No longer subject to the ebbs and flows of his office income, he appreciated the financial security that came with the organization's size. But with each passing year, new and unexpected problems sprouted.

As the medical group added specialists in hand surgery and cranio-facial surgery, Mike no longer took care of patients in need of tendon or cleft-lip repair. He'd always found those procedures fulfilling and resented having to give them up. Slowly, his practice narrowed such that the majority of his patients were either women seeking breast surgeries or elderly patients with lower-extremity ulcers. Occasionally, someone with a cyst or minor skin cancer would get referred his way, or he would be called to the ER to treat a patient with a facial fracture, but those were exceptions. Mike's scope of responsibilities had thinned out, yet his workload was busier than it had been in private practice. The leaders of his medical group were constantly pushing him to generate more RVUs (relative value units, a measure used to calculate a physician's workload and determine fee-for-service reimbursement).

Mike was starting to regret his decision to leave private practice. He knew taking a job as an employed physician would require some sacrifice: less independence for more financial security, a busier workday for a more predictable weekly schedule, and so on. But he never expected he'd feel like such an insignificant cog in a big, plodding machine. And things were about to get much worse.

In the summer of 2018, Mike texted me this tangled, frantic knot of words: *Robbie, I need your help! You know I'm an excellent doctor. I'm being blamed. Can you help me? Let's meet.*

I suggested my favorite Italian restaurant in Palo Alto. Not wanting our conversation overheard, I reserved a table in the piazza, away from the large circular fountain in the center of the outdoor dining area. The waiter handed us dinner menus and recommended Chianti. We ordered two glasses. Eager to hear what was on his mind, I asked my friend what was so urgent. Mike took a generous sip of wine and explained that he was being sued for malpractice.

Using the familiar shorthand of doctors talking shop outside the office, Mike began to reconstruct the events that led him to this moment. The patient was a fifty-two-year-old woman seeking breast reduction surgery. She had a DD cup size and significant lower back pain. As I listened to Mike spell out each step he took, it was obvious why he was such an excellent surgeon. His detailed evaluation and preparation were meticulous and impeccable.

On the day of the surgery, Mike met the patient in the preoperative area and documented the woman's health, noting both normal heart and lung exams. He sat her up and used a pen with permanent ink to measure and mark the planned incision points. Everything sounded perfect to me so far. Mike had done this procedure hundreds of times.

As surgery got under way, Mike incised the left breast, removed the woman's excess skin, then resected the tissue and associated fat. The procedure seemed to be progressing flawlessly; however, after incising through the skin on the right breast, Mike's hand encountered a hard mass directly under the areola.

He sent a small sample to the lab. Fifteen minutes later, the pathologist called to tell him the bad news. The biopsied mass was cancerous. Because the patient was unconscious and couldn't consent to a mastectomy, Mike had no option but to swap out instruments and close the left side. Then he did his best to reapproximate the tissues on the right.

Later that day, while sitting with the patient and her husband, Mike assured them both that everything would be okay. He labeled the operation "a blessing in disguise." *Thank goodness we found the cancer early* on, he told them. He said he would ask his colleague in general surgery to see her later that day. A week later, the surgeon performed a definitive mastectomy. Over the next several months, the woman received radiation therapy and started chemotherapy.

As I watched Mike move his carpaccio around with a fork, he explained that he had just received an "intent to sue" notice from his patient's malpractice attorney. With the woman's cancer having spread to her lungs and liver, Mike told me the lawyer was out for blood. Somehow, at some point between the initial office consultation and surgery, Mike had overlooked a vital piece of information. The results of the mammogram he ordered were logged in the electronic medical record, but he hadn't seen them. The radiology report clearly noted a possible tumor. The radiologist recommended a repeat exam and possible biopsy. The breast reduction surgery never should have taken place.

I could tell that Mike was hurting and afraid. I wasn't sure what to say. Before I could begin, he erupted in anger, listing off by memory all the people who'd let him down and allowed this error to happen. Someone else should have found it, he insisted. He certainly didn't have the time to do it all himself, not with the department chief breathing down his neck, demanding he see more patients than humanly possible. Mike talked about how the office staff had failed to bring the abnormal radiology results to his attention. And what about the nurse who called the patient the night before? Shouldn't she have checked the chart? What about the radiologist who didn't follow up to make sure his recommendations were followed? The list was long. The only person Mike left off it was himself.

"I haven't slept well in days," he told me. Mike was worried about losing his medical license, his job, and his reputation. He wanted to know what I thought he should do about it. Sitting outside, in a piazza reminiscent of old Italy, I was reminded just how far the practice of medicine had come—how much more doctors have to worry about now than ever before. I told him the same things I would have said to any physician in his situation: follow the advice of your attorney, under no circumstances alter any medical records, prepare well for your deposition, and seek professional help if the anxiety worsens.

Mike's frustration re-exploded. "Didn't you hear me? I just told you about all the people who screwed me. Weren't you listening? What should I do about *their* incompetence?" He fired off questions as if mounting a desperate attack. Should he go to the media with his side of the story? What about suing the medical group, the radiologist, or even the patient for making such frivolous accusations? "Robbie, you're supposed to be the expert in these types of situations," he said, "so help me."

It was time to end the dinner. I know that Mike's anger was only an outward reflection of his pain and shame. Getting sued was a blow to his ego and professional pride. And it's true that of the hundreds of steps involved in surgery, Mike missed just one. But it was enough to harm his patient. Rather than admit it or apologize for it, Mike let the worst of physician culture do the thinking and talking for him. Nowhere in his residency training did he learn to say, "I'm sorry; I was wrong; I made a mistake." Instead he blamed the victim and the bystanders for his oversight. Mike was never taught to accept his limitations either. In their training, doctors are expected to be superhuman, which is why so many of them feel invincible—until a crisis reminds them of their fallibility. Mike ignored all the opportunities in front of him to prevent such a costly mistake. The physician culture stood in his way.

Instead of overworking himself to exhaustion, Mike could have dialed back his schedule. Instead of assuming his mind was a steel trap, incapable of forgetting even the slightest detail, he could have embedded a pre-op checklist into his computer, which would have reminded him to review the woman's mammography results. He could have apologized to the family and been present when the general surgeon consulted the frightened patient. Instead, denial and repression got in the way. Mike simply wasn't able to accept the gravity of his error. Sometimes patients sue because they want the money. More often, they sue because they feel hurt and abandoned.

There is no way to know if the patient would have experienced a different outcome had the cancer been found two months earlier. Ultimately, the medical group and the patient settled out of court for an undisclosed amount. Mike continued to practice despite the sense of betrayal he felt, his disdain for those around him, and his ongoing failure to acknowledge his mistake. We still catch up over email now and then, but he never again asked me for my advice.

In Mike I saw how the flaws of physician culture can crush the spirits of even the best doctors. In this next story, you'll see the culture's remarkable beauty through the lens of two physicians who are not so different from Mike.

———

IN 2017, AFTER A MORNING of intense January rainfall in Northern California, I found myself gripping the rail of a stairwell near the entrance to an underground parking garage. My left knee was throbbing. A man twice my size lay below me at the base of the stairs, belly up. As a crowd gathered around us, every face carried the same stunned expression.

"Stay put," said one of the onlookers, "I'm calling 911."

I looked back up the stairs at the puddle of rainwater that pooled halfway down the first flight. It was there the man now groaning below me had slipped and shrieked. Startled by the noise, I had reflexively grabbed the handrail and turned my torso just in time to see his upper body barreling toward me, arms extended like a defensive lineman about to execute a devastating blindside sack. As he slammed into me, the combination of his weight and momentum caused my left knee to buckle. Had I not held firm to the metal bar, I'd probably be facedown beneath him.

Turning back toward him, I could see the man was clutching his ribs in obvious pain, awaiting an ambulance to take him to the closest ER. I convinced a pair of kindly bystanders to help me to my car just twenty yards from the end of the stairwell. With a rush of adrenaline, cortisol, and other hormones temporarily switching off the pain receptors in my brain, I managed to get myself from the garage to the Kaiser Santa Clara medical center, phoning the orthopedic department along the way.

I asked to speak to the physician everyone at the hospital called Vladi, short for Vladimir. He was a Russian-trained surgeon who repeated his full five years of orthopedic residency when he immigrated to the United States. He's a master surgeon, and I couldn't think of anyone more qualified to treat me. As a dedicated runner and skier, I wanted only the best.

By the time I arrived at the hospital entrance, the adrenaline had worn off, and the pain was excruciating. Vladi and another orthopedic colleague met me at the door, transferred me to a wheelchair, and brought me inside. After a series of X-rays, they assessed the damage to my knee and gave it a name: tibial plateau fracture, a devastating injury for which there was little chance of full recovery. Vladi said the best option was to open everything up, reposition the pieces, and insert plates and screws to hold the bony fragments in place until the fractures healed.

Wanting to move forward with the surgical procedure as soon as possible, I asked, "When do you want to operate?"

"If you prefer, I can do it tonight or tomorrow," he said, "but I'd recommend that Jeff do the operation. He's an orthopedic surgeon at the San Jose [Kaiser Permanente] facility."

His response caught me off guard. Vladi had more training, experience, and expertise than any orthopedic surgeon I knew. Why was he referring me to another physician I'd never met who practiced fifteen miles away? Maybe he was about to start a vacation or had another patient scheduled for the OR. He answered before I could ask the question.

"Jeff specializes in this particular procedure, and he is your best chance for an optimal result," he explained, adding, "would you like me to contact him now?"

"Yes, let's do that," I said.

Sitting in front of a video monitor, Vladi and I saw Jeff's face appear. From his office, he waved at us and introduced himself. After typing a few commands into the electronic health record that he and Vladi shared, Jeff brought my X-rays into view and pointed to a dozen or so bony pieces. He confirmed Vladi's diagnosis and concurred with the treatment plan. From the ease and familiarity with which these two doctors spoke, it was clear they had exchanged many patients in the past. This was simply routine for them. I wasn't getting any special treatment.

Before disconnecting, Jeff asked Vladi to write me a prescription for pain medication and to put my knee in a specific splint designed to reduce the discomfort. I was able to go home that night. The next morning at six, I met Jeff (for the first time in person) inside the preoperative area at the San Jose facility. Our video conference the day before, along with

Vladi's endorsement, gave me all the confidence I needed to trust I was in the best of hands. Within fifteen minutes, I was asleep on the operating table.

I awoke six hours later. The hard work was about to begin. I was at the base of a mountain, staring up at a long, arduous journey. Lying in the hospital bed, gazing at the ceiling hour after hour, I feared for the future. I tried imagining what life would be like without running, skiing, and hiking. My body felt flooded with postoperative pain and my mind overwhelmed with dread.

Shortly after sunrise the following day, Jeff knocked on my hospital room door and washed his hands (making sure I saw him do it). He was there to doctor my wounds—all of them. He began with the ones that were visible: the ten- and twelve-inch incisions running up and down my leg. Then he sat down in the chair to the right of my bed, so our faces were at the same level, and he spoke to me with empathy, sympathy, kindness, and humility. We discussed my concerns about never running again and he assured me the pain I felt would eventually go away. Gradually, throughout the conversation, Jeff chipped away at my fears and the futility I felt. Before he left, he asked if there was anything more he could do to help. Only when I said no did he stand, wash his hands again, and walk out.

That evening, Jeff returned and repeated the ritual as he did the following morning and again the next night, prior to my discharge. Of all the physically and emotionally painful hours that filled those days in the hospital, my talks with Jeff are the minutes I remember and cherish most. In the days and weeks that followed, I saw Jeff in his office for ongoing evaluations, X-rays, suture removal, dressing changes, and knee-brace application. In the waiting area, I'd talk to his other patients. All of them described Jeff with the same gratitude and appreciation that I felt.

Four years have passed since my accident, and I'm pain free with near-normal function. I'm fortunate to have made a full recovery. On most days, I have to look down at my scars to remember whether it was the left or right leg that was injured.

I'm back to skiing with friends and running thirty to forty miles a week. I'll be forever grateful for Jeff's technical skill. And I'm equally appreciative of Vladi. If he hadn't checked his ego at the exam room door, I might not have had such a superb outcome.

Ultimately, as I look back on these experiences, I see one culture with two very different outcomes. The values and norms that drove Mike to near ruin are the same ones that created Jeff's compassion and Vladi's selfless humility.

IF YOU ASK ME WHO is the best surgeon, Vladi, Jeff, or Mike, I'd be hard-pressed to choose. All are technically brilliant and passionate about medical care. If you ask me who is the best person or the most ethical doctor, I couldn't answer that either. There is so little that separates their talents, desire, and commitment as physicians. And yet, like raindrops falling on the Great Divide, the stories of these individuals end up as far apart as the Atlantic and Pacific. I suspect Mike will remain bitter for the rest of his career. Vladi and Jeff are likely to continue to be content and fulfilled with their work.

In the end, countless factors determine the care patients receive and the satisfaction doctors feel. Sometimes our experiences are shaped by nothing more than chance. If Mike's patient didn't have breast cancer, the results of her mammogram would have been inconsequential. My surgery could have been complicated by numerous factors, from infection to the failure of bone healing. But in the long run, results in medicine are more than happenstance.

A healthcare organization that is integrated, prepaid, and technolog-ically savvy can bring out the best in physicians—enabling better col-laboration, cooperation, prevention. These systemic influences affect the physician culture, creating a set of behaviors that lead to better clinical outcomes. When doctors work in an isolated, volume-driven, competitive environment, the most problematic parts of the culture are likely to show themselves. Worse clinical outcomes, higher rates of physician burnout, and widespread dissatisfaction ensue.

Depending on the healthcare setting and circumstances, a culture that's capable of inflicting harm can also heal. As a resident I observed the ways it helped doctors cure cancer in children who once stood no chance for survival. On my cardiac surgery rotations I watched doctors stop and restart human hearts to repair life-threatening birth defects. Since then I've shaken hands with colleagues who saved the lives of Ebola victims in Africa and put their own health on the line to keep patients from dying of COVID-19. For those experiences, I am grateful.

Along the way, I've also had to look into the eyes of mothers as they described to me the loss of a child, not from some untreatable disease but from a preventable medical error. I've heard colleagues talk about posh New York dinners they attended as guests of a drug company, and I remember hearing those same doctors deny that an eleven-course meal at a Michelin-starred restaurant could influence the prescriptions they write. I've attended funerals for people who would still be alive had they received the preventive screenings they needed or if all doctors had simply washed their hands before entering the patient's hospital room.

My love for medicine is no longer blind, but it's no less passionate. I remain convinced that there is no group of people more dedicated to helping others in need than doctors. I admire and am personally thankful for the hard work and commitment of the physicians with whom I've worked—and who have taken great care of me and my family in times of sickness and injury. American physicians are among the best in the world. When their culture aligns with what patients desire and deserve, they achieve superlative outcomes in the most compassionate ways imaginable. In the right circumstances, doctors are capable of almost anything. And that's what makes it so heartbreaking when cultural values obstruct their mission and cause harm to patients and themselves.

I have spent my entire career in love with medicine. I feel as passionately about the profession today as I did on my first day of Anatomy 101. The best decision I made in my life was choosing to become a physician. I wrote this book with the hope that future generations of doctors will be able to say the same thing.

ACKNOWLEDGMENTS

WRITING A BOOK LIKE *UNCARING* requires the contributions of many people beyond the author. I am fortunate to have had the support of my family, friends, and colleagues. Without them, this book would not exist.

Growing up, my brother, Ron, sister, Karen, and I could not have asked for better parents. Each night, our dinner table was filled with delicious food that my mother cooked with love. It was also the place our parents served us heaping portions of *culture*. Through stories of their upbringing in times of economic despair, my mother and father taught us the values of hard work, fiscal prudence, and charity. From them, we learned about our religious heritage and the obligations that came with it. We took from them many other lessons, which we turned into the lifelong expectation that all people deserve to be treated with dignity, respect, and kindness.

I dedicated my first book, *Mistreated*, to my father after he died from a preventable medical error caused by a broken healthcare system. In that book, I laid out a plan to fix the system but didn't address the role doctors would need to play. This book, dedicated to my mother, is about the integrity of the relationship between physicians and their patients. Anyone who ever interacted with my mother not only benefited from the experience but felt better because of it. Physician culture would be improved if it adhered to my mother's example. Our patients need more than just positive medical outcomes. They deserve to feel valued.

In addition to my parents and siblings, I want to thank my partner, Janet, with whom I have shared immense joy, happiness, and love. Through our relationship, I have learned the depth of fulfillment two people can achieve when they're unafraid to open their hearts. As a skilled physician and talented surgeon, she has been called on throughout the coronavirus pandemic to care for critically ill patients. Working twelve- and twenty-four-hour shifts, she treated people unable to breathe, pulling many of them back from the edge of death. I thought about her and her incredible colleagues often when writing about the heroism and selflessness of our nation's most dedicated physicians. Laudatory descriptions of the profession followed without effort.

Some of the stories and lessons captured in *Uncaring* span the two decades I spent in medical school, residency, and clinical practice. During that time, I benefited from the teachings and wisdom of far too many professors and colleagues to list here. Although I have not seen many of you since that time, I remember well the lessons you imparted. Most notably, you taught me to be dedicated and to show compassion as a doctor, surgeon, and healer. I worked hard to repay the debts of gratitude I owe by teaching the next generation of physicians what you taught me. And in doing so, I tried my hardest to communicate, not only vast quantities of medical knowledge and advanced surgical technique, but also the values you instilled in me through your courageous and selfless actions.

To the committed and hardworking physicians, nurses, and staff with whom I worked in the Permanente Medical Group and Mid-Atlantic Permanente Group, I say thank you. Your mission-driven spirit and focus inspire me to this day. Years later, I remain grateful to the TPMG Board of Directors who chose me as CEO and to the remarkable physician leaders on both coasts who informed and made possible the Five *C*s of Cultural Change.

In particular, I'd like to recognize the many thousands of doctors I watched, time and again, put the needs of others ahead of themselves. I was energized by the passion you demonstrated while on surgical relief missions around the world. I saw it often in the operating room as you worked to save a patient's limb or life. And I observed you stepping forward and volunteering to help during natural disasters or public health crises, despite the dangers. All of you, alone and together, drove me to be a better physician, inspired me to become a better person, and never let me forget why I chose to become a doctor years before.

I am deeply grateful for the guidance of my friend and writing partner, Ben Lincoln, who helped me translate my thoughts and experiences into a book that both doctors and patients could access and apply to their healthcare experiences. He is as dedicated as I am to improving medical care for all Americans. Between us, hundreds of drafts and thousands of edits moved back and forth. Each exchange got *Uncaring* a step closer to being worthy of print. As a researcher, writer, and second pair of eyes, Ben has skill and expertise second to none.

Others whose talent and dedication made these pages possible include John Maas, literary agent extraordinaire at Park & Fine; Ben Adams, the brilliant and resourceful executive editor at PublicAffairs; along with the helpful and hands-on team at Hachette Book Group, with special thanks to Melissa Veronesi and Melissa Raymond.

The people who volunteered their stories for inclusion in this book deserve recognition for their bravery and their desire to help others. Thank you to Judy and Karen Lively for holding nothing back in our conversation and for having the courage to be exactly who you are. Thank you to Maria and Hunter Jones for proving that there's nothing stronger in this world than two people who believe in each other. Thank you to Nat Gleason, Graham Stratton, Vladimir Khapchik, and Jeff MacLean for your clinical expertise and unbreakable commitment to the highest ideals of medicine. My deepest gratitude goes to Gloria, Kathy, Sam, Bill, Sarah, Jason, Archie, Stephen, Cindy, and Mike, whose names have been changed and identities hidden to protect their privacy. I recognize that each of you suffered, and I wish it hadn't happened. I don't know how many of you or your families will read *Uncaring*, but I hope you understand the reason I retold your story was not to cause you further pain but to help minimize the suffering of others.

To my sister, Karen, I appreciate being able to tell Steve's story. He was a remarkable person, and his death has left a deep hole in your life and in the lives of many others. I miss his wit, intelligence, and dedication to you. To my cousin Alan, aunt Ruthie, uncle Herb, and above all, my parents, Jack and Lillian, I would love nothing more than to thank you in person. I think about my parents every day and am forever grateful for the priceless gifts they gave me in the form of valuable life lessons.

When I began to write *Uncaring* in 2018, the world was a different place. Most coronaviruses in broad circulation then were annoying—producing the common cold, with its sniffling and sneezing symptoms—but they were not particularly lethal. More than halfway through the writing process, a new strain of coronavirus went from bat to Wuhan wet market to the United States, turning the world on its head. Not since the Spanish flu of a century ago has the culture of American medicine been more challenged. In response, physicians from every specialty across the nation stepped forward. Individually and collectively, they reminded us why we both need and respect doctors.

The pandemic shone a light on a medical culture that is scientific and selfless but also stubborn and sometimes narcissistic. In times of catastrophe, physicians can be counted on to put the lives of patients ahead of their own. When the pandemic ends, our country will need to begin healing. I'm optimistic and hopeful that when that day arrives, doctors will once more rise to the occasion. In advance, allow me to thank you all for the work you will do, the time you will dedicate, and the success I believe you will achieve. Let me know how I can help.

BIBLIOGRAPHY

The following bibliography is not intended to be comprehensive. Rather, it is meant as a resource for those who wish to learn more about the cultural and systemic factors that influence doctors, patients, and the health of the nation. It also includes references to some of my journalistic works, including articles published in *Forbes*, the *Wall Street Journal*, and *Harvard Business Review* as well as my podcast *Fixing Healthcare*. Each offers a deeper perspective on the subject matter than was included in these pages. For additional information and insight into the chapters of this book, visit RobertPearlMD.com.

Works cited appear in the order they are referenced within each chapter.

Introduction

Hawryluk, Markian. "Scientist Has 'Invisible Enemy' in Sights with Microscopic Portraits of Coronavirus." *Kaiser Health News*, May 22, 2020. khn.org/news/scientist-has -invisible-enemy-in-sights-with-microscopic-portraits-of-coronavirus.

Wee, Sui-lee, and Vivian Wang. "China Grapples with Mystery Pneumonia-Like Illness." *New York Times*, January 6, 2020.

Aspril, Joshua. "U.S. Health Care Spending Highest Among Developed Countries." Johns Hopkins Bloomberg School of Public Health, January 8, 2019. www.jhsph .edu/news/news-releases/2019/us-health-care-spending-highest-among-developed -countries.html.

"Social Progress Imperative: Global Results." 2020. www.socialprogress.org/index/global /results.

"Commonwealth Fund 2018 Annual Report." 2018. annualreport.commonwealthfund .org/2018.

Miller, Lee J., and Wei Lu. "Healthy Nation Rankings: These Are the Healthiest Countries." Bloomberg, February 24, 2019. www.bloomberg.com/news/articles/2019 -02-24/spain-tops-italy-as-world-s-healthiest-nation-while-u-s-slips.

Solly, Meilan. "U.S. Life Expectancy Drops for Third Year in a Row, Reflecting Rising Drug Overdoses, Suicides." *Smithsonian Magazine*, December 3, 2018.

Gomez, Jessie. "ER Staff in Tears After Man Holds up 'Beautiful' Sign Thanking Them for Saving Wife's Life." *USA Today*, March 27, 2020.

Clark, Andrew, Mark Jit, Charlotte Warren-Gash, Bruce Guthrie, Harry H. X. Wang, Stewart W. Mercer, Colin Sanderson, et al. "Global, Regional, and National Estimates of the Population at Increased Risk of Severe COVID-19 due to Underlying Health Conditions in 2020: A Modelling Study." *Lancet Global Health* 8, no. 8 (2020).

Richardson, Safiya, Jamie S. Hirsch, Mangala Narasimhan, James M. Crawford, Thomas McGinn, Karina W. Davidson, Douglas P. Barnaby, et al. "Presenting Characteristics, Comorbidities, and Outcomes Among 5700 Patients Hospitalized with COVID-19 in the New York City Area." *Journal of the American Medical Association* 323, no. 20 (2020): 2052.

Bar-On, Yinon M., Avi Flamholz, Rob Phillips, and Ron Milo. "SARS-CoV-2 (COVID-19) by the Numbers." *eLife* 9 (2020).

PART ONE: DIAGNOSING PHYSICIAN CULTURE
1. Bloodletting, Handwashing, and Gorilla Watching

Geyer-Kordesch, Johanna, and Fiona MacDonald. *The History of the Royal College of Physicians and Surgeons, 1599–1858: Physicians and Surgeons in Glasgow*. London: Hambledon, 2003.

Chernow, Ron. *Washington: A Life*. New York: Penguin, 2010.

Anders, Eli Osterweil. "'A Plea for the Lancet': Bloodletting, Therapeutic Epistemology, and Professional Identity in Late Nineteenth-Century American Medicine." *Social History of Medicine* 29, no. 4 (2016): 781–801.

Vadakan, Vibul V. "The Asphyxiating and Exsanguinating Death of President George Washington." *Permanente Journal* 8, no. 2 (Spring 2004): 76–79. www.thepermanente journal.org/files/Spring2004/time.pdf.

Knox, Mason. "The Medical History of George Washington, His Physicians, Friends and Advisers." *Bulletin of the Institute of the History of Medicine*, 1933.

NCC Staff. "The Mysterious Death of George Washington." *Constitution Daily* (blog). National Constitution Center, 2019. constitutioncenter.org/blog/the-mysterious -death-of-george-washington.

Thomas, D. P. "The Demise of Bloodletting." *Journal of the Royal College of Physicians of Edinburgh* 44, no. 1 (2014): 72–77.

Morabia, A. "Pierre-Charles-Alexandre Louis and the Evaluation of Bloodletting." *Journal of the Royal Society of Medicine* 99, no. 3 (2006): 158–160.

Stewart, Oliver. "Bloodletting: A Brief Historical Perspective and Modern Medical Applications." Clinical Correlations, October 31, 2019. www.clinicalcorrelations .org/2019/10/31/bloodletting-a-brief-historical-perspective-and-modern-medical -applications.

Parapia, Liakat Ali. "History of Bloodletting by Phlebotomy." *British Journal of Haematology* 143, no. 4 (2008): 490–495.

Ioannidis, John P. A. "How Many Contemporary Medical Practices Are Worse Than Doing Nothing or Doing Less?" *Mayo Clinic Proceedings* 88, no. 8 (2013): 779–781.

Kadar, Nicholas, Roberto Romero, and Zoltán Papp. "Ignaz Semmelweis: The 'Savior of Mothers.'" *American Journal of Obstetrics and Gynecology* 219, no. 6 (2018): 519–522.

Loudon, Irvine. "Ignaz Phillip Semmelweis' Studies of Death in Childbirth." *Journal of the Royal Society of Medicine* 106, no. 11 (2013): 461–463.

Semmelweis, Ignác Fülöp. *The Etiology, Concept, and Prophylaxis of Childbed Fever*. 1861.

Hennessy, Michelle. "One Third of Doctors Don't Wash Their Hands Between Patients—Report." *The Journal* (Dublin, Ireland), November 14, 2012. www.the journal.ie/doctors-was-hands-674108-Nov2012.

Childress, Sarah. "Do Hospital Workers Really Wash Their Hands?" *Frontline*. Public Broadcasting Service, November 15, 2013. www.pbs.org/wgbh/frontline/article/do-hospital-workers-really-wash-their-hands.

Hartocollis, Anemona. "With Money at Risk, Hospitals Push Staff to Wash Hands." *New York Times*, May 28, 2013.

Haque, Mainul, Massimo Sartelli, Judy McKimm, and Muhamad Bin Abu Bakar. "Health Care–Associated Infections: An Overview." *Infection and Drug Resistance* 11 (2018): 2321–2333.

"Nearly Half a Million Americans Suffered from Clostridium Difficile Infections in a Single Year." Centers for Disease Control and Prevention, February 25, 2015. www.cdc.gov/media/releases/2015/p0225-clostridium-difficile.html.

Fitzharris, Lindsey. *The Butchering Art: Joseph Lister's Quest to Transform the Grisly World of Victorian Medicine*. London: Penguin Books, 2018.

Simons, Daniel J., and Christopher F. Chabris. *Selective Attention Test* (video). 1:21. YouTube, March 10, 2010. www.youtube.com/watch?v=vJG698U2Mvo.

Chabris, Christopher F., and Daniel J. Simons. *The Invisible Gorilla: And Other Ways Our Intuitions Deceive Us*. New York: Crown, 2010.

2. A First Look at Physician Culture

Kroeber, Alfred, and Clyde Kluckhohn. "Culture: A Critical Review of Concepts and Definitions." *Journal of Philosophy* 51, no. 19 (1952): 559.

Jena, Anupam B., and Andrew R. Olenski. "How Common Mental Shortcuts Can Cause Major Physician Errors." *New York Times*, February 20, 2020.

Kahneman, Daniel. *Thinking, Fast and Slow*. New York: Farrar, Straus and Giroux, 2015.

Gerstner, Louis V. *Who Says Elephants Can't Dance?* London: HarperCollins, 2003.

Coyle, Daniel. *The Culture Code: The Secrets of Highly Successful Groups*. London: Random House Business Books, 2018.

Newson, Martha. "United in Defeat: The Causes and Consequences of Identity Fusion in Football Fans." PhD diss., University of Oxford, 2017.

Mannix, Rebekah, and Joshua Nagler. "Tribalism in Medicine—Us vs Them." *JAMA Pediatrics* 171, no. 9 (2017): 831.

Hochberg, Mark S. "The Doctor's White Coat: An Historical Perspective." *AMA Journal of Ethics* 9, no. 4 (2007): 310–314.

Hata, Susan R. "The Ritual of the Table." *New England Journal of Medicine* 383 (2020): 1301–1303.

Nurok, Michael, and Thomas H. Lee. "Transforming Culture in Health Care." *New England Journal of Medicine* 381, no. 22 (2019): 2173–2175.

Pearl, Robert. "When Doctors Disappoint Patients, Remember 'It's the Culture, Stupid.'" *Forbes*, March 26, 2019.

3. Heroes and Fools

Philibert, Ingrid, Betty Chang, Timothy Flynn, Paul Friedmann, Rebecca Minter, Eric Scher, and W. T. Williams. "The 2003 Common Duty Hour Limits: Process, Outcome, and Lessons Learned." *Journal of Graduate Medical Education* 1, no. 2 (2009): 334–337.

"History of Duty Hours." Accreditation Council for Graduate Medical Education. www.acgme.org/What-We-Do/Accreditation/Clinical-Experience-and-Education-formerly-Duty-Hours/History-of-Duty-Hours. Accessed October 14, 2020.

Rosenbaum, Lisa, and Daniela Lamas. "Eyes Wide Open—Examining the Data on Duty-Hour Reform." *New England Journal of Medicine* 380, no. 10 (2019): 969–970.

4. A Two-Part History of Today's Physician Culture

Strathern, Paul. *A Brief History of Medicine: From Hippocrates' Four Humours to Crick and Watson's Double Helix*. London: Robinson, 2005.

Bynum, W. F. *The Western Medical Tradition, 1800–2000*. New York: Cambridge University Press, 2006.

Tan, Sy, and Y. Tatsumura. "Alexander Fleming (1881–1955): Discoverer of Penicillin." *Singapore Medical Journal* 56, no. 7 (2015): 366–367.

Mukherjee, Siddhartha. *The Emperor of All Maladies: A Biography of Cancer*. New York: Scribner, 2010.

Anonymous. "The Self-Inflicted Death of the Physician." KevinMD, May 29, 2019. www.kevinmd.com/blog/2019/06/the-self-inflicted-death-of-the-physician.html.

McLeod, Saul. "Defense Mechanisms." Simply Psychology, April 10, 2019. www.simplypsychology.org/defense-mechanisms.html.

Getz, Faye Marie. *Medicine in the English Middle Ages*. Princeton, NJ: Princeton University Press, 1998.

Dreher, Rod. "Oberlin Is an Insane Asylum." *American Conservative*, May 25, 2016.

Rosenberg, Saul A., and Henry S. Kaplan. "The Evolution and Summary Results of the Stanford Randomized Clinical Trials of the Management of Hodgkin's Disease: 1962–1984." *International Journal of Radiation Oncology*Biology*Physics* 11, no. 1 (1985): 5–22.

Melnick, Edward R., Liselotte N. Dyrbye, Christine A. Sinsky, Mickey Trockel, Colin P. West, Laurence Nedelec, Michael A. Tutty, and Tait Shanafelt. "The Association Between Perceived Electronic Health Record Usability and Professional Burnout Among US Physicians." *Mayo Clinic Proceedings* 95, no. 3 (2020): 476–487.

Frakt, Austin. "Reagan, Deregulation and America's Exceptional Rise in Health Care Costs." *New York Times*, June 4, 2018.

Siddiqui, Gina. "Why Doctors Reject Tools That Make Their Jobs Easier." *Observations* (blog). *Scientific American*, October 15, 2018. blogs.scientificamerican.com/observations/why-doctors-reject-tools-that-make-their-jobs-easier.

Chaiyachati, Krisda H., Judy A. Shea, David A. Asch, Manqing Liu, Lisa M. Bellini, C. Jessica Dine, Alice L. Sternberg, et al. "Assessment of Inpatient Time Allocation Among First-Year Internal Medicine Residents Using Time-Motion Observations." *JAMA Internal Medicine* 179, no. 6 (2019): 760.

Gawande, Atul. *Better: A Surgeon's Notes on Performance*. London: Penguin Books, 2008.

Ramsay, G., A. B. Haynes, S. R. Lipsitz, I. Solsky, J. Leitch, A. A. Gawande, and M. Kumar. "Reducing Surgical Mortality in Scotland by Use of the WHO Surgical Safety Checklist." *British Journal of Surgery* 106, no. 8 (2019): 1005–1011.

Mambu, Joseph. "Restoring the Art of Medicine." *American Journal of Medicine* 130, no. 12 (2017): 1340–1341.

Genuis, Stephen J., and Shelagh K. Genuis. "Resisting Cookbook Medicine." *BMJ* 329, no. 7458 (2004).

Newman, Leonard S., Kimberley J. Duff, and Roy F. Baumeister. "A New Look at Defensive Projection: Thought Suppression, Accessibility, and Biased Person Perception." *Journal of Personality and Social Psychology* 72, no. 5 (1997): 980–1001.

Kolbert, Elizabeth, and Maria Konnikova. "Why Facts Don't Change Our Minds." *New Yorker*, February 20, 2017.

Syrek, Ryan. "Medical Student Life & Education Report 2018." Medscape, September 5, 2018. www.medscape.com/slideshow/2018-medical-student-report-6010086#1.

"The Future of Healthcare: A National Survey of Physicians." The Doctors Company, 2018. www.thedoctors.com/about-the-doctors-company/newsroom/the-future-of-healthcare-survey.

Perlmutter, Austin. "What's Happened to Clinician Empathy?" KevinMD, September 23, 2019. www.kevinmd.com/blog/2019/03/whats-happened-to-clinician-empathy .html.

Frellick, Marcia. "Hospitalists Highlight Lack of Respect in 45% Burnout Rate." Medscape, May 13, 2019. www.medscape.com/viewarticle/912897.

5. The People v. Physician Culture

McNeil, Donald G. "Slithery Medical Symbolism: Worm or Snake? One or Two?" *New York Times*, March 8, 2005.

Prakash, M., and J. Carlton Johnny. "Things You Don't Learn in Medical School: Caduceus." *Journal of Pharmacy and Bioallied Sciences* 7, no. 5 (2015): 49.

Makary, Martin A., and Michael Daniel. "Medical Error—the Third Leading Cause of Death in the US." *BMJ* (2016): i2139.

"The Financial and Human Cost of Medical Error." Betsy Lehman Center for Patient Safety, June 2019. betsylehmancenterma.gov/research/costofme.

Misiakos, Evangelos P., George Bagias, Paul Patapis, Dimitrios Sotiropoulos, Prodromos Kanavidis, and Anastasios Machairas. "Current Concepts in the Management of Necrotizing Fasciitis." *Frontiers in Surgery* 1 (2014).

Pereira-Lima, Karina, Douglas A. Mata, Sonia R. Loureiro, José A. Crippa, Lívia M. Bolsoni, and Srijan Sen. "Association Between Physician Depressive Symptoms and Medical Errors." *JAMA Network Open* 2, no. 11 (2019).

Tawfik, Daniel S., Jochen Profit, Timothy I. Morgenthaler, Daniel V. Satele, Christine A. Sinsky, Liselotte N. Dyrbye, Michael A. Tutty, Colin P. West, and Tait D. Shanafelt. "Physician Burnout, Well-Being, and Work Unit Safety Grades in Relationship to Reported Medical Errors." *Mayo Clinic Proceedings* 93, no. 11 (2018): 1571–1580.

Bohnen, Jordan D., Keith D. Lillemoe, Elizabeth A. Mort, and Haytham M. A. Kaafarani. "When Things Go Wrong: The Surgeon as Second Victim." *Annals of Surgery* 269, no. 5 (2019): 808–809.

Caplan, Arthur L. "No, Doctors Who Make Errors Are Not 'Second Victims.'" Medscape, April 25, 2019. www.medscape.com/viewarticle/912206.

Ansari-Winn, Dianne. "It's Time to Advocate for a New Culture in Medicine." KevinMD, October 8, 2018. www.kevinmd.com/blog/2018/10/its-time-to-advocate -for-a-new-culture-in-medicine.html.

PART TWO: THE PHYSICIAN'S PAIN
1. Did We Kill One of Our Own?

Stevenson, Robert Louis. *Strange Case of Dr. Jekyll and Mr. Hyde*. New York: C. Scribner's Sons, 1927.

Pearl, Robert. "Results: The July 2019 Survey on Physician Burnout." RobertPearlMD .com, August 9, 2019. robertpearlmd.com/burnout-survey.

Pearl, Robert, Jeremy Corr, and Donald Berwick. "Episode 5: Don Berwick Brings a Global Perspective to Fixing US Healthcare." *Fixing Healthcare* (podcast), May 29, 2020. fixinghealthcarepodcast.com/2018/12/09/episode-5-don-berwick.

"HEDIS Measures and Technical Resources." National Committee for Quality Assurance, July 22, 2020. www.ncqa.org/hedis/measures.

Anderson, Pauline. "Doctors' Suicide Rate Highest of Any Profession." WebMD, May 8, 2018. www.webmd.com/mental-health/news/20180508/doctors -suicide-rate-highest-of-any-profession.

Andrew, Louise B. "Physician Suicide." Medscape, August 1, 2018. emedicine.medscape
.com/article/806779-overview.

Bright, Robert P., and Lois Krahn. "Depression and Suicide Among Physicians." *Current Psychiatry* 10, no. 4 (April 2011): 16–30.

Kishore, Sandeep, Douglas E. Dandurand, Angela Mathew, and David Rothenberger. "Breaking the Culture of Silence on Physician Suicide." Discussion Paper. *NAM Perspectives* 6, no. 6 (June 3, 2016).

2. *The Rise of Burnout, the Rebirth of Moral Injury*

Reinhart, R. J. "Nurses Continue to Rate Highest in Honesty, Ethics." Gallup Poll. Gallup, September 11, 2020. news.gallup.com/poll/274673/nurses-continue-rate -highest-honesty-ethics.aspx.

Birth, Allyssa. "Prestigious Occupations." The Harris Poll, April 21, 2018. theharrispoll .com/according-to-a-november-2015-harris-poll-the-following-are-prestigious -occupations. Note: "Doctor Tops List of Prestigious Occupations: 9 in 10 Americans See Doctor as a Prestigious Occupation."

Mejia, Zameena. "These Are the 25 Best-Paying Jobs in America in 2019, According to US News & World Report." CNBC, August 26, 2019. www.cnbc.com/2019/01/08 /the-are-the-25-best-paying-jobs-in-america-in-2019-according-to-us-news--world -report--.html. Note: The top twelve best-paying jobs are medical.

Rotenstein, Lisa S., Matthew Torre, Marco A. Ramos, Rachael C. Rosales, Constance Guille, Srijan Sen, and Douglas A. Mata. "Prevalence of Burnout Among Physicians." *JAMA* 320, no. 11 (2018): 1131.

National Academies of Sciences, Engineering, and Medicine. *Taking Action Against Clinician Burnout: A Systems Approach to Professional Well-Being.* Consensus Study Report. Washington, DC: National Academies Press, 2019.

Kane, Leslie. "Medscape National Physician Burnout & Suicide Report 2020." Medscape, January 15, 2020, 1–29. www.medscape.com/slideshow /2020-lifestyle-burnout-6012460.

Freudenberger, Herbert J. "Staff Burn-Out." *Journal of Social Issues* 30, no. 1 (1974): 159–165.

Abbott, Brianna. "Physician Burnout Is Widespread, Especially Among Those in Midcareer." *Wall Street Journal*, January 15, 2020.

Flock, Elizabeth. "Burnout Is Rampant Among Doctors and Nurses. Can the Arts Help?" *PBS News Hour.* Public Broadcasting Service, November 5, 2019. www.pbs.org /newshour/arts/burnout-is-rampant-among-doctors-and-nurses-can-the-arts-help.

Khansa, Ibrahim, and Jeffrey E. Janis. "A Growing Epidemic: Plastic Surgeons and Burnout—a Literature Review." *Plastic and Reconstructive Surgery* 144, no. 2 (2019).

Shanafelt, Tait D., Omar Hasan, Lotte N. Dyrbye, Christine Sinsky, Daniel Satele, Jeff Sloan, and Colin P. West. "Changes in Burnout and Satisfaction with Work-Life Balance in Physicians and the General US Working Population Between 2011 and 2014." *Mayo Clinic Proceedings* 90, no. 12 (2015): 1600–1613.

Jha, Ashish K., Andrew R. Iliff, Alain A. Chaoui, Steven Defossez, Maryanne C. Bombaugh, and Yael R. Miller. *A Crisis in Health Care: A Call to Action on Physician Burnout.* Massachusetts Medical Society, Massachusetts Health and Hospital Association, Harvard T. H. Chan School of Public Health, and Harvard Global Health Institute, 2019. www.massmed.org/News-and-Publications/MMS-News-Releases /Physician-Burnout-Report-2018.

Pearl, Robert, Jeremy Corr, and Halee Fischer-Wright. "Episode 2: Dr. Halee Fischer-Wright Wants to Unify All the Healthcare Players." *Fixing Healthcare* (podcast), September 8, 2018. www.fixinghealthcarepodcast.com/2018/09/08/episode-2.

Talbot, Simon G., and Wendy Dean. "Physicians Aren't 'Burning Out.' They're Suffering from Moral Injury." *STAT News*, July 26, 2018. www.statnews.com/2018/07/26 /physicians-not-burning-out-they-are-suffering-moral-injury.

Dean, Wendy, and Simon G. Talbot. "Moral Injury and Burnout in Medicine: A Year of Lessons Learned." *STAT News*, July 26, 2019. www.statnews.com/2019/07/26 /moral-injury-burnout-medicine-lessons-learned.

Bailey, Melissa. "Beyond Burnout: Docs Decry 'Moral Injury' from Financial Pressures of Health Care." *Kaiser Health News*, February 4, 2020. khn.org/news /beyond-burnout-docs-decry-moral-injury-from-financial-pressures-of-health-care.

Shrank, William H., Teresa L. Rogstad, and Natasha Parekh. "Waste in the US Health Care System." *JAMA* 322, no. 15 (2019): 1501.

Callaghan, Brian C., Kevin A. Kerber, Robert J. Pace, Lesli E. Skolarus, and James F. Burke. "Headaches and Neuroimaging." *JAMA Internal Medicine* 174, no. 5 (2014): 819.

"U.S. Headache Sufferers Get $1 Billion Worth of Brain Scans Each Year." *ScienceDaily*, March 17, 2014. www.sciencedaily.com/releases/2014/03/140317170642.htm.

Dall, Chris. "Price to Pay: Antibiotic-Resistant Infections Cost $2 Billion a Year." Center for Infectious Disease Research and Policy, University of Minnesota, March 22, 2018. www.cidrap.umn.edu/news-perspective/2018/03/price-pay -antibiotic-resistant-infections-cost-2-billion-year.

Gordon, Mara. "Do You Need That Surgery? How to Decide, and How to Pick a Surgeon if You Do." National Public Radio, July 19, 2019. www.npr.org/sections /health-shots/2019/07/19/743248074/do-you-need-that-surgery-how-to-decide -and-how-to-pick-a-surgeon-if-you-do.

Makary, Marty. *The Price We Pay: What Broke American Health Care—and How to Fix It.* New York: Bloomsbury, 2019.

Delitto, Anthony, Sara R. Piva, Charity G. Moore, Julie M. Fritz, Stephen R. Wisniewski, Deborah A. Josbeno, Mark Fye, and William C. Welch. "Surgery Versus Nonsurgical Treatment of Lumbar Spinal Stenosis." *Annals of Internal Medicine* 162, no. 7 (2015): 465.

Brox, J. I., O. P. Nygaard, I. Holm, A. Keller, T. Ingebrigtsen, and O. Reikeras. "Four-Year Follow-up of Surgical Versus Non-Surgical Therapy for Chronic Low Back Pain." *Annals of the Rheumatic Diseases* 69, no. 9 (2009): 1643–1648.

Martin, Keith L. "Medscape Residents Lifestyle & Happiness Report 2019." Medscape, August 7, 2019. www.medscape.com/slideshow/2019-residents -lifestyle-happiness-6011774.

Terry, Ken. "One in 5 Residents Doubt Career Choice Despite Ample Job Offers." Medscape, May 16, 2019. www.medscape.com/viewarticle/913082.

Hu, Yue-Yung, Ryan J. Ellis, D. Brock Hewitt, Anthony D. Yang, Elaine Ooi Cheung, Judith T. Moskowitz, John R. Potts, et al. "Discrimination, Abuse, Harassment, and Burnout in Surgical Residency Training." *New England Journal of Medicine* 381, no. 18 (2019): 1741–1752.

Pearl, Robert. "Saving America's Hospitals: It's Time to Stop Wasting Time and Lives." *Forbes*, January 30, 2018.

"The Value of Time in Healthcare." TeleTracking, August 10, 2015. www.teletracking .com/resources/the-value-of-time.

Adair, Camille. "Burnout vs. Moral Injury: Does It Matter What We Call It?" KevinMD.com, May 9, 2019. www.kevinmd.com/blog/2019/05/burnout-vs-moral -injury-does-it-matter-what-we-call-it.html.

Cheney, Christopher. "Are Your Physicians Suffering from Burnout—or Moral Injury?" HealthLeaders Media, March 25, 2019. www.healthleadersmedia.com/clinical-care /are-your-physicians-suffering-burnout%E2%80%94or-moral-injury.

Macintyre, Michael. "Physician Burnout, Depression Can Lead to Major Medical Errors: Study." ABC News, July 8, 2018. abcnews.go.com/Health /physician-burnout-depression-lead-major-medical-errors-study/story?id=56427381.

3. The Problem with Prestige

Kane, Leslie. "Medscape National Physician Burnout & Suicide Report 2020." Medscape, January 15, 2020, 1–29. www.medscape.com/slideshow/2020 -lifestyle-burnout-6012460.

Kane, Leslie. "Medscape National Physician Burnout, Depression & Suicide Report 2019." Medscape, January 15, 2019, 1–29. www.medscape.com /slideshow/2019-lifestyle-burnout-depression-6011056?faf=1.

Kane, Leslie. "Medscape Physician Compensation Report 2020." Medscape, May 14, 2020, 1–33. www.medscape.com/slideshow/2020-compensation-overview -6012684.

Kane, Leslie. "Medscape Physician Compensation Report 2019." Medscape, April 10, 2019, 1–30. www.medscape.com/slideshow/2019-compensation-overview -6011286.

Berg, Sara. "Physician Burnout: It's Not You, It's Your Medical Specialty." American Medical Association, August 3, 2018. www.ama-assn.org/residents-students /specialty-profiles/physician-burnout-it-s-not-you-it-s-your-medical-specialty.

Marmot, Michael. *The Status Syndrome: How Social Standing Affects Our Health and Longevity.* London: Bloomsbury, 2004.

Venkataramani, Atheendar, Sebastian Daza, and Ezekiel Emanuel. "Association of Social Mobility with the Income-Related Longevity Gap in the United States." *JAMA Internal Medicine* 180, no. 3 (2020): 429.

Pearl, Robert. "The Link Between Burnout and Physician Hierarchy." *Forbes*, July 24, 2019. www.forbes.com/sites/robertpearl/2019/07/24/burnout-and -physician-hierarchy.

"Observation or Active Surveillance for Prostate Cancer." American Cancer Society, 2020. www.cancer.org/cancer/prostate-cancer/treating/watchful-waiting.html.

Lin, Kenneth. *Prostate-Specific Antigen-Based Screening for Prostate Cancer: An Evidence Update for the U.S. Preventive Services Task Force.* Rockville, MD: AHRQ, 2011.

"Prostate Cancer: Screening." U.S. Preventive Services Task Force, May 8, 2018. www .uspreventiveservicestaskforce.org/uspstf/recommendation/prostate-cancer-screening.

Elshaug, Adam G., Amber M. Watt, Linda Mundy, and Cameron D. Willis. "Over 150 Potentially Low-Value Health Care Practices." *Medical Journal of Australia* 197, no. 10 (2012): 556–560.

Castellucci, Maria. "Most Hospitals Fail to Meet Leapfrog's Surgery Volume Standards." Modern Healthcare, July 18, 2019. www.modernhealthcare.com/safety-quality /most-hospitals-fail-meet-leapfrogs-surgery-volume-standards.

Artiga, Samantha, and Elizabeth Hinton. "Beyond Health Care: The Role of Social Determinants in Promoting Health and Health Equity." Kaiser Family Foundation, July 9, 2019. www.kff.org/disparities-policy/issue-brief/beyond-health-care-the-role-of -social-determinants-in-promoting-health-and-health-equity.

4. How the Mighty Fell

Shi, Leiyu. "Primary Care, Specialty Care, and Life Chances." *International Journal of Health Services* 24, no. 3 (1994): 431–458.

Butters, Joan. "Why Utilization Management Matters." Becker's Hospital Review, December 12, 2017. www.beckershospitalreview.com/finance/why-utilization -management-matters.html.

Junod, Suzanne White, and William Thomas Beavers. "FDA and Clinical Drug Trials: A Short History." US Food and Drug Administration, 2008. www.fda.gov/media/110437/download.

Basu, Sanjay, Seth A. Berkowitz, Robert L. Phillips, Asaf Bitton, Bruce E. Landon, and Russell S. Phillips. "Association of Primary Care Physician Supply with Population Mortality in the United States, 2005–2015." *JAMA Internal Medicine* 179, no. 4 (2019): 506.

"More Primary Care Physicians Leads to Longer Life Spans." Stanford Medicine News Center, February 18, 2019. med.stanford.edu/news/all-news/2019/02/more-primary-care-physicians-lead-to-longer-life-spans.html.

Martin, Keith L. "Medscape Internist Compensation Report 2020." Medscape, May 20, 2020. www.medscape.com/slideshow/2020-compensation-internist-6012671.

Pearl, Robert. "Study: Primary Care Doctors Increase Life Expectancy, but Does Anyone Care?" *Forbes*, April 8, 2019.

Starfield, Barbara, Leiyu Shi, and James Macinko. "Contribution of Primary Care to Health Systems and Health." *Milbank Quarterly* 83, no. 3 (2005): 457–502.

Knowles, Megan. "13% of Americans Live in County with Shortage of Primary Care Physicians." Becker's Hospital Review, September 11, 2018. www.beckershospital review.com/hospital-physician-relationships/13-of-americans-live-in-county-with-shortage-of-primary-care-physicians.html.

5. Doctors and Self-Determination Theory

Santos, Laurie. "The Science of Well-Being." Coursera. Yale University, 2020. www.coursera.org/learn/the-science-of-well-being.

"Can Money Buy Happiness? Gallup Poll Asks, and the World Answers." *ScienceDaily*, July 2, 2010. www.sciencedaily.com/releases/2010/07/100701072652.htm.

Ubel, Peter A. *Critical Decisions: How You and Your Doctor Can Make the Right Medical Choices Together.* New York: HarperOne, 2012.

Vedantam, Shankar, and Maggie Penman. "Even Astronauts Get the Blues: Or Why Boredom Drives Us Nuts." *Hidden Brain* (podcast). National Public Radio, March 15, 2016. www.npr.org/2016/03/14/470416797/even-astronauts-get-the-blues-or-why-boredom-drives-us-nuts.

Harlow, H. F., R. O. Dodsworth, and M. K. Harlow. "Total Social Isolation in Monkeys." *Proceedings of the National Academy of Sciences* 54, no. 1 (1965): 90–97.

Pink, Daniel H. *Drive: The Surprising Truth About What Motivates Us.* New York: Riverhead Books, 2011.

Deci, Edward L. "Effects of Externally Mediated Rewards on Intrinsic Motivation." *Journal of Personality and Social Psychology* 18, no. 1 (1971): 105–115.

Deci, Edward L., and Richard M. Ryan. "Conceptualizations of Intrinsic Motivation and Self-Determination." In *Intrinsic Motivation and Self-Determination in Human Behavior,* 11–40. New York: Plenum, 1985.

Hartzband, Pamela, and Jerome Groopman. "Physician Burnout, Interrupted." *New England Journal of Medicine* 382, no. 26 (June 25, 2020): 2485–2487.

Steiner, Claudia, and Zeynal Karaca. "Surgeries in Hospital-Based Ambulatory Surgery and Hospital Inpatient Settings, 2014: Statistical Brief #223." National Center for Biotechnology Information. US National Library of Medicine, July 2020. pubmed.ncbi.nlm.nih.gov/28722845/.

Vemulapalli, Sreekanth, John D. Carroll, Michael J. Mack, Zhuokai Li, David Dai, Andrzej S. Kosinski, Dharam J. Kumbhani, et al. "Procedural Volume and Outcomes for Transcatheter Aortic-Valve Replacement." *New England Journal of Medicine* 380, no. 26 (June 27, 2019): 2541–2550.

Pearl, Robert. "Saving America's Hospitals: It's Time to Stop Wasting Time and Lives." *Forbes*, January 30, 2018.

"Surgeon Volume and Surgical Appropriateness." Leapfrog Group, March 31, 2017. www .leapfroggroup.org/ratings-reports/surgeon-volume-and-surgical-appropriateness.

Sternberg, Steve, and Geoff Dougherty. "Risks Are High at Low-Volume Hospitals." *U.S. News & World Report*, May 18, 2015.

Baker, Laurence, and Maryann O'Sullivan. "Small Numbers Can Have Big Consequences: Many California Hospitals Perform Dangerously Low Numbers of Cancer Surgeries." California Health Care Foundation, June 1, 2017. www.chcf.org /publication/small-numbers-can-have-big-consequences-many-california-hospitals -perform-dangerously-low-numbers-of-cancer-surgeries.

Oldenburg, Ray. *The Great Good Place: Cafes, Coffee Shops, Bookstores, Bars, Hair Salons, and Other Hangouts at the Heart of a Community*. Philadelphia: Da Capo, 1989.

Hayhurst, Chris. "Feeling Isolated Is a Key Driver of Physician Burnout." athenahealth, February 14, 2019. www.athenahealth.com/knowledge-hub/practice-management /disconnected-isolation-and-physician-burnout.

Epley, Nicholas, and Laurie Santos. "Interview with Nicholas Epley: Stuff That Really Makes Us Happy." Coursera. Yale University, 2019. www.coursera.org/lecture /the-science-of-well-being/interview-with-nicholas-epley-x4U9I.

Ubel, Peter. "Your (500) Physician(s) Will See You Now." *Forbes*, May 31, 2019.

Ballard, Jamie. "Millennials Are the Loneliest Generation." YouGov, July 30, 2019. today.yougov.com/topics/lifestyle/articles-reports/2019/07/30/loneliness -friendship-new-friends-poll-survey.

Holt-Lunstad, Julianne, Timothy B. Smith, and J. Bradley Layton. "Social Relationships and Mortality Risk: A Meta-Analytic Review." *PLoS Medicine* 7, no. 7 (July 27, 2010).

Alimi, Yewande, Maria Altieri, and Jeremy Kauffman. "A Sense of Belonging and Community Can Mitigate Physician Burnout." *Bulletin of the American College of Surgeons*, September 5, 2019.

6. Bored Stiff

Wilson, Timothy D., David A. Reinhard, Erin C. Westgate, Daniel T. Gilbert, Nicole Ellerbeck, Cheryl Hahn, Casey L. Brown, and Adi Shaked. "Just Think: The Challenges of the Disengaged Mind." *Science* 345, no. 6192 (July 3, 2014): 75–77.

Staiger, Douglas O. "Trends in the Work Hours of Physicians in the United States." *JAMA* 303, no. 8 (February 24, 2010): 747–753.

Gaskill, J. Richard. "Recollections of Internship." July 1, 1959. Note: Image included in this book was provided via email.

PART THREE: HELPING OR HARMING PATIENTS?
1. Quality Isn't a Given

"Survey of America's Patients: An Examination of How Patients Experience the American Health Care System." The Physicians Foundation, October 1, 2019. physicians foundation.org/research-insights/the-physicians-foundation-2019-patient-survey.

McCarthy, Justin. "Seven in 10 Maintain Negative View of U.S. Healthcare System." Gallup, January 14, 2019. news.gallup.com/poll/245873/seven-maintain-negative -view-healthcare-system.aspx.

Kohn, Linda T., Janet Corrigan, and Molla S. Donaldson. *To Err Is Human: Building a Safer Health System*. Washington, DC: National Academy Press, 2000.

Institute of Medicine (IOM). *Crossing the Quality Chasm: A New Health System for the 21st Century*. Washington, DC: National Academy Press, 2005.

Institute of Medicine (IOM). *Performance Measurement: Accelerating Improvement*. Washington, DC: National Academies Press, 2006.

Robbins, Alexandra. "The Problem with Satisfied Patients." *Atlantic*, April 17, 2015.

Roosa, Tikkanen, and Melinda K. Abrams. "U.S. Health Care from a Global Perspective, 2019: Higher Spending, Worse Outcomes?" The Commonwealth Fund, January 30, 2020. www.commonwealthfund.org/publications/issue-briefs/2020/jan/us-health-care-global-perspective-2019.

"Social Progress Imperative: Global Results." 2020. www.socialprogress.org/index/global/results.

2. A Tale of Two Emergencies

Marisa Lagos, Kevin Fagan, and Justin Berton. "San Bruno Fire Levels Neighborhood—Gas Explosion." *San Francisco Chronicle*, February 9, 2012.

"Heart Disease Facts." Centers for Disease Control and Prevention, September 8, 2020. www.cdc.gov/heartdisease/facts.htm.

"How Heart Attacks Became Less Deadly." Harvard Medical School. Harvard Health Publishing, 2020. www.health.harvard.edu/healthbeat/how-heart-attacks-became-less-deadly.

Elflein, John. "Number of Specialist Doctors in U.S. by Field." Statista, 2020. www.statista.com/statistics/209424/us-number-of-active-physicians-by-specialty-area.

Pauls, Lynn, Rebecca Johnson-Paben, John McGready, Jamie Murphy, Peter Pronovost, and Christopher Wu. "The Weekend Effect in Hospitalized Patients: A Meta-Analysis." *Journal of Hospital Medicine* 12, no. 9 (2017): 760–766.

Bray, Benjamin D., and Adam Steventon. "What Have We Learnt After 15 Years of Research into the 'Weekend Effect'?" *BMJ Quality & Safety* 26, no. 8 (November 30, 2016): 607–610.

Jena, Anupam B., Vinay Prasad, Dana P. Goldman, and John Romley. "Mortality and Treatment Patterns Among Patients Hospitalized with Acute Cardiovascular Conditions During Dates of National Cardiology Meetings." *JAMA Internal Medicine* 175, no. 2 (February 1, 2015): 237.

3. Human Shields

Blumberg, Alex, and Adam Davidson. "Accidents of History Created U.S. Health System." *All Things Considered*. National Public Radio, October 22, 2009. www.npr.org/templates/story/story.php?storyId=114045132.

Code of Ethics of the American Medical Association: Adopted May, 1847. Philadelphia: William F. Fell, 1888. ethics.iit.edu/ecodes/sites/default/files/Americaan%20Medical%20Association%20Code%20of%20Medical%20Ethics%20%281847%29.pdf.

Sawyer, Bradley, and Cynthia Cox. "How Does Health Spending in the U.S. Compare to Other Countries?" Peterson-KFF Health System Tracker, December 7, 2018. www.healthsystemtracker.org/chart-collection/health-spending-u-s-compare-countries.

Picchi, Aimee. "Vast Number of Americans (8 in 10) Live Paycheck to Paycheck." CBS News, August 24, 2017. www.cbsnews.com/news/americans-living-paycheck-to-paycheck.

Martinez, Gina. "GoFundMe CEO: One-Third of Fundraisers Are for Medical Costs." *Time*, January 30, 2019.

Konish, Lorie. "This Is the Real Reason Most Americans File for Bankruptcy." CNBC, February 11, 2019. www.cnbc.com/2019/02/11/this-is-the-real-reason-most-americans-file-for-bankruptcy.html.

Khazan, Olga. "Americans Are Going Bankrupt from Getting Sick." *Atlantic*, September 3, 2019.

Herman, Bob. "Health Care Is Gobbling Up Your Wages." Axios, August 5, 2019. www .axios.com/health-care-costs-wages-insurance-employers-6cfb79ef-92fb-4f22 -a231-16a6df9b0da8.html.

"The Real Cost of Health Care: Interactive Calculator Estimates Both Direct and Hidden Household Spending." Kaiser Family Foundation, June 7, 2019. www.kff.org/health-costs/press-release/interactive-calculator-estimates -both-direct-and-hidden-household-spending.

Olen, Helaine. "Even the Insured Often Can't Afford Their Medical Bills." *Atlantic*, September 12, 2017.

Stevens, Rosemary A. "Health Care in the Early 1960s." *Health Care Financing Review* 18, no. 2 (1996): 11–22.

Catlin, Aaron, and Cathy Cowan. "National Health Spending 1960–2013." *Health Affairs* (blog), November 23, 2015. www.healthaffairs.org/do/10.1377 /hblog20151123.051904/full.

"National Health Expenditure Accounts (NHEA)." Centers for Medicare & Medicaid Services, 2018. www.cms.gov/Research-Statistics-Data-and-Systems /Statistics-Trends-and-Reports/NationalHealthExpendData/NationalHealth AccountsHistorical.

Garmon, Christopher, and Benjamin Chartock. "One in Five Inpatient Emergency Department Cases May Lead to Surprise Bills." *Health Affairs* 36, no. 1 (January 2017): 177–181.

Chhabra, Karan R., Kyle H. Sheetz, Ushapoorna Nuliyalu, Mihir S. Dekhne, Andrew M. Ryan, and Justin B. Dimick. "Out-of-Network Bills for Privately Insured Patients Undergoing Elective Surgery with In-Network Primary Surgeons and Facilities." *JAMA* 323, no. 6 (February 11, 2020): 538.

Harris, Richard. "For Her Head Cold, Insurer Coughed Up $25,865." *Kaiser Health News*, December 23, 2019. khn.org/news/medical-bill-of-the-month-head-cold -throat-swab-dna-tests-insurer-coughed-up-25k.

Ostrov, Barbara Feder. "That's a Lot of Scratch: The $48,329 Allergy Test." *Kaiser Health News*, October 29, 2018. khn.org/news/thats-a-lot-of-scratch-the-48329-allergy-test.

Sanger-Katz, Margot. "In the U.S., an Angioplasty Costs $32,000. Elsewhere? Maybe $6,400." *New York Times*, December 27, 2019.

Scott, Dylan. "Nearly Half of Americans Say They've Been Hit with a Surprise Medical Bill." *Vox*, November 13, 2019. www.vox.com/policy-and-politics/2019/11/13 /20961663/poll-stop-surprise-medical-bills-legislation.

"Mission, Vision & Values." American College of Emergency Physicians, 2020. www .acep.org/what-we-believe/mission-vision--values.

Luthi, Susannah. "Surprise Medical Billing Legislation Threatened by Provider Lobbying." Modern Healthcare, August 26, 2019. www.modernhealthcare.com /government/surprise-medical-billing-legislation-threatened-provider-lobbying.

Bluth, Rachel, and Emmarie Huetteman. "Investor-Backed Physician Groups Emerge as Loudest Opponents of Proposals to End Surprise Medical Bills." *St. Louis Post-Dispatch*, September 11, 2019.

Farmer, Blake. "It's Not Just Hospitals That Sue Patients Who Can't Pay." *Kaiser Health News*, February 21, 2020. khn.org/news/its-not-just-hospitals -that-sue-patients-who-cant-pay.

Owens, Caitlin. "Hospitals Still Suing Patients in Coronavirus Hotspots." Axios, August 21, 2020. www.axios.com/hospitals-lawsuits-patients-coronavirus -7133bf3e-4fab-4880-93ff-246ec0c4b0fc.html.

Thomas, Wendi C., Maya Miller, Beena Raghavendran, and Doris Burke. "This Doctors Group Is Owned by a Private Equity Firm and Repeatedly Sued the Poor Until We Called Them." ProPublica, November 19, 2019. www.propublica.org/article/this -doctors-group-is-owned-by-a-private-equity-firm-and-repeatedly-sued-the-poor -until-we-called-them.

4. The Real Price of Rx

Crow, David. "Pharma Chief Defends 400% Drug Price Rise as a 'Moral Requirement.'" *Financial Times*, September 11, 2018.

Crow, Kelly. "Leonardo Da Vinci Painting 'Salvator Mundi' Smashes Records with $450.3 Million Sale." *Wall Street Journal*, November 16, 2017.

Grochowski Jones, Ryann, Mike Tigas, Charles Ornstein, and Lena Groeger. "Dollars for Docs." ProPublica, October 17, 2019. projects.propublica.org/docdollars.

Fresques, Hannah. "Doctors Prescribe More of a Drug if They Receive Money from a Pharma Company Tied to It." ProPublica, December 20, 2019. www.propublica.org /article/doctors-prescribe-more-of-a-drug-if-they-receive-money-from-a-pharma -company-tied-to-it.

Weber, Tracy, Charles Ornstein, and Ryann Grochowski Jones. "We Found Over 700 Doctors Who Were Paid More Than a Million Dollars by Drug and Medical Device Companies." ProPublica, October 17, 2019. www.propublica.org/article/we -found-over-700-doctors-who-were-paid-more-than-a-million-dollars-by-drug-and -medical-device-companies.

Frellick, Marcia. "More Than Half of Doctors Get Industry Payments/Meals: Poll." Medscape, December 20, 2019. www.medscape.com/viewarticle/922816.

Pearl, Robert. "Shame, Scandal Plague Healthcare Providers in 2018." *Forbes*, December 11, 2018.

Fickweiler, Freek, Ward Fickweiler, and Ewout Urbach. "Interactions Between Physicians and the Pharmaceutical Industry Generally and Sales Representatives Specifically and Their Association with Physicians' Attitudes and Prescribing Habits: A Systematic Review." *BMJ Open* 7, no. 9 (August 2017).

Dejong, Colette, Thomas Aguilar, Chien-Wen Tseng, Grace A. Lin, W. John Boscardin, and R. Adams Dudley. "Pharmaceutical Industry–Sponsored Meals and Physician Prescribing Patterns for Medicare Beneficiaries." *JAMA Internal Medicine* 176, no. 8 (August 2016): 1114.

Elliott, Carl. "The Drug Pushers." *Atlantic*, April 1, 2006.

Harrison, Pam. "Half of NCI Cancer Center Directors Collect Industry Payments." Medscape, August 7, 2019. www.medscape.com/viewarticle/916550.

Bala, Ram, and Pradeep Bhardwaj. "Detailing vs. Direct-to-Consumer Advertising in the Prescription Pharmaceutical Industry." *Management Science* 56, no. 1 (2010): 148–160.

Pearl, Robert. "The $2.1 Million Question: What Are the Medical, Ethical Implications of the World's Priciest Drug?" *Forbes*, June 10, 2019.

Pearl, Robert. "The Immorality of Prescription Drug Pricing in America." *Forbes*, September 26, 2018.

"Public Opinion on Prescription Drugs and Their Prices." Kaiser Family Foundation, November 20, 2019. www.kff.org/slideshow/public-opinion-on-prescription -drugs-and-their-prices.

Raymond, Nate. "Doctor in Insys Opioid Kickback Scheme Gets Four Years in Prison." Reuters, March 9, 2018. www.reuters.com/article/us-insys-opioids/doctor-in-insys -opioid-kickback-scheme-gets-four-years-in-prison-idUSKCN1GL1DP.

5. *A Great Inconvenience*

Ganguli, Ishani, Zhuo Shi, E. John Orav, Aarti Rao, Kristin N. Ray, and Ateev Mehrotra. "Declining Use of Primary Care Among Commercially Insured Adults in the United States, 2008–2016." *Annals of Internal Medicine* 172, no. 4 (February 2020): 240.

Burda, David. "How the COVID-19 Pandemic Is Dulling the Point of All Those Healthcare Regulations." 4sight Health, April 23, 2020. www.4sighthealth.com /how-the-covid-19-pandemic-is-dulling-the-point-of-all-those-healthcare-regulations.

Patel, V., and C. Johnson. "Individuals' Use of Online Medical Records and Technology for Health Needs." Office of the National Coordinator for Health Information Technology. *ONC Data Brief*, no. 40 (April 2018). www.healthit.gov/sites/default/files /page/2018-03/HINTS-2017-Consumer-Data-Brief-3.21.18.pdf.

HealthGrades. "Assessing Online Scheduling as an Emerging Trend in Scheduling Physician Appointments." HealthLeaders, November 6, 2017. www.healt hleadersmedia.com/innovation/assessing-online-scheduling-emerging-trend -scheduling-physician-appointments.

Lutton, Logan. "American Patients Vastly Prefer Healthcare Price Transparency, According to New Survey." *Medical Economics*, April 2, 2020.

Becker's Hospital Review and Envera Health and Evariant. *Embracing the Experience: How VCU Drives More Volume by Transitioning from Traditional Marketing to Personalized Experiences.* Video. 59:22. YouTube, May 29, 2018. www.youtube.com /watch?v=Gu2IpplrjL4.

"Study: 96 Percent of Online Complaints About Doctors Fault Customer Service, Not Quality of Care." GlobeNewswire News Room, April 26, 2016. www.globenew swire.com/news-release/2016/04/26/832480/0/en/Study-96-Percent-of-Online -Complaints-About-Doctors-Fault-Customer-Service-Not-Quality-of-Care.html.

The Road Ahead in U.S. Healthcare: Will Patients Take the Wheel? A Healthcare White Paper. PNC Healthcare, 2015. www.pnc.com/content/dam/pnc-com /pdf/corporateandinstitutional/Treasury%20Management/Healthcare/patients -take-wheel-Whitepaper_cib-healthcare.pdf.

Kane, Leslie. "Medscape Physician Compensation Report 2019." Medscape, May 14, 2020, 24. www.medscape.com/slideshow/2020-compensation-overview-6012684.

"Special Report: The State of Consumer Trust." Most Trusted Brands 2020. Morning Consult, 2020. morningconsult.com/most-trusted-brands.

Zgierska, Aleksandra, David Rabago, and Michael Miller. "Impact of Patient Satisfaction Ratings on Physicians and Clinical Care." *Patient Preference and Adherence* 8 (2014): 437–446.

"Telehealth Index: 2019 Consumer Survey." Amwell, March 9, 2020. business.amwell .com/resources/telehealth-index-2019-consumer-survey.

6. *The Language Barrier*

"Medical Dictionary (App)." Farlex Inc., August 17, 2015. apps.apple.com/us/app /medical-dictionary-by-farlex/id1015991271.

Castro, Cesar M., et al. "Babel Babble: Physicians' Use of Unclarified Medical Jargon with Patients." *American Journal of Health Behavior* 31 (2007): 85–95.

Goldman, Brian. *The Secret Language of Doctors: Cracking the Code of Hospital Culture.* Toronto: HarperCollins, 2015.

Shem, Samuel. *The House of God: A Novel.* New York: Richard Marek Publishers, 1978.

Raven, Kathleen. "Medical Buzzwords Decoded." Yale Medicine, January 31, 2020. www.yalemedicine.org/stories/medical-buzzwords.

Weiss, Jennifer. "'Physician' Not 'Provider' Is Better for Doctor and Patient." Permanente Medicine, January 8, 2020. permanente.org/physician-not-provider-is-better-for-doctor-and-patient.

"Provider, Use of Term (Position Paper)." American Academy of Family Physicians, 2018. www.aafp.org/about/policies/all/provider.html.

Caplan, Arthur L. "No, Patients Are NOT Consumers, and MDs Are NOT Providers." Medscape, April 23, 2019. www.medscape.com/viewarticle/911562.

Ospina, Naykky Singh, Kari A. Phillips, Rene Rodriguez-Gutierrez, Ana Castaneda-Guarderas, Michael R. Gionfriddo, Megan E. Branda, and Victor M. Montori. "Eliciting the Patient's Agenda: Secondary Analysis of Recorded Clinical Encounters." *Journal of General Internal Medicine* 34, no. 1 (July 2, 2018): 36–40.

7. Impersonalized Medicine

Gawande, Atul. "Cowboys and Pit Crews." *New Yorker*, May 26, 2011.

8. The Truth Is Complicated

Bivens, Matt. "The Dishonesty of Informed Consent Rituals." *New England Journal of Medicine* 382, no. 12 (March 19, 2020): 1089–1091.

Fojo, Tito, Sham Mailankody, and Andrew Lo. "Unintended Consequences of Expensive Cancer Therapeutics—the Pursuit of Marginal Indications and a Me-Too Mentality That Stifles Innovation and Creativity." *JAMA Otolaryngology—Head & Neck Surgery* 140, no. 12 (December 2014): 1225.

Jacobson, Mireille, A. James O'Malley, Craig C. Earle, Juliana Pakes, Peter Gaccione, and Joseph P. Newhouse. "Does Reimbursement Influence Chemotherapy Treatment for Cancer Patients?" *Health Affairs* 25, no. 2 (2006): 437–443.

Pearl, Robert. "John McCain Did Not 'Give Up.'" *Forbes*, August 26, 2018.

Mogul, Fred. "Why So Many People Die in Hospitals Instead of at Home." *PBS News Hour*. Public Broadcasting Service, September 22, 2014. www.pbs.org/newshour/health/many-people-die-hospitals-instead-home.

Frellick, Marcia. "Few Physicians Using CMS Advance Care Planning Codes." Medscape, March 11, 2019. www.medscape.com/viewarticle/910204.

Ambroze, W. L., and J. H. Pemberton. "A Chance to Cut Is a Chance to Cure?" *American Journal of Gastroenterology* 85 (1990): 1531–1532.

Frellick, Marcia. "Clinicians' Comfort Levels Low with Life Expectancy Discussions." Medscape, April 24, 2019. www.medscape.com/viewarticle/912047.

9. The Doctor's Double Standard

Bauer, Hartwig, and Kim C. Honselmann. "Minimum Volume Standards in Surgery—Are We There Yet?" *Visceral Medicine* 33, no. 2 (May 2017): 106–116.

Reich, Harry, John Decaprio, and Fran Mcglynn. "Laparoscopic Hysterectomy." *Journal of Gynecologic Surgery* 5, no. 2 (February 2009): 213–216.

Mostafavi, Beata. "Plotting the Downward Trend in Traditional Hysterectomy." *Rounds* (blog). M Health Lab, University of Michigan, January 23, 2018. labblog.uofmhealth.org/rounds/plotting-downward-trend-traditional-hysterectomy.

Fahrenheit, Daniel Gabriel, and Pieter van der Star. *Fahrenheit's Letters to Leibniz and Boerhaave*. Leiden: Rodopi, 1983.

Siddiqui, Gina. "Why Doctors Reject Tools That Make Their Jobs Easier." *Observations* (blog). *Scientific American*, October 15, 2018. blogs.scientificamerican.com/observations/why-doctors-reject-tools-that-make-their-jobs-easier.

Joy, Janet Elizabeth, Edward E. Penhoet, and Diana B. Petitti. *Saving Women's Lives: Strategies for Improving Breast Cancer Detection and Diagnosis.* Washington, DC: National Academies Press, 2005.

PART FOUR: THE SOCIAL LADDER

1. A Culture Without Answers

Gould, Wendy Rose. "The Real Reason That Going to the Doctor Gives You Anxiety." NBC News, August 25, 2017. www.nbcnews.com/better/health/real-reason-going -doctor-gives-you-anxiety-ncna795566.

Hippocrates. "Hippocratic Corpus [Excerpts]." *Academic Medicine* 88, no. 1 (January 2013): 80.

2. On Death and Dying

"Code of Medical Ethics Opinion 5.7: Physician-Assisted Suicide." American Medical Association, 2017. www.ama-assn.org/delivering-care/ethics/physician -assisted-suicide.

Frellick, Marcia. "AMA Will Revisit Stance Against Physician-Assisted Dying." Medscape, June 11, 2018. www.medscape.com/viewarticle/897896.

"States with Legal Physician-Assisted Suicide." Britannica ProCon.org, February 18, 2020. euthanasia.procon.org/states-with-legal-physician-assisted-suicide.

Tinker, Ben. "111 People Died Under CA's New Right-to-Die Law." CNN, June 29, 2017. www.cnn.com/2017/06/28/health/california-end-of-life-2016-bn/index.html.

Cain, Cindy L., Barbara A. Koenig, Helene Starks, Judy Thomas, Lindsay Forbes, Sara McCleskey, and Neil S. Wenger. "Hospital and Health System Policies Concerning the California End of Life Option Act." *Journal of Palliative Medicine* 23, no. 1 (December 23, 2019): 60–66.

Parikh, Ravi B. "Opinion: Why I Won't Stop Treating Patients at the End of Life." Medscape, March 11, 2020. www.medscape.com/viewarticle/926414.

Wu, Bryan, Liz Hamel, and Mollyann Brodie. "Views and Experiences with End-of-Life Medical Care in the U.S.—Findings." Kaiser Family Foundation, May 11, 2017. www.kff.org/report-section/views-and-experiences-with-end-of-life-medical -care-in-the-us-findings.

Ostrov, Barbara Feder. "Most Doctors Unsure How to Discuss End-of-Life Care, Survey Says." *Kaiser Health News*, April 14, 2016. khn.org/news/most-doctors -unsure-how-to-discuss-end-of-life-care-survey-says.

Tolliver, Kevin. "The Nuances Between Palliative Care vs. Physician-Assisted Suicide." KevinMD.com, May 15, 2019. www.kevinmd.com/blog/2019/05/the-nuances -between-palliative-care-vs-physician-assisted-suicide.html.

3. The Young and the Breathless

Verghese, Abraham. "The Gordon Wilson Lecture: 'The Doctor in Our Own Time': Fildes' Famous Painting and Perceptions of Physician Attentiveness." *Transactions of the American Clinical and Climatological Association* 119 (2008): 117–126.

Verghese, Abraham. *Cutting for Stone: A Novel.* New York: Alfred A. Knopf, 2016.

"Hydrocephalus Fact Sheet." National Institute of Neurological Disorders and Stroke. US Department of Health and Human Services, 2020. www.ninds.nih.gov/disorders /patient-caregiver-education/fact-sheets/hydrocephalus-fact-sheet.

Kaszuba, Beth. "Facing Down Two Cancers Without Fear." Geisinger Stories. Geisinger, March 2020. www.geisinger.org/health-and-wellness/geisingerstories /2020/03/12/14/03/facing-down-cancer-hunter-jones.

Hiller, Mark. "'Hope for Hunter' Helping Cancer Patients." PAhomepage.com, January 11, 2017. www.pahomepage.com/news/hope-for-hunter-helping-cancer-patients.

Verheggen, François, Katelynn A. Perrault, Rudy Caparros Megido, Lena M. Dubois, Frédéric Francis, Eric Haubruge, Shari L. Forbes, Jean-François Focant, and Pierre-Hugues Stefanuto. "The Odor of Death: An Overview of Current Knowledge on Characterization and Applications." *BioScience* 67, no. 7 (July 7, 2017): 600–613.

4. Colorblind

Axelrod, Jim. "The Immortal Henrietta Lacks." *CBS Sunday Morning*, March 15, 2010. www.cbsnews.com/news/the-immortal-henrietta-lacks.

"The Tuskegee Timeline." Centers for Disease Control and Prevention, March 2, 2020. www.cdc.gov/tuskegee/timeline.htm.

Jones, James H. *Bad Blood: The Tuskegee Syphilis Experiment*. New York: Free Press, 1993.

Pearl, Robert. "Coronavirus Deaths Show How Little Black Lives Matter in American Healthcare." *Forbes*, June 16, 2020.

Pilkington, Ed. "Black Americans Dying of Covid-19 at Three Times the Rate of White People." *Guardian* (London), May 20, 2020.

"Health Disparities: Race and Hispanic Origin—Provisional Death Counts for Coronavirus Disease 2019 (COVID-19)." Centers for Disease Control and Prevention. www.cdc.gov/nchs/nvss/vsrr/covid19/health_disparities.htm. Accessed September 16, 2020.

Fisher, Max, and Emma Bubola. "As Coronavirus Deepens Inequality, Inequality Worsens Its Spread." *New York Times*, March 15, 2020.

COVID-19 and Minority Health Access: Illustrating Symptomatic Cases from Reported Minority Communities and Healthcare Gaps due to COVID-19. Rubix Life Sciences, March 2020. rubixls.com/wp-content/uploads/2020/04/COVID-19-Minority -Health-Access-7-1.pdf.

Lavizzo-Mourey, Risa, and David Williams. "Being Black Is Bad for Your Health." *U.S. News & World Report*, April 14, 2016.

Williams, David, and Ronald Wyatt. "Racial Bias in Health Care and Health." *JAMA* 314, no. 6 (2015): 555.

Shah, Nilay S., Rebecca Molsberry, Jamal S. Rana, Stephen Sidney, Simon Capewell, Martin O'Flaherty, Mercedes Carnethon, Donald M. Lloyd-Jones, and Sadiya S. Khan. "Heterogeneous Trends in Burden of Heart Disease Mortality by Subtypes in the United States, 1999–2018: Observational Analysis of Vital Statistics." *BMJ* 370 (2020): m2688.

Ledford, Heidi. "Millions of Black People Affected by Racial Bias in Health-Care Algorithms." *Nature* 574, no. 7780 (October 2019): 608–609.

Reid, Maryann. "Why Going to the Doctor as a Black Person Is Hard." *Forbes*, February 11, 2020.

Ramaswamy, Swapna Venugopal. "Without an 'Ounce of Empathy': Their Stories Show the Dangers of Being Black and Pregnant." *USA Today*, September 9, 2020.

Rho, Hye Jin, Hayley Brown, and Shawn Fremstad. "A Basic Demographic Profile of Workers in Frontline Industries." Center for Economic and Policy Research, April 7, 2020. cepr.net/a-basic-demographic-profile-of-workers-in-frontline-industries.

Yasmin, Seema. "How Medicine Perpetuates the Fallacy of Race." Medscape, March 11, 2020. www.medscape.com/viewarticle/926549.

Hoffman, Kelly M., Sophie Trawalter, Jordan R. Axt, and M. Norman Oliver. "Racial Bias in Pain Assessment and Treatment Recommendations, and False Beliefs About Biological Differences Between Blacks and Whites." *Proceedings of the National Academy of Sciences* 113, no. 16 (April 4, 2016): 4296–4301.

Haglage, Abby. "'White Coats for Black Lives': How Nurses and Doctors Are Sounding the Alarm About Medical Racism." *Yahoo! News*, June 12, 2020. www.yahoo.com /lifestyle/white-coats-for-black-lives-how-nurses-and-doctors-are-sounding-the -alarm-about-medical-racism-151450054.html.

Desmond-Harris, Jenée. "Implicit Bias Means We're All Probably at Least a Little Bit Racist." *Vox*, December 26, 2014. www.vox.com/2014/12/26/7443979 /racism-implicit-racial-bias.

"Implicit Association Tests." Project Implicit, 2020. implicit.harvard.edu/implicit /education.html.

Blair, I. V., J. F. Steiner, D. L. Fairclough, R. Hanratty, D. W. Price, H. K. Hirsh, L. A. Wright, et al. "Clinicians' Implicit Ethnic/Racial Bias and Perceptions of Care Among Black and Latino Patients." *Annals of Family Medicine* 11, no. 1 (January 2013): 43–52.

Alsan, Marcella, Owen Garrick, and Grant Graziani. *Does Diversity Matter for Health? Experimental Evidence from Oakland.* American Economic Review: Working Paper. Stanford Institute for Economic Policy Research, September 2018. siepr.stanford.edu /research/publications/does-diversity-matter-health-experimental-evidence-oakland.

Khullar, Dhruv. "Even as the U.S. Grows More Diverse, the Medical Profession Is Slow to Follow." *Washington Post*, September 24, 2018.

Logan, Trevon. "In American Health Care, Prejudice Is Deadly." Bloomberg, August 25, 2020. www.bloomberg.com/opinion/articles/2020-08-25/in-american-health -care-prejudice-is-deadly.

Belkin, Douglas. "Why We Need More Black Doctors—and How to Get There." *Wall Street Journal*, September 8, 2020.

Campbell, Kendall M., Irma Corral, Jhojana L. Infante Linares, and Dmitry Tumin. "Projected Estimates of African American Medical Graduates of Closed Historically Black Medical Schools." *JAMA Network Open* 3, no. 8 (August 20, 2020).

Greenwood, Brad N., Rachel R. Hardeman, Laura Huang, and Aaron Sojourner. "Physician–Patient Racial Concordance and Disparities in Birthing Mortality for Newborns." *Proceedings of the National Academy of Sciences* 117, no. 35 (August 17, 2020): 21194–21200.

5. Does Sex Matter?

Preez, Michael Du, and Jeremy Dronfield. *Dr. James Barry: A Woman Ahead of Her Time.* London: Oneworld, 2016.

Rae, Isobel. *The Strange Story of Dr. James Barry: Army Surgeon, Inspector-General of Hospitals, Discovered on Death to Be a Woman.* London: Longmans, Green, 1958.

Hume, Robert. "The Anatomy of a Lie: The Irish Woman Who Lived as a Man to Practice Medicine." *Irish Examiner*, August 1, 2014.

Conley, Frances K. *Walking Out on the Boys.* New York: Farrar, Straus and Giroux, 1998.

Hu, Yue-Yung, Ryan J. Ellis, D. Brock Hewitt, Anthony D. Yang, Elaine Ooi Cheung, Judith T. Moskowitz, John R. Potts, et al. "Discrimination, Abuse, Harassment, and Burnout in Surgical Residency Training." *New England Journal of Medicine* 381, no. 18 (October 31, 2019): 1741–1752.

"Only 1 in 20 Neurosurgeons Is a Woman." Information on Women in Neurosurgery. Northwest Neurosurgery Institute, 2020. www.northwestneurosurgery.com /resources/information-on-women-in-neurosurgery.

Anonymous. "Don't Make Me Choose Between Motherhood and My Career." KevinMD.com, August 19, 2019. www.kevinmd.com/blog/2019/08/dont-make-me -choose-between-motherhood-and-my-career.html.

Hussein, Qaali. "The Stigma of Motherhood in Medicine." KevinMD.com, October 25, 2019. www.kevinmd.com/blog/2019/10/the-stigma-of-motherhood-in-medicine .html.

"Women Paid Less Than Men Even at Highest Levels of Academic Medicine." Stanford Medicine News Center, March 2, 2020. med.stanford.edu/news/all-news/2020/02 /women-paid-less-than-men-even-at-highest-levels-of-academic-medi.html.

6. Discomfort with Difference

Vlessides, Michael. "High Percentage of Transgender Youth Don't Disclose It to HCPs." Medscape, March 11, 2020. www.medscape.com/viewarticle/926619.

Sequeira, Gina M., Kristin N. Ray, Elizabeth Miller, and Robert W. S. Coulter. "Transgender Youth's Disclosure of Gender Identity to Providers Outside of Specialized Gender Centers." *Journal of Adolescent Health* 66, no. 6 (June 1, 2020): 691–698.

Canner, Joseph K., Omar Harfouch, Lisa M. Kodadek, Danielle Pelaez, Devin Coon, Anaeze C. Offodile, Adil H. Haider, and Brandyn D. Lau. "Temporal Trends in Gender-Affirming Surgery Among Transgender Patients in the United States." *JAMA Surgery* 153, no. 7 (July 2018): 609.

Greenberg, Daniel, Maxine Najle, Natalie Jackson, Oyindamola Bola, and Robert P. Jones. "America's Growing Support for Transgender Rights." Public Religion Research Institute, June 11, 2019. www.prri.org/research/americas-growing -support-for-transgender-rights.

DeFao, Janine. "Male or Female, Always a Doctor: Top Physician Tells Colleagues, Patients at Kaiser That He Is Finally Becoming a Woman." *San Francisco Chronicle*, March 16, 2005.

7. The Last Straw

Chisolm, Julian John. *A Manual of Military Surgery.* Richmond, VA: West & Johnson, 1861.

Bernard, Claude, and Charles Huette. *Illustrated Manual of Operative Surgery and Surgical Anatomy.* San Francisco: Norman Publications, 1861.

Whitman, Walt. "All-Nighter: Walt Whitman Tends to the Wounded the Best He Can." *Lapham's Quarterly*, January 1, 1684.

"What Did Civil War Surgeons Feel?" National Museum of Civil War Medicine, March 23, 2018. www.civilwarmed.org/surgeons-cope.

Studdert, David M., Yifan Zhang, Sonja A. Swanson, Lea Prince, Jonathan A. Rodden, Erin E. Holsinger, Matthew J. Spittal, Garen J. Wintemute, and Matthew Miller. "Handgun Ownership and Suicide in California." *New England Journal of Medicine* 382, no. 23 (June 4, 2020): 2220–2229.

Butkus, Renee, Robert Doherty, and Sue S. Bornstein. "Reducing Firearm Injuries and Deaths in the United States: A Position Paper from the American College of Physicians." *Annals of Internal Medicine* 169, no. 10 (November 20, 2018): 704–707.

National Rifle Association (@NRA). "Someone should tell self-important anti-gun doctors to stay in their lane. Half of the articles in Annals of Internal Medicine are pushing for gun control. Most upsetting, however, the medical community seems to have consulted NO ONE but themselves." Twitter, November 7, 2018. twitter.com/NRA /status/1060256567914909702.

Ho, Vivian. "'Do You Know How Many Bullets I Pull out of Corpses Weekly?'— Doctors to NRA." *Guardian*, November 10, 2018.

Williams, Timothy. "What Are 'Red Flag' Gun Laws, and How Do They Work?" *New York Times*, August 6, 2019.

Greenfieldboyce, Nell. "Spending Bill Lets CDC Study Gun Violence; but Researchers Are Skeptical It Will Help." National Public Radio, March 23, 2018. www.npr .org/sections/health-shots/2018/03/23/596413510/proposed-budget-allows-cdc-to -study-gun-violence-researchers-skeptical.

Studdert, David. "Owning Handgun Associated with Dramatically Higher Risk of Suicide." Stanford Health Policy. Freeman Spogli Institute for International Studies and the Stanford School of Medicine, June 3, 2020. healthpolicy.fsi.stanford.edu/news /handgun-ownership-associated-dramatically-higher-risk-suicide.

"Code of Medical Ethics Opinion 1.1.7: Physician Exercise of Conscience." American Medical Association, 2017. www.ama-assn.org/delivering-care/ethics /physician-exercise-conscience.

Lucas, Elizabeth, and Julie Appleby. "Doctors Can Change Opioid Prescribing Habits, but Progress Comes in Small Doses." *Kaiser Health News*, August 15, 2019. khn.org /news/doctors-opioid-prescribing-habits-change-comes-in-small-doses.

Stack, Liam. "Measles Cases Reach Highest Level in More Than 25 Years, C.D.C. Says." *New York Times*, May 30, 2019.

Halperin, Beth, Ryan Melnychuk, Jocelyn Downie, and Noni MacDonald. "When Is It Permissible to Dismiss a Family Who Refuses Vaccines? Legal, Ethical and Public Health Perspectives." *Paediatrics & Child Health* 12, no. 10 (December 2007): 843–845.

Salas, Renee N. "The Climate Crisis and Clinical Practice." *New England Journal of Medicine* 382, no. 7 (February 13, 2020): 589–591.

Cummings, Mike. "Healthcare Industry Is a Major Source of Harmful Emissions." *Yale News*, August 2, 2019.

Abbott, Brianna. "Medical Schools Are Pushed to Train Doctors for Climate Change." *Wall Street Journal*, August 7, 2019.

PART FIVE: THE EVOLUTION OF PHYSICIAN CULTURE

1. Economic Desperation

Konkel, Lindsey. "Life for the Average Family During the Great Depression." History.com, April 19, 2018. www.history.com/news/life-for-the-average -family-during-the-great-depression.

Wilbur, Ray Lyman. *Medical Care for the American People: The Final Report of the Committee on the Costs of Medical Care.* Chicago: University of Chicago Press, 1932.

Gore, Thomas B. "A Forgotten Landmark Medical Study from 1932 by the Committee on the Cost of Medical Care." *Baylor University Medical Center Proceedings* 26, no. 2 (April 2013): 142–143.

Falk, I. S. "Medical Care in the USA: 1932–1972. Problems, Proposals and Programs from the Committee on the Costs of Medical Care to the Committee for National Health Insurance." *Milbank Memorial Fund Quarterly: Health and Society* 51, no. 1 (1973): 1–32.

Falk, I. S. "Some Lessons from the Fifty Years Since the CCMC Final Report, 1932." *Journal of Public Health Policy* 4, no. 2 (June 1983): 135.

Baker, Paula, Donald T. Critchlow, and Christie Ford Chapin. "Chapter 25: Health Policy." Essay. In *The Oxford Handbook of American Political History*, edited by Paula Baker and Donald T. Crtichlow, 464–467. New York: Oxford University Press, 2020.

Moser, Whet. "When America First Realized It Had a Problem with Health-Care Costs." *Chicago Magazine*, July 28, 2017.

Walker, Forrest A. "Americanism Versus Sovietism: A Study of the Reaction to the Committee on the Costs of Medical Care." *Bulletin of the History of Medicine* 53, no. 4 (1979): 489–504.

Barr, Donald A. *Introduction to U.S. Health Policy: The Organization, Financing, and Delivery of Health Care in America.* Baltimore, MD: Johns Hopkins University Press, 2011.

Byrd, W. Michael, and Linda A. Clayton. *The American Health Dilemma: Race, Medicine, and Health Care in the United States, 1900–2000.* London: Routledge, 2015.

Siegel, Rachel, and Andrew Van Dam. "U.S. Economy Contracted at Fastest Quarterly Rate on Record from April to June as Coronavirus Walloped Workers, Businesses." *Washington Post,* July 31, 2020.

Casselman, Ben. "A Collapse That Wiped Out 5 Years of Growth, with No Bounce in Sight." *New York Times,* July 30, 2020.

Schrager, Allison, Allen C. Guelzo, and Brian Riedl. "Pandemic Adds $8 Trillion to Debt Avalanche." Manhattan Institute, June 11, 2020. www.manhattan-institute .org/pandemic-adds-8-trillion-debt-avalanche.

Riedl, Brian. "Who Will Fund $24 Trillion in New Government Debt?" *National Review,* July 28, 2020.

Hansen, Sarah. "Federal Budget Deficit Will Approach $4 Trillion in 2020, CBO Says, as the Economy Continues to Nosedive." *Forbes,* April 24, 2020.

"The Great Lockdown: Worst Economic Downturn Since the Great Depression." International Monetary Fund, March 23, 2020. www.imf.org/en/News /Articles/2020/03/23/pr2098-imf-managing-director-statement-following-a-g20 -ministerial-call-on-the-coronavirus-emergency.

Long, Heather, and Andrew Van Dam. "U.S. Unemployment Rate Soars to 14.7 Percent, the Worst Since the Depression Era." *Washington Post,* May 9, 2020.

Lowrey, Annie. "The Second Great Depression." *Atlantic,* June 23, 2020.

Walsh, Mary Williams. "A Tidal Wave of Bankruptcies Is Coming." *New York Times,* June 18, 2020.

Sisko, Andrea M., Sean P. Keehan, John A. Poisal, Gigi A. Cuckler, Sheila D. Smith, Andrew J. Madison, Kathryn E. Rennie, and James C. Hardesty. "National Health Expenditure Projections, 2018–27: Economic and Demographic Trends Drive Spending and Enrollment Growth." *Health Affairs* 38, no. 3 (February 20, 2019): 491–501.

Altman, Drew. "Many Poor and Minority Families Can't Afford Food or Rent Because of Coronavirus." Axios, May 29, 2020. www.axios.com/coronavirus-economy -jobs-unemployent-racial-disparities-29e3c6c4-bb43-4eaf-bf90-04697ca66b2d .html.

Irwin, Neil. "Don't Lose the Thread: The Economy Is Experiencing an Epic Collapse of Demand." *New York Times,* June 6, 2020.

Thomas, Lauren. "25,000 Stores Are Predicted to Close in 2020, as the Coronavirus Pandemic Accelerates Industry Upheaval." CNBC, June 9, 2020. www.cnbc .com/2020/06/09/coresight-predicts-record-25000-retail-stores-will-close-in-2020 .html.

Thomas, Patrick, Sarah Chaney, and Chip Cutter. "New Covid-19 Layoffs Make Job Reductions Permanent." *Wall Street Journal,* August 28, 2020.

Davidson, Kate. "U.S. Debt Is Set to Exceed Size of the Economy Next Year, a First Since World War II." *Wall Street Journal,* September 2, 2020.

Rabouin, Dion. "Here Comes the Real Recession." Axios, September 2, 2020. www .axios.com/recession-within-recession-coronavirus-0bcb2af4-4c1a-4ded-9579 -096214c5b2d6.html.

Rovner, Julie. "Another Problem on the Health Horizon: Medicare Is Running out of Money." *Kaiser Health News*, July 22, 2020. khn.org/news/another-problem -on-the-health-horizon-medicare-is-running-out-of-money.

"PwC US CFO Pulse Survey." PwC, 2020. www.pwc.com/us/en/library/covid-19/pwc -covid-19-cfo-pulse-survey.html.

2. Between Scylla and Charybdis

"History of SSA During the Johnson Administration 1963–1968." Social Security History, 2020. www.ssa.gov/history/lbjstmts.html.

Amadeo, Kimberly. "President Jimmy Carter's Economic Policies and Accomplishments." *The Balance*, May 7, 2020. www.thebalance.com/president-jimmy-carter -s-economic-policies-4586571.

Clymer, Adam. "After 3 Decades Working in Senate, Kennedy Gets a Turn for His Agenda." *New York Times*, March 8, 1993.

Enthoven, Alain. "The Rise and Fall of HMOs Shows How a Worthy Idea Went Wrong." *CommonWealth*, August 2, 2014.

Kleinfield, N. R. "The King of the H.M.O. Mountain." *New York Times*, July 31, 1983.

Enthoven, Alain C. "The History and Principles of Managed Competition." *Health Affairs* 12, Supplement (1993): 24–48.

Pear, Robert. "A.M.A. Rebels over Health Plan in Major Challenge to President." *New York Times*, September 30, 1993.

"Summary of the Affordable Care Act." Kaiser Family Foundation, April 25, 2013. kff .org/health-reform/fact-sheet/summary-of-the-affordable-care-act.

Blumenthal, David, Sara R. Collins, and Mart Beth Hamel. "Health Care Coverage Under the Affordable Care Act—a Progress Report." *New England Journal of Medicine* 371, no. 3 (July 17, 2014): 275–281.

Physician Perspectives About Health Care Reform and the Future of the Medical Profession. Deloitte 2013 Survey of Physicians. Deloitte Center for Health Solutions, 2013. www2.deloitte.com/content/dam/Deloitte/us/Documents/life-sciences-health-care/ us-lshc-deloitte-2013-physician-survey-10012014.pdf.

ACC News Story. "Medicare Access and CHIP Reauthorization Act of 2015: What You Need to Know." American College of Cardiology, April 28, 2015. www .acc.org/latest-in-cardiology/articles/2015/04/28/15/59/medicare-access-and -chip-reauthorization-act-of-2015-what-you-need-to-know.

Joszt, Laura. "CMS' Verma: Upend the Status Quo to Move to Value-Based Care." *American Journal of Managed Care*, April 25, 2019.

Terry, Ken. "CMS Modifies Policies, Timelines for Alternative Payment Models." Medscape, June 4, 2020. www.medscape.com/viewarticle/931801.

3. Two Paths, Both Fraught with Peril

Tikkanen, Roosa, Robin Osborn, Elias Mossialos, Ana Djordjevic, and George A. Wharton. "India: International Healthcare System Profiles." Commonwealth Fund, June 5, 2020. www.commonwealthfund.org/international-health-policy-center /countries/india.

"Maternal, Newborn and Child Health." The Bill & Melinda Gates Foundation. www .gatesfoundation.org/what-we-do/global-development/maternal-newborn-and -child-health. Accessed September 24, 2020.

Kasthuri, Arvind. "Challenges to Healthcare in India—the Five A's." *Indian Journal of Community Medicine* 43, no. 3 (2018): 141–143.

Perry, Philip A., and Timothy Hotze. "Oregon's Experiment with Prioritizing Public Health Care Services." *AMA Journal of Ethics* 13, no. 4 (April 2011): 241–247.

Oberlander, Jonathan, Theodore Marmor, and Lawrence Jacobs. "Rationing Medical Care: Rhetoric and Reality in the Oregon Health Plan." *Canadian Medical Association Journal* 164, no. 11 (May 29, 2001): 1583–1587.

Glionna, John M. "Avoiding Care During the Pandemic Could Mean Life or Death." *Kaiser Health News*, July 31, 2020. khn.org/news/avoiding-care-during-the -pandemic-could-mean-life-or-death.

Abelson, Reed. "Why People Are Still Avoiding the Doctor (It's Not the Virus)." *New York Times*, June 16, 2020.

Frellick, Marcia. "High-Deductible Plans Push Physicians to Change Practice." Medscape, June 18, 2020. www.medscape.com/viewarticle/932614.

Young, Samantha. "'Why Do We Always Get Hit First?' Proposed Budget Cuts Target Vulnerable Californians." California Healthline, June 1, 2020. california healthline.org/news/california-proposed-budget-cuts-target-vulnerable-medicaid -beneficiaries.

"California Assembly Slams Governor's Proposed Budget Cuts." *Los Angeles Times*, May 27, 2020.

Senz, Kristen. "Small Businesses Are Worse Off Than We Thought." Working Knowledge, Harvard Business School, April 13, 2020. hbswk.hbs.edu/item/small -businesses-are-worse-off-than-we-thought.

Pearl, Robert, and Philip Madvig. "Managing the Most Expensive Patients." *Harvard Business Review*, February 26, 2020.

Sidney, Stephen, Michael E. Sorel, Charles P. Quesenberry, Marc G. Jaffe, Matthew D. Solomon, Mai N. Nguyen-Huynh, Alan S. Go, and Jamal S. Rana. "Comparative Trends in Heart Disease, Stroke, and All-Cause Mortality in the United States and a Large Integrated Healthcare Delivery System." *American Journal of Medicine* 131, no. 7 (2018).

Pearl, Robert. "3 Lessons in Rapid Change from an Unlikely Source: Health Care." *Forbes*, May 29, 2014.

"Why Accountable Healthcare? It Promotes Health and Is Readily Available." Council of Accountable Physician Practices (CAPP), 2020. accountablecaredoctors.org /accountable-care-pillars.

Galewitz, Phil. "A Mexican Hospital, an American Surgeon, and a $5,000 Check (Yes, a Check)." *New York Times*, August 9, 2019.

Galewitz, Phil. "Need a Knee Replacement? This Company Pays Employees to Meet a Doctor in Cancun." *Dallas News*, August 20, 2019.

Leisure, Larry. "Why Walmart Centers of Excellence Model Could Redefine How Employers Deliver Quality Care." Healthcare IT News, March 31, 2019. hitconsultant .net/2019/03/06/walmart-centers-of-excellence-model-quality-care/.

Pearl, Robert. "Lessons from HLTH: What Happens if We Fail to Change Healthcare?" RobertPearlMD.com, October 28, 2019. robertpearlmd.com/hlth.

Keckley, Paul. "MedPAC Report to Congress: No Surprises but Incomplete." *Keckley Report*, June 22, 2020. www.paulkeckley.com/the-keckley-report/2020/6/22 /medpac-report-to-congress-no-surprises-but-incomplete.

4. Denial, Anger, Bargaining, and Depression

Kübler-Ross, Elisabeth, and David Kessler. *On Grief and Grieving: Finding the Meaning of Grief Through the Five Stages of Loss*. New York: Scribner, 2005.

Kessler, David. "Five Stages of Grief by Elisabeth Kübler-Ross & David Kessler." Grief .com, 2020. grief.com/the-five-stages-of-grief.

Gibler, Kyle, Omar Kattan, Rupal Malani, and Laura Medford-Davis. "Physician Employment: The Path Forward in the COVID-19 Era." McKinsey & Company, July 17,

2020. www.mckinsey.com/industries/healthcare-systems-and-services/our-insights/physician-employment-the-path-forward-in-the-covid-19-era.

Kane, Leslie. "Medscape Physician Compensation Report 2020." Medscape, May 14, 2020. www.medscape.com/slideshow/2020-compensation-overview-6012684.

Ault, Alicia. "Ob/Gyns, Peds, Other PCPs Seeking COVID-19 Financial Relief." Medscape, April 30, 2020. www.medscape.com/viewarticle/929699.

Terry, Ken. "As COVID-19 Shutters Practices Virtual Doc-Patient Activity Soars." Medscape, April 30, 2020. www.medscape.com/viewarticle/929702.

Balasubramanian, Sai. "Physician Practices Are in Critical Condition due to Coronavirus." *Forbes*, July 27, 2020.

Feldman, David B. "Why the Five Stages of Grief Are Wrong: Lessons from the (Non-) Stages of Grief." *Psychology Today*, July 7, 2017.

Grove, Andrew S. *Only the Paranoid Survive*. New York: Doubleday Business, 1996.

Markoff, John. "Intel's Big Shift After Hitting Technical Wall." *New York Times*, May 17, 2004.

Seltzer, Leon F. "Anger: How We Transfer Feelings of Guilt, Hurt, and Fear." *Psychology Today*, June 14, 2013.

Bailey, Melissa. "Too Many Tests, Too Little Time: Doctors Say They Face 'Moral Injury' Because of a Business Model That Interferes with Patient Care." *Washington Post*, February 1, 2020.

Shrank, William H., Teresa L. Rogstad, and Natasha Parekh. "Special Communication: Waste in the US Health Care System." *JAMA* 322, no. 15 (2019): 1501–1509.

Topol, Eric. "Why Doctors Should Organize." *New Yorker*, August 5, 2019.

"The Physicians Foundation 2020 Physician Survey: Covid-19 Impact Edition." The Physicians Foundation, August 18, 2020. physiciansfoundation.org/research-insights/2020physiciansurvey.

"Public's Views of Doctors, Nurses, Insurance Companies, and Drug Companies Survey." Kaiser Family Foundation, August 3, 2020.

LaPointe, Jacqueline. "Less Than a Third of Docs Owned Independent Practices in 2018." RevCycleIntelligence, September 20, 2018. revcycleintelligence.com/news/less-than-a-third-of-docs-owned-independent-practices-in-2018.

Furukawa, Michael F., Laura Kimmey, David J. Jones, Rachel M. Machta, Jing Guo, and Eugene C. Rich. "Consolidation of Providers into Health Systems Increased Substantially, 2016–18." *Health Affairs* 39, no. 8 (August 2020): 1321–1325.

Lindmark, Augie W., Micah A. Johnson, and Alec M. Feuerbach. "Doctors and Dark Money: A Bad Prescription for Health Reform." Medscape, March 6, 2020. www.medscape.com/viewarticle/926307.

Moir, Fiona, Jill Yielder, Jasmine Sanson, and Yan Chen. "Depression in Medical Students: Current Insights." *Advances in Medical Education and Practice* 9 (May 2018): 323–333.

Mata, Douglas A., Marco A. Ramos, Narinder Bansal, Rida Khan, Constance Guille, Emanuele Di Angelantonio, and Srijan Sen. "Prevalence of Depression and Depressive Symptoms Among Resident Physicians." *JAMA* 314, no. 22 (December 2015): 2373–2383.

Schernhammer, Eva S., and Graham A. Colditz. "Suicide Rates Among Physicians: A Quantitative and Gender Assessment (Meta-Analysis)." *American Journal of Psychiatry* 161, no. 12 (December 2004): 2295–2302.

5. Acceptance and the Five Cs of Cultural Change

Kane, Leslie, and Debra A. Shute. "Medscape Malpractice Report 2019." Medscape, November 20, 2019. www.medscape.com/slideshow/2019-malpractice-report-6012303.

Guardado, José R. *Medical Professional Liability Insurance Premiums: An Overview of the Market from 2010 to 2019.* American Medical Association, 2019. www.ama-assn.org /system/files/2020-02/prp-mlm-premiums.pdf.

Montgomery, A., E. Panagopoulou, A. Esmail, T. Richards, and C. Maslach. "Burnout in Healthcare: The Case for Organisational Change." *BMJ* 366 (July 30, 2019).

Dooley Young, Kerry. "Tackling Economic, Emotional Toll of Clinician Burnout Critical." Medscape, May 31, 2019. www.medscape.com/viewarticle/913778.

Levinson, John, Bruce H. Price, and Vikas Saini. "Death by a Thousand Clicks: Leading Boston Doctors Decry Electronic Medical Records." *Common-Health.* WBUR, May 12, 2017. www.wbur.org/commonhealth/2017/05/12 /boston-electronic-medical-records.

Pearl, Robert. "The Mystery of the Hospital Industry's Silence over EHR Rule Proposal." *Forbes*, March 9, 2020.

Pearl, Robert. "Blockchain, Bitcoin and the Electronic Health Record." *Forbes*, April 10, 2018.

Melnick, Edward R., Liselotte N. Dyrbye, Christine A. Sinsky, Mickey Trockel, Colin P. West, Laurence Nedelec, Michael A. Tutty, and Tait Shanafelt. "The Association Between Perceived Electronic Health Record Usability and Professional Burnout Among US Physicians." *Mayo Clinic Proceedings* 95, no. 3 (March 2020): 476–487.

Bresnick, Jennifer. "Have EHRs, Health IT Adoption Really Made Progress Since 1990?" EHRIntelligence, September 24, 2014. ehrintelligence.com/news /have-ehrs-health-it-adoption-really-made-progress-since-1990.

Aspden, Philip. *Preventing Medication Errors.* Washington, DC: National Academies Press, 2007.

Hutchinson, Sean. "How Lethal Is My Doctor's Sloppy Handwriting?" Mental Floss, August 20, 2014. www.mentalfloss.com/article/58441/how-lethal-my -doctors-sloppy-handwriting.

McCarthy, Douglas, Kimberly Mueller, and Jennifer Wrenn. "Kaiser Permanente: Bridging the Quality Divide with Integrated Practice, Group Accountability, and Health Information Technology." Commonwealth Fund, June 22, 2009. www .commonwealthfund.org/publications/case-study/2009/jun/kaiser-permanente -bridging-quality-divide-integrated-practice.

Rhee, Chanu, Travis M. Jones, Yasir Hamad, Anupam Pande, Jack Varon, Cara O'Brien, Deverick J. Anderson, et al. "Prevalence, Underlying Causes, and Preventability of Sepsis-Associated Mortality in US Acute Care Hospitals." *JAMA Network Open* 2, no. 2 (February 15, 2019).

Whippy, Alan, Melinda Skeath, Barbara Crawford, Carmen Adams, Gregory Marelich, Mezhgan Alamshahi, and Josefina Borbon. "Kaiser Permanente's Performance Improvement System, Part 3: Multisite Improvements in Care for Patients with Sepsis." *The Joint Commission Journal on Quality and Patient Safety* 37, no. 11 (November 2011): 483–493.

Orgera, Kendal, Rachel Garfield, and Anthony Damico. "The Uninsured and the ACA: A Primer—Key Facts About Health Insurance and the Uninsured Amidst Changes to the Affordable Care Act—How Many People Are Uninsured?" Kaiser Family Foundation, May 13, 2020. www.kff.org/report-section/the-uninsured-and-the-aca -a-primer-key-facts-about-health-insurance-and-the-uninsured-amidst-changes-to -the-affordable-care-act-how-many-people-are-uninsured.

Pascale, Richard T., Jerry Sternin, and Monique Sternin. *The Power of Positive Deviance: How Unlikely Innovators Solve the World's Toughest Problems.* Boston: Harvard Business Press, 2010.

Heath, Chip, and Dan Heath. *Switch: How to Change Things When Change Is Hard*. New York: Random House Business, 2010.

Dweck, Carol S. *Mindset: The New Psychology of Success*. New York: Ballantine Books, 2006.

Pearl, Robert. "The Unspoken Causes of Physician Burnout." *Forbes*, July 10, 2019.

Shanafelt, Tait. "Collaboration Aims to Battle Physician Burnout." Stanford Medicine News Center, June 5, 2019. med.stanford.edu/news/all-news/2019/06/collaboration-aims-to-battle-physician-burnout.html.

Russell, Sabin. "Doctors Heading to Sri Lanka as Part of Kaiser's Effort to Help." *San Francisco Chronicle*, January 12, 2005.

Pearl, Robert. "3 Things U.S. Medicine Can Learn from a Global Humanitarian Nonprofit." *Forbes*, August 14, 2017.

6. The Virtues of Being Difficult

Crittenden, Jennifer. "The Package (The 'Difficult' Patient)." *Seinfeld* season 8, episode 139. NBC, December 17, 1996.

Chhabra, Karan R., Kyle H. Sheetz, Ushapoorna Nuliyalu, Mihir S. Dekhne, Andrew M. Ryan, and Justin B. Dimick. "Out-of-Network Bills for Privately Insured Patients Undergoing Elective Surgery with In-Network Primary Surgeons and Facilities." *JAMA* 323, no. 6 (February 11, 2020): 538.

Hennessy, Michelle. "One Third of Doctors Don't Wash Their Hands Between Patients—Report." *The Journal*, November 14, 2012. www.thejournal.ie/doctors-was-hands-674108-Nov2012.

"Nearly Half a Million Americans Suffered from Clostridium Difficile Infections in a Single Year." Centers for Disease Control and Prevention, February 25, 2015. www.cdc.gov/media/releases/2015/p0225-clostridium-difficile.html.

Pearl, Robert. "Six Ways to Make the U.S. Economic and Health Care Systems Stronger After the Coronavirus Pandemic." *Forbes*, May 12, 2020.

Makary, Martin A., and Michael Daniel. "Medical Error—the Third Leading Cause of Death in the US." *BMJ* 353 (2016): i2139.

Pearl, Robert. "Medical Conflicts of Interest Are Dangerous." *Wall Street Journal*, April 24, 2013.

Grochowski Jones, Ryann, Mike Tigas, Charles Ornstein, and Lena Groeger. "Dollars for Docs." ProPublica, October 17, 2019. projects.propublica.org/docdollars.

Gawande, Atul. "Cowboys and Pit Crews." *New Yorker*, May 26, 2011.

Shrank, William H., Teresa L. Rogstad, and Natasha Parekh. "Waste in the US Health Care System." *JAMA* 322, no. 15 (2019): 1501.

"U.S. Headache Sufferers Get $1 Billion Worth of Brain Scans Each Year." *ScienceDaily*, March 17, 2014. www.sciencedaily.com/releases/2014/03/140317170642.htm.

Gordon, Mara. "Why Do Doctors Overtreat? For Many, It's What They're Trained to Do." National Public Radio, April 19, 2019. www.npr.org/sections/health-shots/2019/04/19/715113208/why-do-doctors-overtreat-for-many-its-what-they-re-trained-to-do.

Piller, Charles. "FDA and NIH Let Clinical Trial Sponsors Keep Results Secret and Break the Law." *Science*, January 13, 2020.

Castellucci, Maria. "Most Hospitals Fail to Meet Leapfrog's Surgery Volume Standards." Modern Healthcare, July 18, 2019. www.modernhealthcare.com/safety-quality/most-hospitals-fail-meet-leapfrogs-surgery-volume-standards.

Marsa, Linda. "How to Choose a Surgeon, Doctor for Medical Surgeries." AARP, August 24, 2017. www.aarp.org/health/conditions-treatments/info-2017/choose-a-surgeon-doctor-surgeries.html.

Ostrov, Barbara Feder. "Most Doctors Unsure How to Discuss End-of-Life Care, Survey Says." *Kaiser Health News*, April 14, 2016. khn.org/news/most-doctors-unsure-how-to-discuss-end-of-life-care-survey-says.

7. Medicine: A Love Story

Pearl, Robert. "It's a Wonder People Survive More Than Three Nights in a Hospital." *Forbes*, March 31, 2017.

INDEX

acceptance
  depression and, 294, 297
  finding, 249–251
  grief model and, 295–297
  physician culture and, 249–251,
    294–297
Accountable Care Organizations,
  274–275, 282, 306
achromatopsia, 308
Advancing Health Equity, 224
Affordable Care Act (ACA), 101, 274,
  303
Alan (cousin), 38–43, 134
allegiances, 27–28
Amazon, 150, 152, 286, 287
American Board of Pediatrics, 235
American College of Emergency
  Physicians (ACEP), 139–140
American College of Physicians (ACP),
  254–257
American Conservative (magazine), 39
American Foundation of Suicide
  Prevention, 294
American Journal of Health Behavior
  (journal), 156
American Medical Association
  (AMA), 134, 193, 226–227, 258,
  266–267, 274–276, 281, 285
amyotrophic lateral sclerosis (ALS),
  203–204
anger, managing, 289, 291–292,
  328–330
Annals of Internal Medicine (journal),
  152, 255
antibiotics, 37, 60–64, 165–167, 220

Anversa, Piero, 143
"art of medicine," 46–48, 57
Asclepius, 50–51
Ashley Furniture, 286
asthma, 73, 162
autonomy, 106–112, 307

bacterial infections, 58–64, 165–167
barber pole, 16, 28
bargaining process, 289, 293–294
Barry, James, 230–231
Baselga, José, 143
Basu, Sanjay, 102–103
battlefield surgeons, 252–254
behaviors, modifying, 312–321
Berkshire Hathaway, 286
Berwick, Don, 73
Biden, Joe, 287
Bill & Melinda Gates Foundation, 278
Black Lives Matter movement, 228
Blackstock, Uché, 224
bloodletting, 13–17
Boerhaave, Herman, 182–183
boredom, 114–118
brain cancer, 172, 212–213
brain surgery, 86, 213
brain tumor, 86, 212–213
breast cancer, 94, 180, 224, 333
Brigham and Women's Hospital,
  85–86, 143
British Journal of Haematology (journal),
  17
Brooklyn College, 170
Brown v. Board of Education of Topeka
  (legal case), 227

Buckley, William F., 39
Bulkley, Margaret, 231
burnout, 81–94, 106, 112, 296
burnout survey, 83, 90–91

Caduceus, 50–51
Callaghan, Brian, 87
cancer
    brain cancer, 172, 212–213
    breast cancer, 94, 180, 224, 333
    cervical cancer, 180
    colon cancer, 33, 73, 212–216
    diagnosis of, 39–40
    fight against, 37, 40–43, 49
    Hodgkin's lymphoma, 40, 43
    leukemia, 37–43, 58–60, 170
    lung cancer, 33, 73, 166
    ovarian cancer, 171, 214
    pancreatic cancer, 175–176
    preventing, 73–75, 97
    prostate cancer, 93
    screenings, 180
    skin cancer, 96, 326
    surgery for, 94–95, 224, 327–328
    treating, 37, 40–42, 58–60, 93–95,
        171–173, 212–216, 327–328
capitation model, 264–265, 273–276,
    283–285, 305. *See also* healthcare
    system
cardiac surgery, 95, 98, 100–101, 232,
    280
cardiovascular disease, 44, 73, 224,
    228. *See also* heart disease
care. *See also* healthcare system; primary
    care
    commitment to, 300–303
    coordinating, 318–319
    quality care, 84–86, 123–126,
        153–154, 266, 283–286
Carlin, George, 123
Carter, Jimmy, 272–273
Case Western Reserve University,
    245
cellulitis, 60–61
Centers for Disease Control and
    Prevention (CDC), 2, 87, 222,
    224, 257–259, 280

Centers for Medicare & Medicaid
    Services (CMS), 73, 154, 266,
    269–270, 287
cervical cancer, 180
Chabris, Christopher, 22–23
Charles II, King, 15
Charybdis, 271–276, 283–284
childbirth, 18–19, 109, 133, 224, 278
Circe, 271
Civil Rights Movement, 221
Civil War, 252–254
climate change, 258, 260
Clinton, Bill, 273–274
Code of Medical Ethics (book), 193, 258
collaboration, 282–283, 301, 305–307
College of William & Mary, 243
colon cancer, 33, 73, 212–216
colorblind, being, 219–229
commitment to care, 300–303
Committee on the Costs of Medical
    Care (CCMC), 264–267, 272–
    275, 282
communicating, 28–29, 155–160
competence, 106–112
computer era, 43–49. *See also*
    technological changes
conflicts of interest, 317–318
confronting problems, 297–300
Conley, Frances, 233–235
connectedness, 104–113, 303–305
contributions, importance of, 307–311
"cookbook medicine," 47
coronavirus
    description of, 1–2
    fight against, 49
    healthcare system and, 2–7
    healthcare workers and, 2–4
    impact of, 2–7, 149–150, 268–269,
        289
    racism and, 221–223, 228
    vaccines for, 259
Council of Accountable Physician
    Practices (CAPP), 283
COVID-19
    description of, 1–2
    fight against, 49
    healthcare system and, 2–7

healthcare workers and, 2–4
impact of, 2–7, 149–150, 268–269, 289
racism and, 221–223, 228
vaccines for, 259
Craik, James, 15
CT scans, 36, 86–87, 100, 280–281
cultural allegiances, 27–28
cultural change
  collaboration, 282–283, 301, 305–307
  commitment to care, 300–303
  confronting problems, 297–300
  connectedness, 104–113, 303–305
  contributions, 307–311
  five Cs of, 295, 297–311
  health records and, 244, 300–306
  healthcare system and, 244, 297–311
  physician culture and, 26–27, 295, 297–311
cultural conditioning, 24–25. *See also* physician culture
cultural symbols, 28–29
Cures Act, 150
customer service, 124–125, 149–154, 307
Cutting for Stone (book), 206

da Vinci, Leonardo, 142
Dana Farber Institute, 37
Dartmouth College, 198
Dean, Wendy, 86
Death with Dignity laws, 193–194
death/dying. *See also* life expectancy
  with dignity, 193–194
  discussing, 320–321
  end-of-life options, 170–172, 194, 204–207, 282, 290, 320–321
  fear of, 38
  medically assisted death, 193–194, 204–205
  mortality statistics, 18–20, 44, 99–101, 173–175, 180, 222–228, 278
  prolonging life, 171–173, 192–194
  relationship with, 216–218
"Decades of Physician Excellence," 114

Deci, Edward, 106–107, 109
defense mechanisms, 4, 38, 43, 48–49, 62–65, 77–78, 140
denial, handling, 38, 48, 140, 289–291, 328–330
depression
  acceptance and, 294, 297
  causes of, 294, 297
  physician culture and, 76–79, 81–83, 88–89, 92–94, 289, 294, 296–297
dermatology, 96, 138, 326
diabetes, 6, 73, 75, 98, 158, 217, 223, 228, 279
diagnostic tools, 35–37, 69–71, 100–101, 125–130, 175–176
Diener, Ed, 105
difficult, being, 312–321
disasters, 127–132, 309–311
diseases. *See also* cancer
  asthma, 73, 162
  cardiovascular disease, 44, 73, 224, 228
  chronic diseases, 6–7, 84, 87, 117, 178, 192, 223, 228, 260, 282–287
  climate change and, 258, 260
  diabetes, 6, 73, 75, 98, 158, 217, 223, 228, 279
  diagnosing, 28–29, 35–40, 69–71, 93, 100–101, 125–134, 150–153, 160–167, 175–176, 206–207, 220–221
  disinfectants and, 1, 19–21, 187
  germ theory of, 19–21
  heart disease, 6, 44, 73, 99–101, 129–131, 143, 162, 200–201, 220–224, 282, 303
  hygiene and, 13, 19–22, 314–315
  hypertension, 6, 44, 48, 75, 97–98, 223
  miasma theory of, 18, 20
  obesity, 6
  osteoporosis, 73, 159, 220
  pre-existing conditions, 101, 274
  preventing, 6–7, 45, 73–75, 97–100, 178, 265, 282–287, 333–334
  sexually transmitted diseases, 219–221

diseases. *See also* cancer (*continued*)
 strokes, 44, 73, 100, 170, 224, 282, 303
 transmitting, 18–21
 treating, 43–44, 48, 87–88, 95–98, 129–131, 319
disinfectants, 1, 19–21, 187
Doctor, The (artwork), 206–207
doctor-patient relationship
 benefits of, 330–334
 changes in, 107, 151–159, 274–275, 312–321
 end-of-life options, 170–172, 194
 imbalance in, 77, 151–159
 power in, 151–159
"doctor's doctor," 72
Doctors Helping Doctors program, 305
double standards, 177–183
drug epidemics, 2, 115–116, 147–148, 259
Duke University, 105

economic desperation, 4, 8, 263–272, 289–290
economic devastation, 269, 277–280, 285, 304
electronic health records (EHRs)
 benefits of, 44–46, 79, 282–283, 287, 300–303, 331
 creation of, 44–46
 cultural change and, 244, 300–306
 description of, 44–46, 79
 issues with, 89–92, 168, 244
 learning system, 300–303
Eli Lilly & Company, 145
emergencies
 cost of, 136–140
 disasters, 127–132, 309–311
 racism and, 222–223
 surgeries, 30–33
 treating, 30–33, 114–119, 129–130, 200–201, 220–223, 254–256, 330–331
emotions
 acceptance, 294–297
 anger, 289, 291–292, 328–330

bargaining, 289, 293–294
burnout, 81–94, 106, 112, 296
defense mechanisms, 4, 38, 43, 48–49, 62–65, 77–78, 140
denial, 38, 48, 140, 289–291, 328–330
depression, 76–79, 81–83, 88–89, 92–94, 289, 294, 296–297
grieving process, 289–297
handling, 38–49, 62–65, 77–94, 140, 157, 219, 248–249, 289–298
happiness, 104–111
humor, 157–159, 248–249
love, 322–334
repression, 38, 48, 140, 329–330
satisfaction, 104–111
Emperor of All Maladies, The (book), 37
End of Life Option Act, 194, 204
end-of-life options, 170–172, 194, 204–207, 282, 290, 320–321
Etiology, Concept, and Prophylaxis of Childbed Fever (book), 19

Fahrenheit, Daniel, 182
Fauci, Anthony, 221–223
fee-for-service (FFS), 264–265, 273–276, 282–285, 305. *See also* healthcare system
female doctors, 221–236
Fildes, Luke, 206–207
financial devastation, 4, 139, 149, 300–301
Financial Times (newspaper), 141
Fleming, Alexander, 37
Floyd, George, 221, 228
fools, 30–34, 271
Forbes (magazine), 224
Freudenberger, Herbert, 82

Gallup, 81, 105
gas pipeline explosion, 127–128
Gaskill, J. Richard, 119
Gawande, Atul, 164
Geisinger Health, 212, 216, 283
gender discrimination, 230–251
gender reassignment surgery, 243–245, 249

George Washington University School of Medicine and Health Sciences, 308
germ theory, 19–21
Gerstner, Lou, 26
God's Love We Deliver, 165
Godwin, William, 13
Goldman, Brian, 156–157
gonorrhea, 221
Google, 151, 152
gorilla watching, 13, 22–23
Gray, Darrell, 225–226
Great Depression, 221, 263–269, 277, 291–294
grief, model of, 289–290, 296
grieving process, 289–297
Groopman, Jerome, 112
gross domestic product (GDP), 134–135, 255, 268–269, 278
Grove, Andy, 291
gun violence, 254–258
gunshot wounds, 254–256

handwashing importance, 13, 19–22, 314–315
Hanks, Tom, 152
happiness, pursuit of, 104–111
Harlow, Harry F., 105–106
harming patients, 4–8, 35, 85, 121–183, 189, 225, 312–319
Hartzband, Pamela, 112
Harvard University, 22–23, 39, 41, 82, 102, 106, 112, 143, 226
Haven, 286–287
Health Maintenance Organization (HMO) Act, 273
Healthcare Effectiveness Data and Information Set (HEDIS), 74
healthcare reform, 4–5, 267–290
healthcare system
    administrative issues, 4
    benefits of, 333–334
    capitation model, 264–265, 273–276, 283–285, 305
    collaboration within, 282–283, 301, 305–307
    commitment to, 300–303
    confronting problems, 297–300
    connectedness, 104–113, 303–305
    contribution to, 307–311
    costs of, 2, 133–148, 263–276, 289–290, 314
    COVID-19 and, 2–7
    cultural change, 244, 297–311
    decline of, 23, 51–52, 82, 103, 224–225, 290
    description of, 2–3
    failures of, 23, 84, 292
    fee-for-service model, 264–265, 273–276, 282–285, 305
    fixing, 4–5, 267–290
    Great Depression and, 263–269
    healthcare access, 278–282
    healthcare coverage, 270, 278–281
    healthcare rationing, 270, 279–281, 285
    healthcare workers and, 2–4, 7
    insurance costs, 101, 134–135, 146, 274, 303, 314
    integration model, 266, 273–276, 282–285
    issues with, 2, 4, 23, 81–87, 97–98, 165–168, 277–292
    life expectancy and, 99–103, 126, 290
    navigating through, 271–276
    new model, 281–285
    pre-existing conditions, 101, 274
    prepayment model, 264–267, 273–274, 282–285
    prevention model, 282–287
    quality care, 84–86, 123–126, 153–154, 266, 283–286
    ranking systems, 53, 74, 92–96, 117, 126, 159, 177–178
    reform for, 4–5, 267–290
    reimbursement model, 264–268, 273–276, 282
    risks to, 277–288
    teamwork, 282, 305–307, 319
    two-tier system, 278–281, 285, 288
healthcare workers
    characteristics of, 3–4
    COVID-19 and, 2–3

healthcare workers (*continued*)
  healthcare system and, 2–4
  helping patients, 4–9, 121–183
  heroism and, 3–4, 7, 30–35, 49, 123,
    139–140, 164, 271
health-coverage expansions, 270
heart disease, 6, 44, 73, 99–101,
    129–131, 143, 162, 200–201,
    220–224, 282, 303
heart machines, 17
heart surgery, 95, 98, 100–101, 232,
    280
Heath, Chip, 304
Heath, Dan, 304
helping patients, 4–9, 121–183
hemangioma, 55–57
hemochromatosis, 16
Herb (uncle), 39–40, 43, 94, 134
Hermes, 51
heroism, 3–4, 7, 30–35, 49, 123,
    139–140, 164, 271
Hidden Brain (NPR show), 105
Hill, Anita, 234
Hippocrates, 35, 85, 225
Hippocratic Oath, 35, 85, 189, 225
HIV/AIDS, 43, 303
Hodgkin's lymphoma, 40, 43
Holt, Daniel, 254
Homer, 191, 271, 277
Hope for Hunter Fund, 216
hospital-acquired infections (HAIs),
    19–21, 314–315
House of God, The (book), 158
human shields, 133–140
humor, using, 157–159, 248–249
hydrocephalus, 208–210
hygiene, 13, 19–22, 314–315
Hymn to Aphrodite (poem), 191
hypertension, 6, 44, 48, 75, 97–98,
    223
hysterectomy, 180–182

IBM, 26–27
*Illustrated Manual of Operative Surgery
    and Surgical Anatomy* (book), 252
immigration concerns, 258–259

impersonalized medicine, 161–168
Implicit Association Test, 226
incomes/salaries, 91, 104–105
inconveniences, handling, 149–154
infection
  antibiotics for, 60–64, 165–167
  bacterial infections, 58–64,
    165–167
  description of, 1–2
  hospital-acquired infections, 19–21,
    314–315
  risks of, 87–88
information technology, 6, 44–55,
    81–82, 125–126, 151–152
innovations, 81–82, 183–184, 243–244,
    254–255, 303–309. *See also*
    medical discoveries
Institute for Healthcare Improvement,
    73
Institute of Medicine, 124, 177, 316
insurance costs, 101, 134–135, 146,
    274, 303, 314. *See also* healthcare
    system
integration model, 266, 273–276,
    282–285
Intel, 291
International Journal of Health Services
    (journal), 99
International Monetary Fund, 269
internship recollections, 118, 119
Invisible Gorilla, The (book), 22

JAMA Internal Medicine (journal), 102,
    144
Janoff-Bulman, Ronnie, 290
J.D. Power, 307
Jobs, Steve, 164
Johns Hopkins Hospital, 219, 239, 243,
    245
Johnson, Lyndon, 135, 272–273
joint replacements, 101, 109, 280,
    286
Jordan, Michael, 108
*Journal of the American Medical
    Association* (journal), 87
JPMorgan Chase, 286

Kahneman, Daniel, 25
Kaiser Permanente, 55, 70–73, 114, 117–118, 127–128, 177–182, 195–196, 238–240, 249–250, 283, 298–310, 326, 331
Kaiser Santa Clara, 58, 71, 118, 330–331
Karen (sister), 164–168
Kay, Isaac, 254
Kennedy, John F., 135
Kennedy, Ted, 272
Kessler, David, 290
Kluckhohn, Clyde, 24
Kroeber, Alfred, 24
Kübler-Ross, Elisabeth, 290, 296

Lacks, Henrietta, 219
language barriers, 155–160
"last straw," 252–260
Leapfrog Group, 266, 320
Lear, Tobias, 14
Leaves of Grass (book), 253
leukemia, 37–43, 58–60, 170
life expectancy
   decline in, 2
   denial and, 290
   examination of, 99–103
   healthcare and, 99–103, 126, 290
   increase in, 36
   mortality statistics, 18–20, 44, 99–101, 173–175, 180, 222–228, 278
   prolonging life, 171–173, 192–194
Lively, Judy, 238–251
lives, saving, 5, 40–45, 95, 129, 155, 224, 300–302
lockdowns, 3–4, 268–269
Louis, Pierre Charles Alexandre, 16
love for medicine, 323–334
love story, 322–323
lung cancer, 33, 73, 166
Lyft, 285
lymphoma, 40, 43

Madonna, 175
malpractice claims, 77, 82, 298–299, 327–329
Manual of Military Surgery (book), 252
Marmot, Michael, 92
Marywood University, 211, 216
MASH units, 254
mastectomies, 94, 224, 327–328
Mayo Clinic, 286
Mayo Clinic Proceedings (journal), 17
Mayo Health System, 283
McCain, John, 172
Medicaid, 135, 272–273, 279, 287, 293
medical costs, 2, 133–148, 263–276, 289–290, 314
medical discoveries, 17–19, 35–49, 100–101, 183–184, 231. *See also* technological changes
medical errors, 52, 88, 111, 177–179, 284–298, 300–302, 316–318
medical practice contradictions, 13–17
medical practice progress, 17–18
medical terms, clarifying, 155–160
Medicare, 135, 272–275, 287
Medicare Access and CHIP Reauthorization Act (MACRA), 275
Medicare for All, 270
Medice, cura te ipsum (quote), 296
medicine
   algorithmic approaches, 44–49, 55–57, 107, 245
   antibiotics, 37, 60–64, 165–167, 220
   "art of medicine," 46–48, 57
   conflicts of interest, 317–318
   "cookbook medicine," 47
   costs of, 141–148
   drug epidemics, 2, 115–116, 147–148, 259
   evidence-based practices, 6, 44–51, 55–57, 86–87, 106–107, 112, 126, 180, 254–256, 283, 297
   impersonalized medicine, 161–168
   love for, 323–334
   necessity of, 319
   opioid crisis, 147, 259

medicine (*continued*)
  pre-existing conditions, 101, 274
  prescriptions, 2, 87, 115–116,
    133–134, 141–148, 259
  private practice, 95, 267–268, 273,
    325–326
  trauma medicine, 95, 133, 175,
    254–256, 290
Medscape, 83, 90–91
Melinek, Judy, 187, 256
Memorial Sloan Kettering Cancer
  Center, 143
mental health, 76–79, 81–83, 96, 258
mental shortcuts, 25–26
metrics, 45–48, 72–79, 112, 178, 302
mighty, falling of, 99–103
military surgery, 252–254
minorities, 219–229
mobile army surgical hospitals, 254
Moore, Gordon, 291
Moore, James, 254
moral injury, 81–89, 139, 288, 292
mortality and morbidity (M&M),
  173–175
mortality statistics, 18–20, 44, 99–101,
  173–175, 180, 222–228, 278. *See
  also* life expectancy
MRI scans, 17, 36, 86–87, 100, 213,
  280–281
Mukherjee, Siddhartha, 37–38
Mulye, Nirmal, 141–142

Napoleon, 281
National Academy of Medicine, 124,
  177
National African American Male
  Wellness Initiative, 225
National Committee for Quality
  Assurance, 74, 117, 182, 266, 307
National Institutes of Health, 17
National Rifle Association (NRA),
  256–257
necrotizing fasciitis, 61–64
neurology, 28, 86–87, 155, 201–203,
  226
New England Journal of Medicine
  (journal), 17, 106, 234

New York Times (newspaper), 2, 143,
  286
New Yorker (magazine), 164
Newsom, Gavin, 279
Newton, Isaac, 13
Nixon, Richard, 273, 275
Nostrum Laboratories, 141

Obama, Barack, 274–275
Obamacare, 101, 274
Oberlin College, 39
Odysseus, 271–273, 277
Odyssey, The (book), 271, 277
Ohio State University, 225
Oldenburg, Ray, 110
Only the Paranoid Survive (book), 291
Open Notes, 150
opioid crisis, 147, 259
Oprah, 152
organ transplants, 5, 95–97
orthopedic surgery, 88, 101–102, 109,
  280, 286, 331–332
Osler, William, 16
osteoporosis, 73, 159, 220
ovarian cancer, 171, 214

Pacific Gas and Electric, 127
pancreatic cancer, 175–176
pandemic
  description of, 1–2
  healthcare system and, 2–7
  healthcare workers and, 2–4
  impact of, 2–7, 149–150, 268–269,
    289
  racism and, 221–223, 228
Pasteur, Louis, 18
patients
  "colorblind" concerns, 219–229
  customer service, 124–125, 149–154,
    307
  discomfort with difference,
    237–251
  doctor-patient relationship, 77,
    107, 151–159, 170–172, 274, 307,
    312–321, 330–334
  double standards, 177–183
  emergencies and, 127–132

harming, 4–8, 35, 85, 121–183, 189, 225, 312–319
helping, 4–9, 121–183
human shields, 133–140
impersonalized medicine, 161–168
inconveniences, 149–154
language barriers, 155–160
"last straw," 252–260
prescription costs, 141–148
quality care, 84–86, 123–126, 153–154, 266, 283–286
questions for doctors, 314–321
safety concerns, 316–317
sexuality and, 230–251
truth complications, 62–64, 169–176
virtual visits, 153–154, 287, 315–316
Patterson, Paul, 31–32
pay rates, 91, 104–105
Pearl, Jack, 170, 293, 322–325
Pearl, Lillian, 169–171, 293, 322–325
Pearl Harbor attack, 322
penicillin, 37, 220
People (magazine), 161
performance metrics, 45–48, 72–79, 112, 178, 302
perils, facing, 277–288
Permanente Medical Group, 70–71, 114, 195, 240, 298, 304–306, 309–310. *See also* Kaiser Permanente
PET scans, 36
"Physician, heal thyself," 296
"Physician Burnout, Interrupted," 106, 112
physician culture
absorbing, 24–25
acceptance and, 249–251, 294–297
acquiring, 24–25
allegiances in, 27–28
anger, 289, 291–292, 328–330
bargaining, 289, 293–294
being difficult, 312–321
bloodletting, 13–17
burnout and, 81–94, 106, 112, 296
collaboration, 282–283, 301, 305–307
"colorblind" concerns, 219–229
commitment to care, 300–303
communicating, 28–29, 155–160
computer era, 43–49
confronting problems, 297–300
connectedness, 303–305
contributions, 307–311
cultural change, 26–27, 295, 297–311
customer service, 149–154
defending, 52–65
defense mechanisms, 4, 38, 43, 48–49, 62–65, 77–78, 140
denial, 38, 48, 140, 289–291, 328–330
depression, 76–79, 81–83, 88–89, 92–94, 289, 294, 296–297
diagnostic tools, 35–37, 69–71, 100–101, 125–130, 175–176
discomfort with difference, 237–251
doctor-patient relationship, 77, 107, 151–159, 170–172, 274, 307, 312–321, 330–334
double standards, 177–183
economic desperation, 4, 8, 263–272, 289–290
emergencies and, 127–132
evaluation of, 27–28
evidence-based practices, 6, 44–51, 55–57, 86–87, 106–107, 112, 126, 180, 254–256, 283, 297
evolution of, 26–27, 261–334
facets of, 24–29
factions in, 27–28
female doctors and, 221–236
five Cs of change, 295, 297–311
focusing on, 4–5
fools, 30–34, 271
gender discrimination, 230–251
gorilla watching, 13, 22–23
handwashing importance, 13, 19–22, 314–315
harming patients, 4–8, 35, 85, 121–183, 189, 225, 312–319
healthcare reform, 4–5, 267–290
helping patients, 4–9, 121–183
heroism and, 3–4, 7, 30–35, 49, 123, 139–140, 164, 271
hierarchy of, 27–28

physician culture (*continued*)
 history of, 35–49
 human shields, 133–140
 impersonalized medicine, 161–168
 inconveniences, 149–154
 issues with, 4–5
 language barriers, 155–160
 language of, 28–29
 "last straw," 252–260
 mental shortcuts, 25–26
 people versus, 50–65
 perils, 277–288
 prescription costs, 141–148
 quality care, 84–86, 123–126,
    153–154, 266, 283–286
 racism and, 221–229
 ranking systems, 53, 74, 92–96, 117,
    126, 159, 177–178
 repression, 38, 48, 140, 329–330
 saving lives, 5, 40–45, 95, 129, 155,
    224, 300–302
 sexuality and, 230–251
 shift in, 69–82
 sleep deprivation, 32–34
 social ladder, 185–260
 societal concerns, 187–190, 221–260
 symbols in, 16, 28–29, 50–51
 systems of thought, 25–26
 teamwork, 282, 305–307, 319
 technological changes, 4–6, 35–55,
    69–82, 100–101, 125–126, 151–
    152, 207, 291, 300–301, 315–316
 of today, 35–49
 transgender concerns, 238–251
 tribalism in, 27–28
 truth complications, 62–64, 169–176
 understanding, 11–65
"Physician Exercise of Conscience," 258
physician pain
 boredom, 114–118
 burnout, 81–94, 106, 112, 296
 falling of mighty, 99–103
 moral injury, 81–89, 139, 288, 292
 prestige problem, 90–98
 self-determination theory, 104–113
 understanding, 67–118
Physician Payments Sunshine Act, 142

plagues, 4, 35, 38
Planned Parenthood, 165
plastic surgery, 51, 55–60, 85, 95,
    187–188, 195, 243. *See also*
    reconstructive surgery
polio, 202
pre-existing medical conditions, 101,
    274
prepayment model, 264–267, 273–274,
    282–285. *See also* healthcare
    system
prescriptions, 2, 87, 115–116, 133–134,
    141–148, 259. *See also* medicine
prestige, problem with, 90–98
prevention, importance of, 6–7,
    282–287
Preventive Services Task force, 93
primary care
 accountability for, 74
 burnout and, 90–91
 finding, 150–152, 182
 managing, 83–84, 95–110, 118–119
 value of, 6, 27–28, 73–74, 95–110,
    282–283, 309, 318–319
"Primary Care, Specialty Care, and
    Life Chances," 99
Prince, 175
Principles and Practice of Medicine, The
    (book), 16
private practice, 95, 267–268, 273,
    325–326
problems, confronting, 297–300
*Proceedings of the National Academy of
    Sciences* (journal), 227
projection, 48, 140
prostate cancer, 93
prostate specific antigen (PSA), 93

quality care, 84–86, 123–126, 153–154,
    266, 283–286
quality-improvement plans, 97–98
questions for doctors, 314–321

racism, 221–229
ranking systems, 53, 74, 92–96, 117,
    126, 159, 177–178
Rawlins, Albin, 14

"Recollections of Internship," 118, 119
reconstructive surgery, 51, 55–58, 85,
 195, 224. *See also* plastic surgery
Reid, Maryann, 224
reimbursement model, 264–268,
 273–276, 282
relatedness, 106–113
repression, handling, 38, 48, 140,
 329–330
Revolutionary War, 189
Robert Wood Johnson Foundation, 223
Robinson, Jackie, 227
robotic prostatectomy, 93
Rod of Asclepius, 50–51
Roosevelt, Franklin D., 263, 267, 273,
 282
Ruthie (aunt), 161–162

safety concerns, 316–317
salary rates, 91, 104–105
Salvator Mundi (artwork), 142
Samuelson, Dr., 201–202
San Francisco Chronicle (newspaper), 250
Santos, Laurie, 104–105
SARS-CoV-2, 1–2. *See also* COVID-19
satisfaction, achieving, 104–111
Save the Children program, 304–305
saving lives, 5, 40–45, 95, 129, 155,
 224, 300–302
scientific progress, 17–19, 35–49,
 69–82, 100–101, 125–126. *See also*
 technological changes
Scylla, 271–276, 283–284
Secret Language of Doctors, The (book),
 156
Seinfeld (TV show), 313
self-determination theory, 104–113
Semmelweis, Ignaz, 17–21, 46, 183,
 230, 292
sepsis, 73, 303
Sex Pistols, 38
sexuality, 230–251
sexually transmitted diseases, 219–221
Simons, Daniel, 22–23
skin cancer, 96, 326
sleep deprivation, 32–34
smallpox, 3

Smith, Adam, 13
Smith, William Kennedy, 234
social ladder
 "colorblind" concerns, 219–229
 concerns about, 185–260
 culture without answers, 187–190
 discomfort with difference, 237–251
 gender discrimination, 230–251
 "last straw," 252–260
 physician culture, 185–260
 sexuality and, 230–251
 societal concerns, 187–190, 221–260
 transgender concerns, 238–251
social media, 154, 187, 211, 256–257,
 292
Social Security Act, 267, 272
societal concerns, 187–190, 221–260
Spanish flu, 3
spinal fusions, 88
Stanford University, 27, 30–31, 38–41,
 102, 195–196, 206, 226–227,
 232–234, 243
Stanford University Hospital, 30–31,
 195–196, 232–234
Sternin, Jerry, 304–305
Sternin, Monique, 304–305
Steve (brother-in-law), 164–168
Stevenson, Robert Louis, 69, 70
Sting, 175
*Strange Case of Dr. Jekyll and Mr. Hyde,
The* (book), 70
strokes, 44, 73, 100, 170, 224, 282, 303
suicide, 76–79, 81–83, 189, 193, 217,
 242, 294
surgeries
 brain surgery, 86, 213
 for cancer, 94–95, 224, 327–328
 cardiac surgery, 95, 98, 100–101,
 232–233, 280, 334
 cosmetic surgery, 56, 248
 emergency surgery, 30–33
 gender reassignment surgery,
 243–245, 249
 heart surgery, 95, 98, 100–101,
 232–233, 280, 334
 joint replacements, 101–102, 109,
 280, 286

surgeries (*continued*)
   military surgery, 252–254
   organ transplants, 5, 95–97
   orthopedic surgery, 88, 101–102, 109, 280, 286, 331–332
   plastic surgery, 51, 55–60, 85, 95, 187–188, 195, 243
   reconstructive surgery, 51, 55–58, 85, 195, 224
Switch (book), 304
symbols, 16, 28–29, 50–51
syphilis, 219–220
Systems and Solutions Group, 164
systems of thought, 25–26

Talbot, Simon, 85–86
teamwork, 282, 305–307, 319
technological changes
   commitment to, 300–301
   computer era, 43–49
   future and, 291, 333–334
   history of, 35–55
   information technology, 6, 44–55, 81–82, 125–126, 151–152
   innovations, 81–82, 183–184, 243–244, 254–255, 303–309
   medical discoveries, 17–19, 35–49, 100–101, 183–184, 231
   reliance on, 207
   scientific progress, 17–19, 35–49, 69–82, 100–101, 125–126
   virtual visits, 153–154, 287, 315–316
telehealth, 153–154, 287, 315–316
thermometer, 182–183
Thinking, Fast and Slow (book), 25
Thomas, Clarence, 234
Thompson, Craig B., 143
thought, systems of, 25–26
"To Err Is Human," 177, 316
transgender concerns, 238–251
transplants, 5, 95–97
trauma medicine, 95, 133, 175, 254–256, 290
tribalism, 27–28
Trump, Donald, 275
truth, complications of, 62–64, 169–176

tumors
   brain tumor, 86, 212–213
   pancreatic tumor, 175–176
   treating, 17, 55–57, 86, 175–176, 212–214, 219
Tuskegee Institute, 219
Twitter, 187, 256–257
two-tier healthcare system, 278–281, 285, 288. *See also* healthcare system

Ubel, Peter, 105
Uber, 285
UCSF Health, 309
"Unintended Consequences of Expensive Cancer Therapeutics," 171
University of California, 145
University of Illinois, 22
University of Michigan, 87
University of Rochester, 106
University of San Diego, 196
University of Wisconsin, 105
urology, 91–93, 100
Us Weekly (magazine), 161

vaccines, 187, 259
venesection, 13–17
Verghese, Abraham, 206–207
Virginia Commonwealth University, 151
virtual visits, 153–154, 287, 315–316
virus
   description of, 1–2
   fight against, 49
   healthcare system and, 2–7
   healthcare workers and, 2–4
   impact of, 2–7, 149–150, 268–269, 289
   racism and, 221–223, 228
   vaccines for, 259

Walking Out on the Boys (book), 233
Walmart, 286
War of 1812, 237
Washington, George, 14–15
Whipple, Allan, 175

Whipple operation, 175
Whitman, Walt, 253
women's health
  breast cancer, 94–95, 180, 224, 333
  cervical cancer, 180
  childbirth and, 18–19, 109, 133, 224, 278
  gynecology, 95, 179–182
  hysterectomies, 180–182
  mastectomies, 94, 224, 327–328
  maternal mortality, 18–19, 126, 180, 224, 278

  ovarian cancer, 171, 214
  workload concerns, 116–118, 130–131, 305–306, 326–329
World Health Organization (WHO), 50, 92, 141, 222
World War I, 254
World War II, 37, 254, 281, 322–323
Wren, Christopher, 311
Wunderlich, Carl Reinhold, 183

Yale Medical School, 195
Yale University, 104, 195, 198–200, 324

 **Dr. Robert Pearl** is the former CEO of the Permanente Medical Group. Named one of *Modern Healthcare*'s fifty most influential physician leaders, Pearl is a clinical professor of plastic surgery at Stanford University School of Medicine and is on the faculty of the Stanford Graduate School of Business, where he teaches courses on strategy and leadership, and lectures on information technology and healthcare policy. He is the author of the *Washington Post* best seller *Mistreated*, hosts the popular podcast *Fixing Healthcare*, publishes a newsletter with over ten thousand subscribers, and is a regular contributor to *Forbes*. He has been featured on *CBS This Morning*, CNBC, and NPR and in *Time*, *USA Today*, and the *Wall Street Journal*. He is a frequent keynote speaker at healthcare and medical technology conferences.